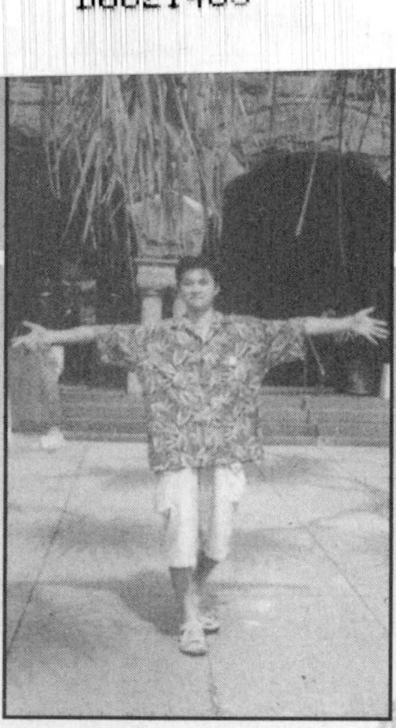

We've been in print for two years—thanks to your support! I plan to keep going, with the motto, "What's worthwhile is never easy."

I want to build this comic along with you, so please participate when you can!

Takeshi Konomi

About Takeshi Konomi

Takeshi Konomi exploded onto the manga scene with the incredible **THE PRINCE OF TENNIS**. His refined art style and sleek character designs proved popular with **Weekly Shonen Jump** readers, and **THE PRINCE OF TENNIS** became the No. 1 sports manga in Japan almost overnight. Its cast of fascinating male tennis players attracted legions of female readers even though it was originally intended to be a boys' comic. The manga continues to be a success in Japan. A hit anime series was created, as well as several video games and mountains of merchandise.

THE PRINCE OF TENNIS
VOL. 9
The SHONEN JUMP Graphic Novel

STORY AND ART BY
TAKESHI KONOMI

English Adaptation/Gerard Jones
Translation/Joe Yamazaki
Touch-up Art & Lettering/Andy Ristaino
Cover Design/Terry Bennett
Interior Design/Janet Piercy
Editor/Michelle Pangilinan

Managing Editor/Elizabeth Kawasaki
Director of Production/Noboru Watanabe
Vice President of Publishing/Alvin Lu
Vice President & Editor in Chief/ Yumi Hoashi
Sr. Director of Acquisitions/Rika Inouye
Vice President of Sales & Marketing/Liza Coppola
Publisher/Hyoe Narita

Printed in the U.S.A.

Published by VIZ Media, LLC
P.O. Box 77010
San Francisco, CA 94107

SHONEN JUMP Graphic Novel Edition
10 9 8 7 6 5 4 3 2 1
First printing, August 2005

PARENTAL ADVISORY
THE PRINCE OF TENNIS
is rated A and is suitable
for readers of all ages.

THE WORLD'S
MOST POPULAR MANGA

SHONEN JUMP
GRAPHIC NOVEL
www.shonenjump.com

www.viz.com

Shonen Jump Graphic Novel

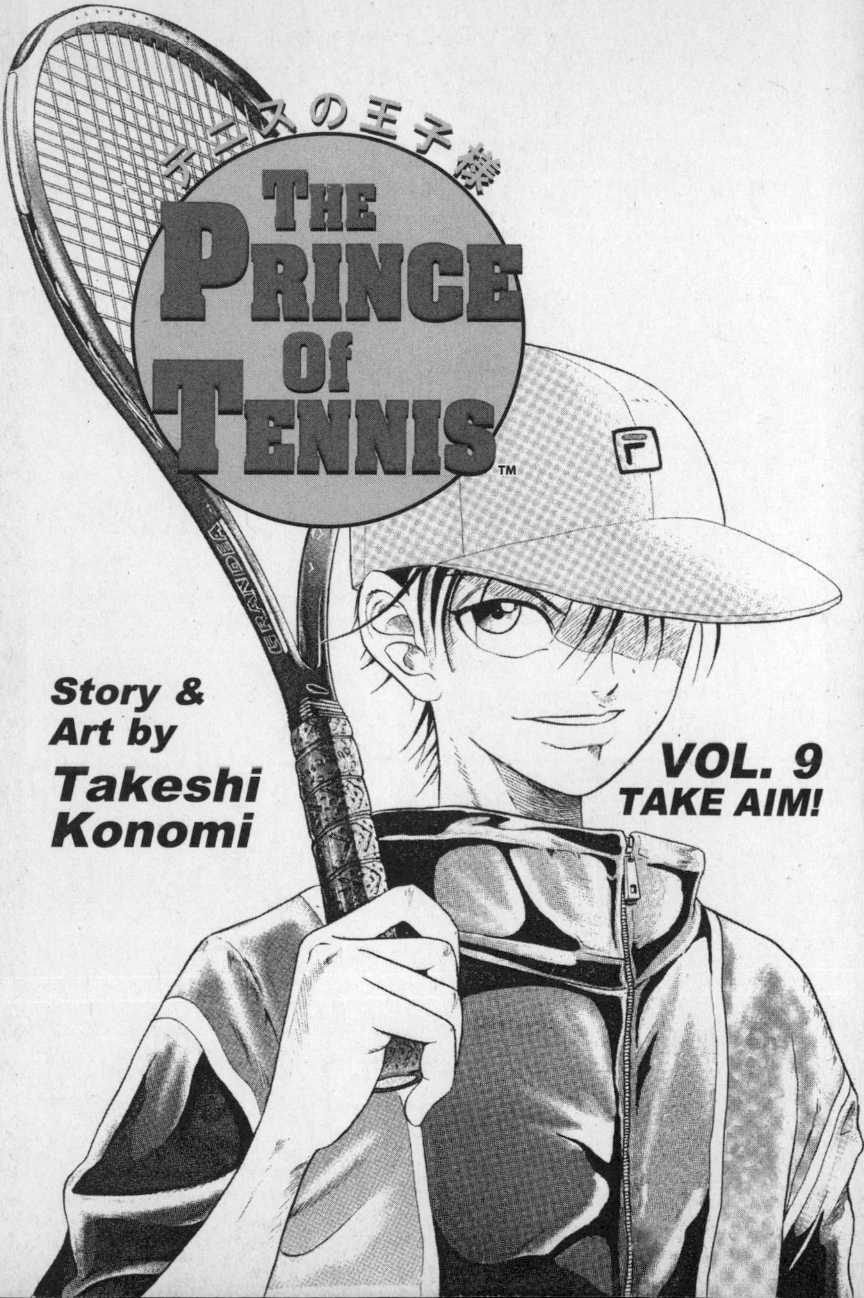

テニスの王子様

THE PRINCE OF TENNIS™

Story & Art by
Takeshi Konomi

VOL. 9
TAKE AIM!

THE PRINCE OF TENNIS

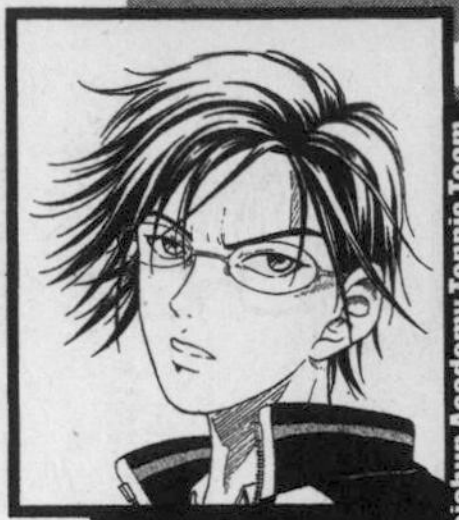

Kunimitsu Tezuka
Seishun Academy Tennis Team Captain (9th Grade)

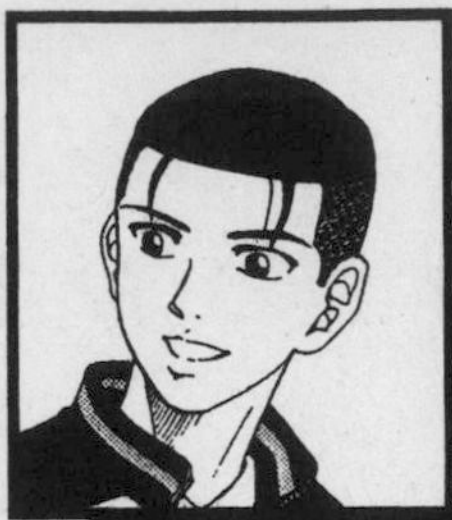

Shuichiro Oishi
Seishun Academy Tennis Team Alternate Captain (9th Grade)

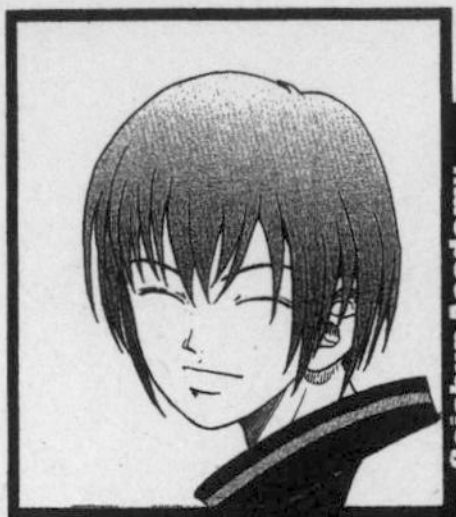

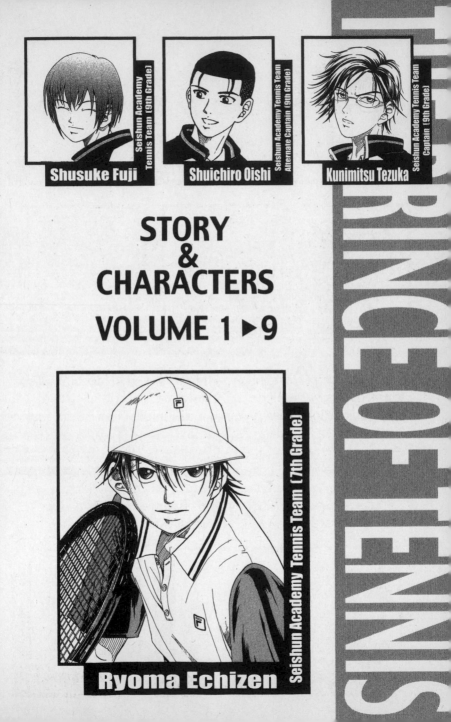

Shusuke Fuji
Seishun Academy Tennis Team (9th Grade)

STORY & CHARACTERS

VOLUME 1 ▶ 9

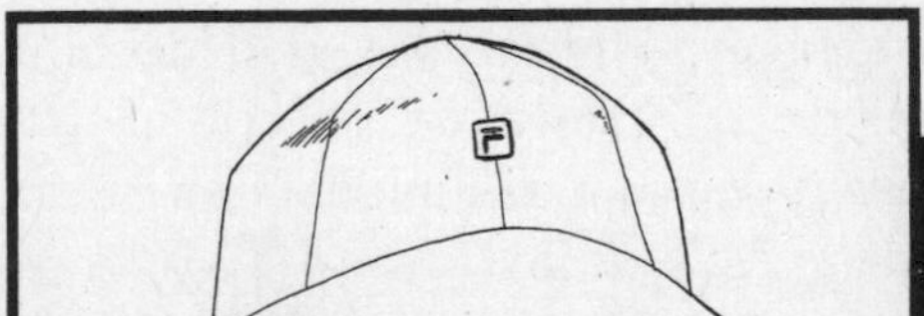

Ryoma Echizen
Seishun Academy Tennis Team (7th Grade)

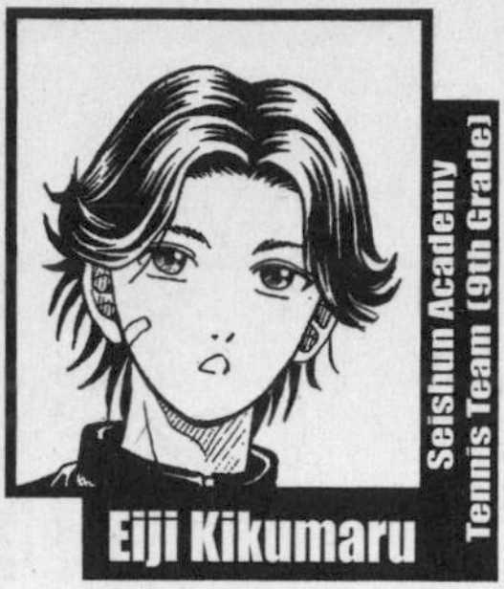
Eiji Kikumaru
Seishun Academy Tennis Team (9th Grade)

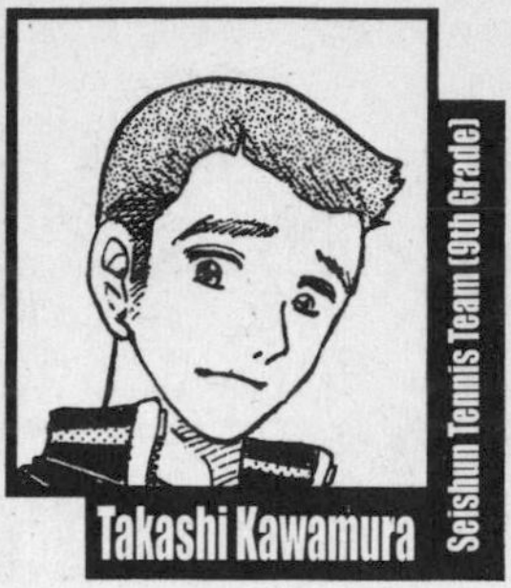
Takashi Kawamura
Seishun Tennis Team (9th Grade)

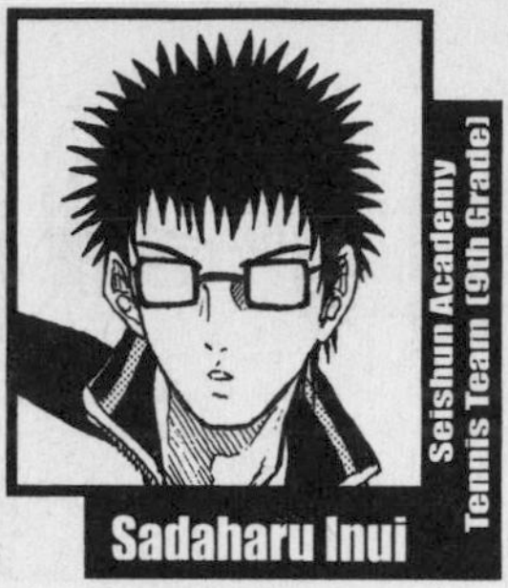
Sadaharu Inui
Seishun Academy Tennis Team (9th Grade)

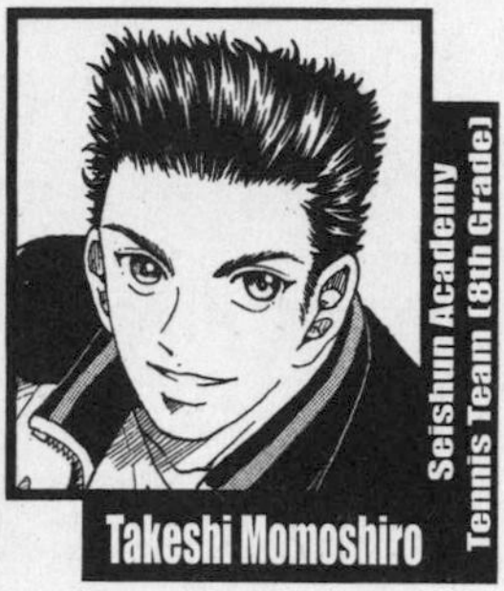
Takeshi Momoshiro
Seishun Academy Tennis Team (8th Grade)

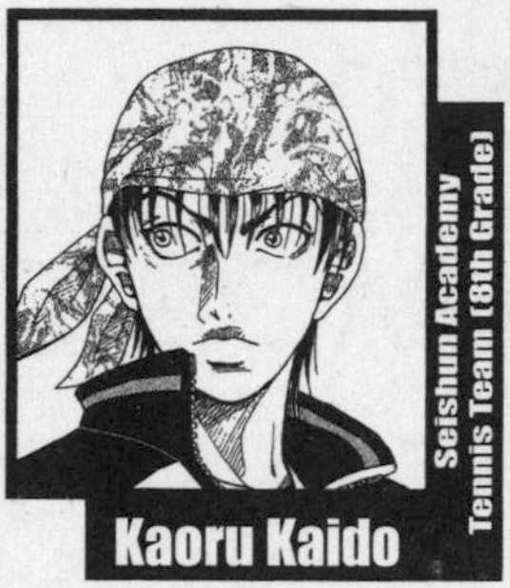
Kaoru Kaido
Seishun Academy Tennis Team (8th Grade)

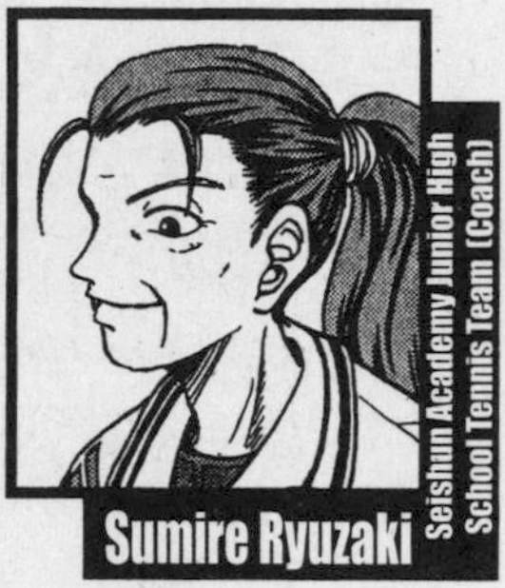
Sumire Ryuzaki
Seishun Academy Junior High School Tennis Team (Coach)

Ryoma Echizen, a tennis prodigy and winner of four U.S. Junior tournaments, has returned to Japan and enrolled at Seishun Academy Junior High. To everyone's astonishment, he becomes a starter in the District Preliminaries, while still in the 7th grade, and helps Seishun earn a berth in the City Tournament. Seishun advances easily until they meet St. Rudolph Academy, but they find themselves with one win and one loss at the end of the No. 2 Doubles match. Now, in the No. 3 Singles match, Ryoma faces Yuta—the younger brother of his brilliant teammate Shusuke!

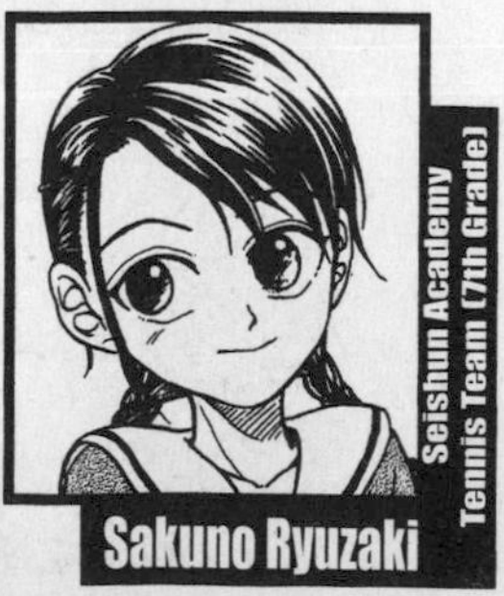
Sakuno Ryuzaki
Seishun Academy Tennis Team (7th Grade)

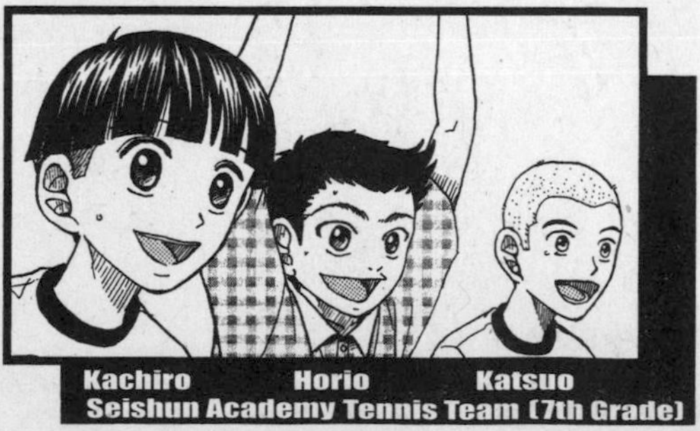
Kachiro
Horio
Katsuo
Seishun Academy Tennis Team (7th Grade)

CONTENTS

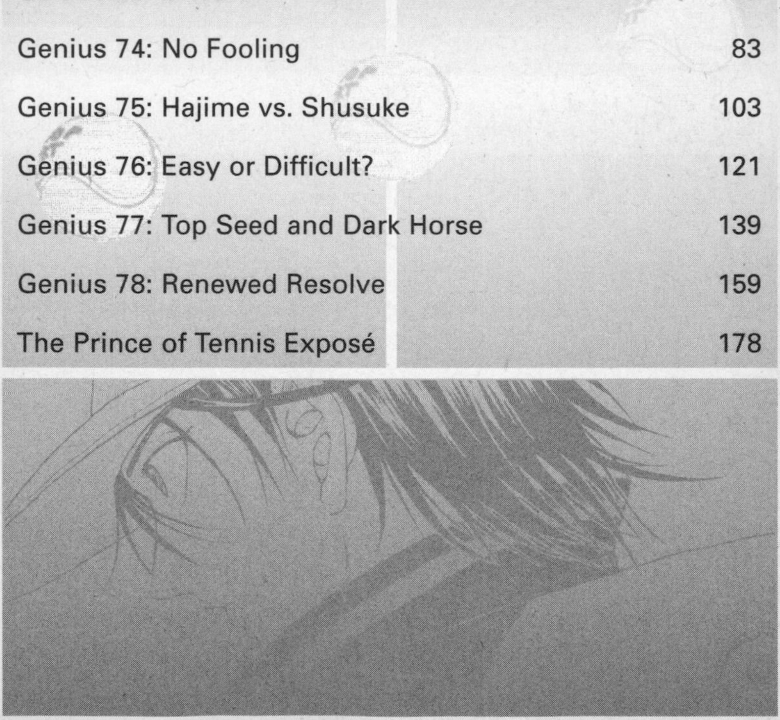

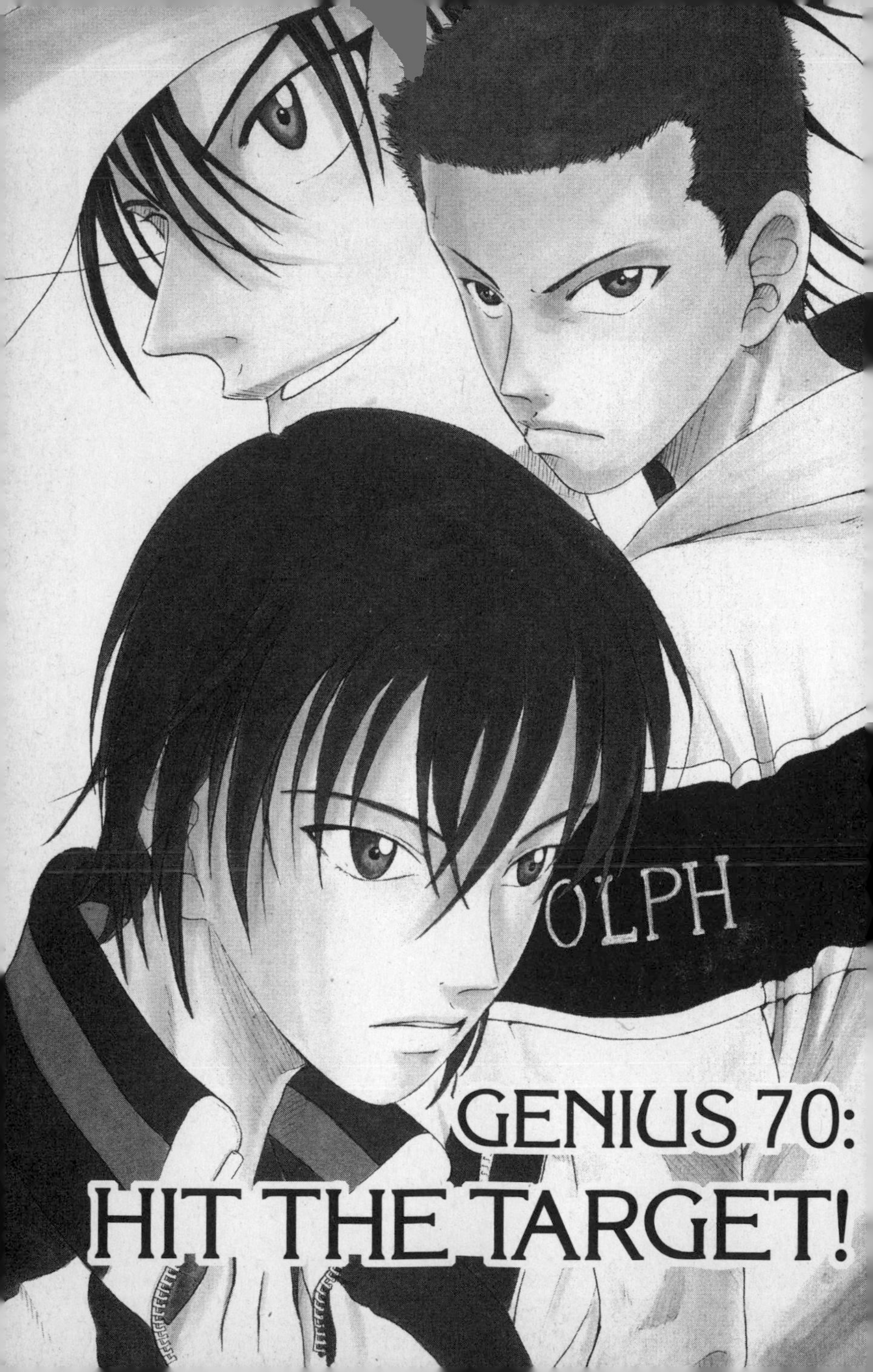
OLPH
GENIUS 70:
HIT THE TARGET!

テニスの王子様

THE PRINCE OF TENNIS™

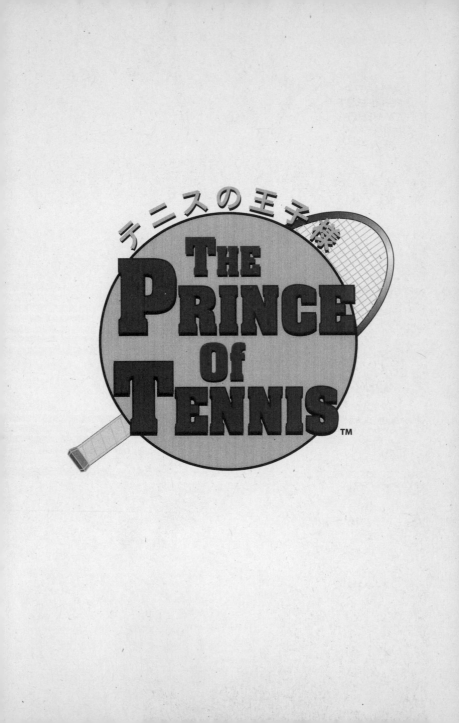

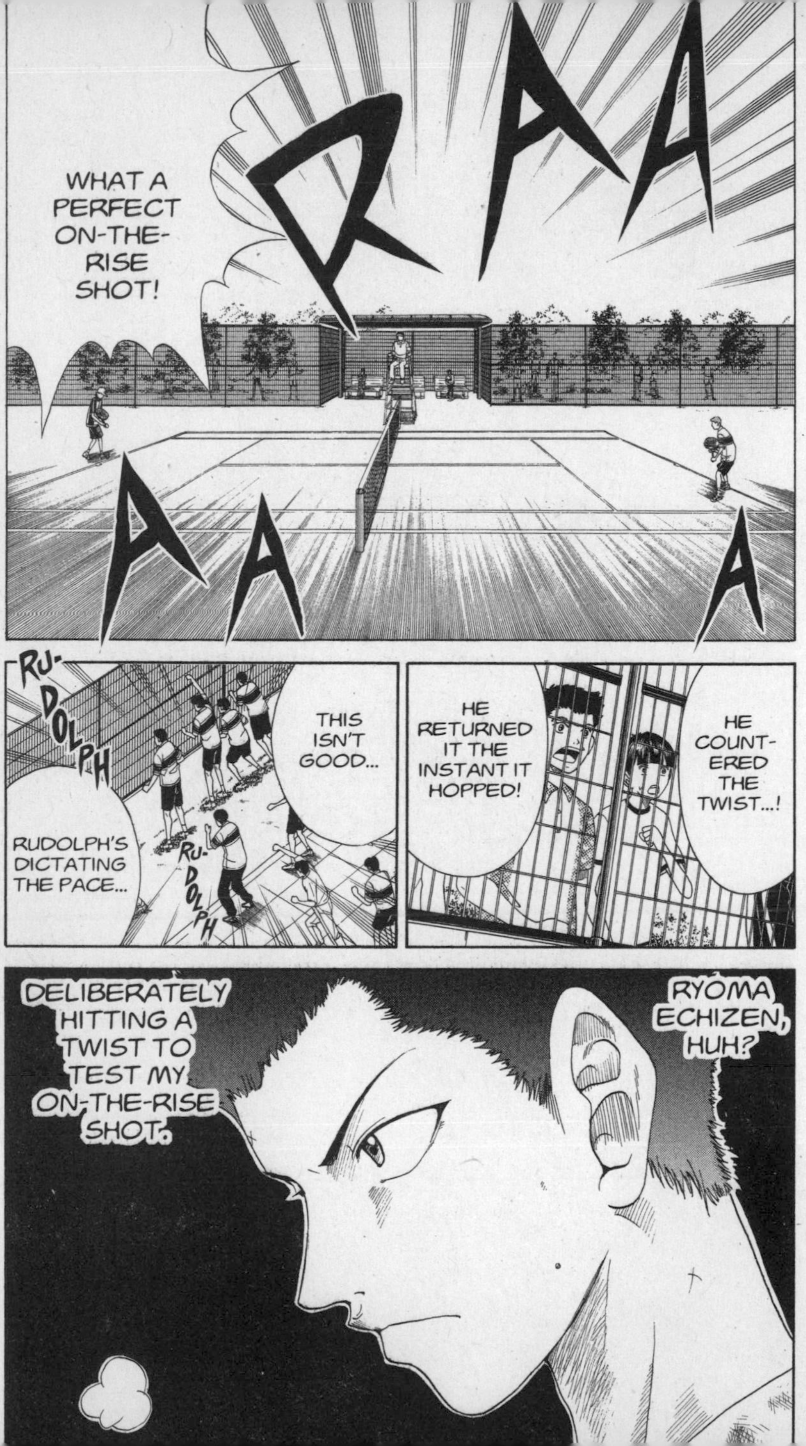
RAAAAA
WHAT A PERFECT ON-THE-RISE SHOT!
HE COUNTERED THE TWIST...!
HE RETURNED IT THE INSTANT IT HOPPED!
THIS ISN'T GOOD...
RU-DOLPH
RUDOLPH'S DICTATING THE PACE...
RU-DOLPH
RYOMA ECHIZEN, HUH?
DELIBERATELY HITTING A TWIST TO TEST MY ON-THE-RISE SHOT.

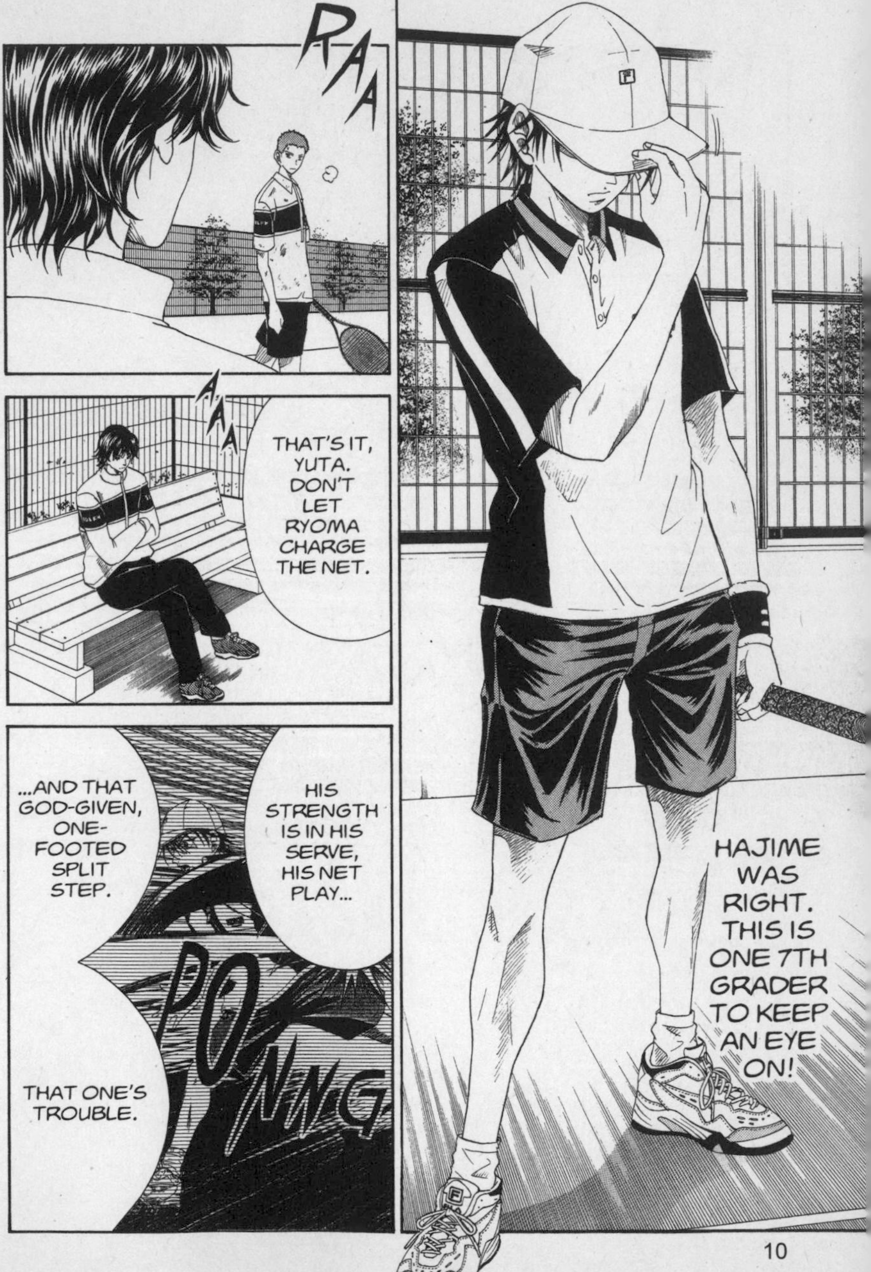
HAJIME WAS RIGHT. THIS IS ONE 7TH GRADER TO KEEP AN EYE ON!
RAAA
AAA
THAT'S IT, YUTA. DON'T LET RYOMA CHARGE THE NET.
HIS STRENGTH IS IN HIS SERVE, HIS NET PLAY...
...AND THAT GOD-GIVEN, ONE-FOOTED SPLIT STEP.
PONNG
THAT ONE'S TROUBLE.

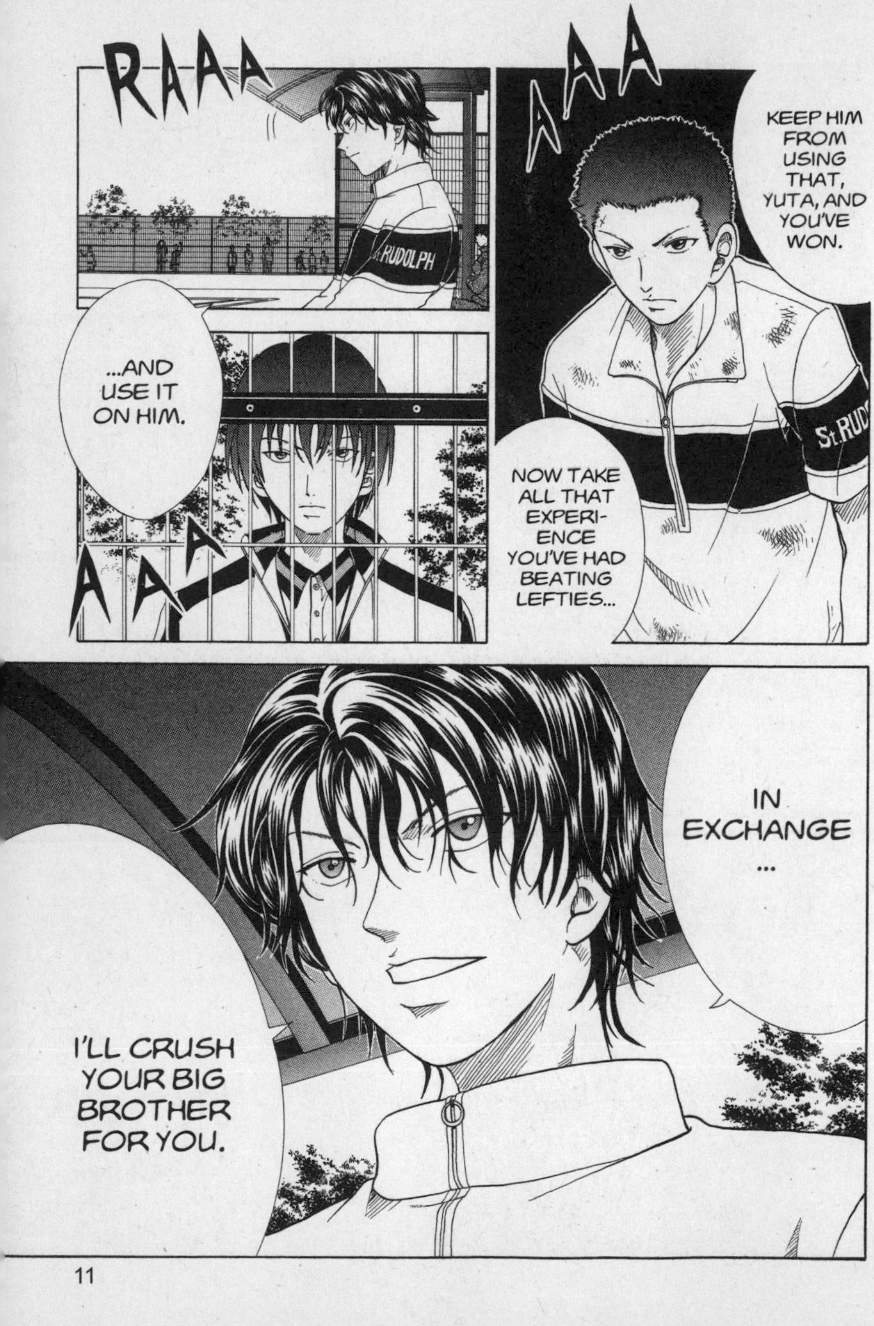
AAA
KEEP HIM FROM USING THAT, YUTA, AND YOU'VE WON.
NOW TAKE ALL THAT EXPERIENCE YOU'VE HAD BEATING LEFTIES...
RAAA
St. RUDOLPH
...AND USE IT ON HIM.
AAA
IN EXCHANGE ...
I'LL CRUSH YOUR BIG BROTHER FOR YOU.

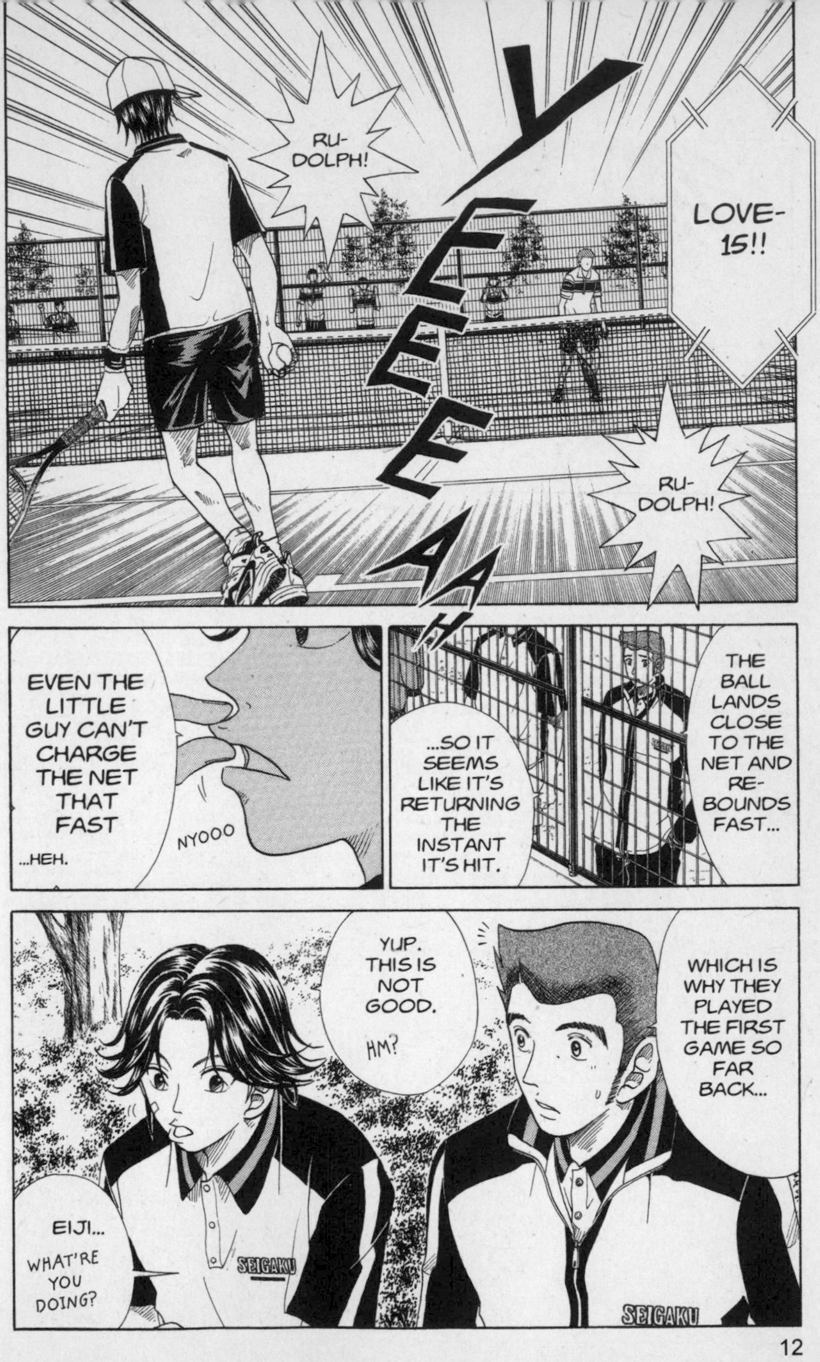
LOVE-15!!
YEEEAAH
RU-DOLPH!
RU-DOLPH!
THE BALL LANDS CLOSE TO THE NET AND RE-BOUNDS FAST...
...SO IT SEEMS LIKE IT'S RETURNING THE INSTANT IT'S HIT.
EVEN THE LITTLE GUY CAN'T CHARGE THE NET THAT FAST
NYOOO
...HEH.
WHICH IS WHY THEY PLAYED THE FIRST GAME SO FAR BACK...
YUP. THIS IS NOT GOOD.
HM?
SEIGAKU
SEIGAKU
EIJI...
WHAT'RE YOU DOING?

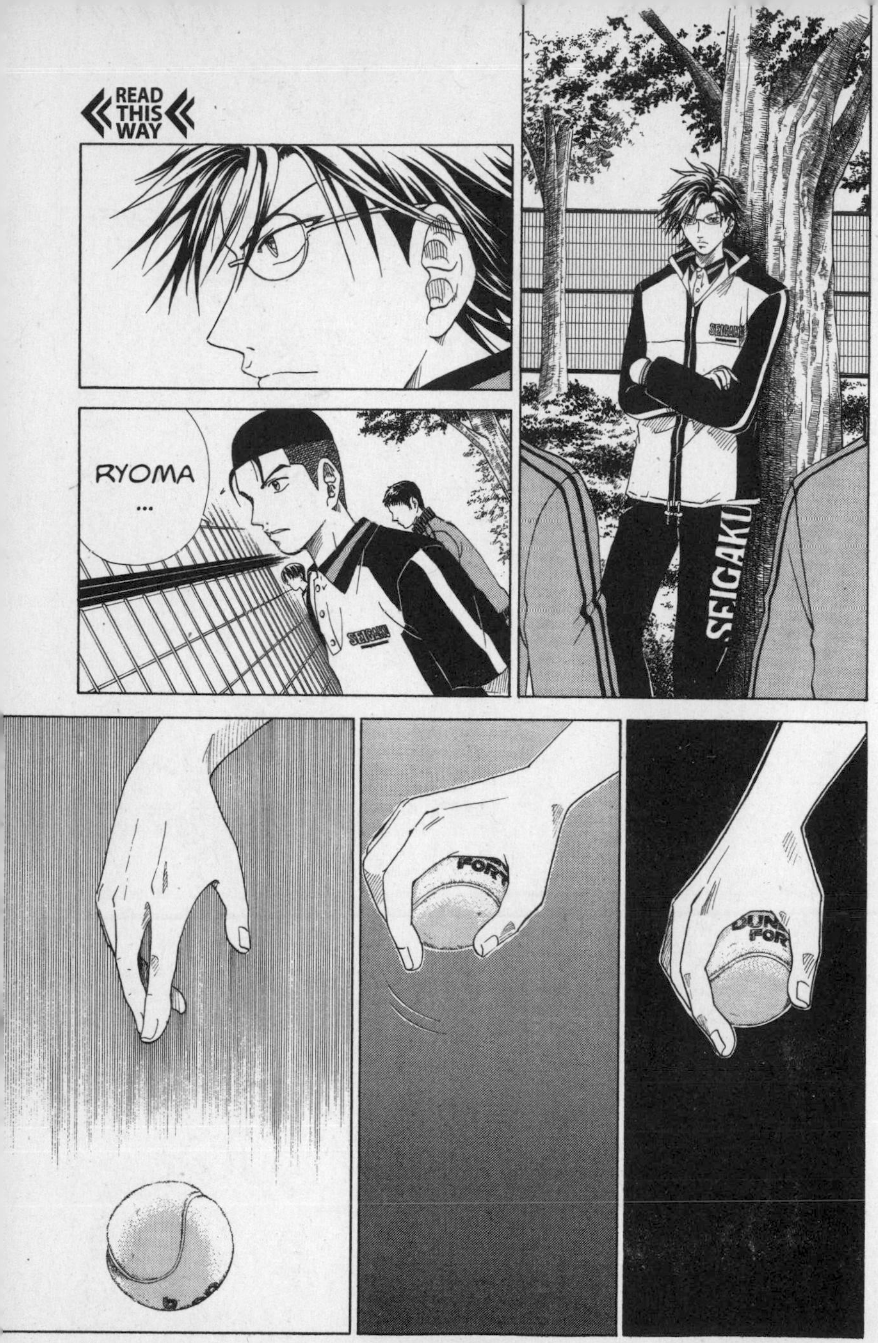
READ THIS WAY
RYOMA ...

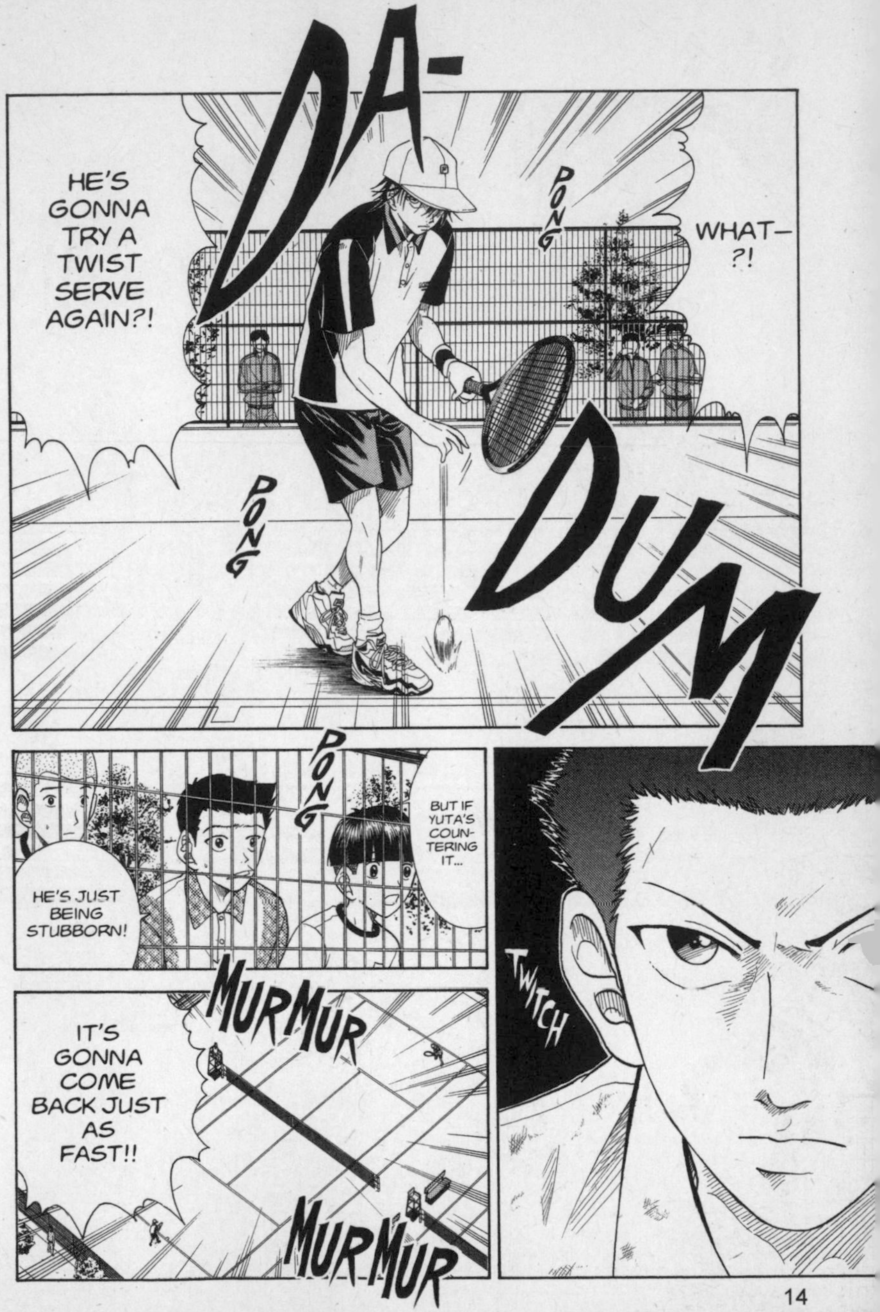
WHAT—?!
PONG
HE'S GONNA TRY A TWIST SERVE AGAIN?!
DA-DUM
PONG
TWITCH
PONG
BUT IF YUTA'S COUNTERING IT...
HE'S JUST BEING STUBBORN!
MURMUR
IT'S GONNA COME BACK JUST AS FAST!!
MURMUR

READ THIS WAY

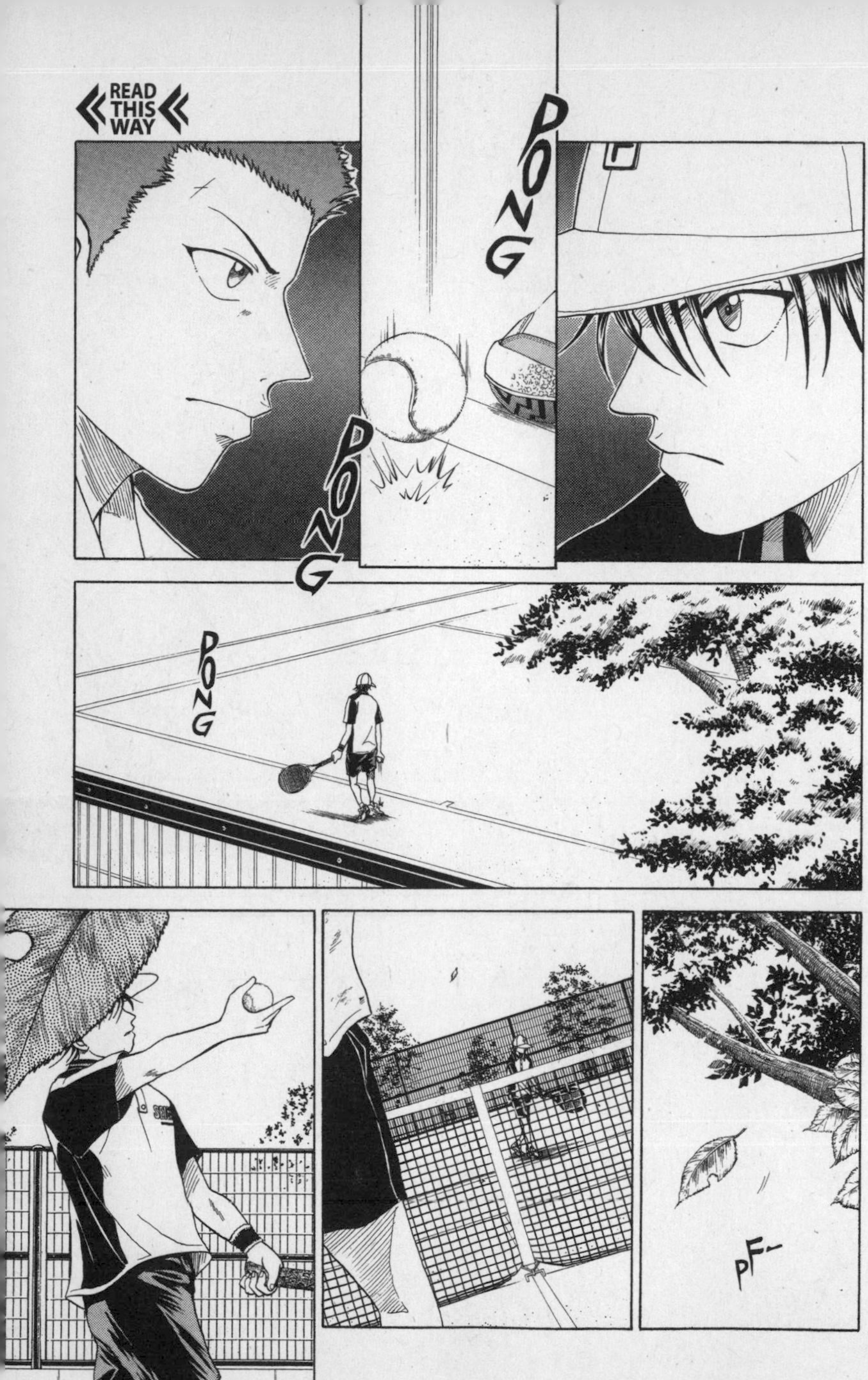
PONG
PONG
PONG
PF~

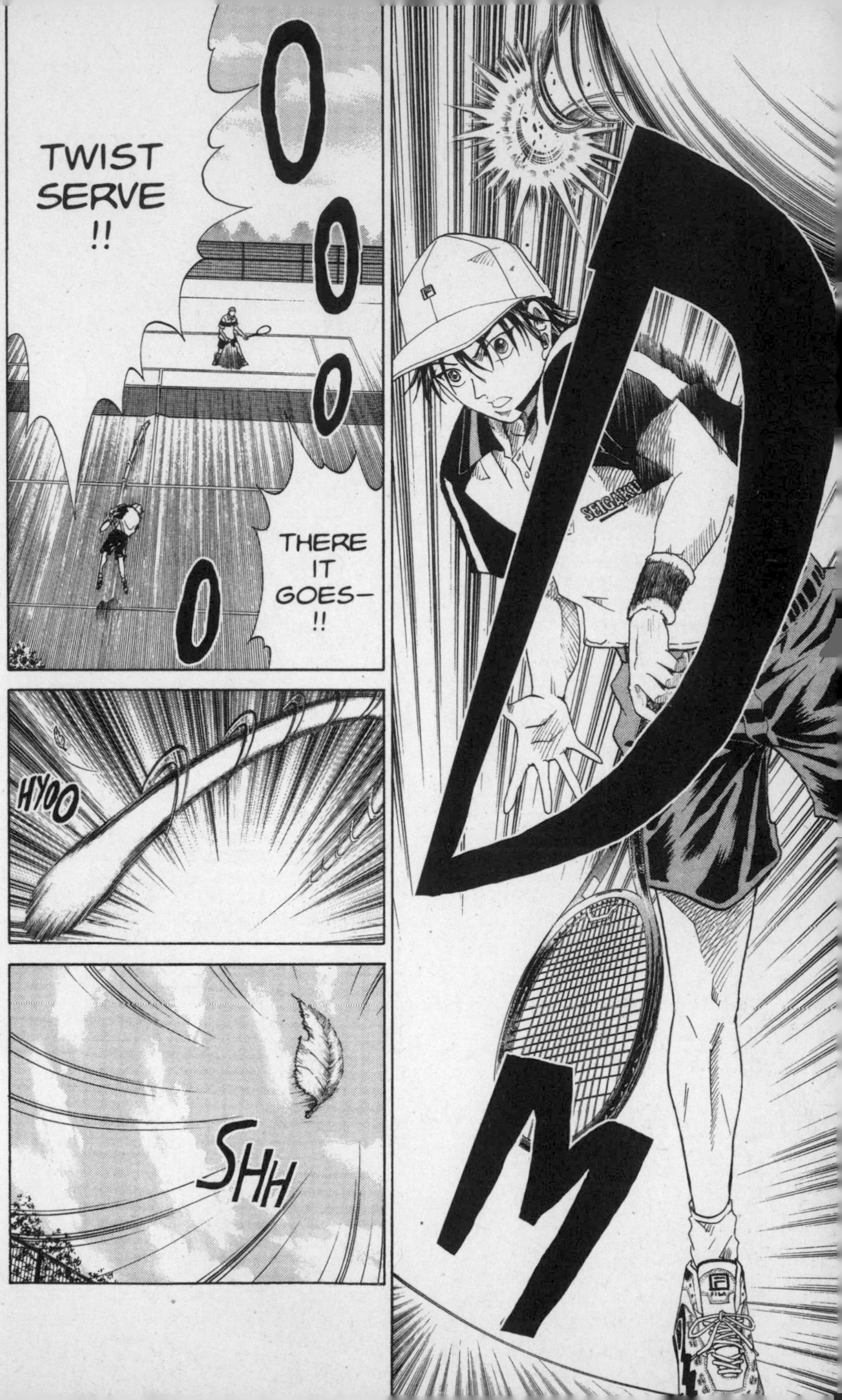
TWIST SERVE !!
THERE IT GOES— !!
HYOO
SHH

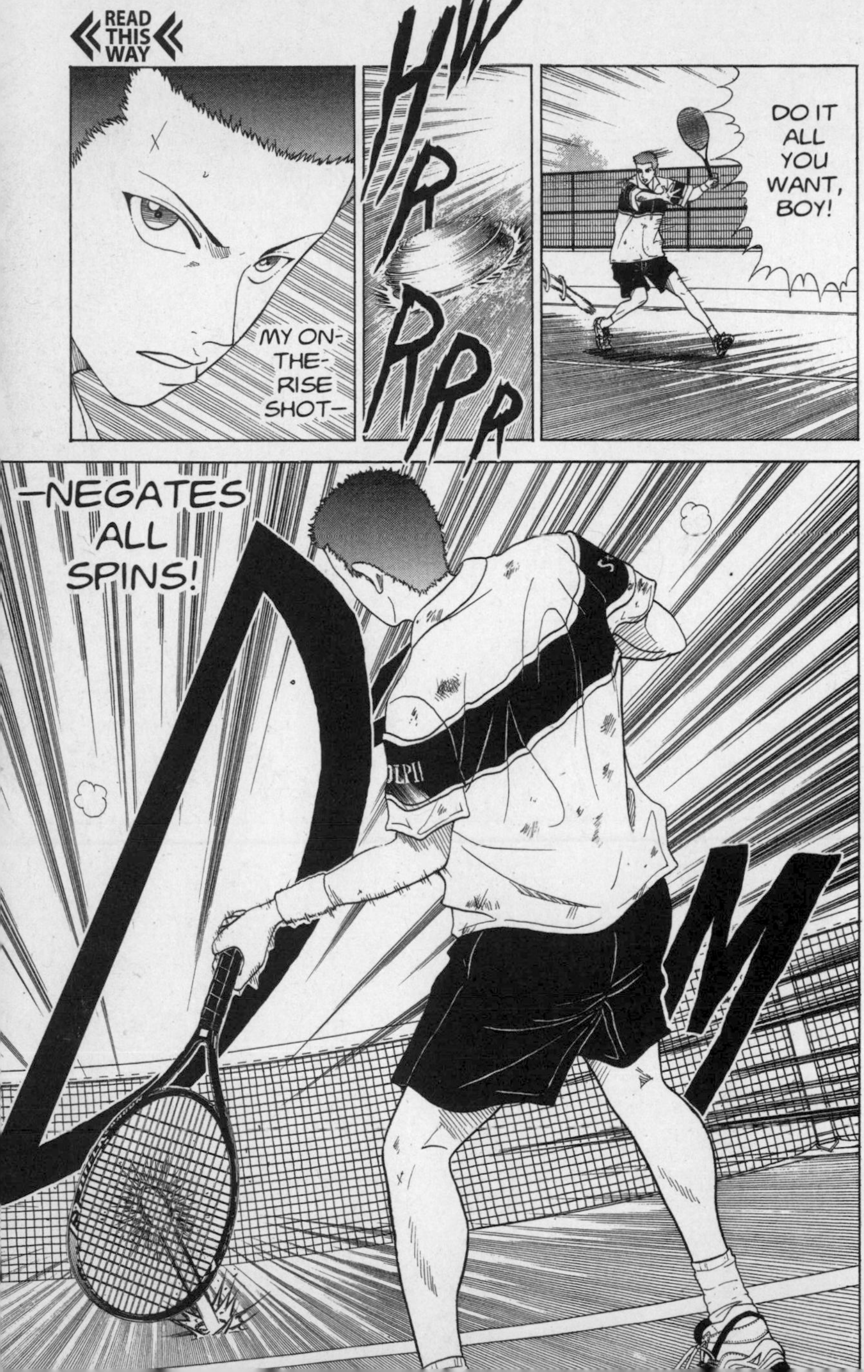
READ THIS WAY
DO IT ALL YOU WANT, BOY!
MY ON-THE-RISE SHOT—
—NEGATES ALL SPINS!

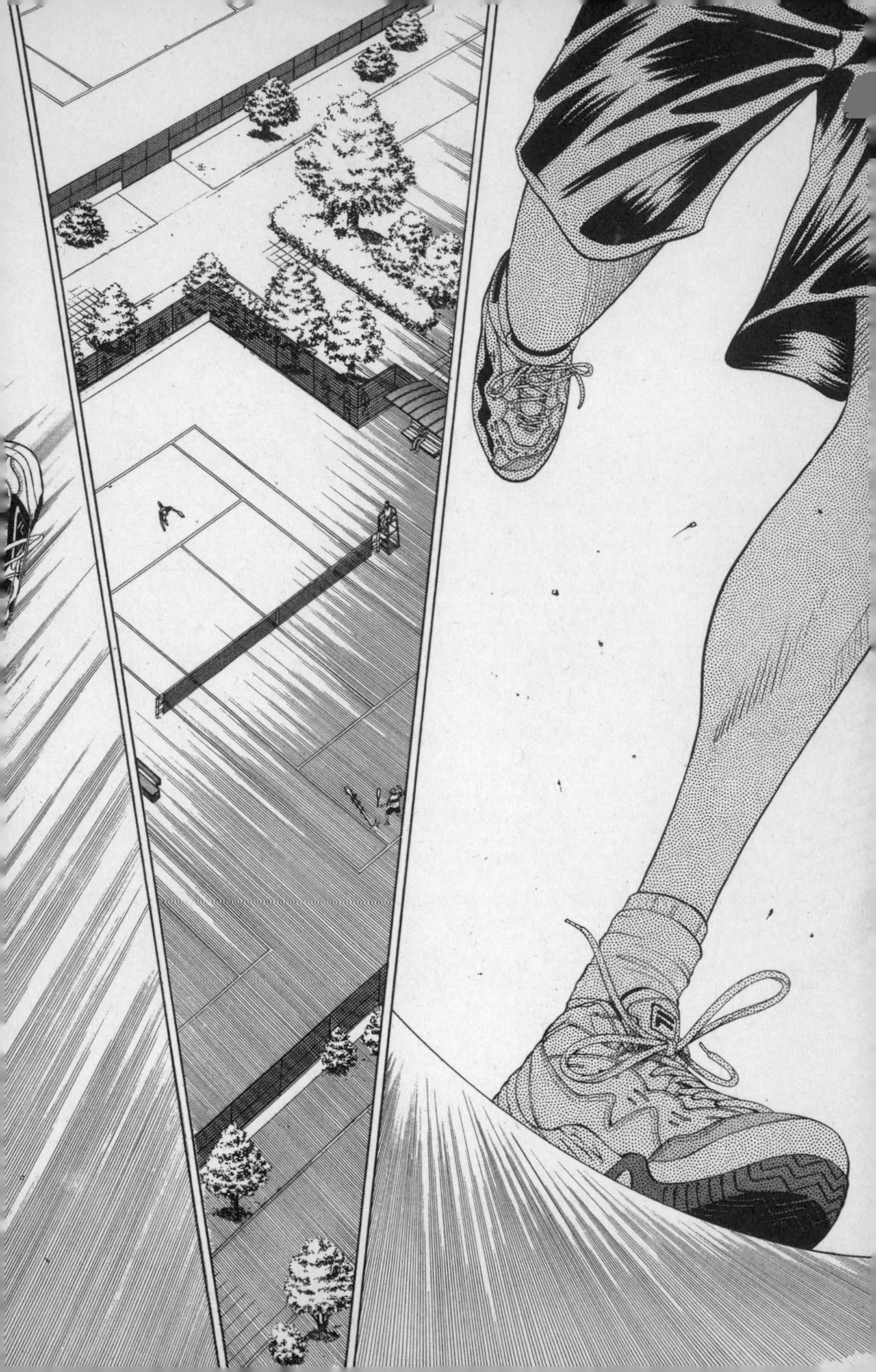

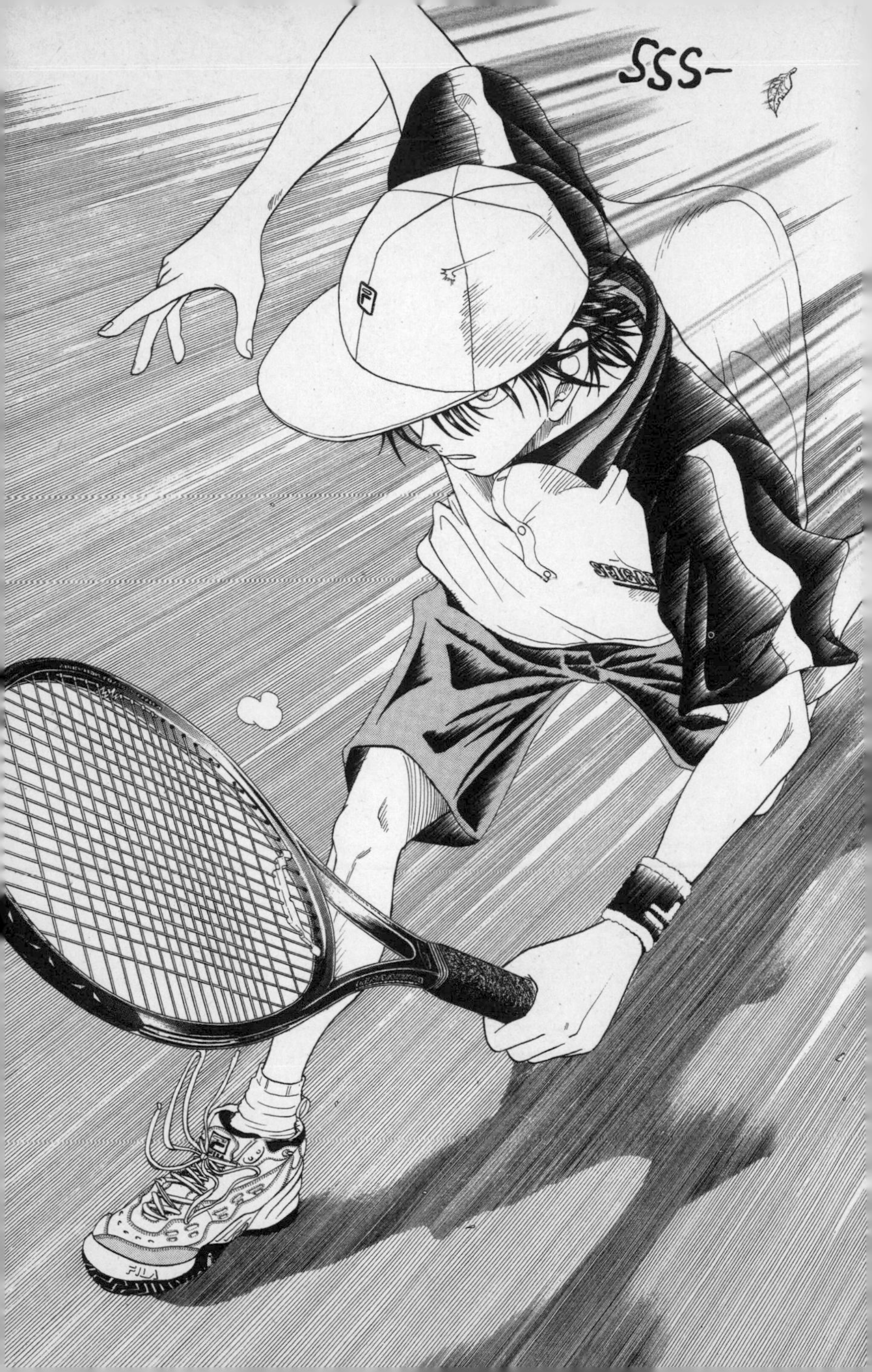
SSS-
FILA

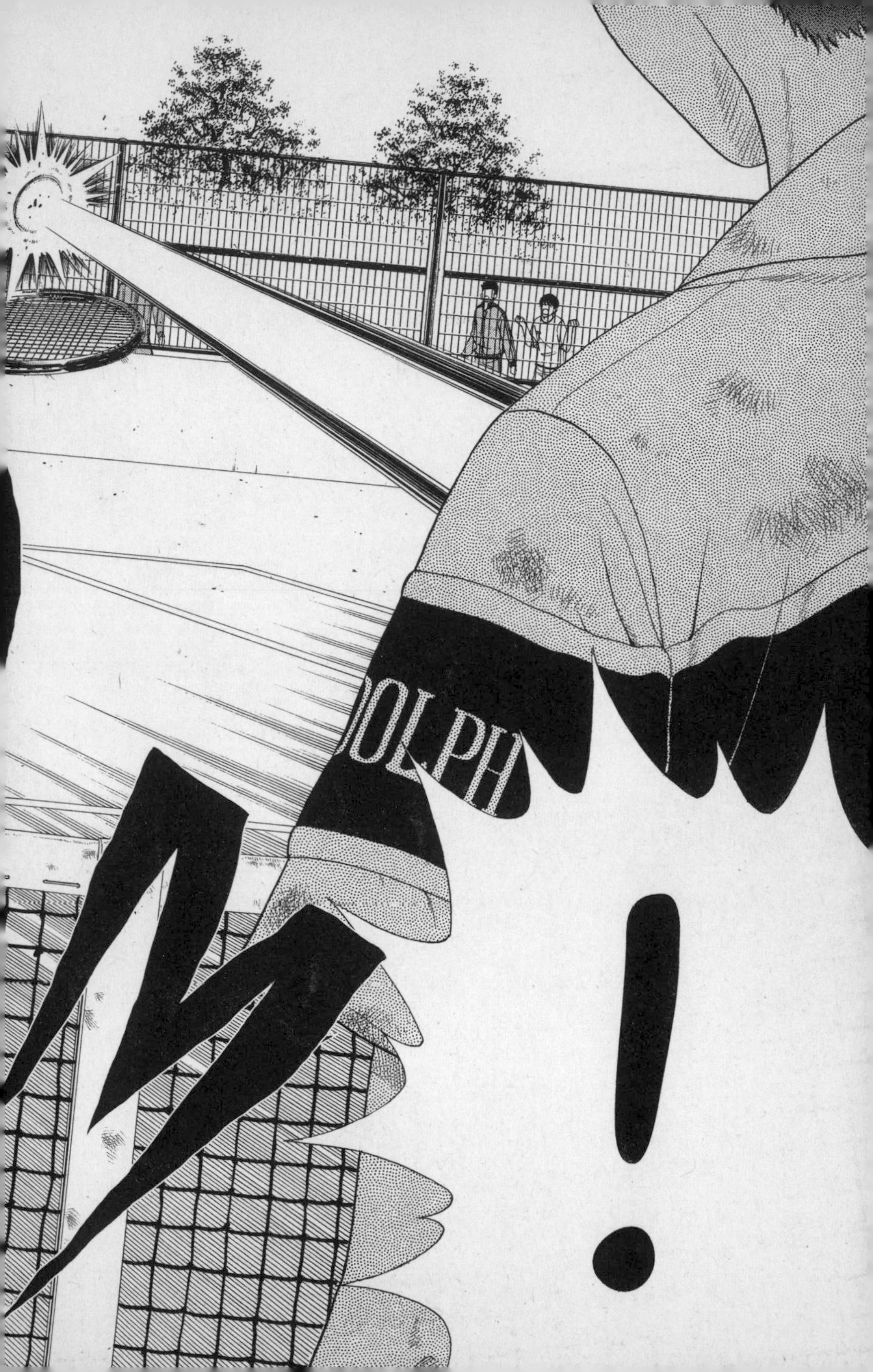
DOLPH
!

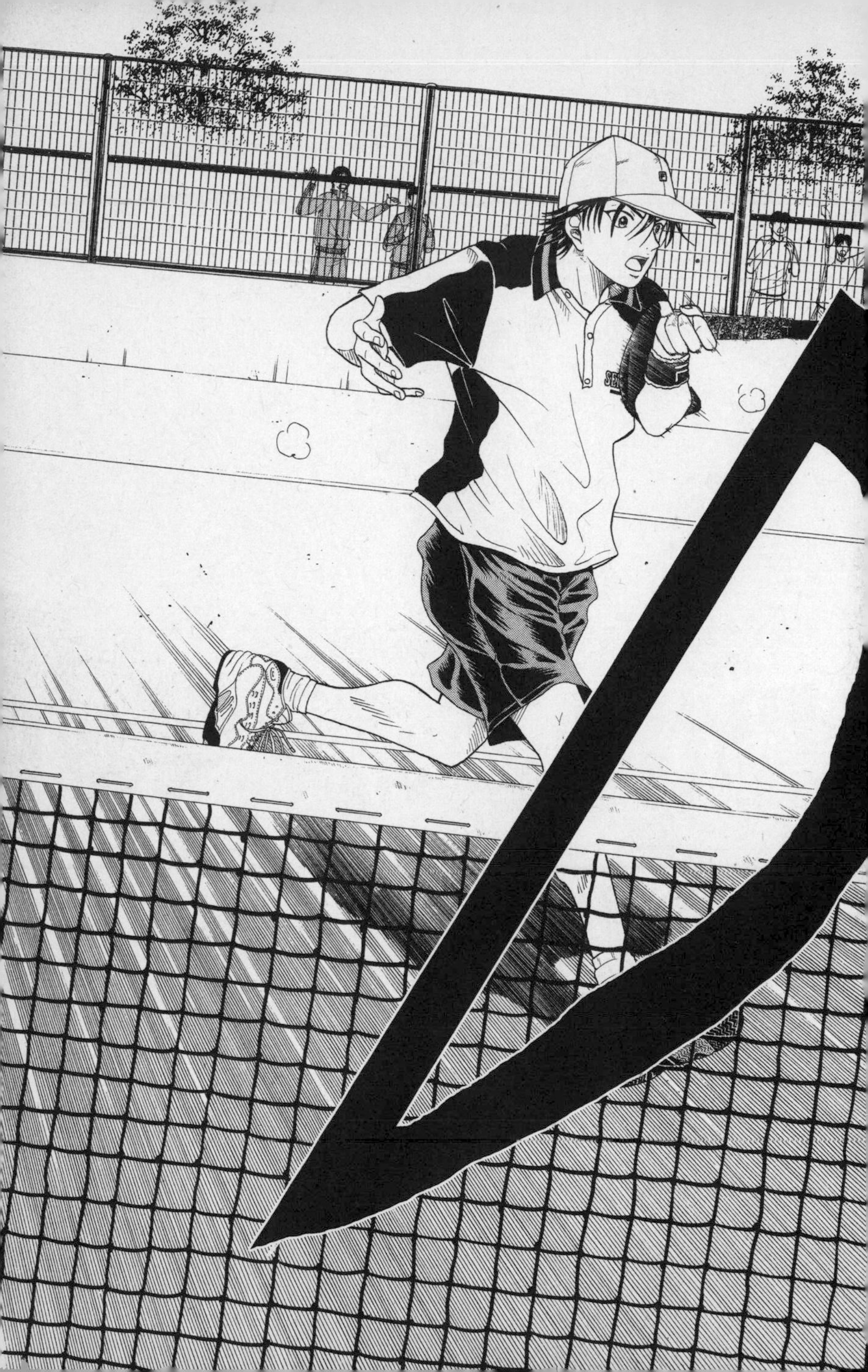

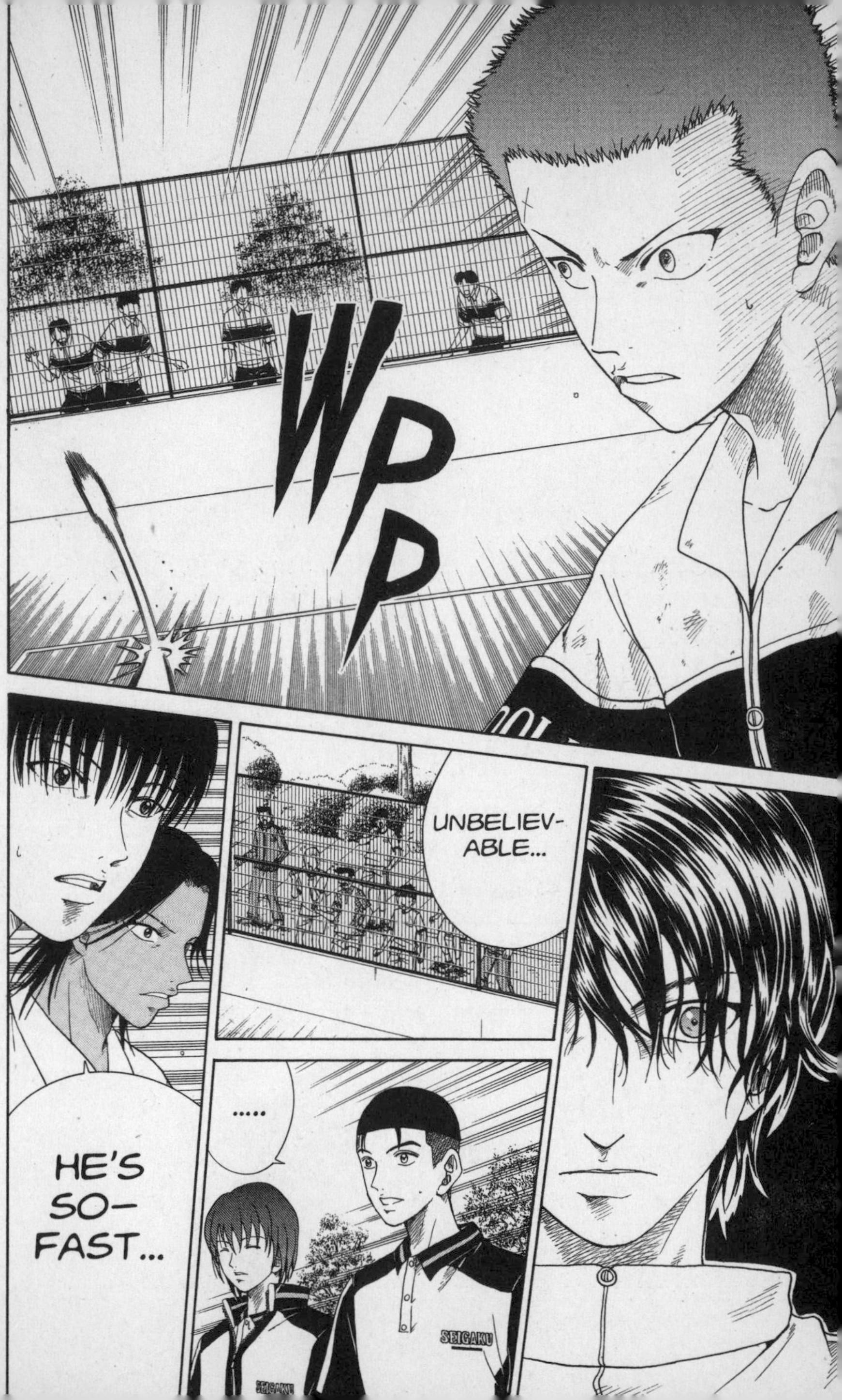
WPP
UNBELIEV-ABLE...
.....
SEIGAKU
HE'S SO-FAST...

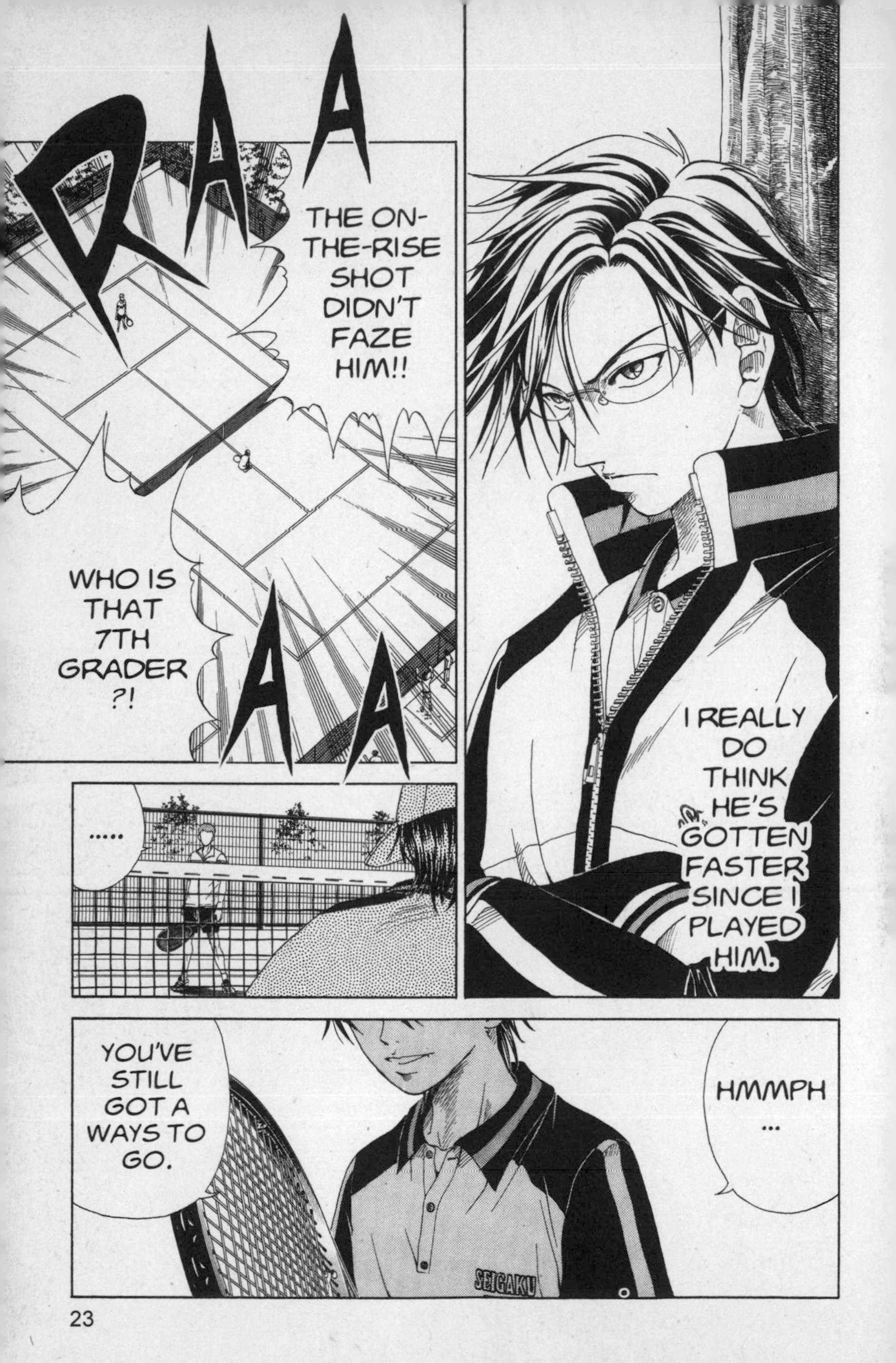
I REALLY DO THINK HE'S GOTTEN FASTER SINCE I PLAYED HIM.
RAAAA
THE ON-THE-RISE SHOT DIDN'T FAZE HIM!!
WHO IS THAT 7TH GRADER?!
.....
HMMPH...
YOU'VE STILL GOT A WAYS TO GO.

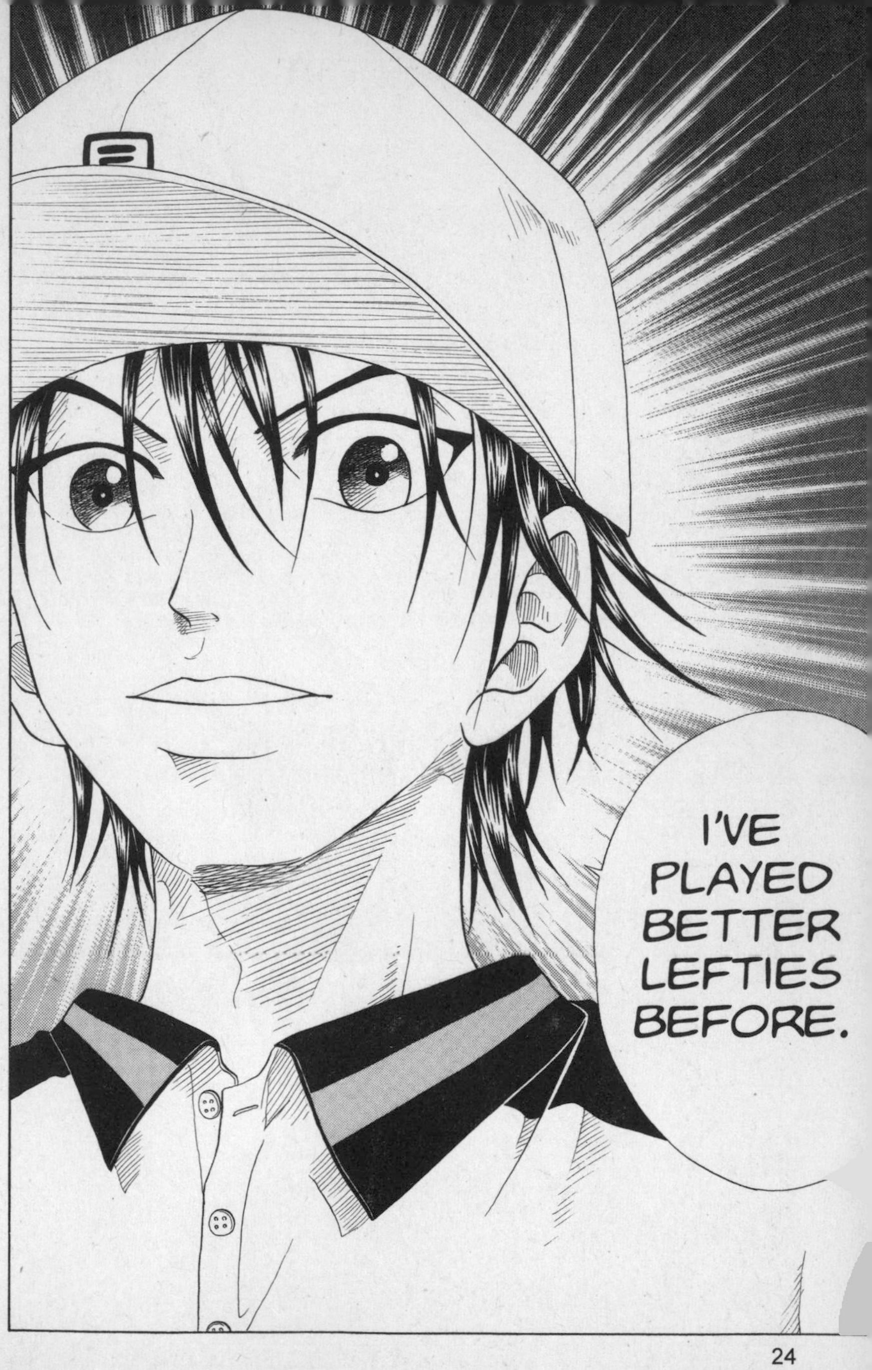
I'VE PLAYED BETTER LEFTIES BEFORE.

GENIUS 71: YUTA'S RETORT

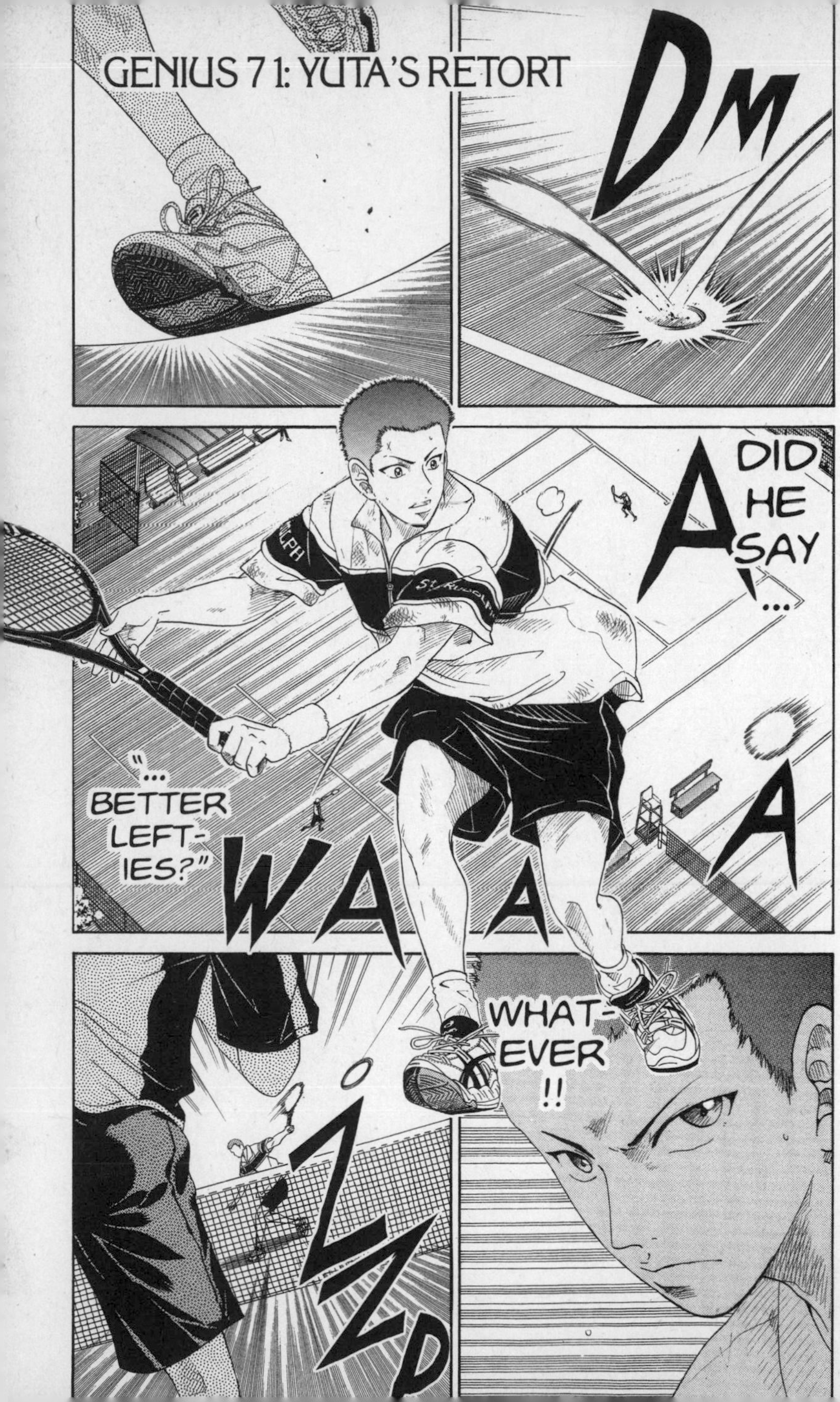
DM
DID HE SAY ...
"... BETTER LEFT-IES?"
A A
WA A A
WHAT-EVER !!
ZZZD

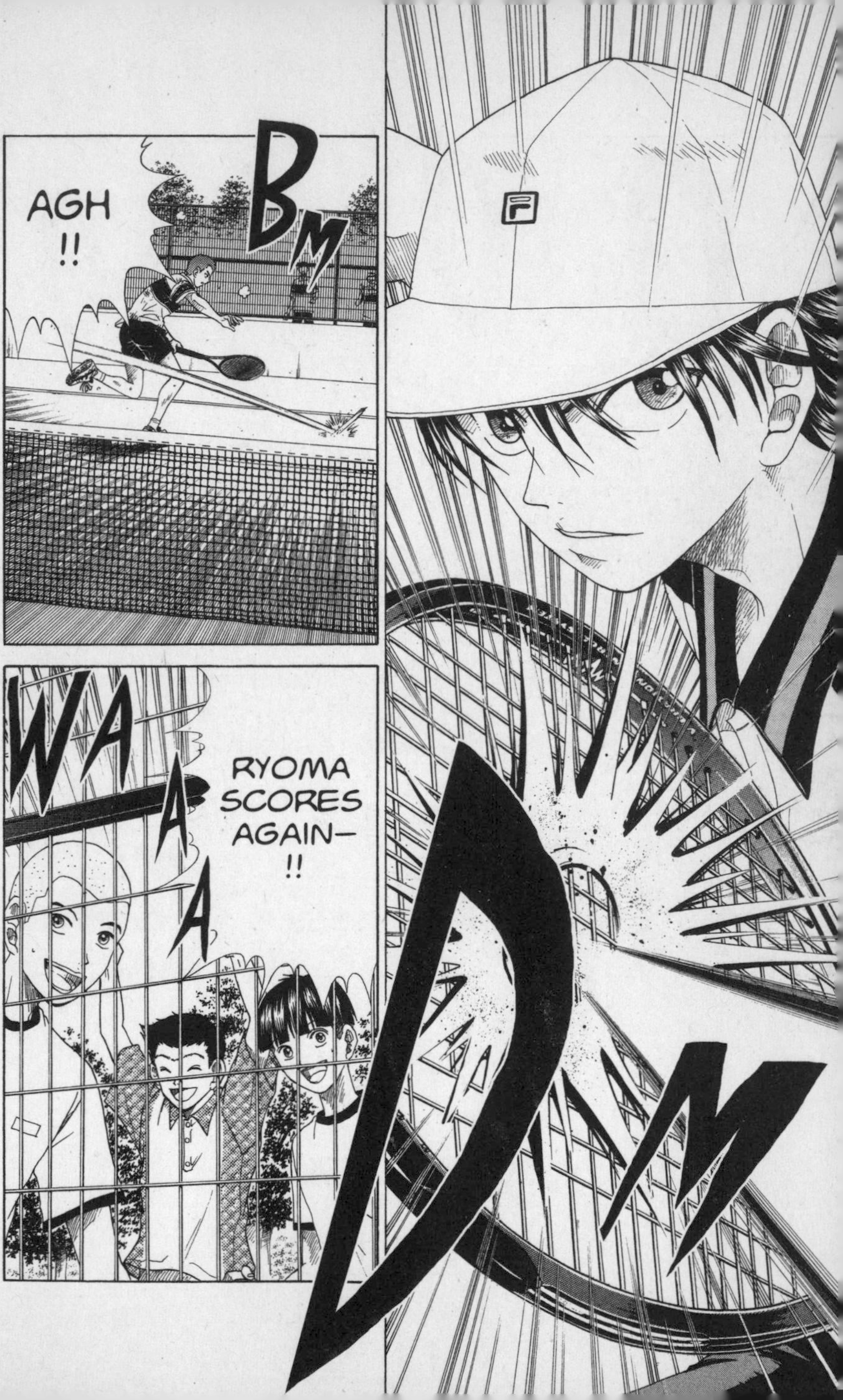
DM
BM
AGH !!
RYOMA SCORES AGAIN— !!
WAAAA

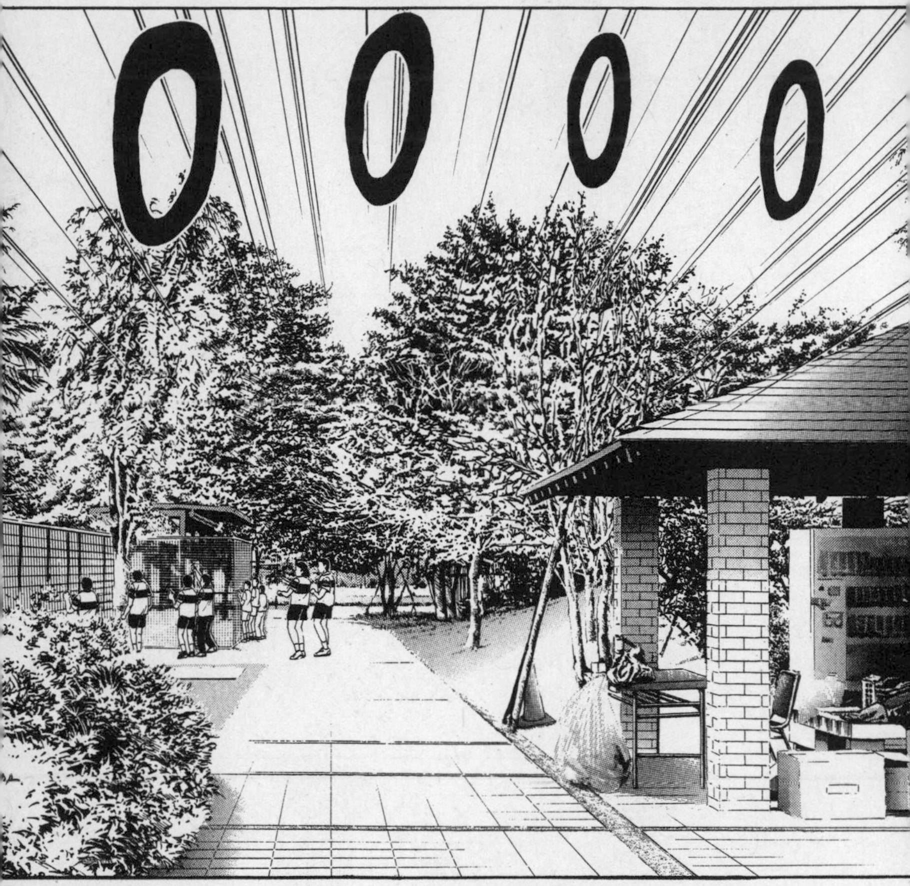

OOOO

GENIUS 71: YUTA'S RETORT

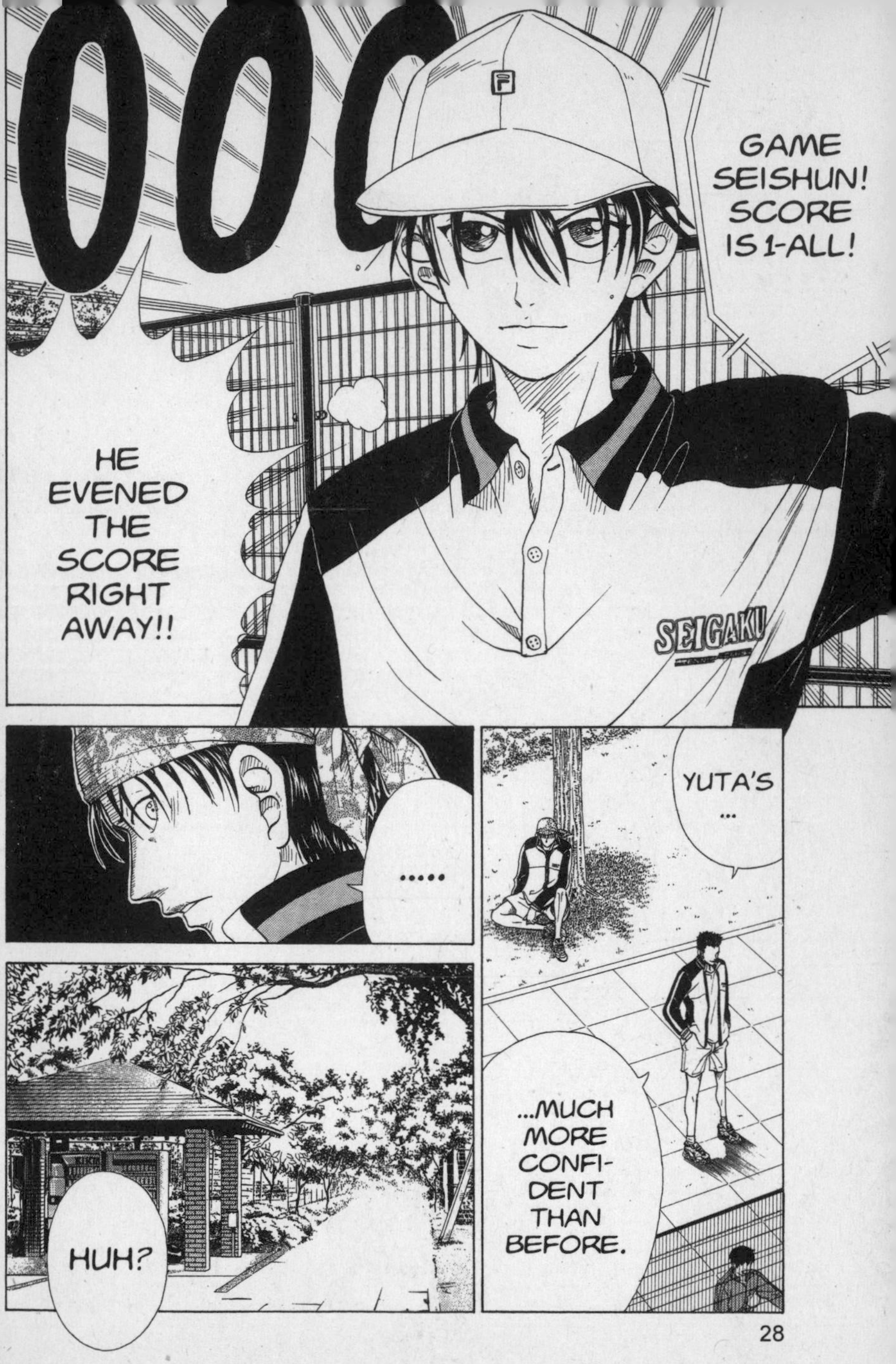
GAME SEISHUN! SCORE IS 1-ALL!
OOO
HE EVENED THE SCORE RIGHT AWAY!!
YUTA'S ...
.....
...MUCH MORE CONFI-DENT THAN BEFORE.
HUH?

READ THIS WAY

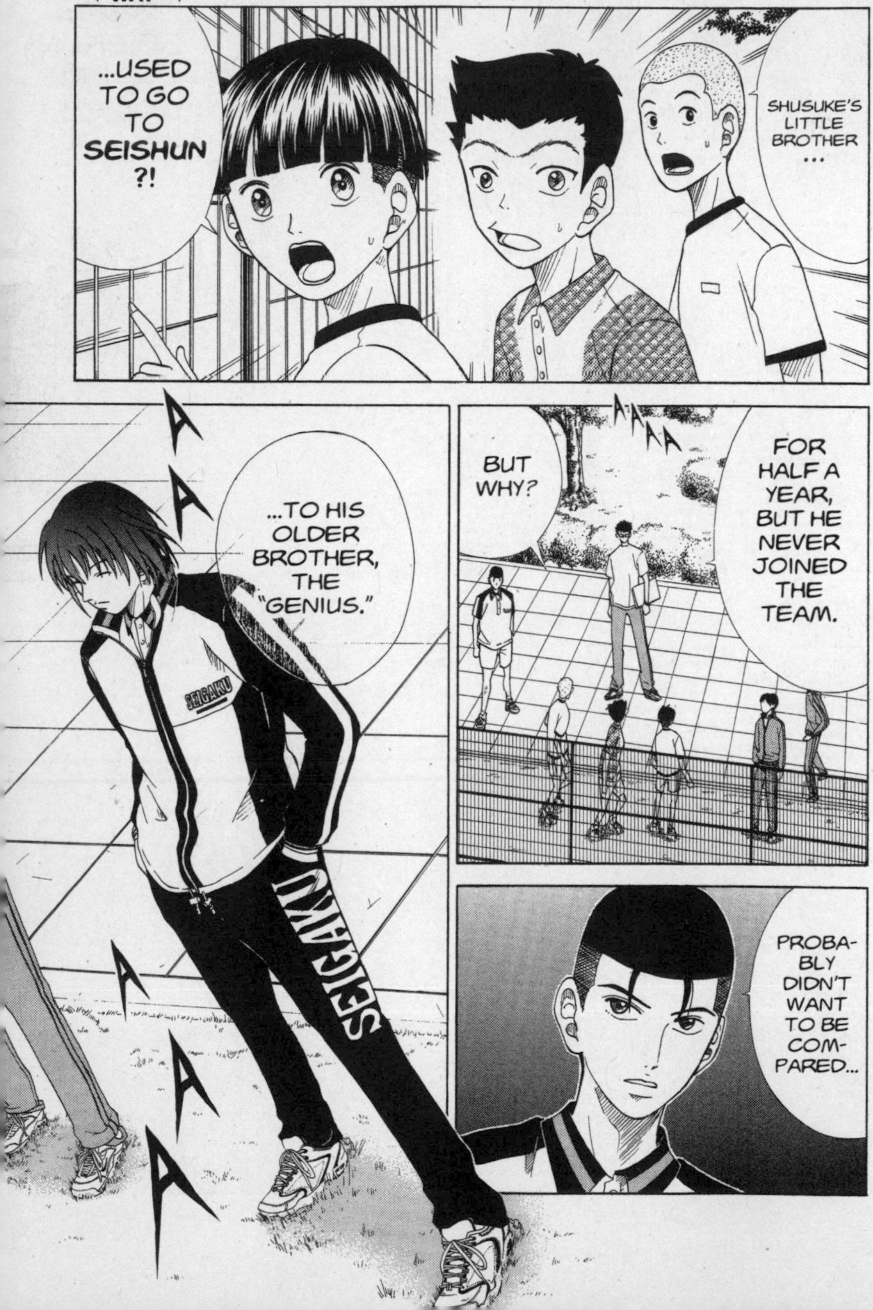
SHUSUKE'S LITTLE BROTHER...
...USED TO GO TO SEISHUN?!
FOR HALF A YEAR, BUT HE NEVER JOINED THE TEAM.
BUT WHY?
PROBABLY DIDN'T WANT TO BE COMPARED...
...TO HIS OLDER BROTHER, THE "GENIUS."
SEIGAKU

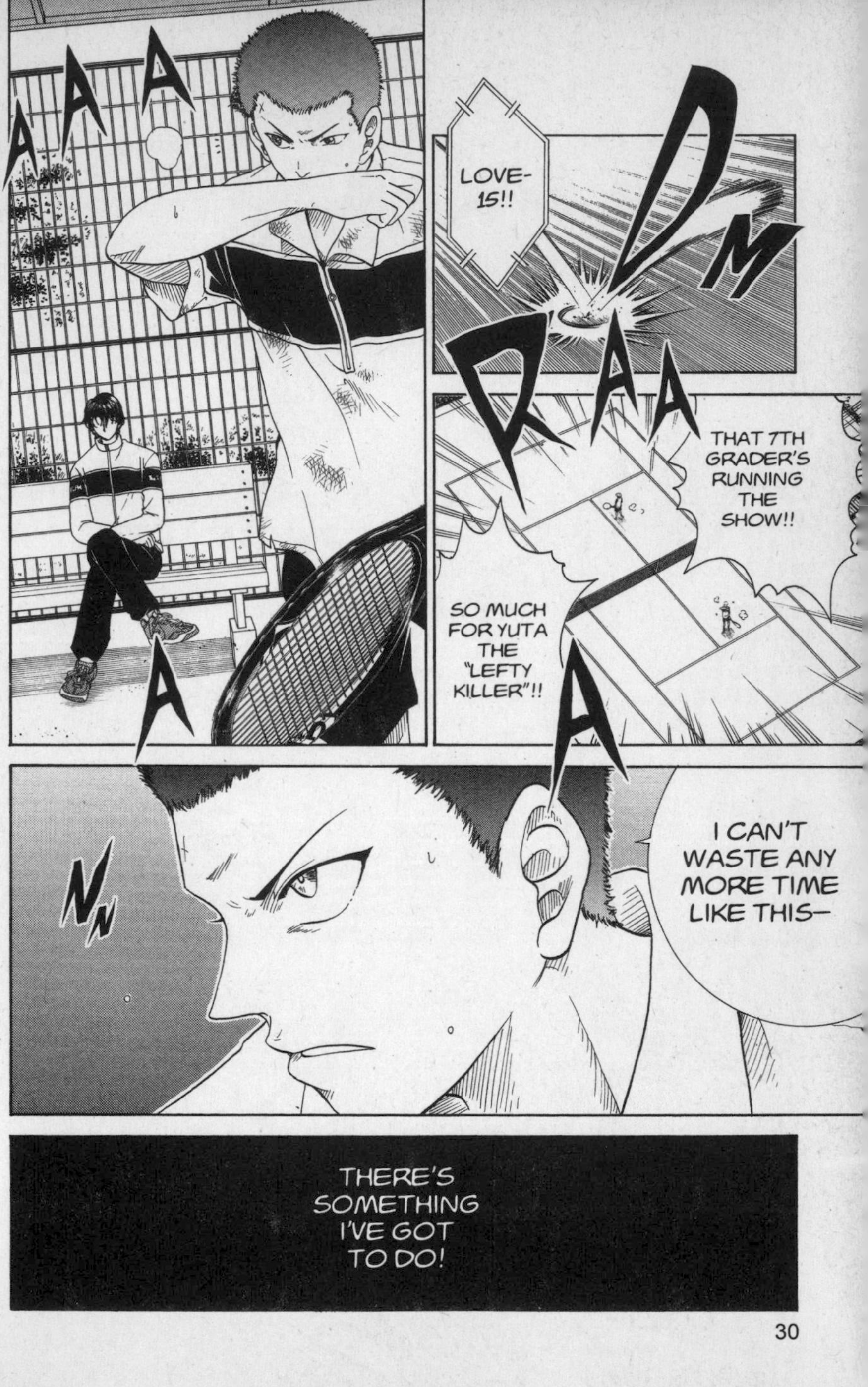
LOVE-15!!
DM
DRAA
THAT 7TH GRADER'S RUNNING THE SHOW!!
SO MUCH FOR YUTA THE "LEFTY KILLER"!!
A
AAAA
A
I CAN'T WASTE ANY MORE TIME LIKE THIS—
NN
THERE'S SOMETHING I'VE GOT TO DO!

READ THIS WAY

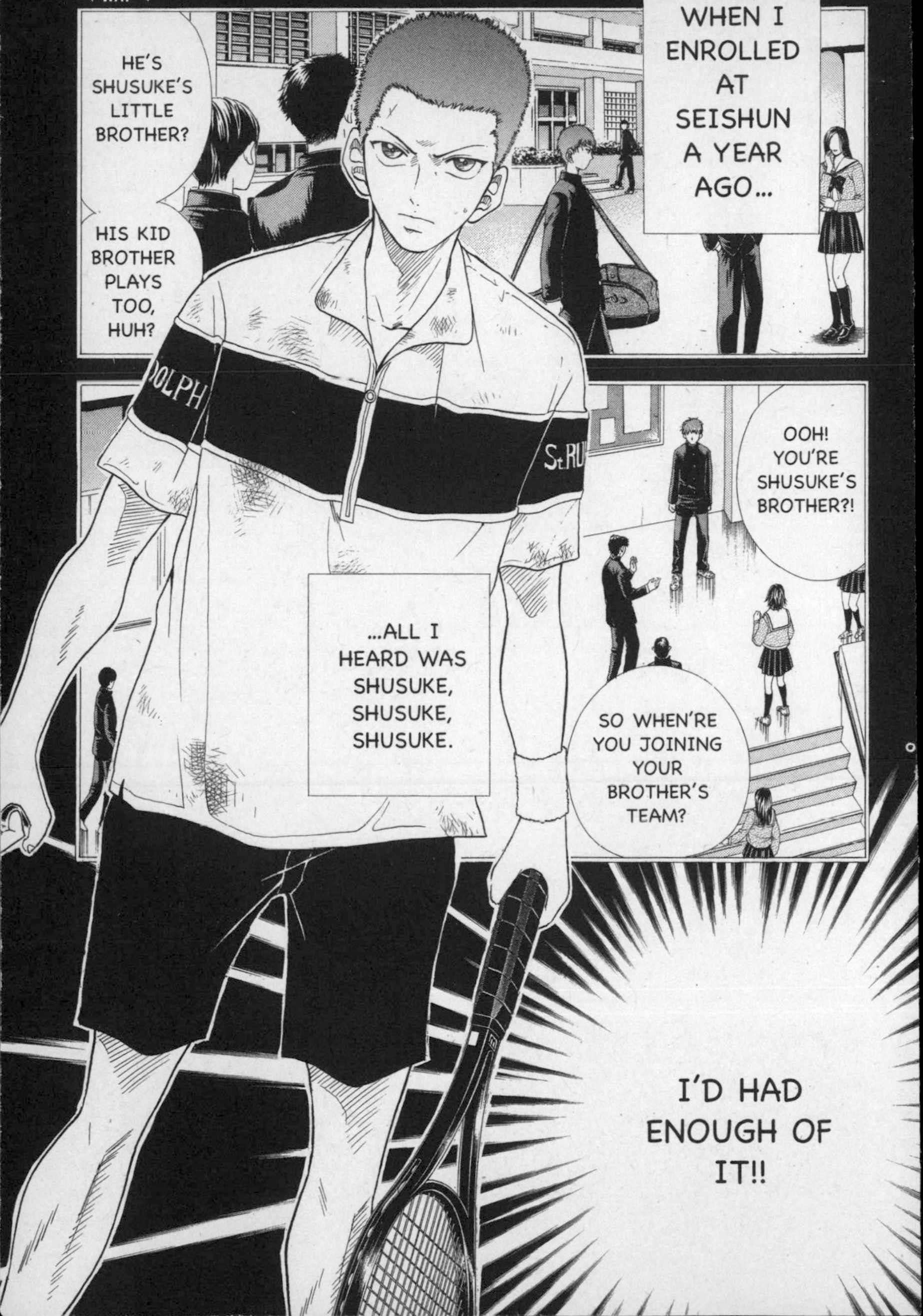
WHEN I ENROLLED AT SEISHUN A YEAR AGO...
HE'S SHUSUKE'S LITTLE BROTHER?
HIS KID BROTHER PLAYS TOO, HUH?
OOH! YOU'RE SHUSUKE'S BROTHER?!
SO WHEN'RE YOU JOINING YOUR BROTHER'S TEAM?
...ALL I HEARD WAS SHUSUKE, SHUSUKE, SHUSUKE.
I'D HAD ENOUGH OF IT!!

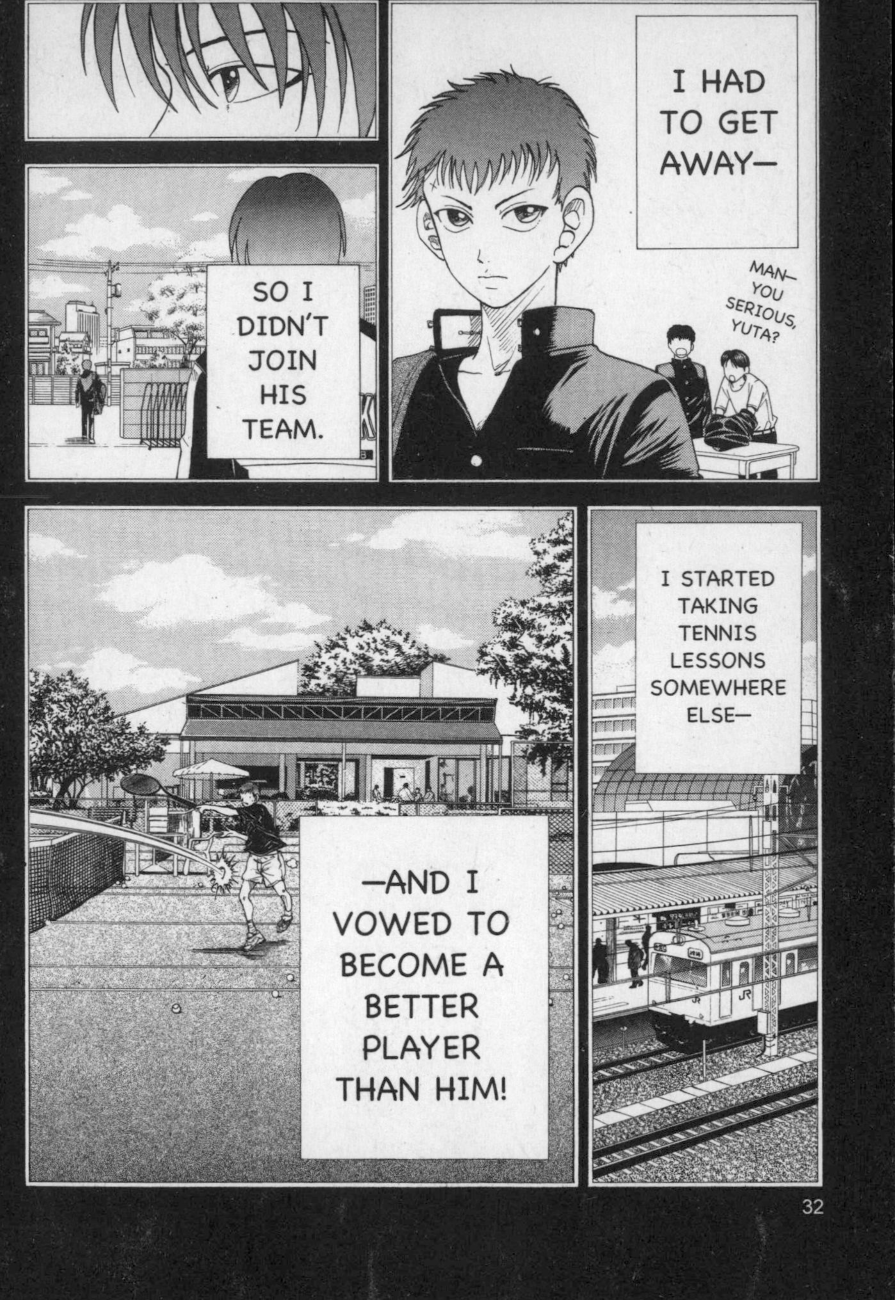
I HAD TO GET AWAY—
MAN— YOU SERIOUS, YUTA?
SO I DIDN'T JOIN HIS TEAM.
I STARTED TAKING TENNIS LESSONS SOMEWHERE ELSE—
—AND I VOWED TO BECOME A BETTER PLAYER THAN HIM!

READ THIS WAY

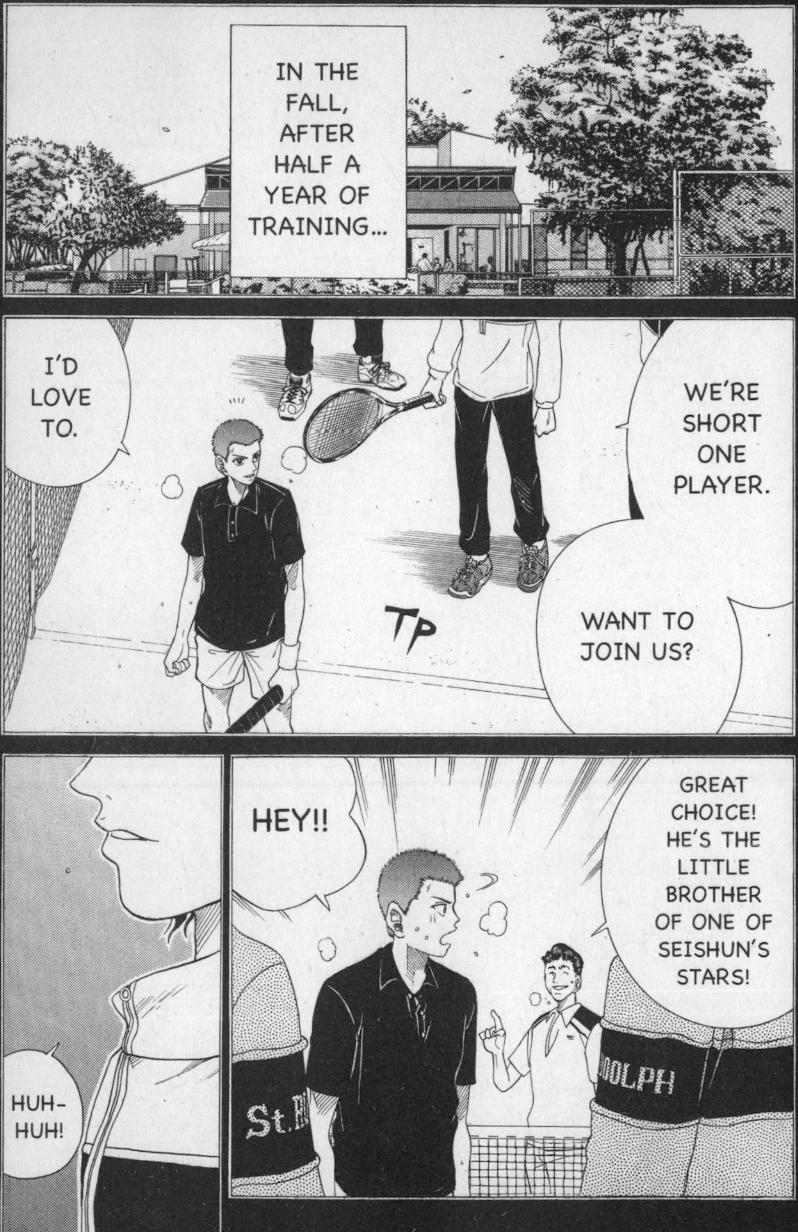
IN THE FALL, AFTER HALF A YEAR OF TRAINING...
WE'RE SHORT ONE PLAYER.
WANT TO JOIN US?
TP
I'D LOVE TO.
GREAT CHOICE! HE'S THE LITTLE BROTHER OF ONE OF SEISHUN'S STARS!
HEY!!
HUH-HUH!

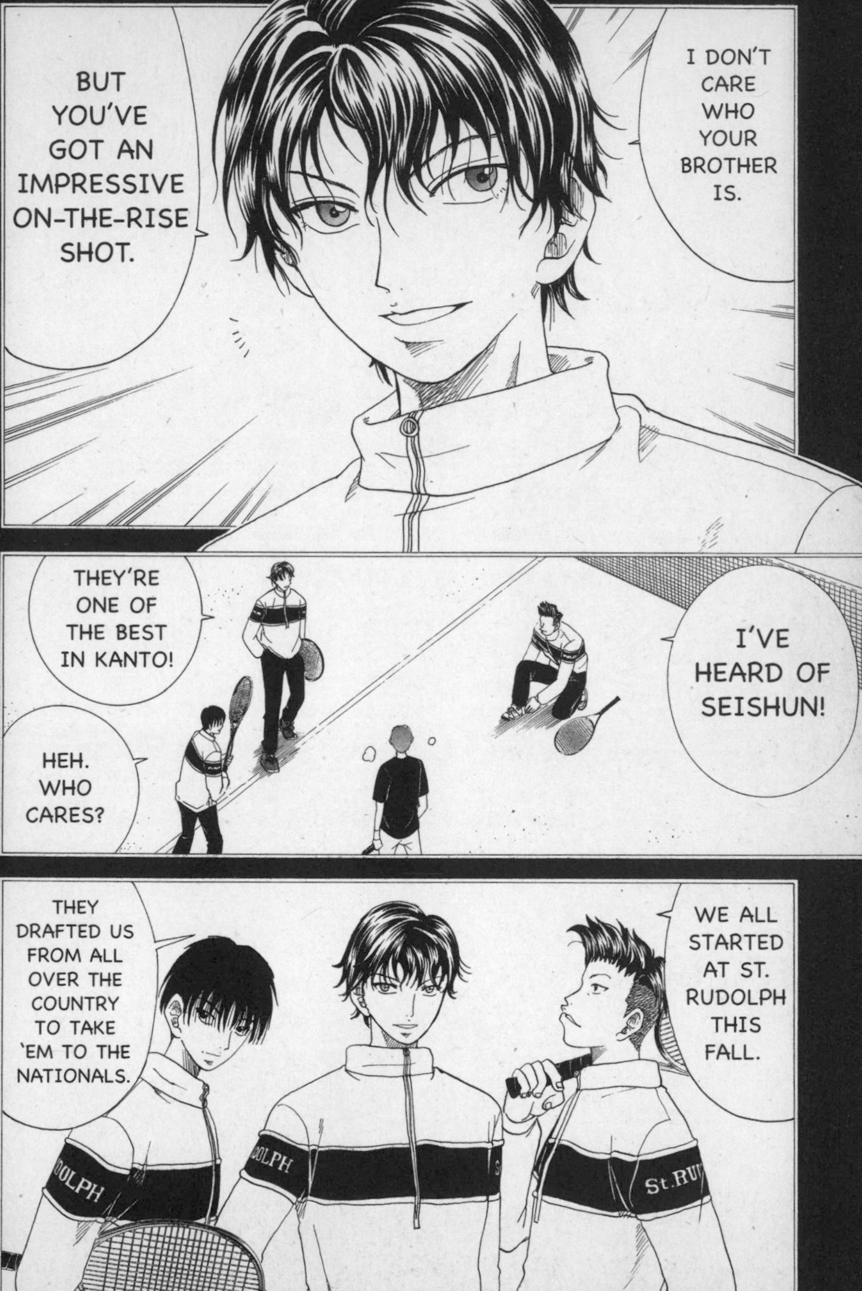
I DON'T CARE WHO YOUR BROTHER IS.
BUT YOU'VE GOT AN IMPRESSIVE ON-THE-RISE SHOT.
I'VE HEARD OF SEISHUN!
THEY'RE ONE OF THE BEST IN KANTO!
HEH. WHO CARES?
WE ALL STARTED AT ST. RUDOLPH THIS FALL.
THEY DRAFTED US FROM ALL OVER THE COUNTRY TO TAKE 'EM TO THE NATIONALS.

READ THIS WAY

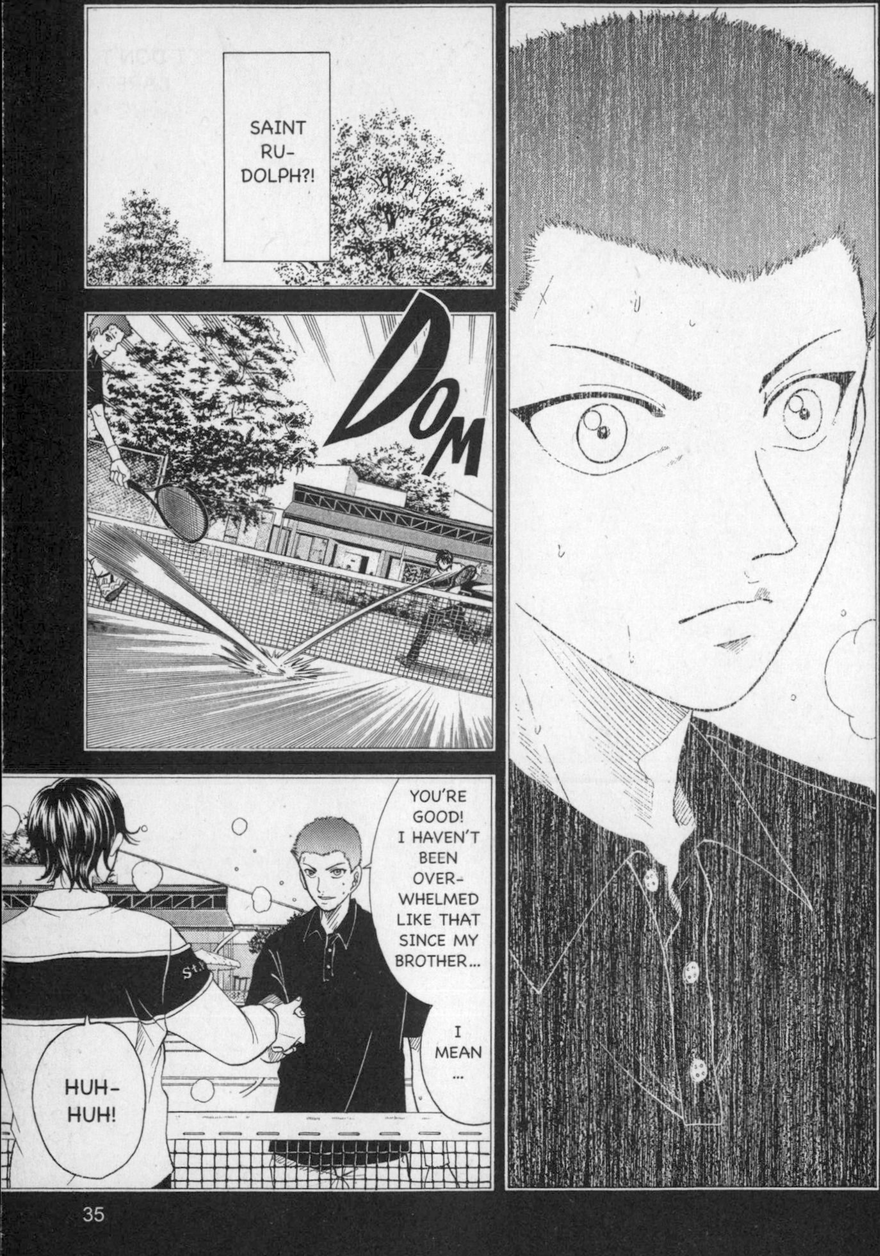
SAINT RU-DOLPH?!
DOM
YOU'RE GOOD! I HAVEN'T BEEN OVER-WHELMED LIKE THAT SINCE MY BROTHER...
I MEAN ...
HUH-HUH!

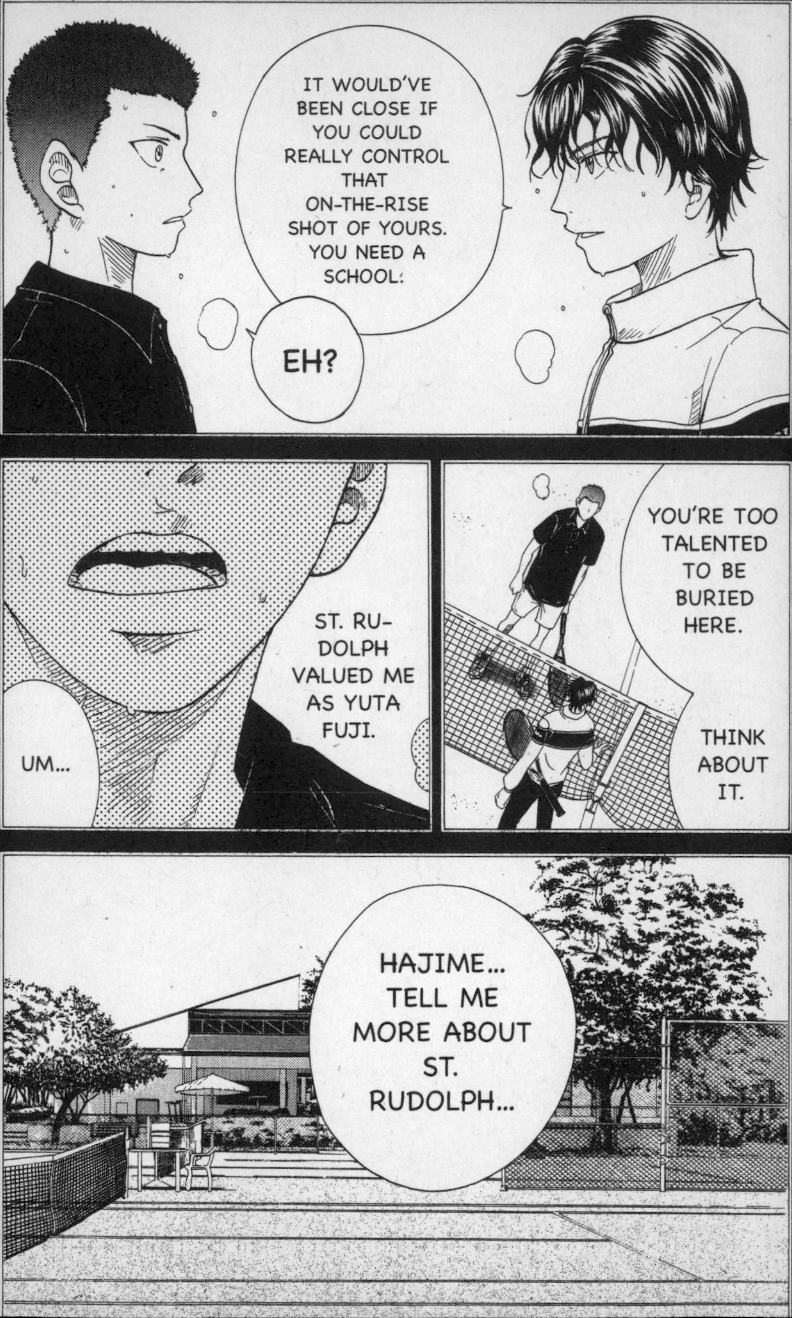
IT WOULD'VE BEEN CLOSE IF YOU COULD REALLY CONTROL THAT ON-THE-RISE SHOT OF YOURS. YOU NEED A SCHOOL:
EH?
YOU'RE TOO TALENTED TO BE BURIED HERE.
THINK ABOUT IT.
ST. RU-DOLPH VALUED ME AS YUTA FUJI.
UM...
HAJIME... TELL ME MORE ABOUT ST. RUDOLPH...

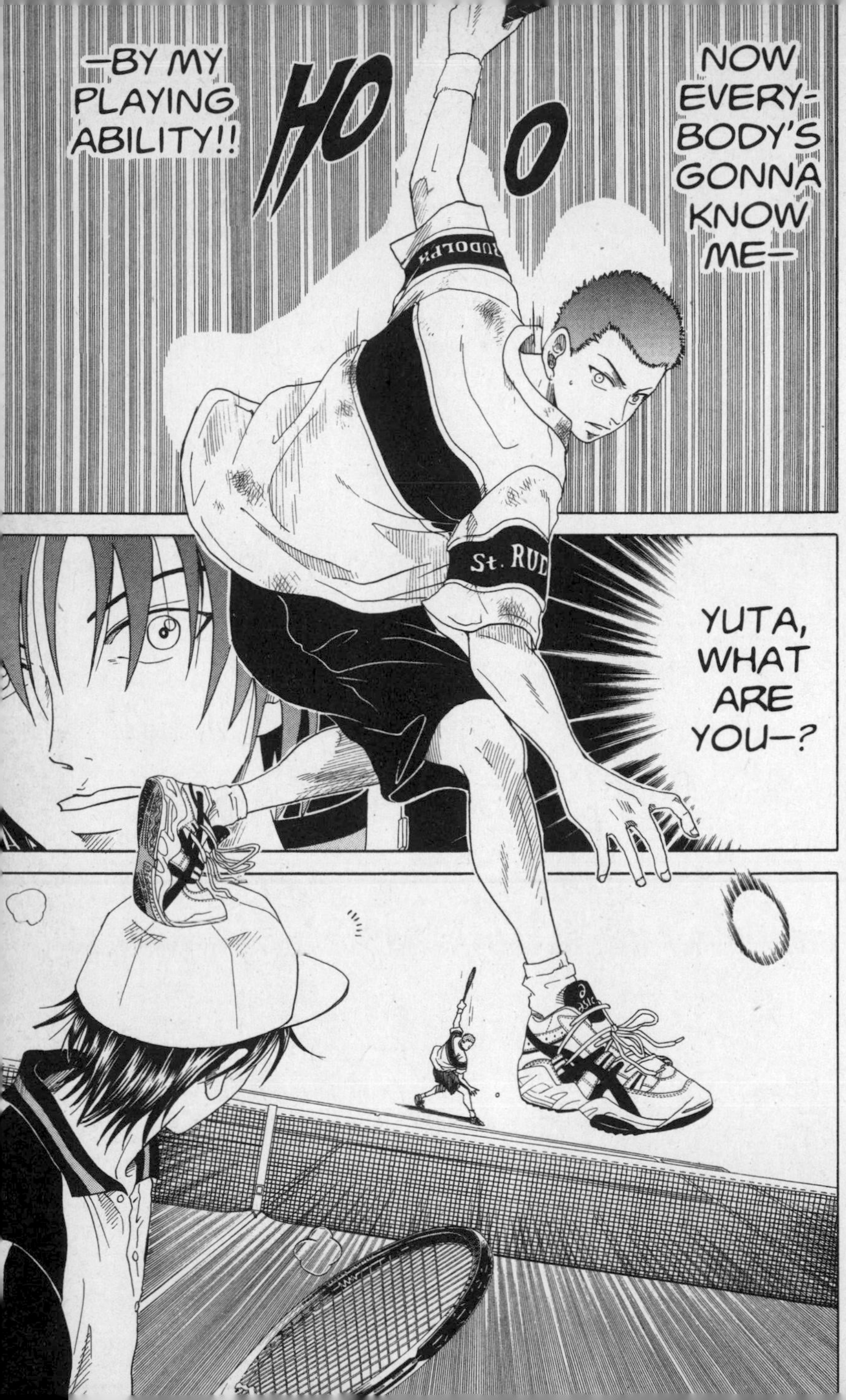
NOW EVERY-BODY'S GONNA KNOW ME—
HO O
—BY MY PLAYING ABILITY!!
YUTA, WHAT ARE YOU—?

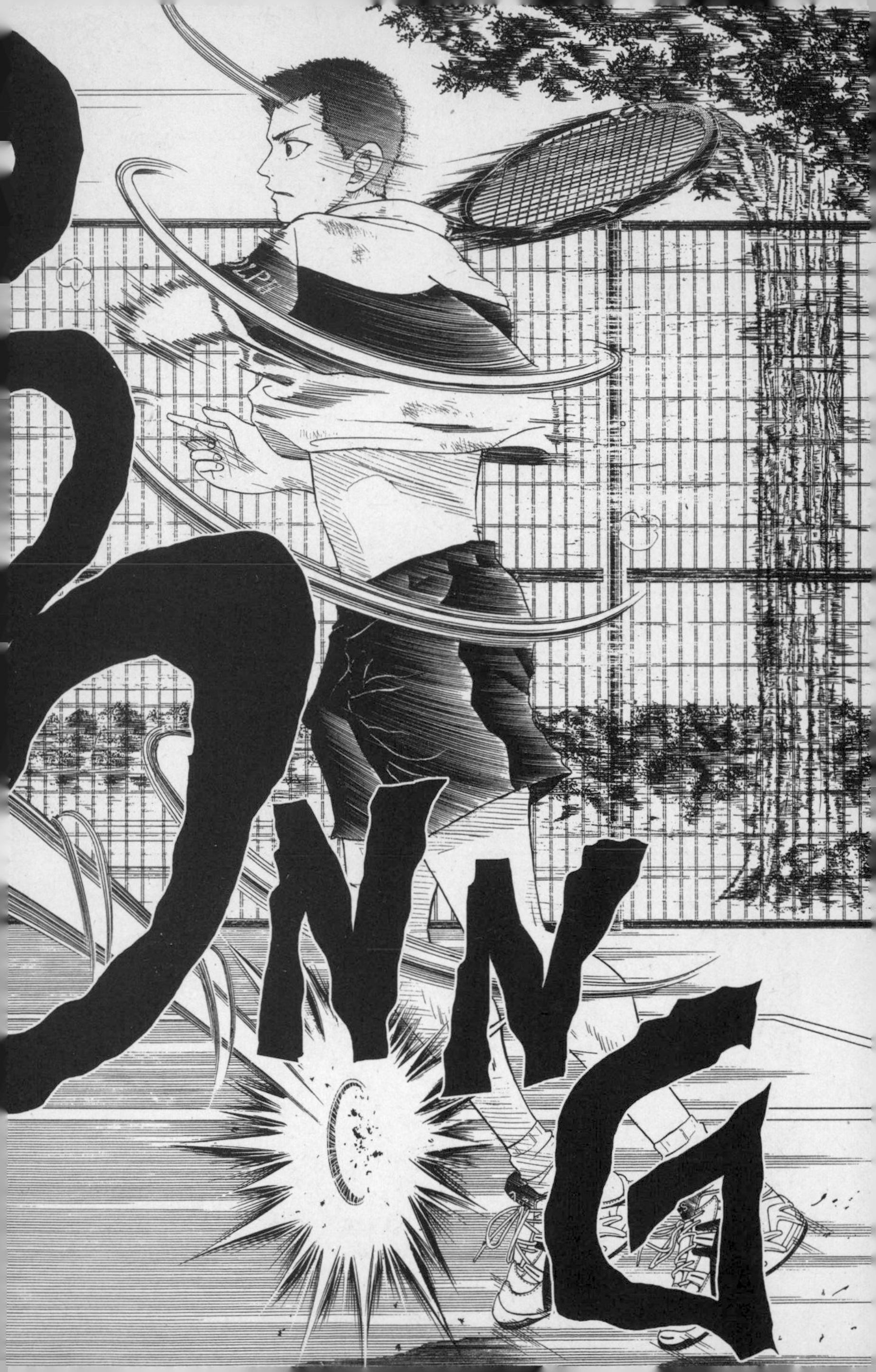
ZNNG

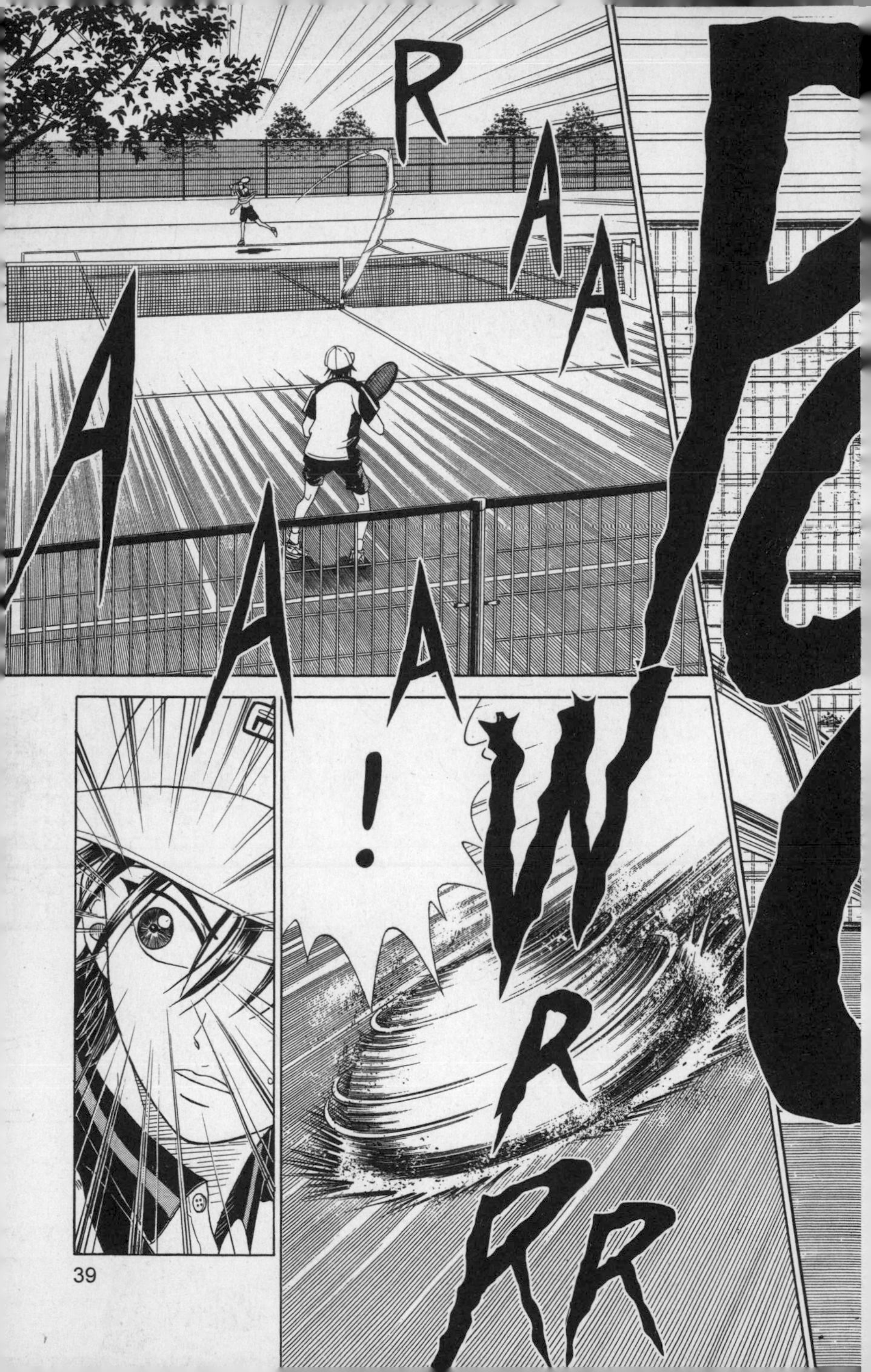
RAAAAA!
WRRR

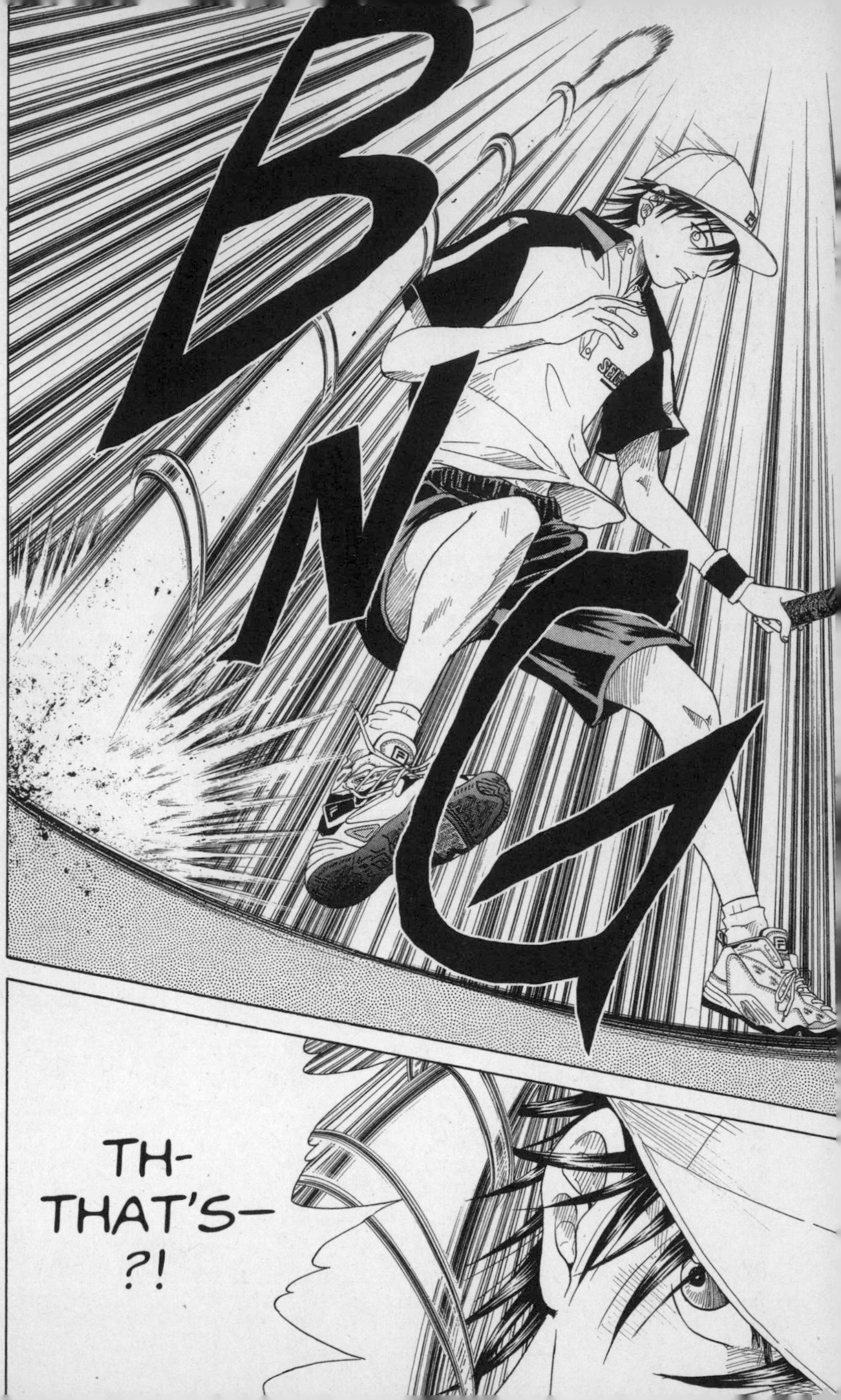
TH-
THAT'S—
?!

READ THIS WAY

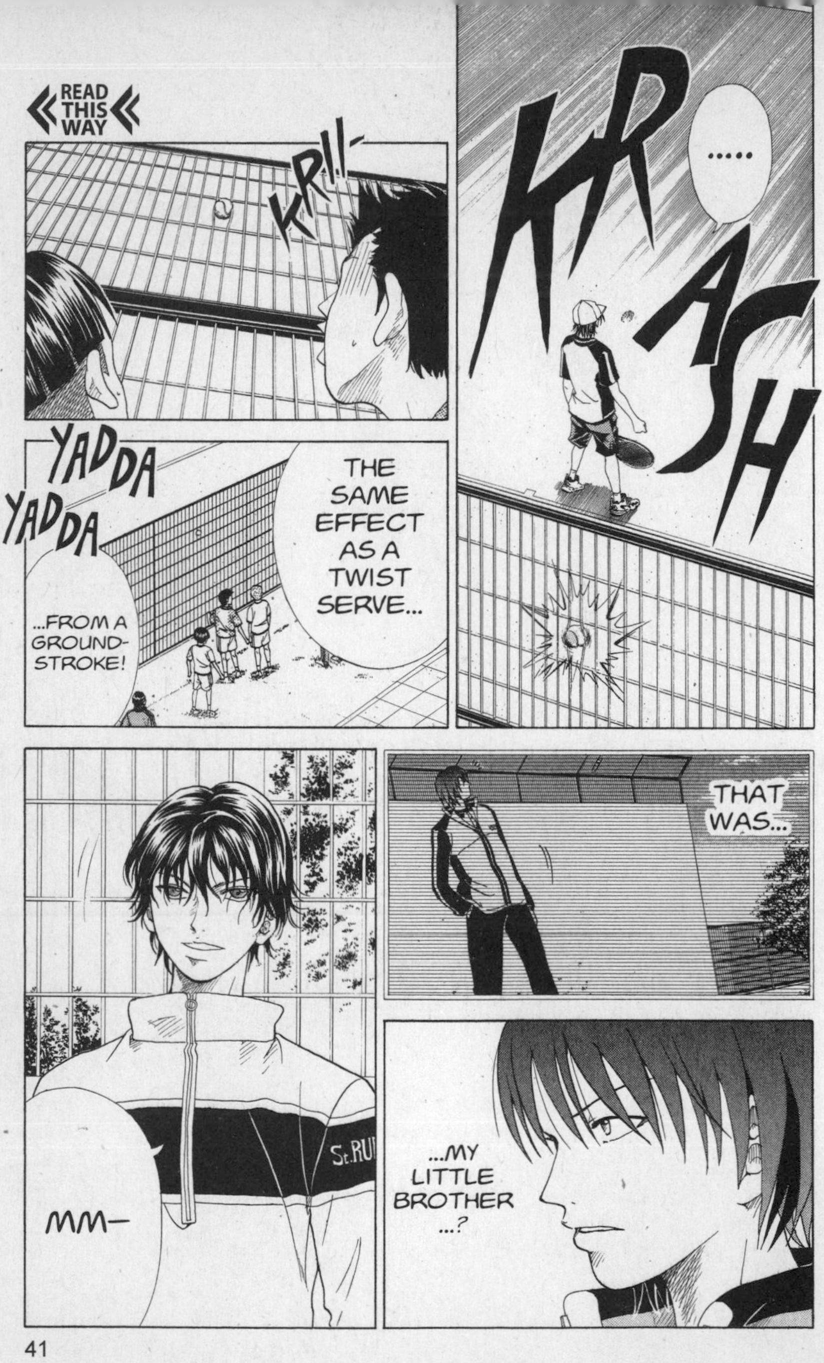

......
KRASH
KRII-
THE SAME EFFECT AS A TWIST SERVE...
YADDA YADDA
...FROM A GROUND-STROKE!
THAT WAS...
...MY LITTLE BROTHER ...?
MM—

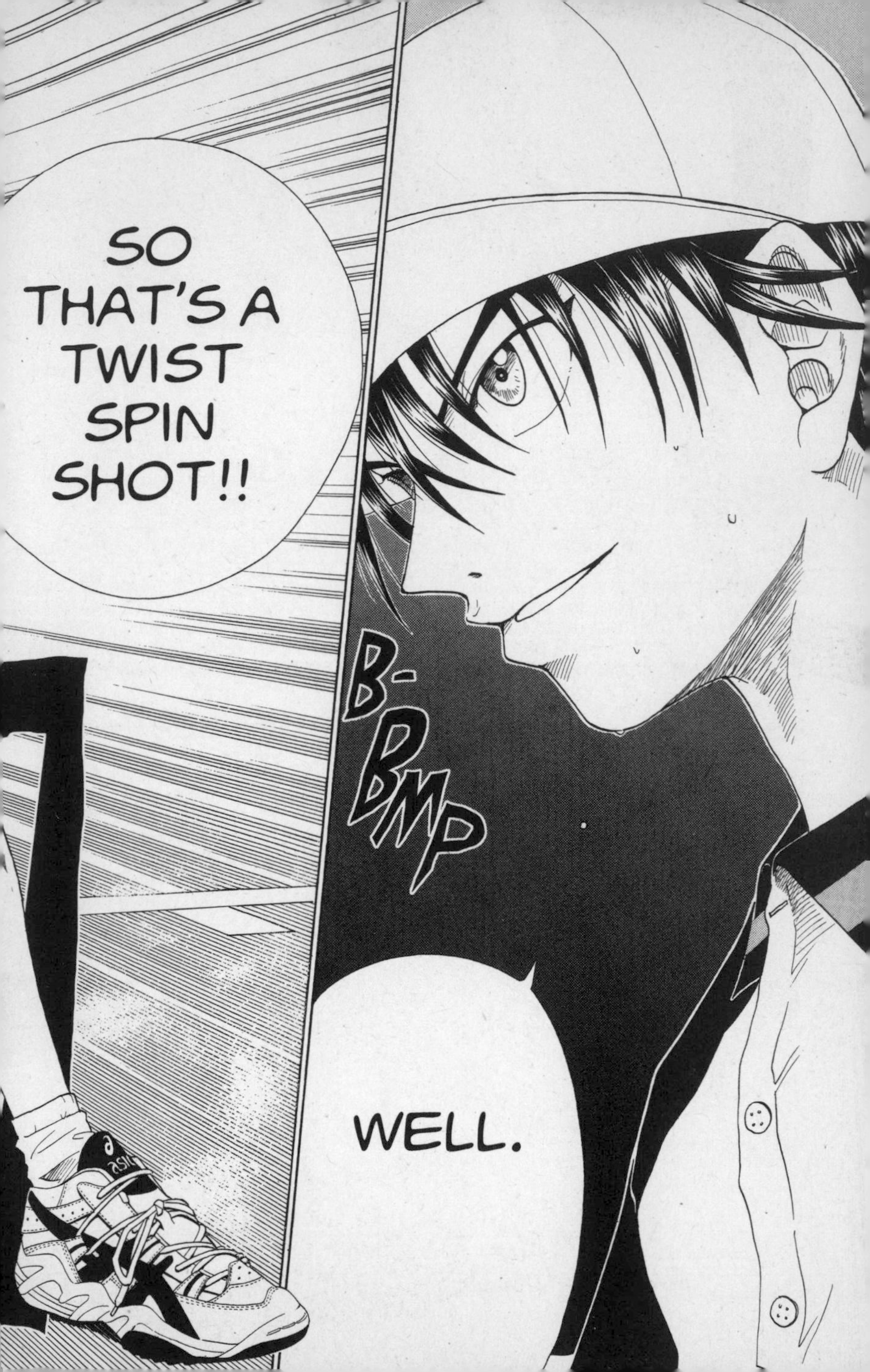
B-BMP
WELL.
SO THAT'S A TWIST SPIN SHOT!!

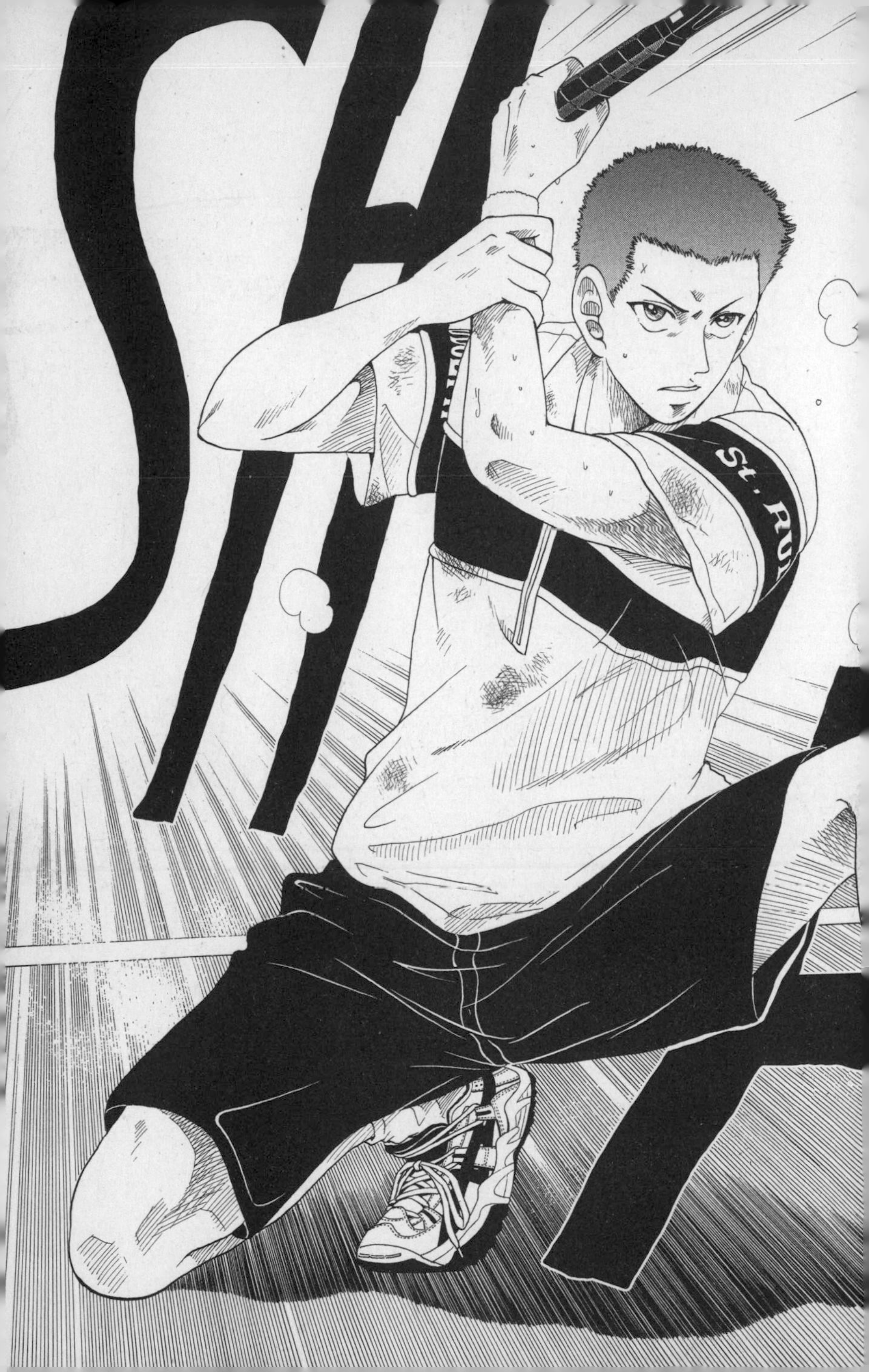
St. RU

Thanks for reading The Prince of Tennis Volume 9!

We got a lot of responses from female readers for the "Valentine Chocolate Acquisition Ranking" we ran in Volume 8.

It seems like people enjoyed it, so I'm glad we took the time to count! But we did get letters saying, "You didn't list the character I sent chocolates to." I'm sorry!

Candies that were sent in standard fan letters instead of the actual Valentines that were sent to me from the editorial office couldn't be counted in time for the deadline. Some of you asked, "Didn't you read it? Did it arrive?" But I humbly read every one of them! I know they were heartfelt! (For now, I'll add one vote for Shinji. 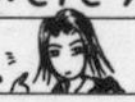)

We're about to hit the second anniversary for the Jump serialization. Like the first anniversary, we're thinking of new projects for this one. To those of you who only read the collected volumes and hate missing projects announced in the magazine, check out Jump #34, on sale July 24th 2001. And please participate in the project! (Editor's Note: This promo was held only in Japan.)

I thought I'd try to place my personal message toward the beginning of the book this time. I hope you enjoy the rest of the volume!

Keep supporting The Prince of Tennis and Ryoma! See you next time!!

テニスの王子様☆
KONOMI
2001.6.5

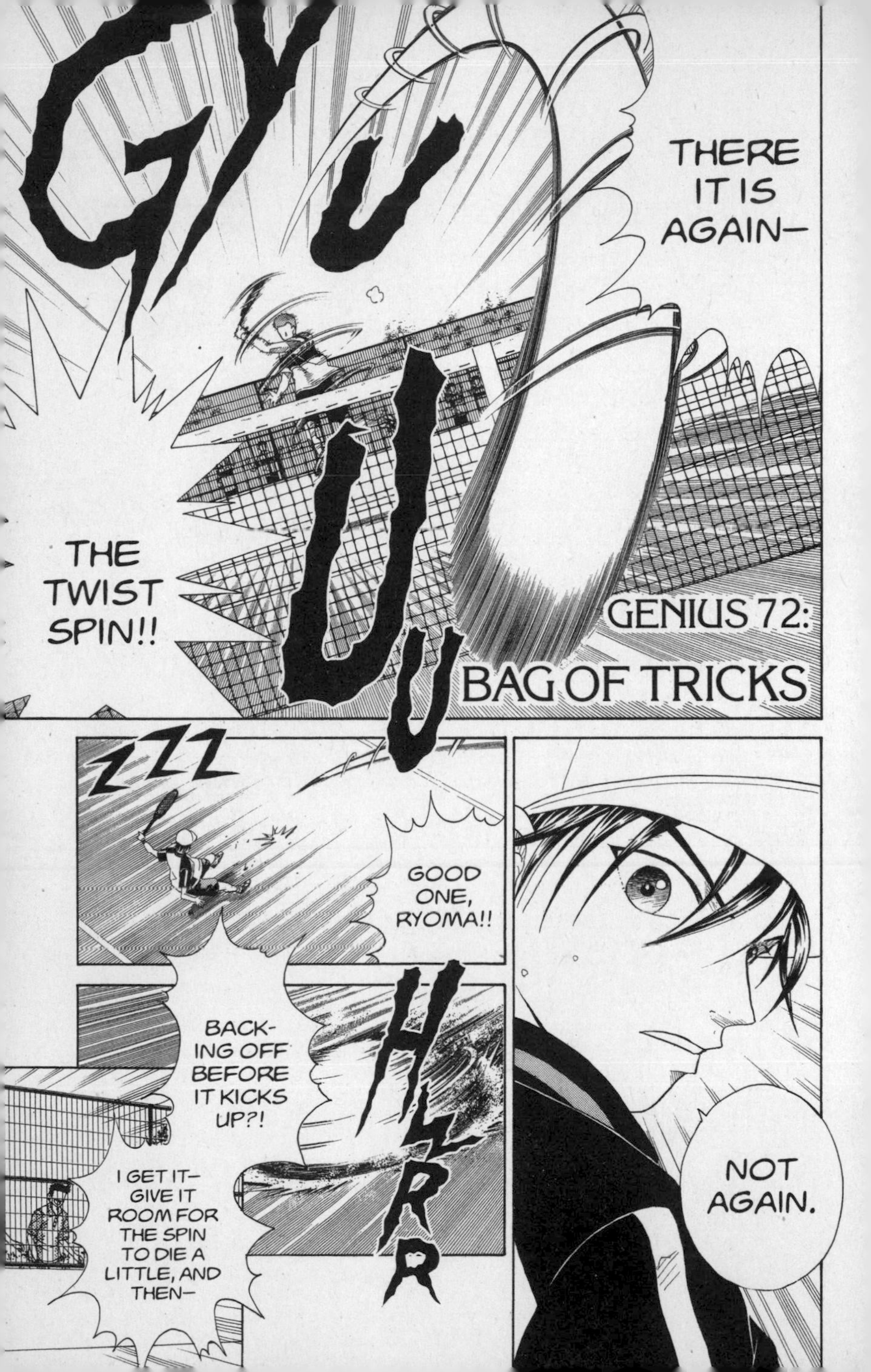
THERE IT IS AGAIN—
GYUU
GENIUS 72: BAG OF TRICKS
THE TWIST SPIN!!
NOT AGAIN.
ZZZ
GOOD ONE, RYOMA!!
BACK-ING OFF BEFORE IT KICKS UP?!
HURR
I GET IT— GIVE IT ROOM FOR THE SPIN TO DIE A LITTLE, AND THEN—

GENIUS 72: BAG OF TRICKS

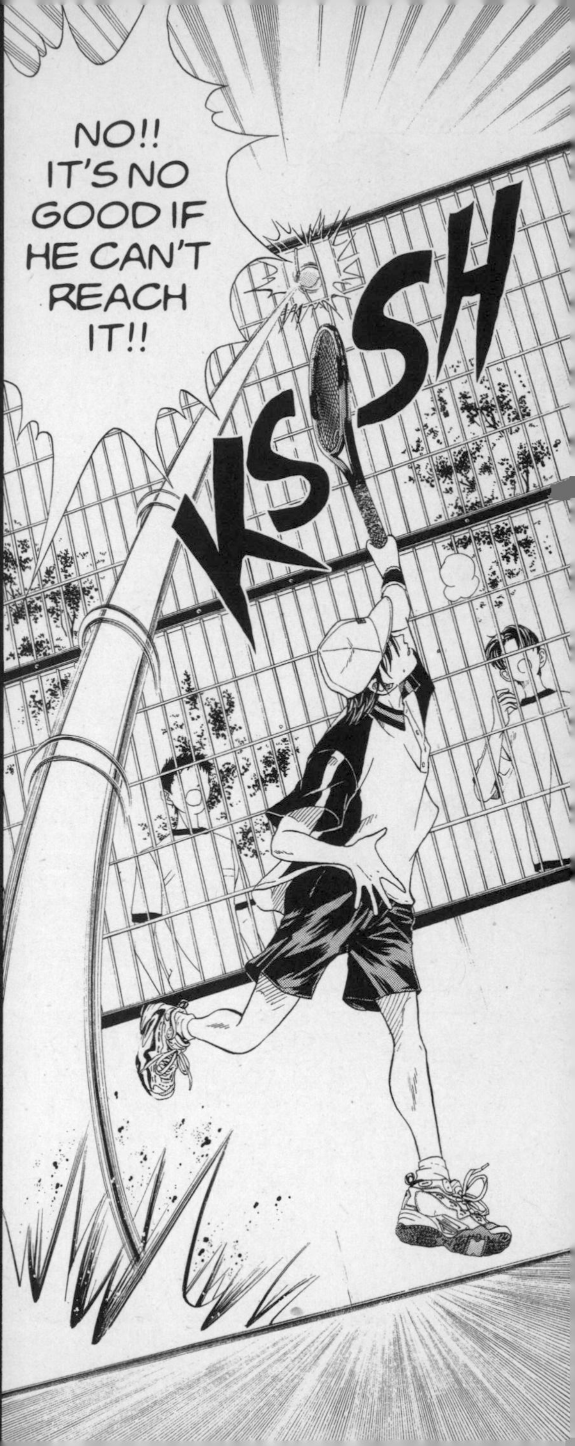
NO!! IT'S NO GOOD IF HE CAN'T REACH IT!!
KSSH

READ THIS WAY

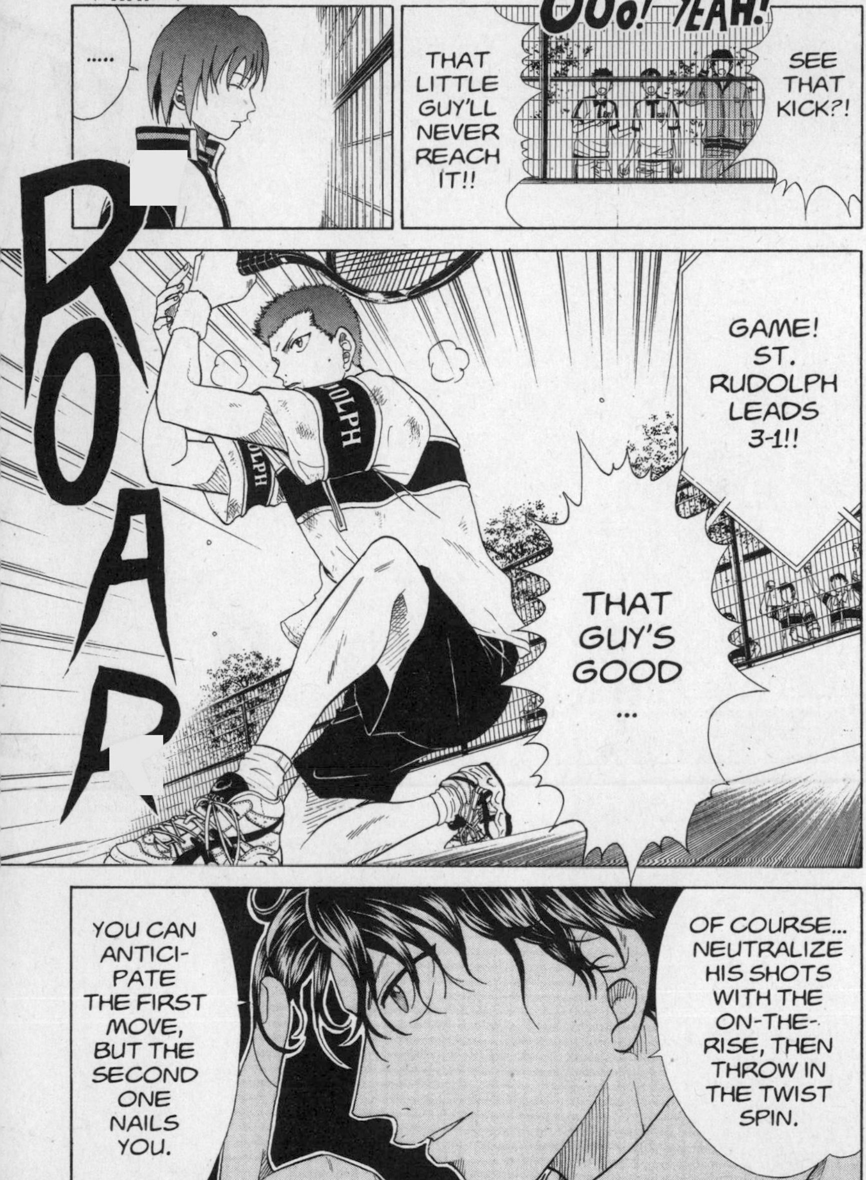

OOo! YEAH!
SEE THAT KICK?!
THAT LITTLE GUY'LL NEVER REACH IT!!
.....
GAME! ST. RUDOLPH LEADS 3-1!!
THAT GUY'S GOOD ...
ROAR
OF COURSE... NEUTRALIZE HIS SHOTS WITH THE ON-THE-RISE, THEN THROW IN THE TWIST SPIN.
YOU CAN ANTICIPATE THE FIRST MOVE, BUT THE SECOND ONE NAILS YOU.

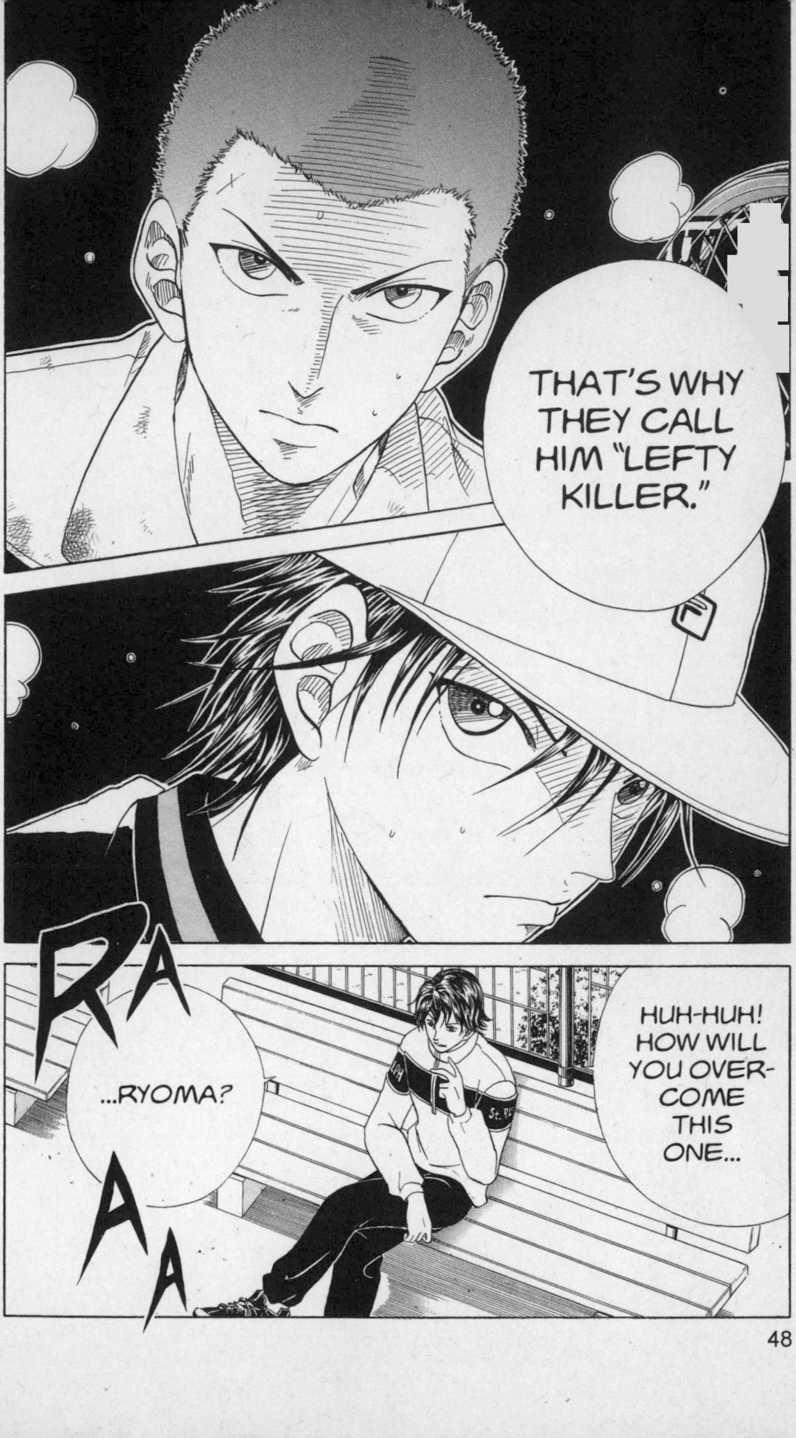
THAT'S WHY THEY CALL HIM "LEFTY KILLER."
HUH-HUH! HOW WILL YOU OVER-COME THIS ONE...
...RYOMA?
RAAAA

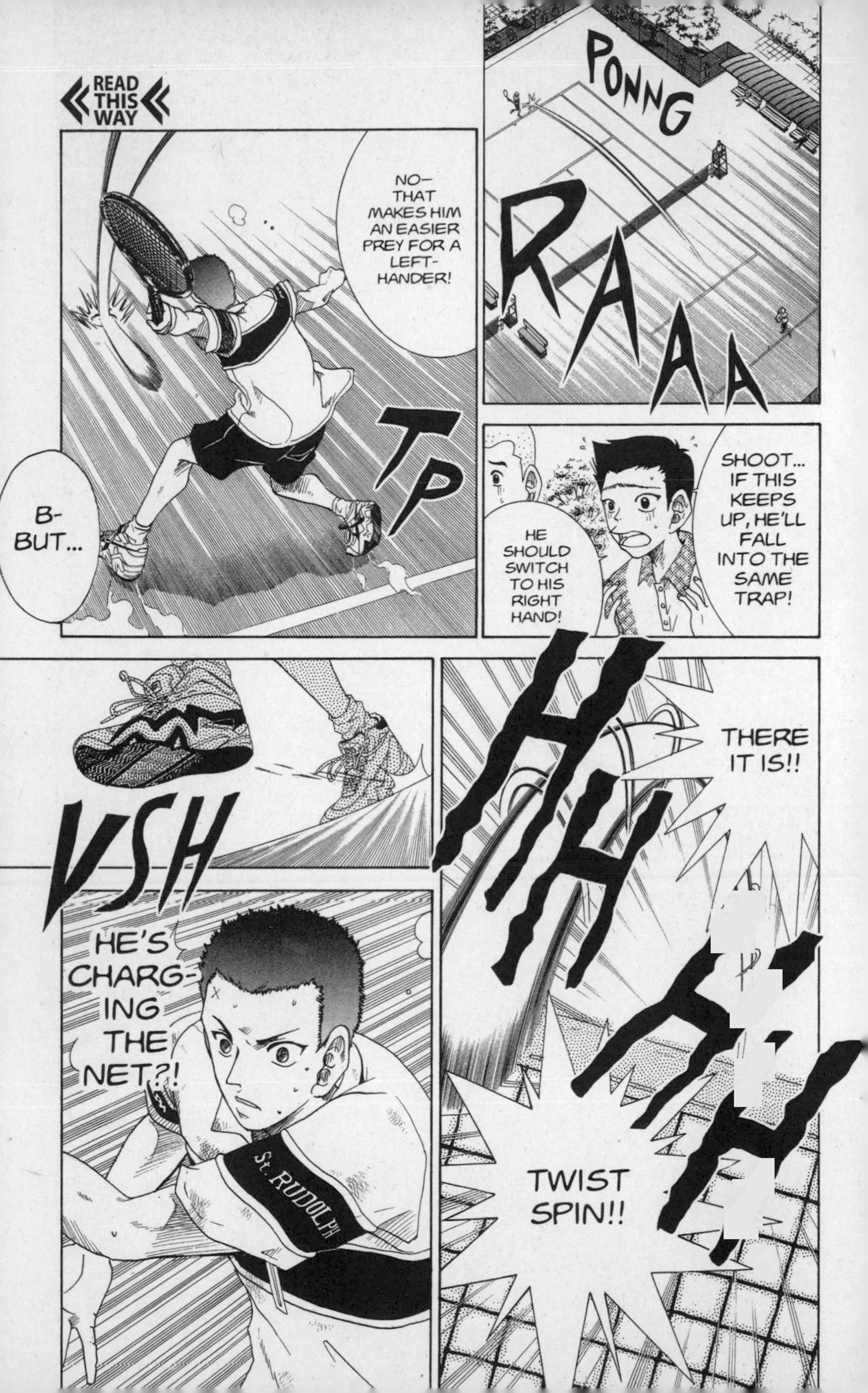
READ THIS WAY
PONNG
RAAAA
SHOOT... IF THIS KEEPS UP, HE'LL FALL INTO THE SAME TRAP!
HE SHOULD SWITCH TO HIS RIGHT HAND!
NO— THAT MAKES HIM AN EASIER PREY FOR A LEFT-HANDER!
TP
B-BUT...
THERE IT IS!!
TWIST SPIN!!
VSH
HE'S CHARG-ING THE NET?!
St. RUDOLPH

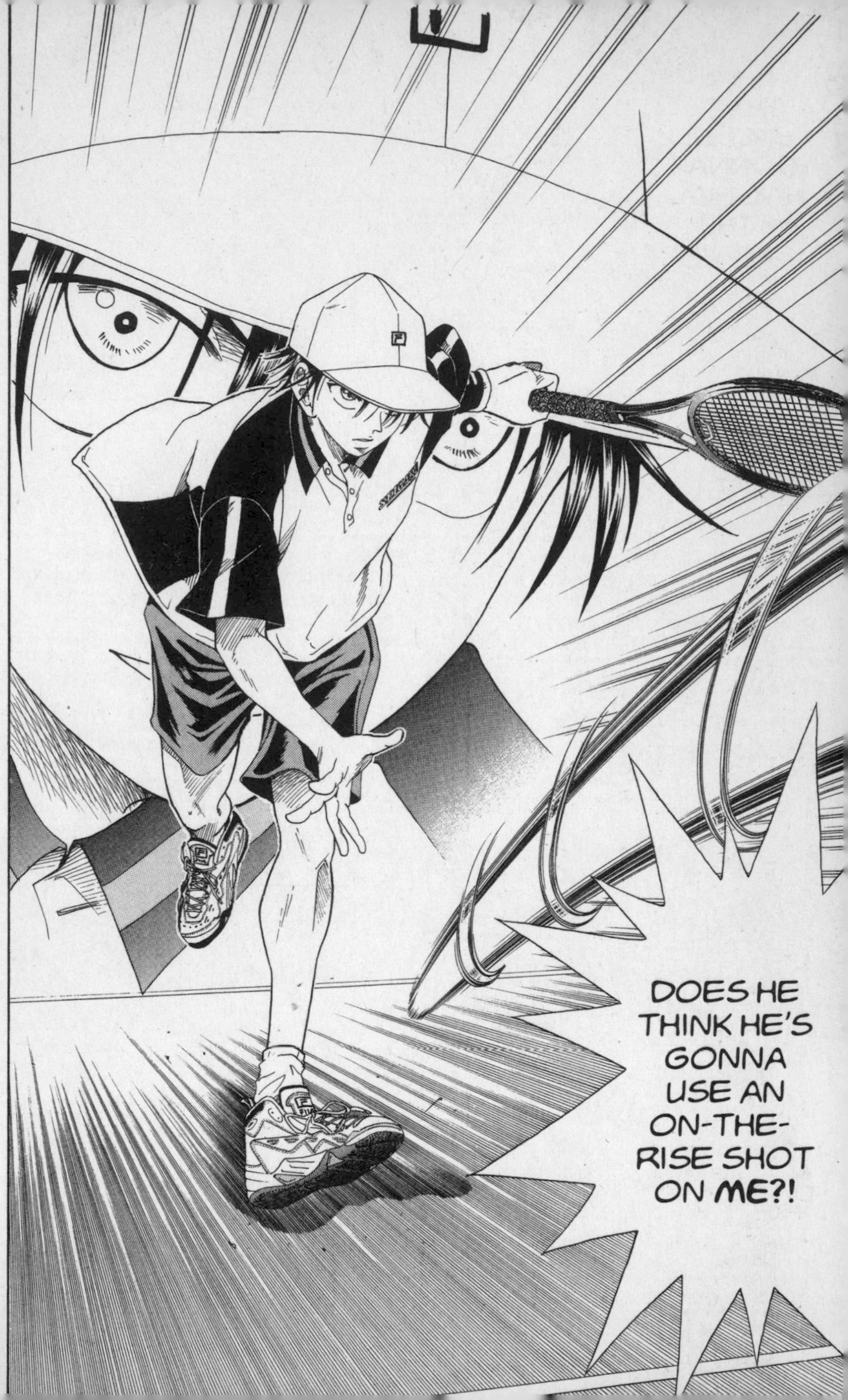
DOES HE THINK HE'S GONNA USE AN ON-THE-RISE SHOT ON ME?!

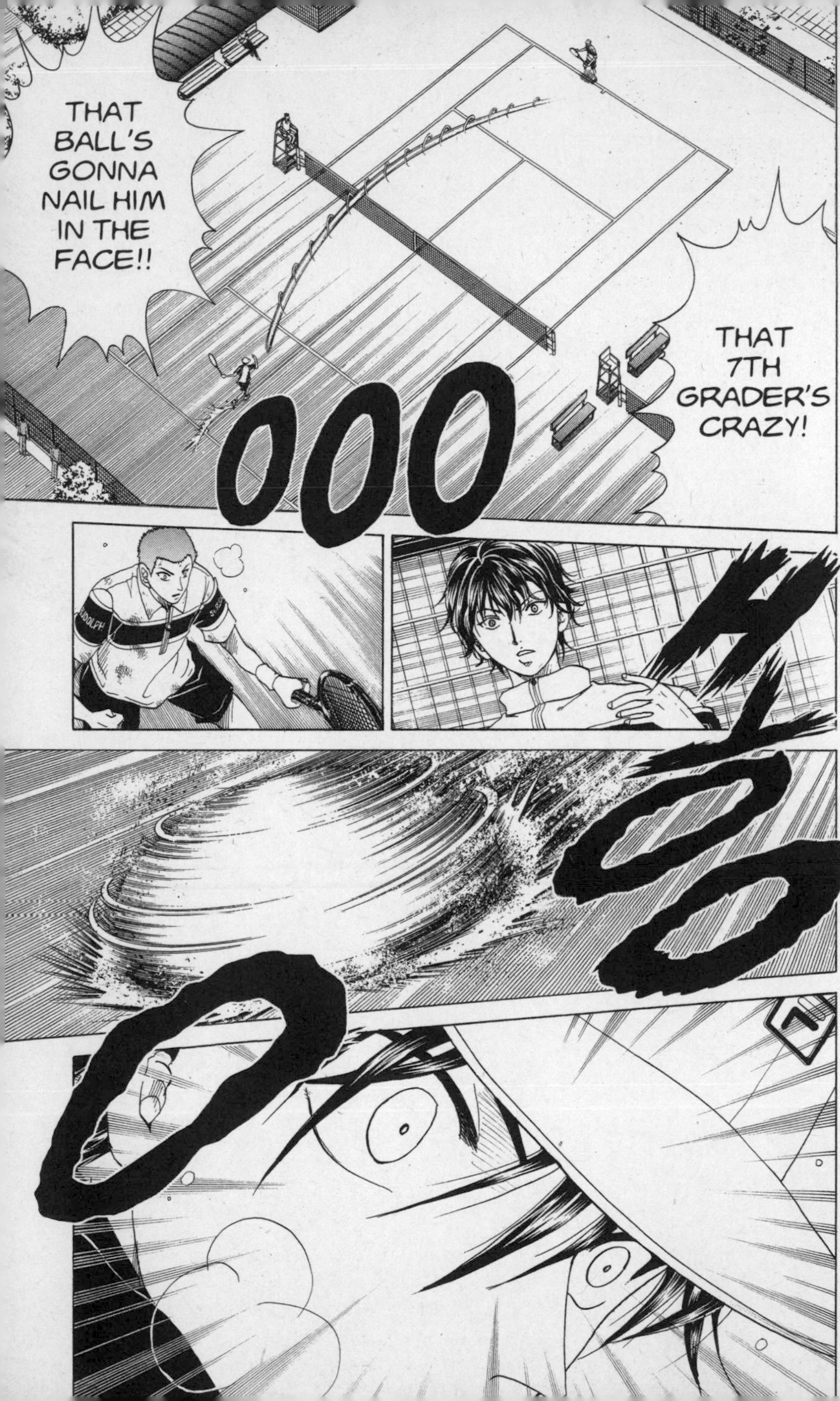
THAT 7TH GRADER'S CRAZY!
THAT BALL'S GONNA NAIL HIM IN THE FACE!!
OOO

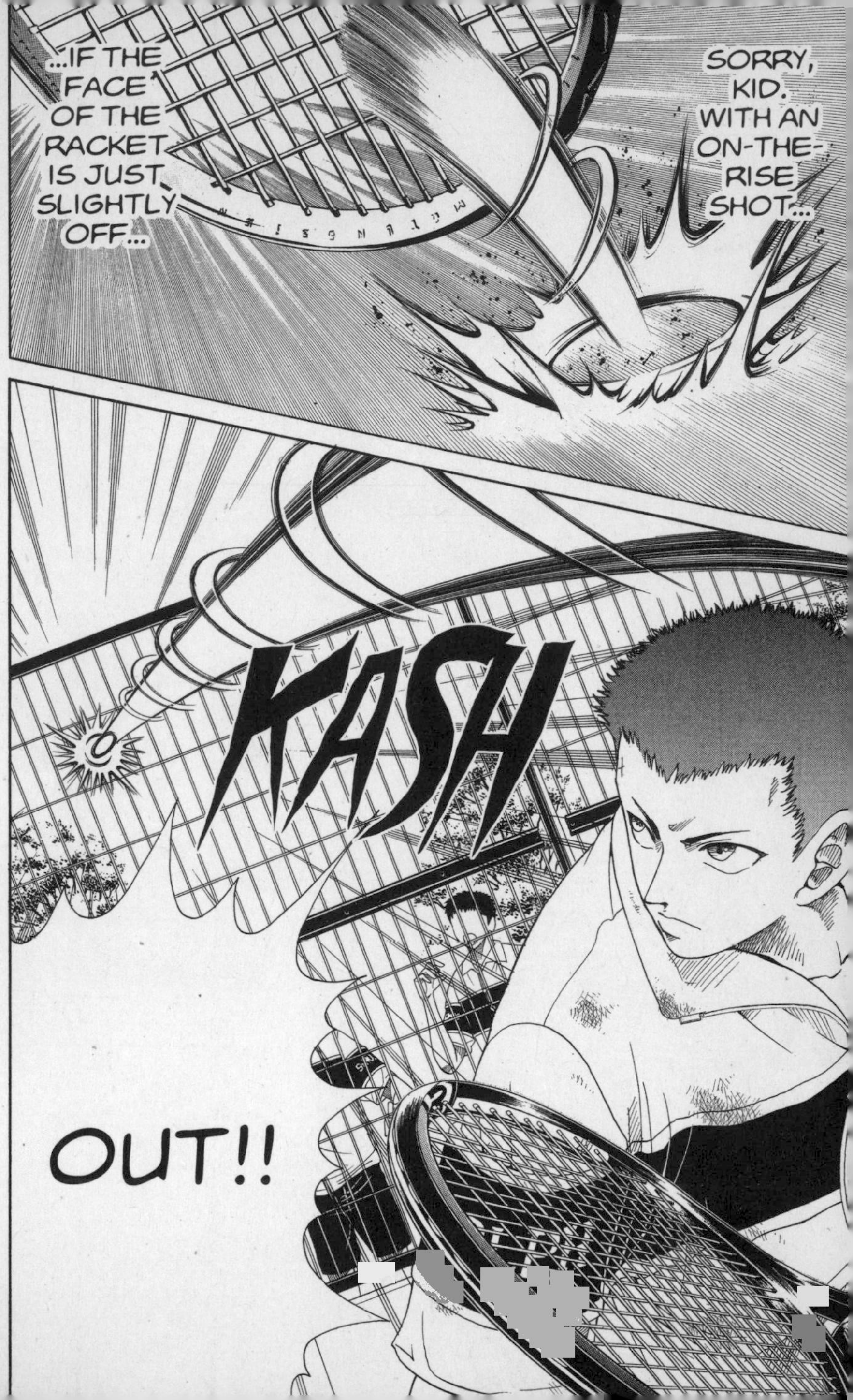
SORRY, KID. WITH AN ON-THE-RISE SHOT...
...IF THE FACE OF THE RACKET IS JUST SLIGHTLY OFF...
KASH
OUT!!

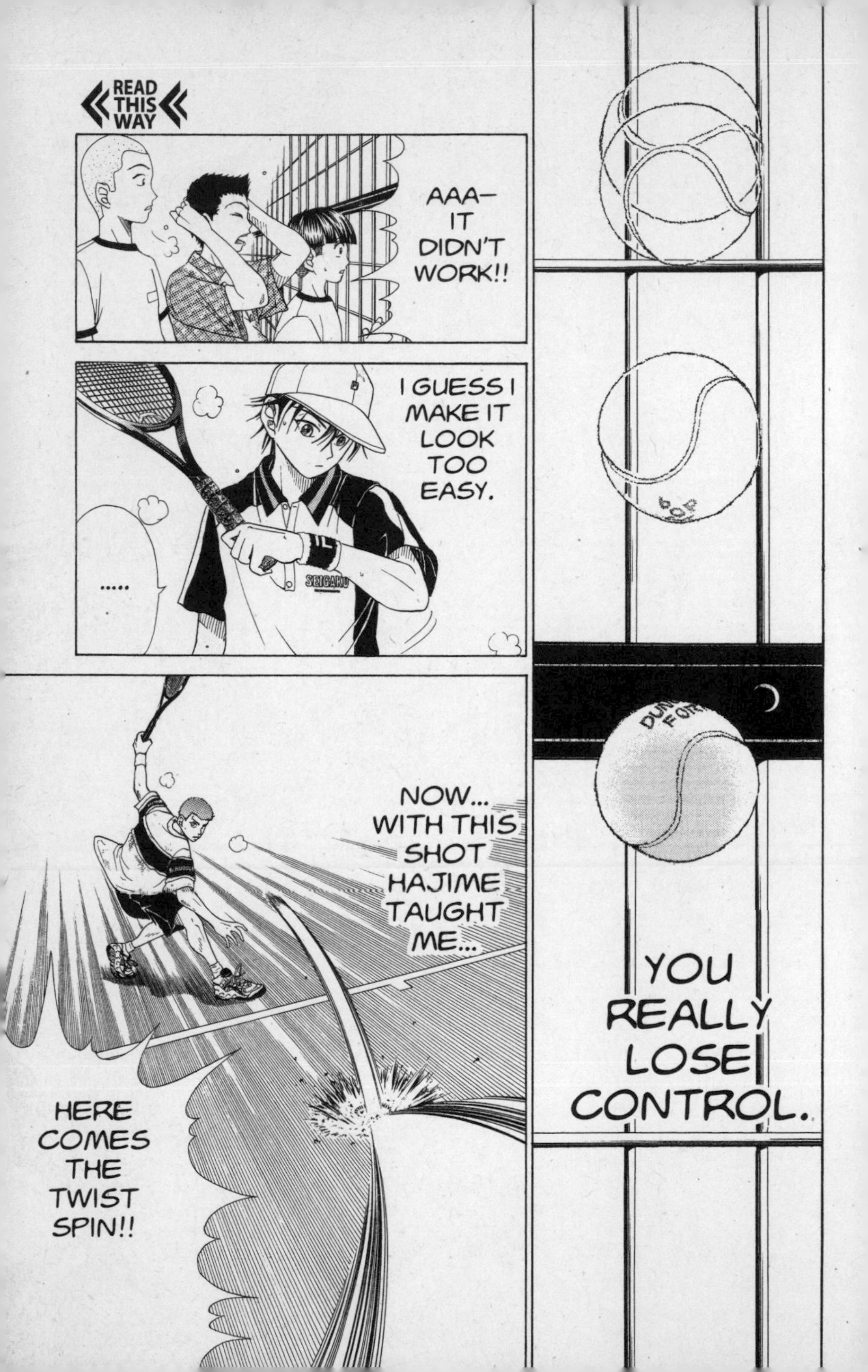
READ THIS WAY
YOU REALLY LOSE CONTROL.
AAA— IT DIDN'T WORK!!
I GUESS I MAKE IT LOOK TOO EASY.
SEIGAKU
.....
NOW... WITH THIS SHOT HAJIME TAUGHT ME...
HERE COMES THE TWIST SPIN!!

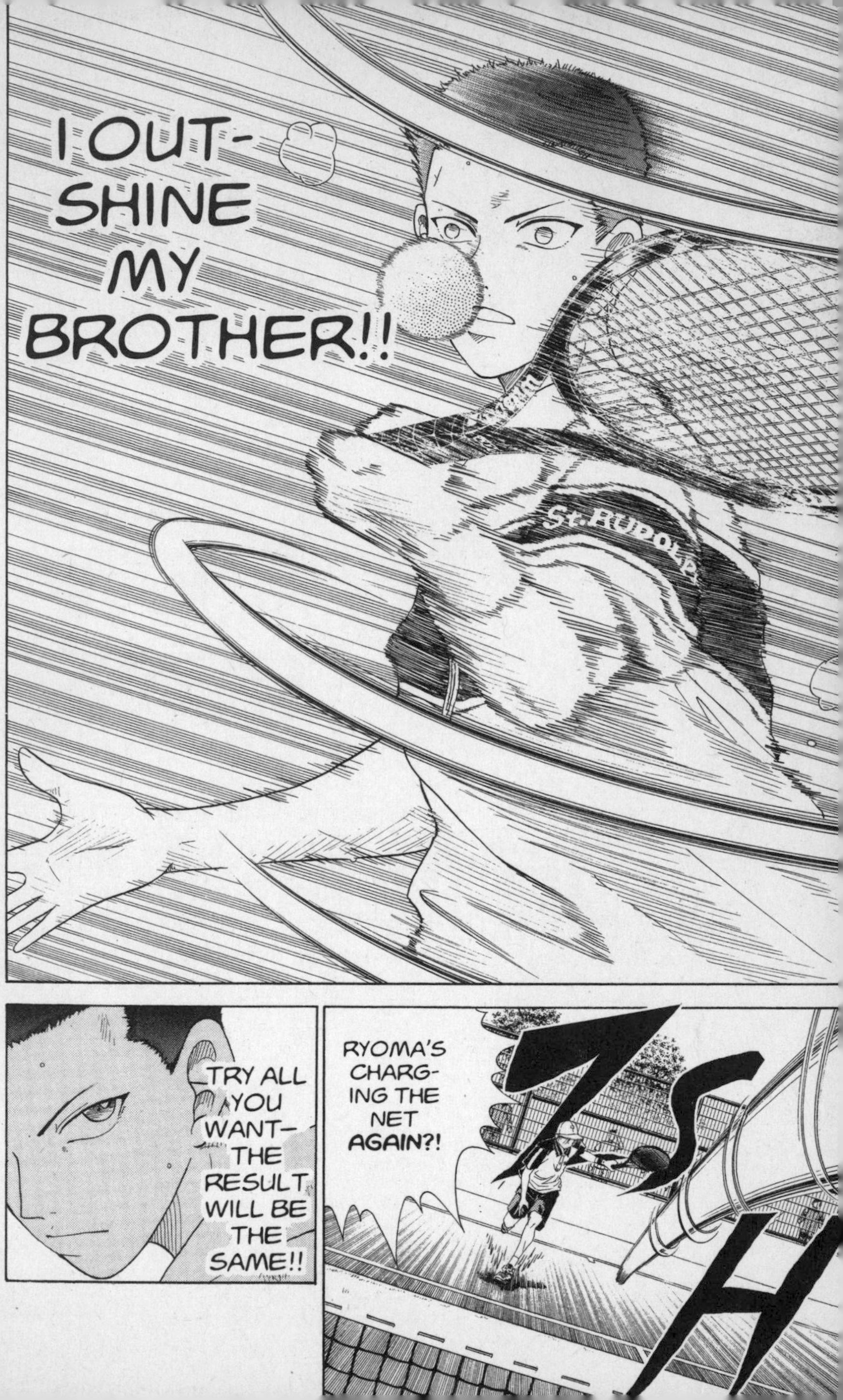
I OUT-SHINE MY BROTHER!!
St. RUDOLP
RYOMA'S CHARGING THE NET AGAIN?!
TRY ALL YOU WANT—THE RESULT WILL BE THE SAME!!
ZSH

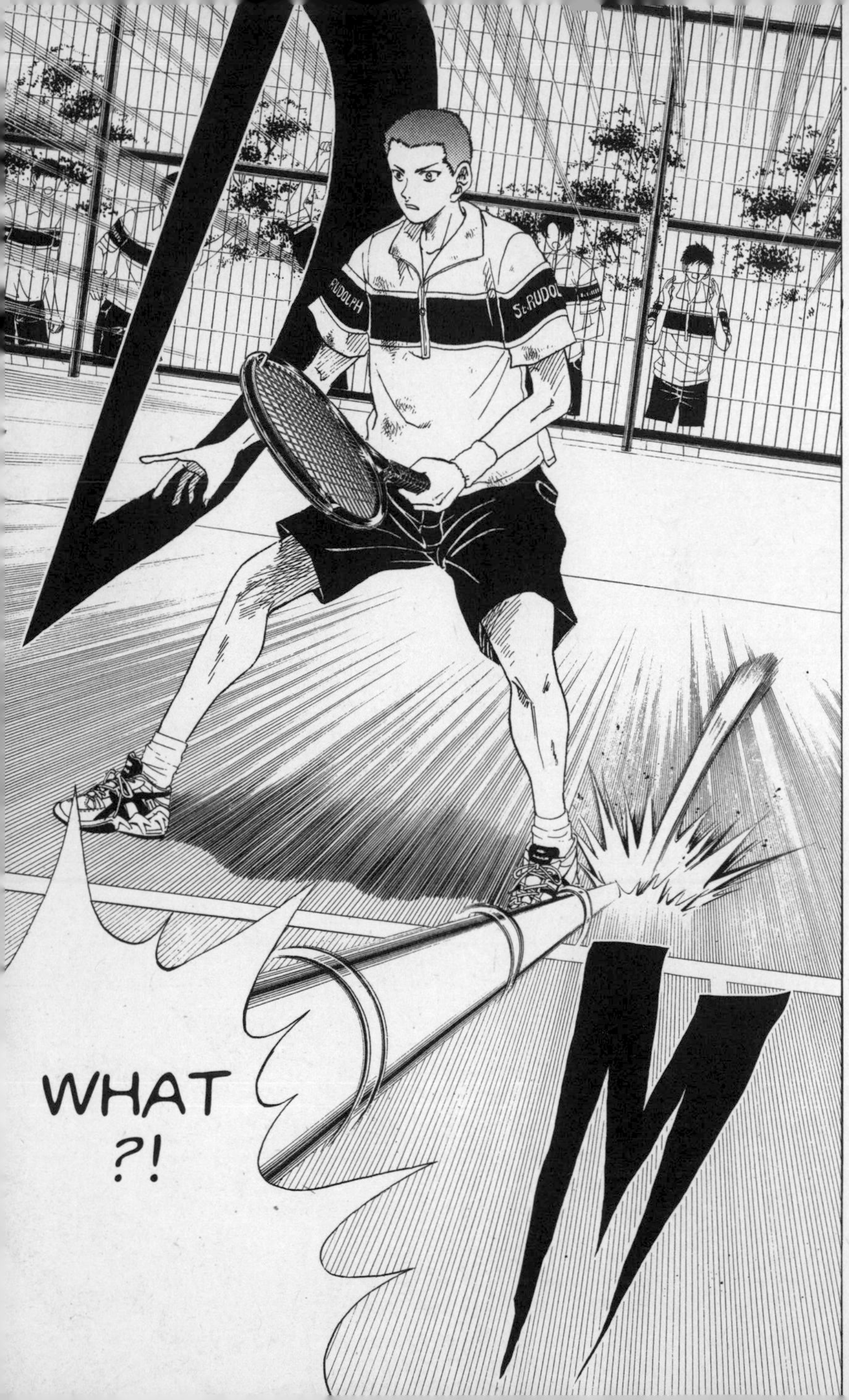
ST. RUDOLPH
WHAT ?!

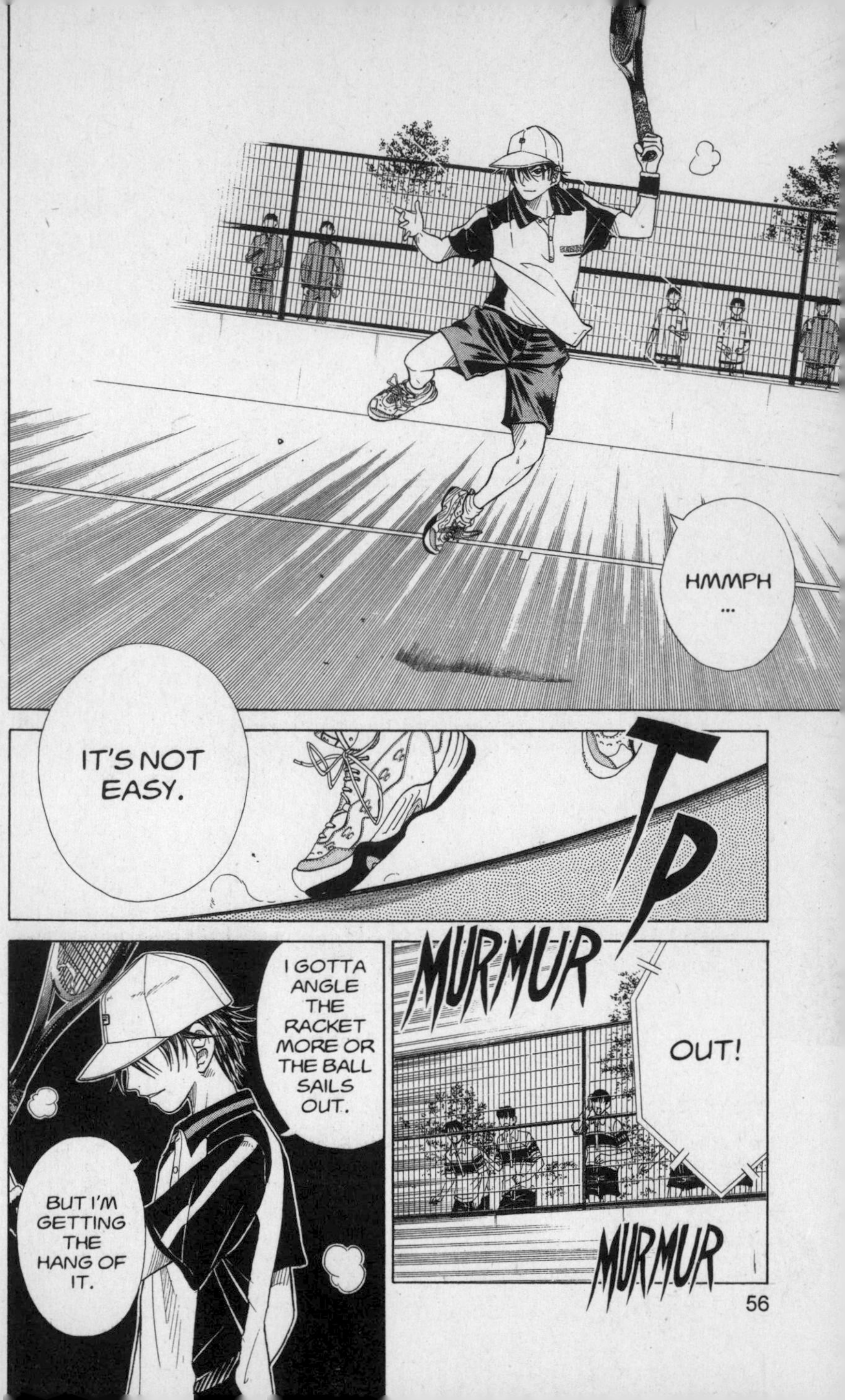
HMMPH ...
IT'S NOT EASY.
TP
MURMUR
OUT!
MURMUR
I GOTTA ANGLE THE RACKET MORE OR THE BALL SAILS OUT.
BUT I'M GETTING THE HANG OF IT.

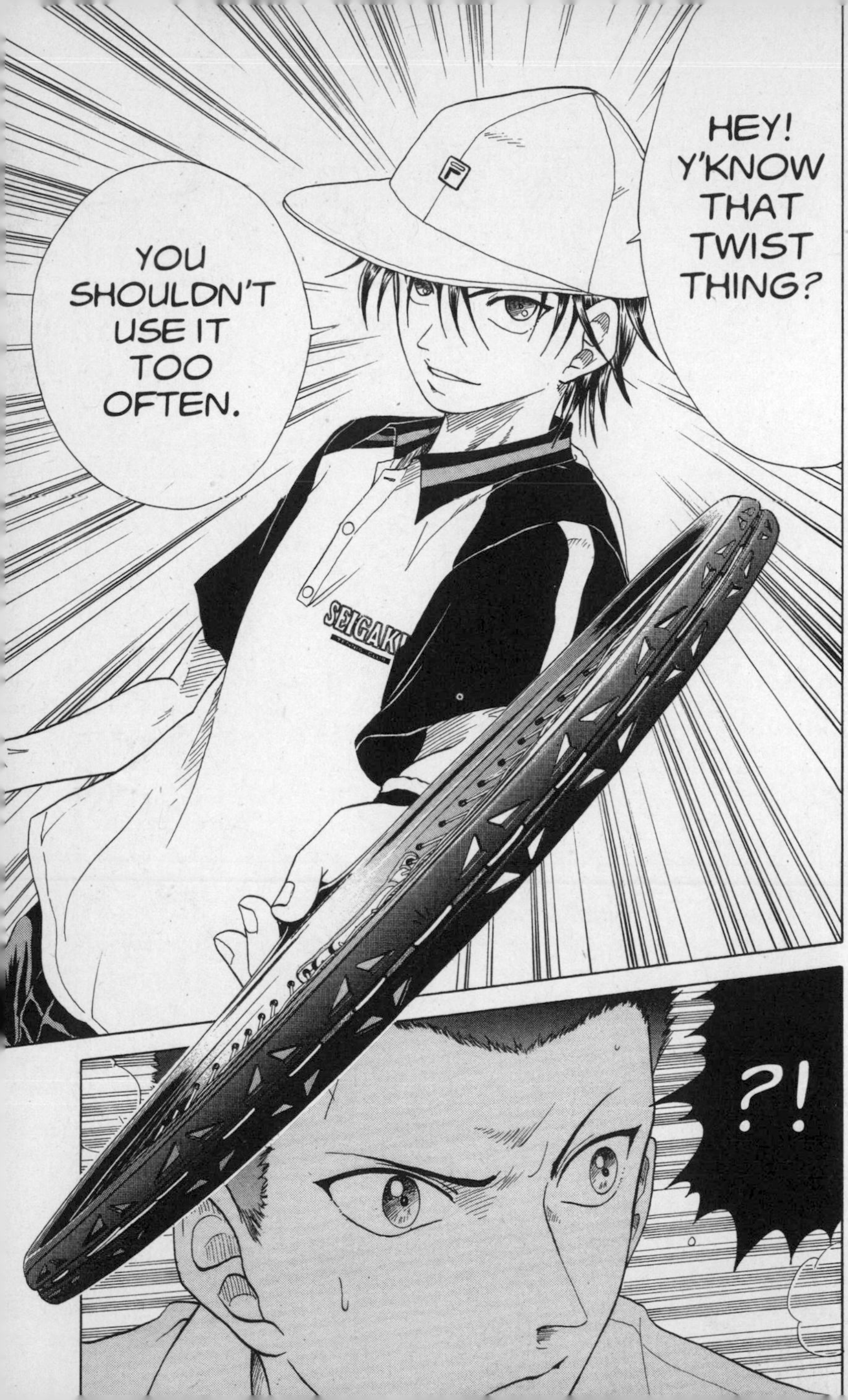
HEY! Y'KNOW THAT TWIST THING?
YOU SHOULDN'T USE IT TOO OFTEN.
?!

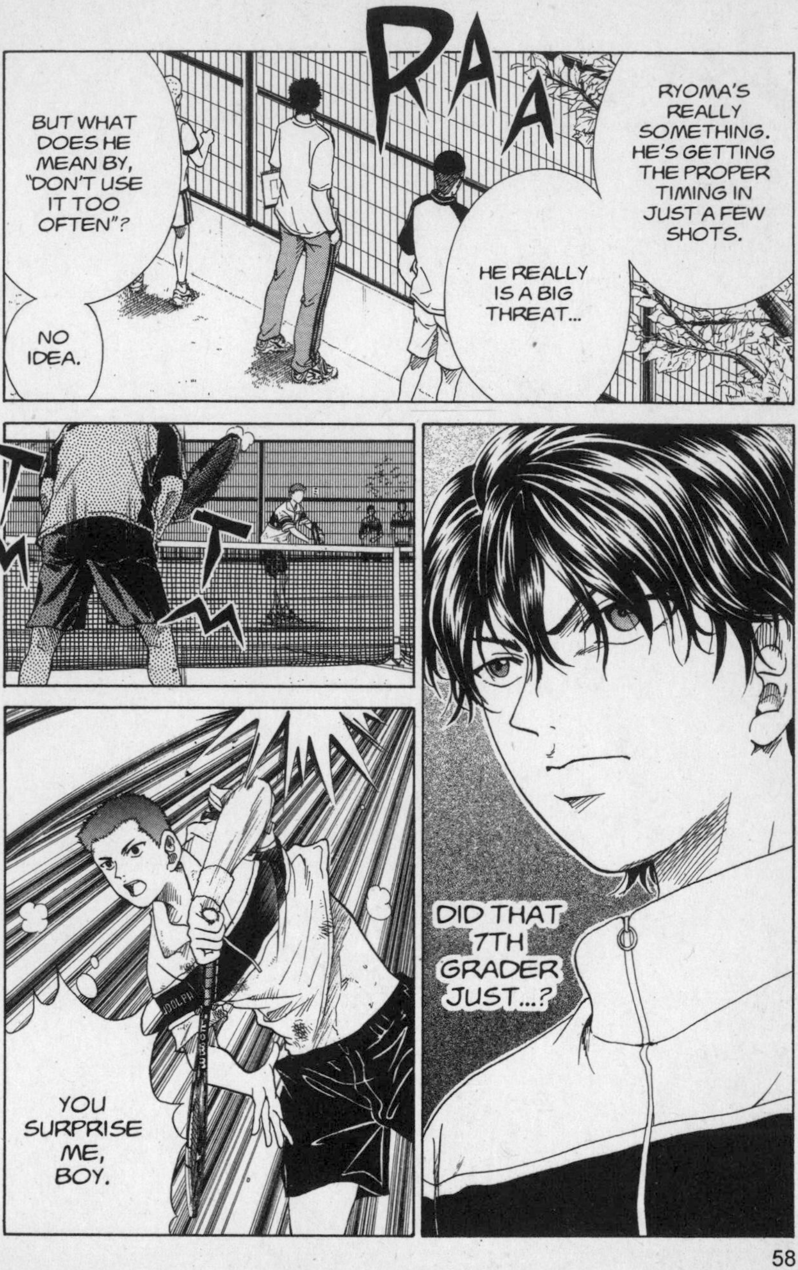
RAA
RYOMA'S REALLY SOMETHING. HE'S GETTING THE PROPER TIMING IN JUST A FEW SHOTS.
HE REALLY IS A BIG THREAT...
BUT WHAT DOES HE MEAN BY, "DON'T USE IT TOO OFTEN"?
NO IDEA.
DID THAT 7TH GRADER JUST...?
TM
TM
YOU SURPRISE ME, BOY.

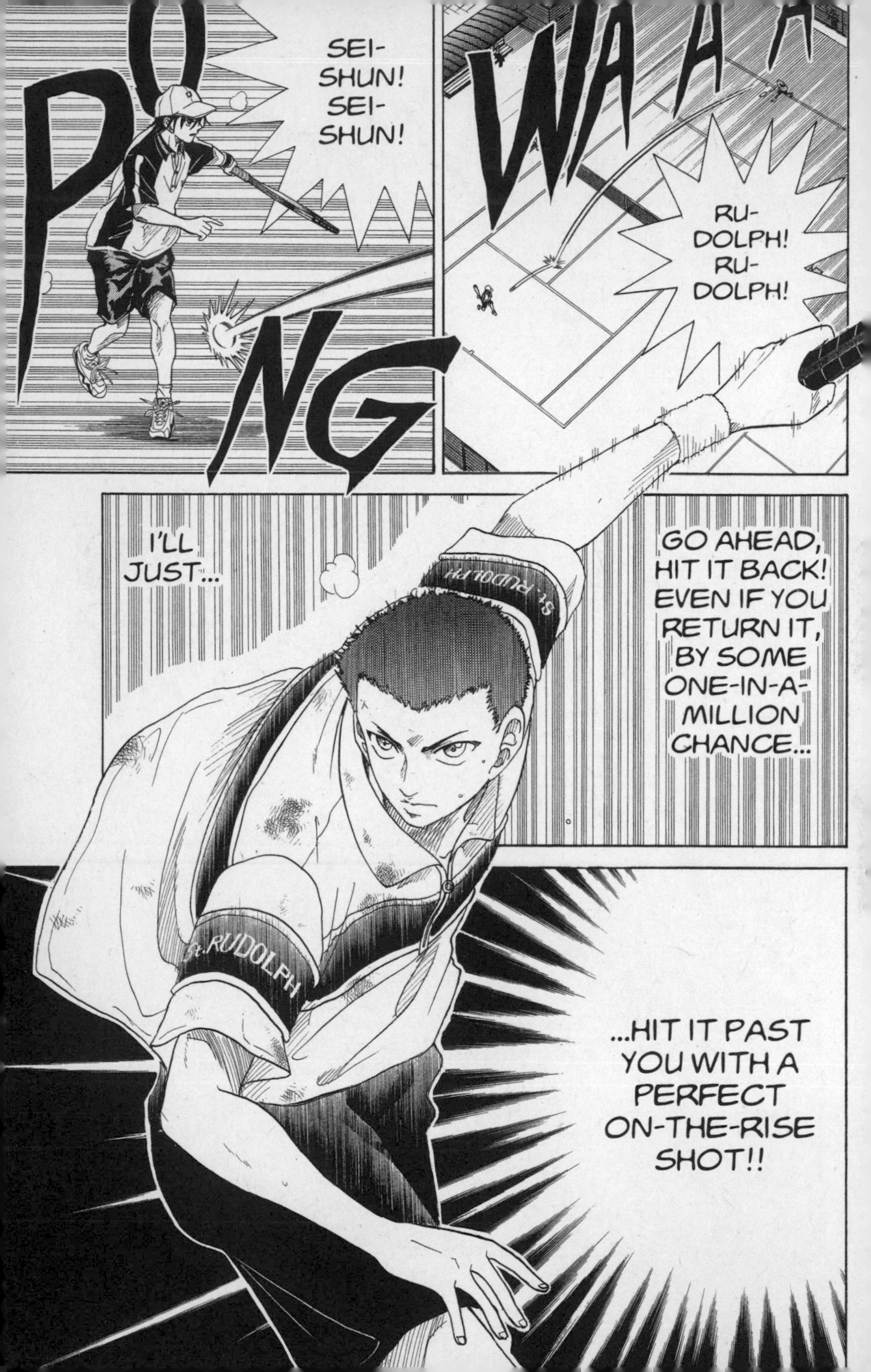
WAAA
RU-DOLPH! RU-DOLPH!
SEI-SHUN! SEI-SHUN!
PONG
GO AHEAD, HIT IT BACK! EVEN IF YOU RETURN IT, BY SOME ONE-IN-A-MILLION CHANCE...
I'LL JUST...
...HIT IT PAST YOU WITH A PERFECT ON-THE-RISE SHOT!!
St. RUDOLPH
St. RUDOLPH

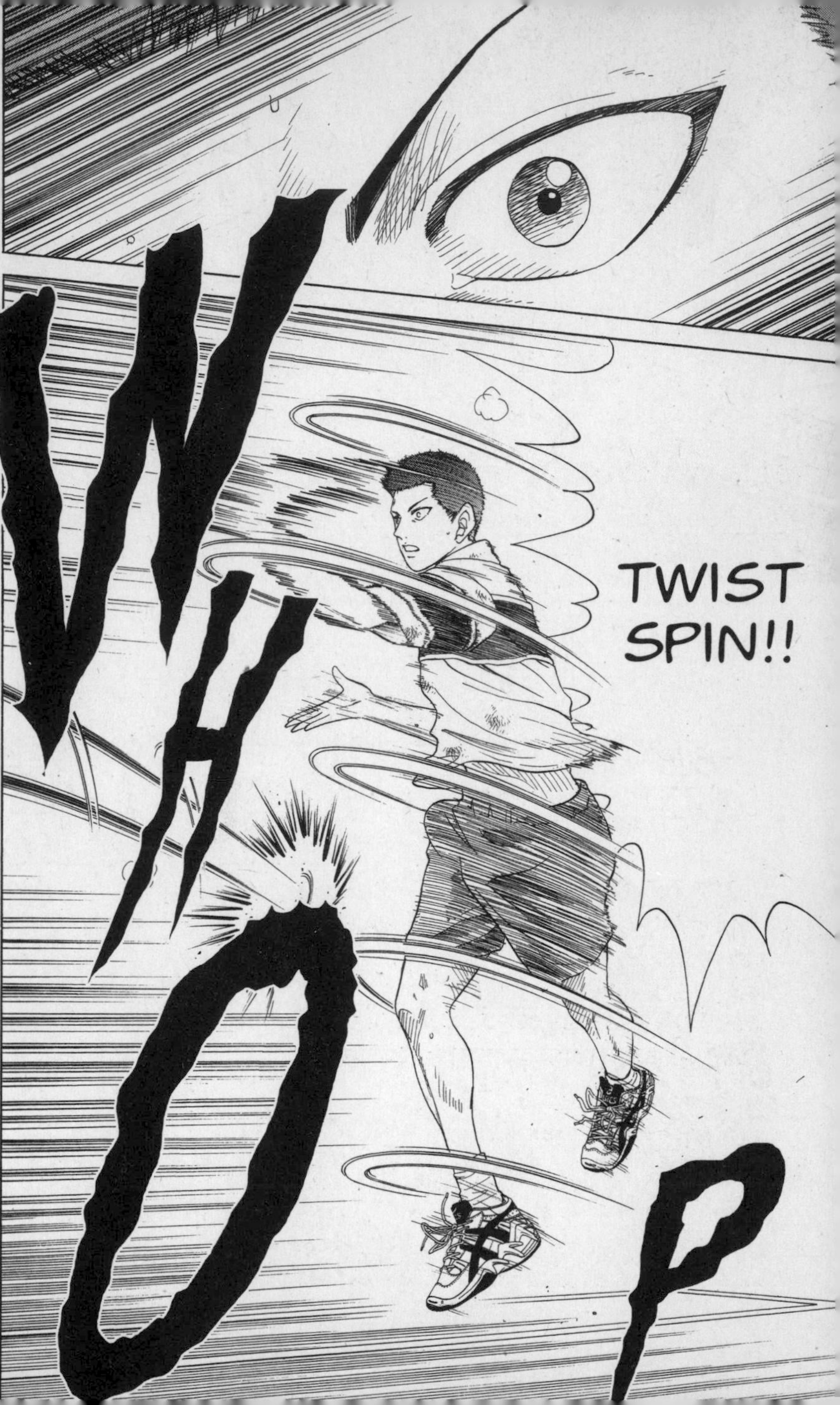
TWIST SPIN!!
WHOP

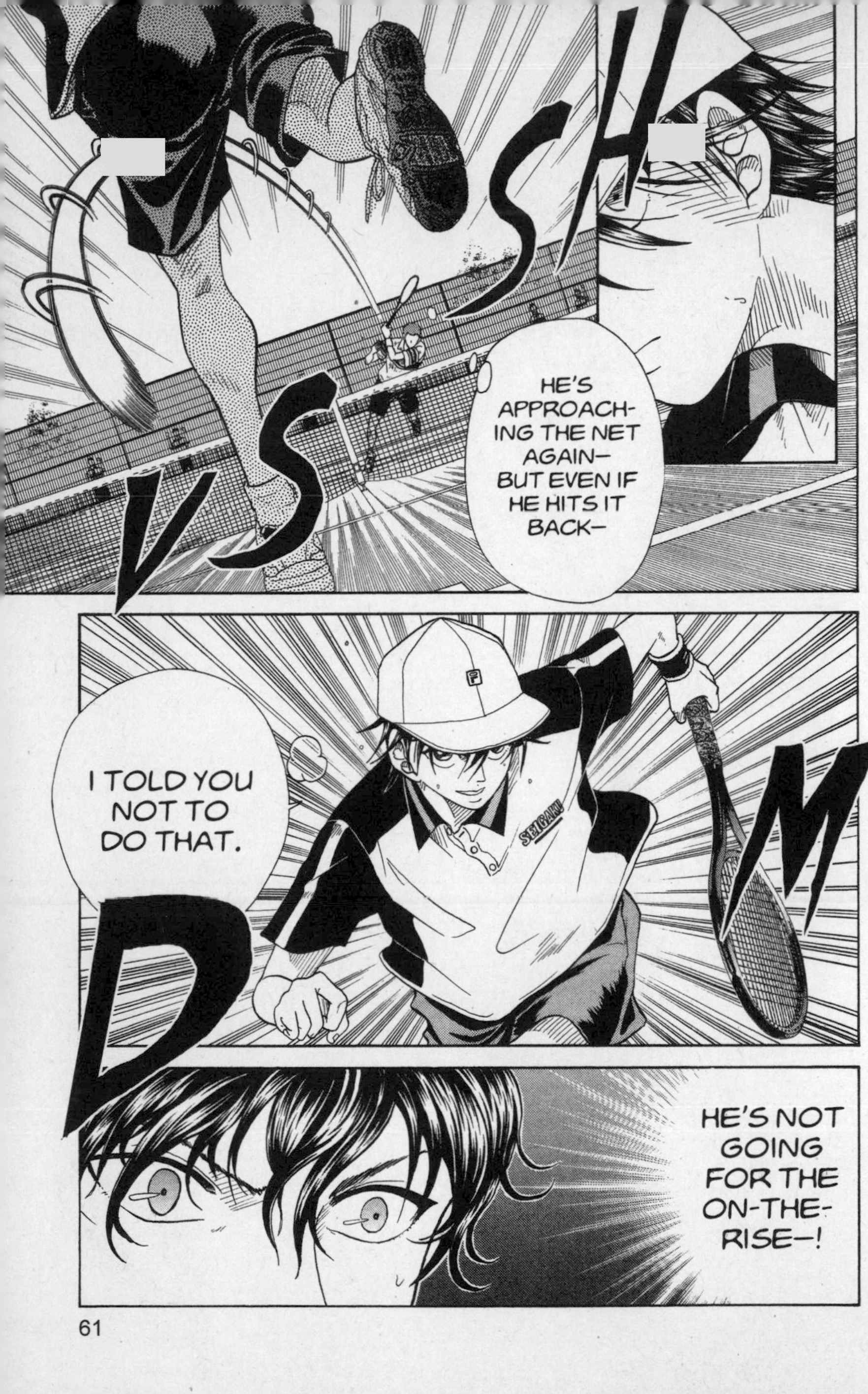
HE'S APPROACHING THE NET AGAIN– BUT EVEN IF HE HITS IT BACK–
VS
SH
I TOLD YOU NOT TO DO THAT.
D
M
HE'S NOT GOING FOR THE ON-THE-RISE–!

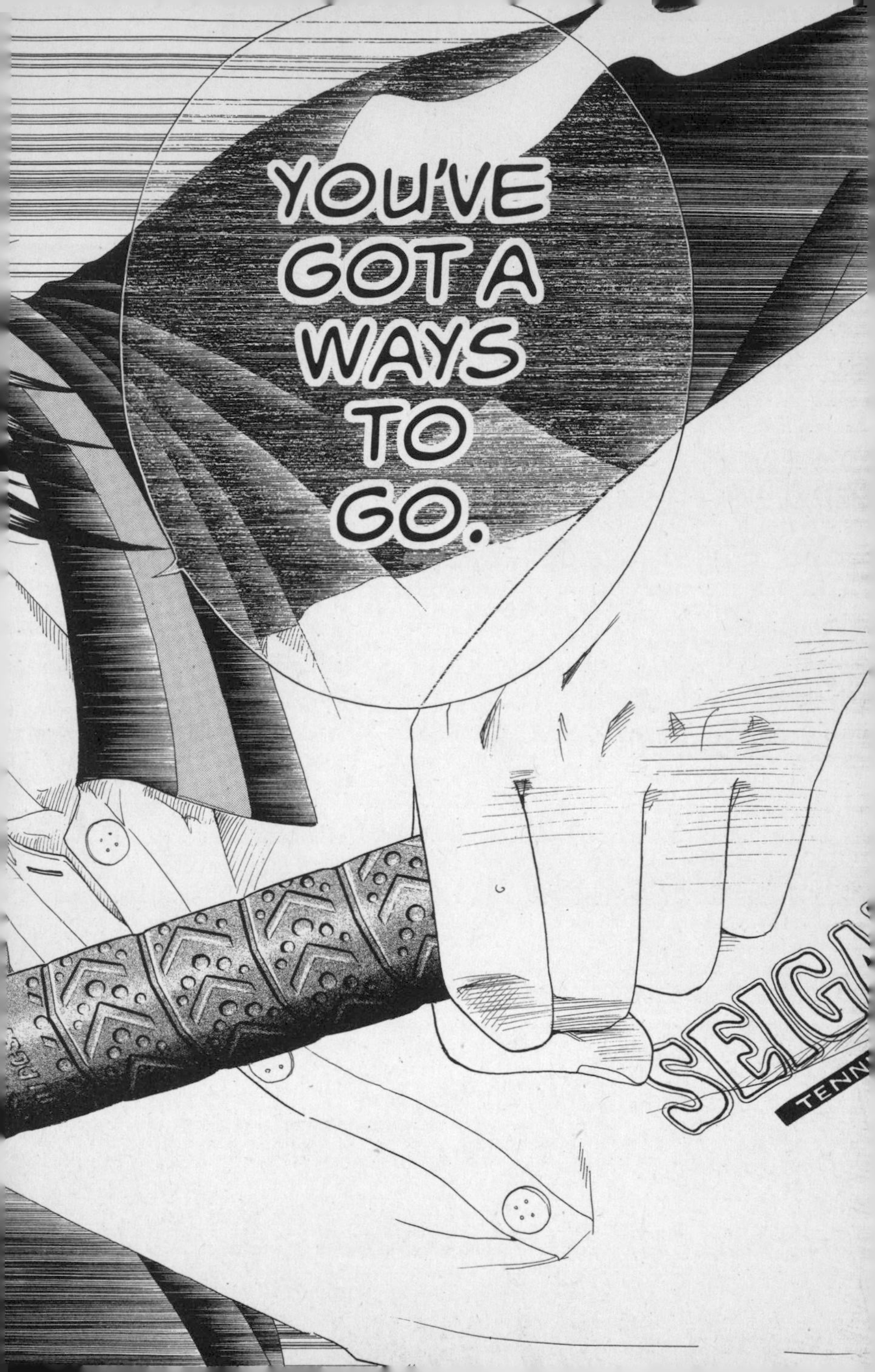
YOU'VE GOT A WAYS TO GO.

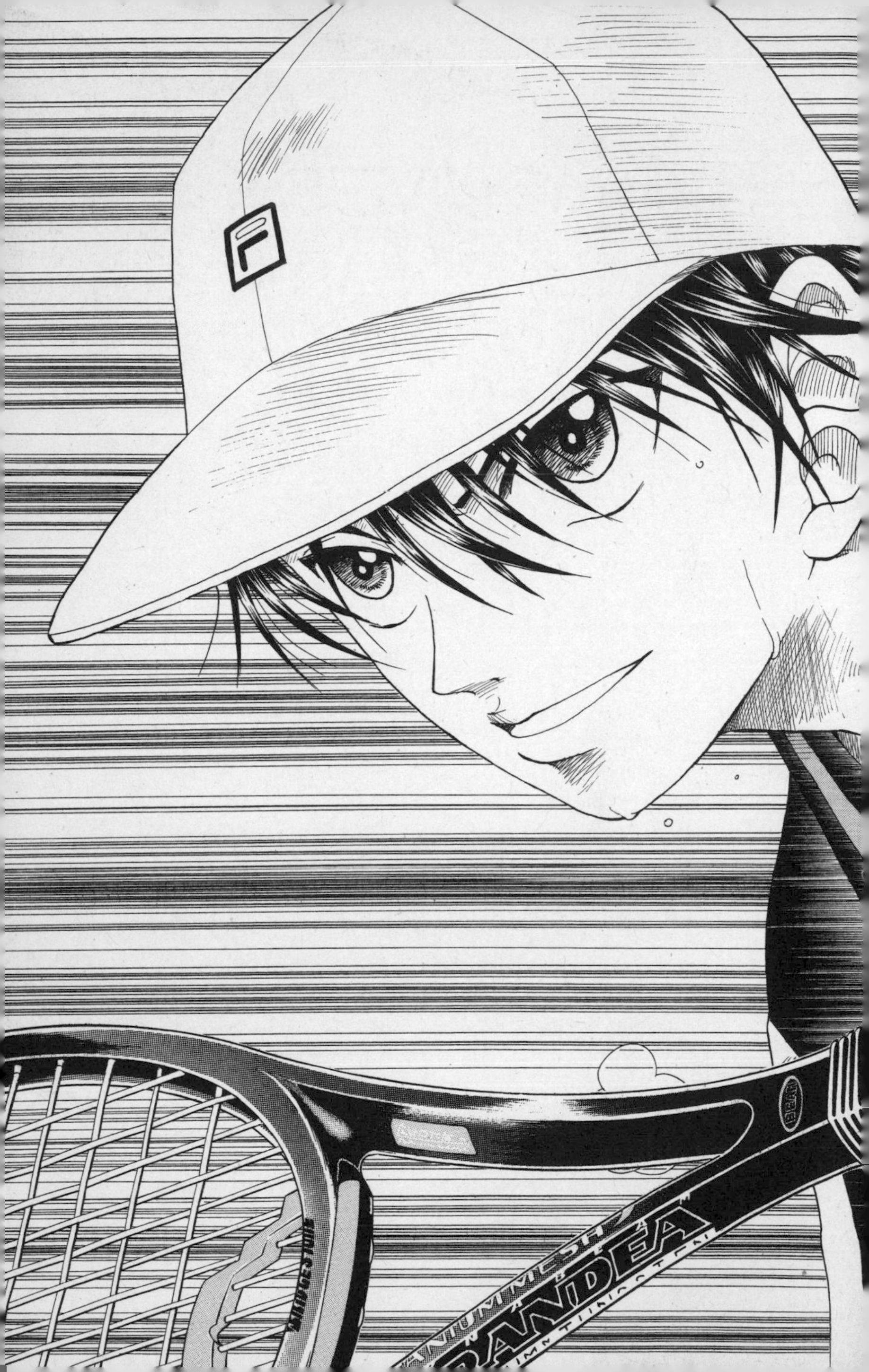

Fan Project!!

Kaoru Kaido 8th Grade Classmate Announcement—!!

This is the classmate project we announced last volume. I think I underestimated the popularity of Kaoru Kaido a bit. Amazing!! Check out the number of applicants!! The passionate love messages!!! The editorial office kept sending me huge cardboard boxes! I couldn't believe it. And, as if reflecting the character, a lot of the letters were passionate, earnest, and devoted. (Kunimitsu, by contrast, is more popular with older brothers and sisters.)

This project gets more and more difficult... I can't decide!! Thank you to all the Kaoru fans out there who applied! Now, the winners of this closely contested race are...

8th Grade Class 7 Number

(Boys)		(Girls)	
1	Reona Abe	1	Tomomi Aoki
2	Masato Ichinowatari	2	Aiko Ito
3	Norikazu Okada	3	Nobue Inamura
4	Kaoru Kaido	4	Narumi Inoue
5	Ichinari Kamon	5	Kan Uehara
6	Hide Kumatani	6	Saya Uozumi
7	Kunio Kojima	7	Satoko Oura
8	Kazuo Komoda	8	Eri Katsutani
9	Kenji Sagane	9	Mayo Sano
10	Norihiro Tsukhira	10	Kanami Shiino
11	Daisuke Tsuchiya	11	Kaori Takada
12	Katsuya Nakamura	12	TomokoTakeyama
13	Motoki Nakamura	13	Sho Nagano
14	Junichi Hashiba	14	Maki Hasegawa
15	Shinji Mitsuaki	15	Aika Yamazaki
16	Shinya Mizusawa	16	Mao Yamamura
17	Keigo Yokoi	17	Mika Yutani
18	Hayao Yoshimura	18	Kazumi Watanabe
19	Suguru Yoshimura		

Total: 36

These are the winners. But thanks to everyone who responded!!
(I don't want to nag, but it might be worth checking out the second anniversary in JUMP 34!)

Ed. Note: This "project" was held only in Japan.

GENIUS 73: DRIVE V

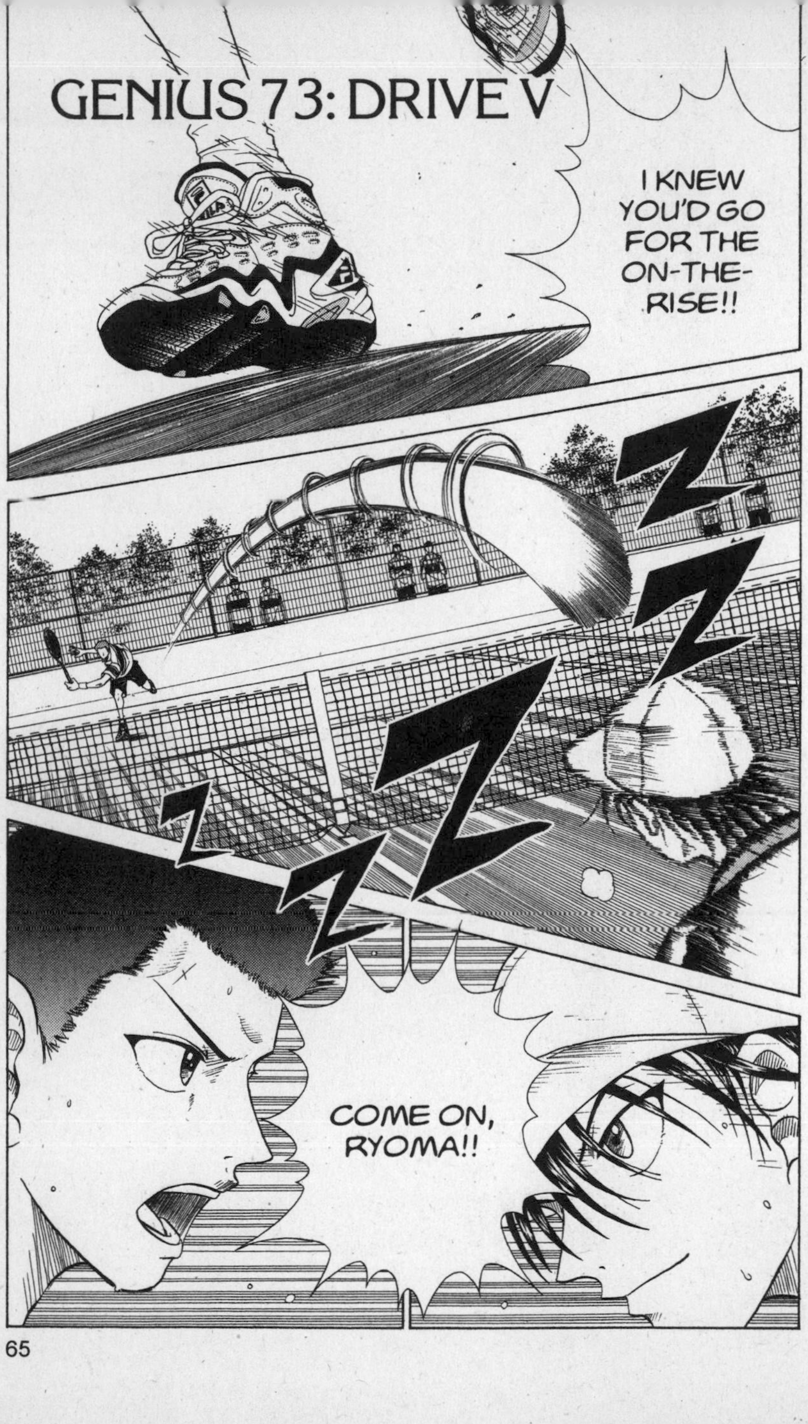
I KNEW YOU'D GO FOR THE ON-THE-RISE!!
COME ON, RYOMA!!

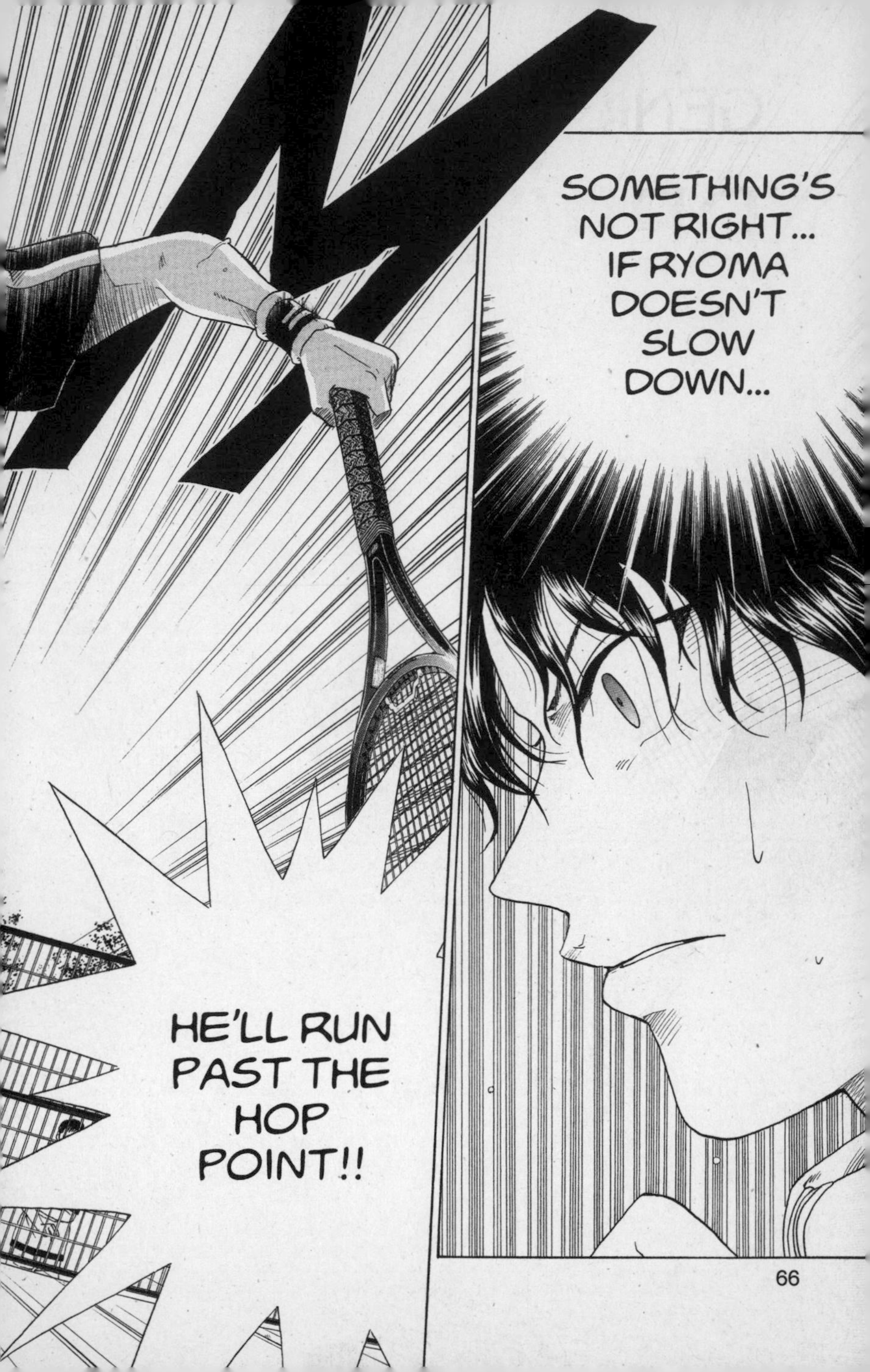
SOMETHING'S NOT RIGHT... IF RYOMA DOESN'T SLOW DOWN...
HE'LL RUN PAST THE HOP POINT!!

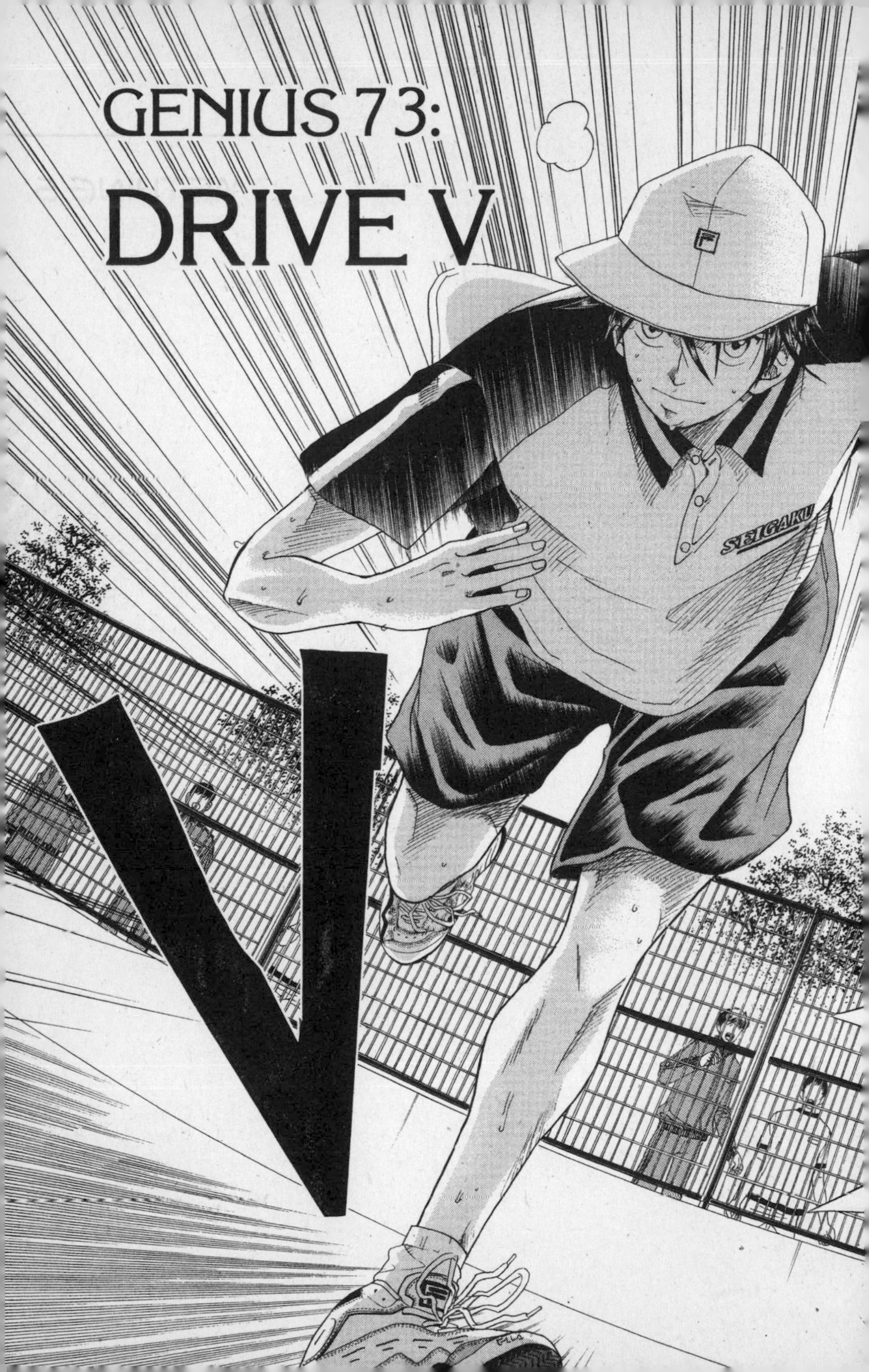
GENIUS 73:
DRIVE V
SEIGAKU
V

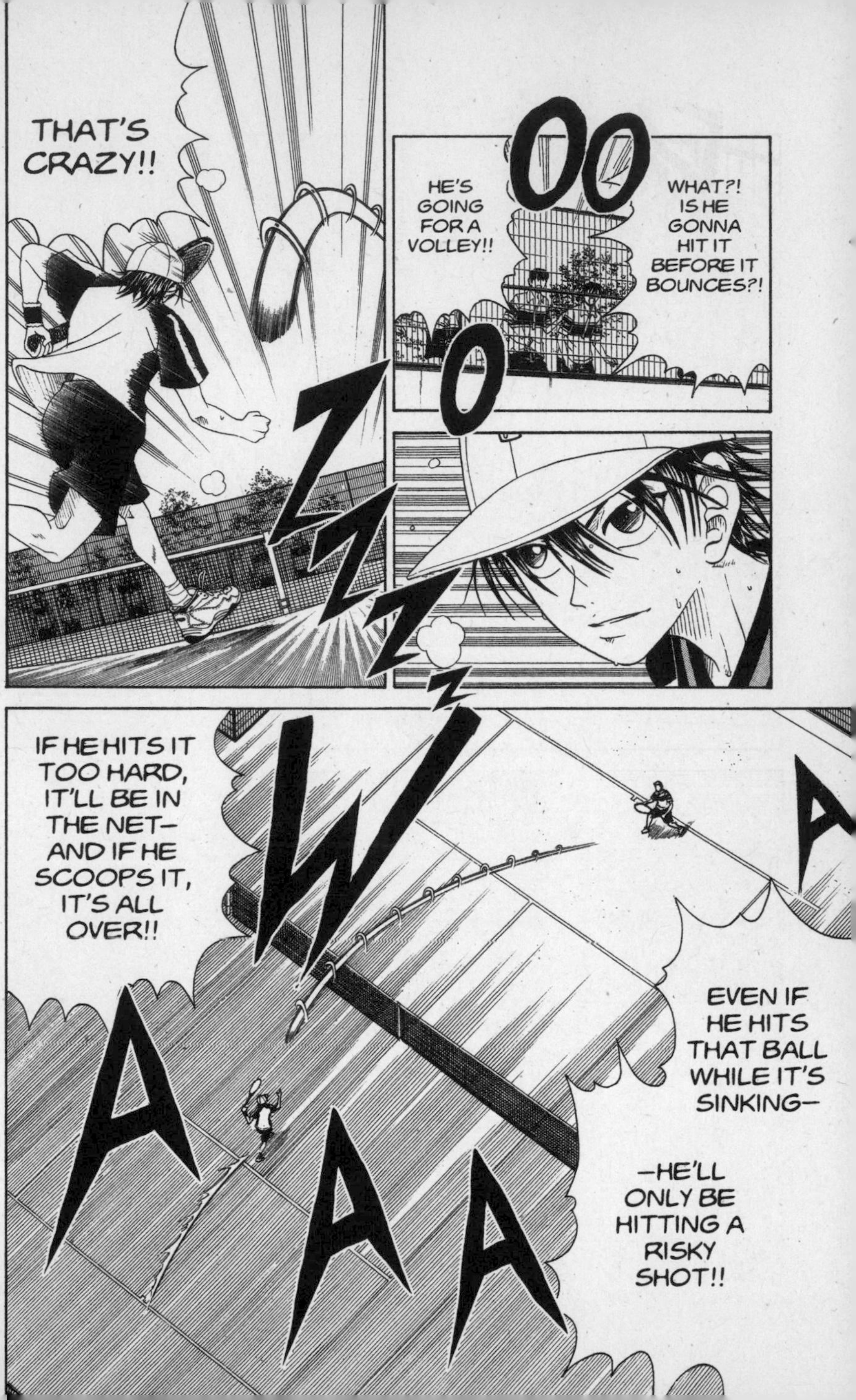
WHAT?! IS HE GONNA HIT IT BEFORE IT BOUNCES?!
HE'S GOING FOR A VOLLEY!!
ZZZZOOO
THAT'S CRAZY!!
WAAAA
EVEN IF HE HITS THAT BALL WHILE IT'S SINKING—
—HE'LL ONLY BE HITTING A RISKY SHOT!!
IF HE HITS IT TOO HARD, IT'LL BE IN THE NET—AND IF HE SCOOPS IT, IT'S ALL OVER!!

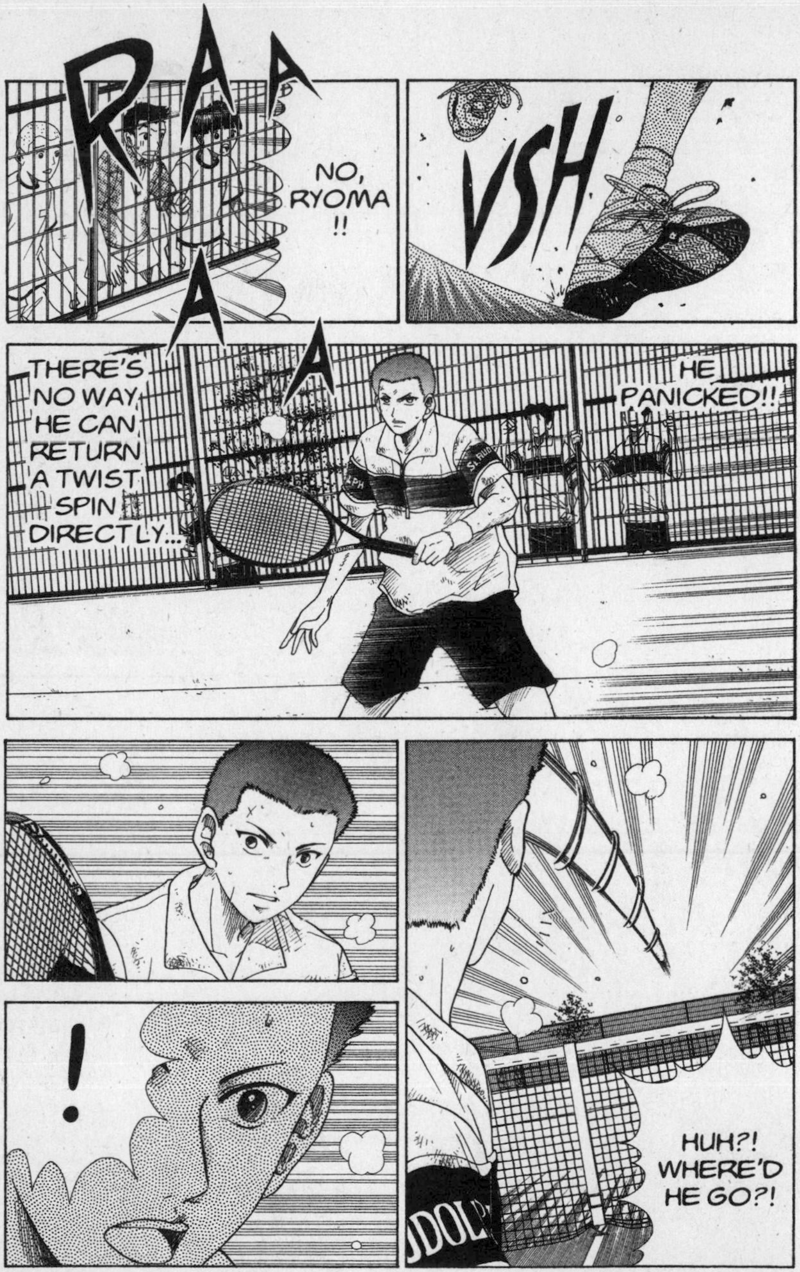
VSH
RAAAAA
NO, RYOMA!!
HE PANICKED!!
THERE'S NO WAY HE CAN RETURN A TWIST SPIN DIRECTLY...
HUH?! WHERE'D HE GO?!
!

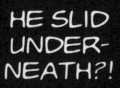

HE SLID UNDER-
NEATH?!

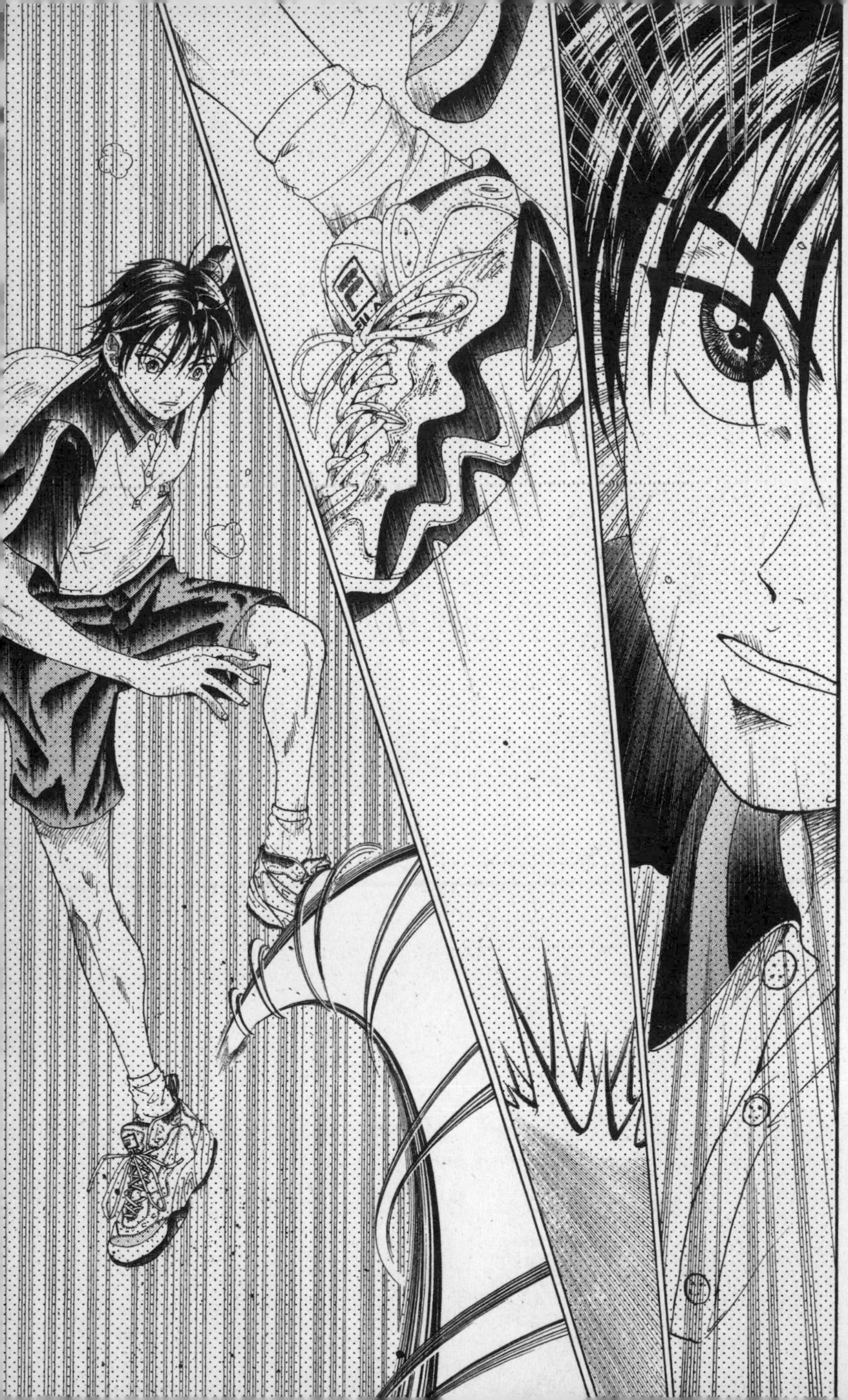

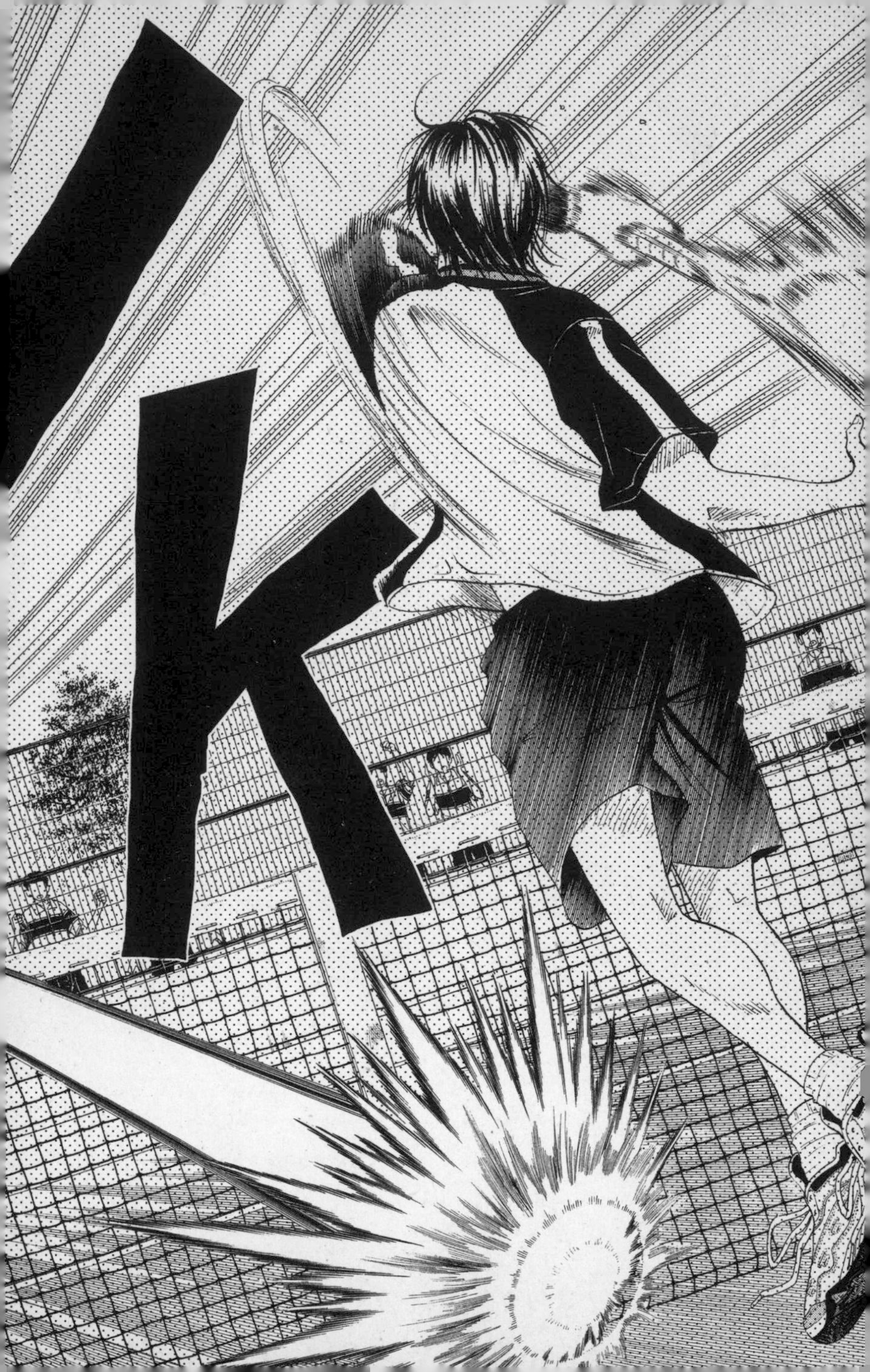
K

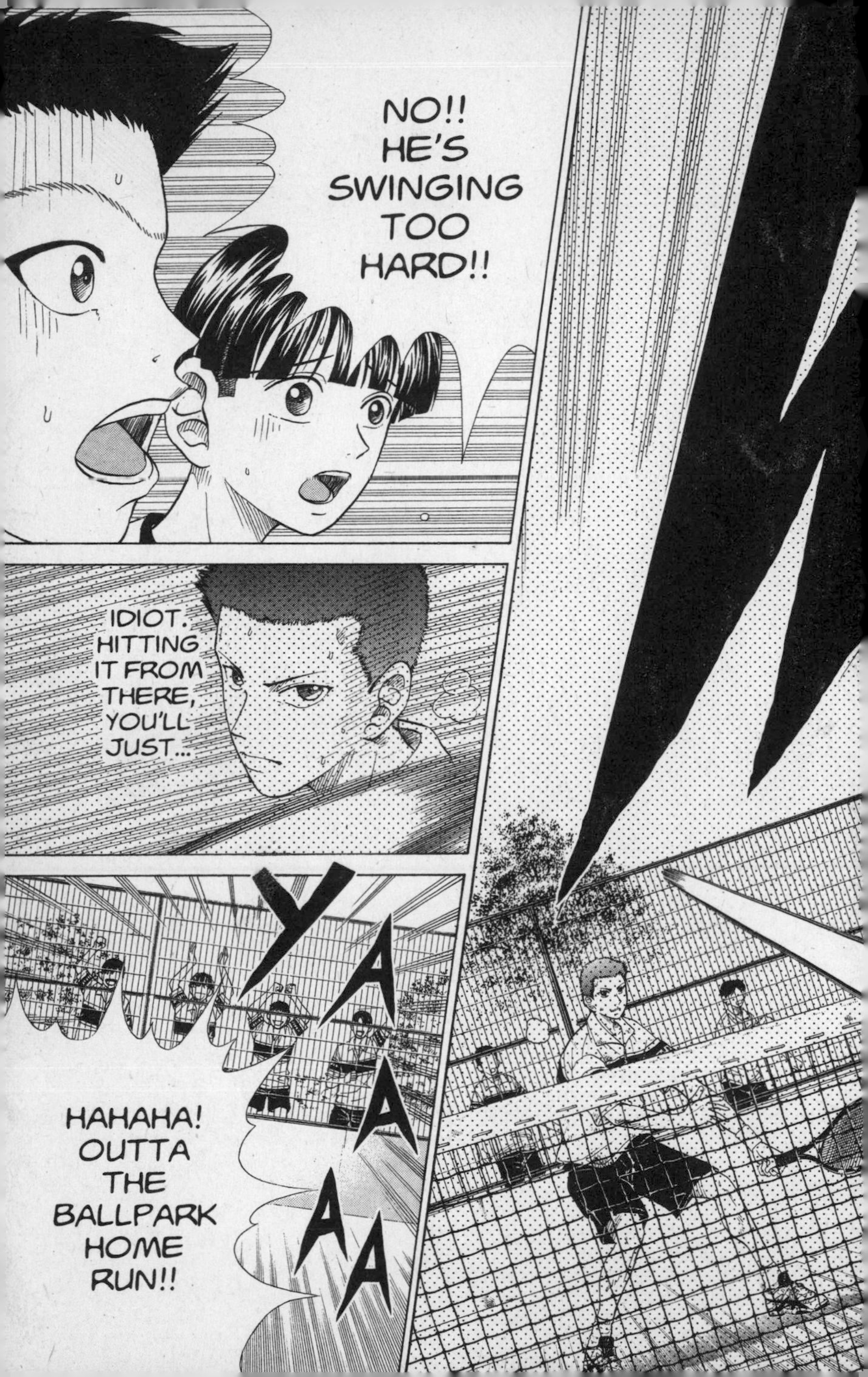
NO!! HE'S SWINGING TOO HARD!!
IDIOT. HITTING IT FROM THERE, YOU'LL JUST...
YAAAA
HAHAHA! OUTTA THE BALLPARK HOME RUN!!

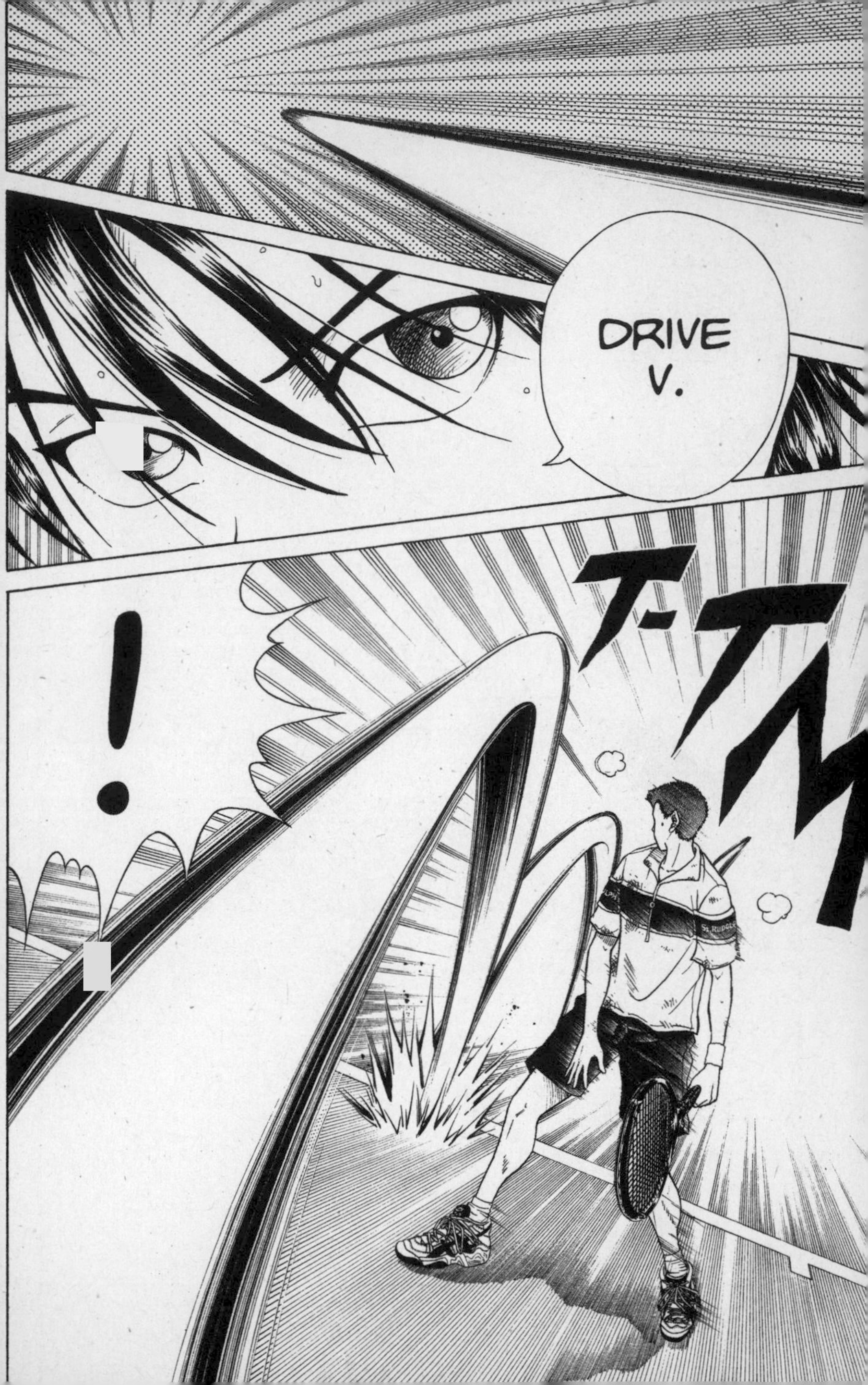
DRIVE V.
T-TM
!

READ THIS WAY

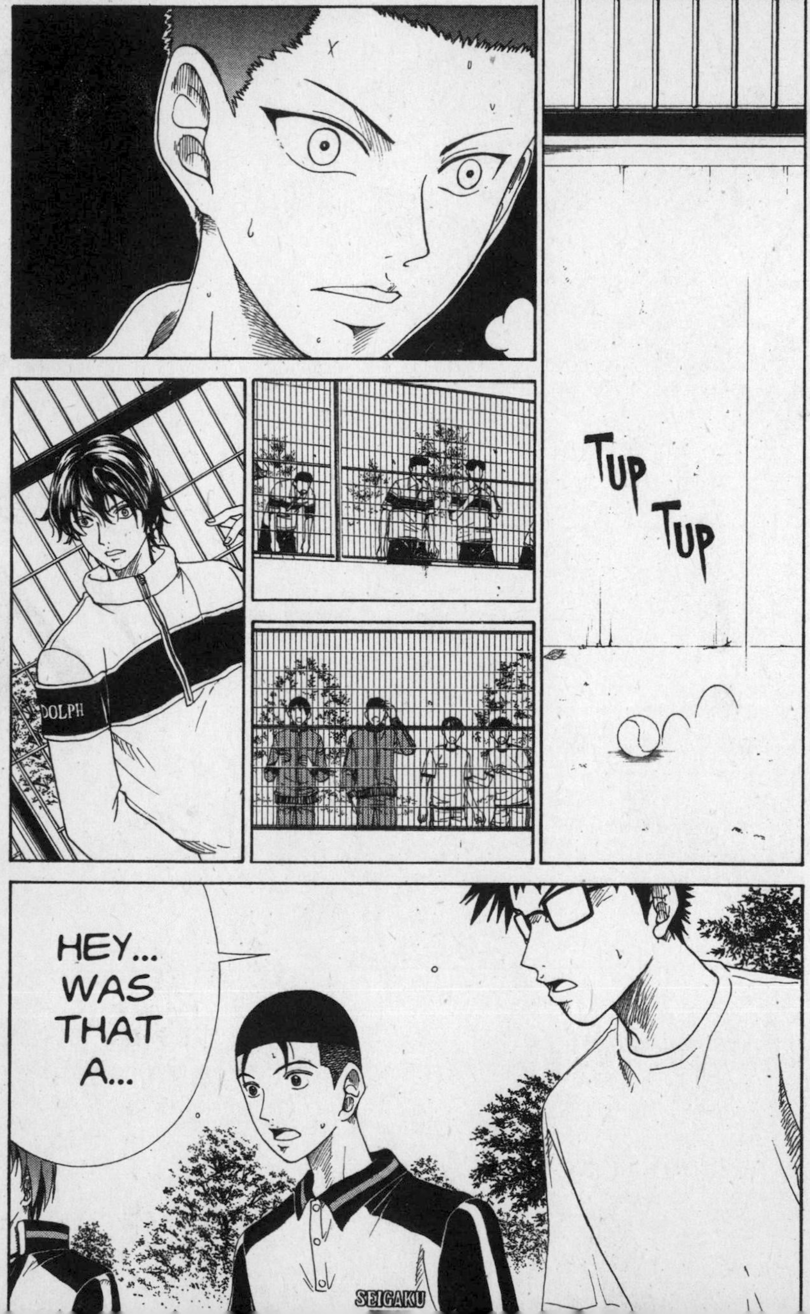
TUP TUP
DOLPH
HEY... WAS THAT A...
SEIGAKU

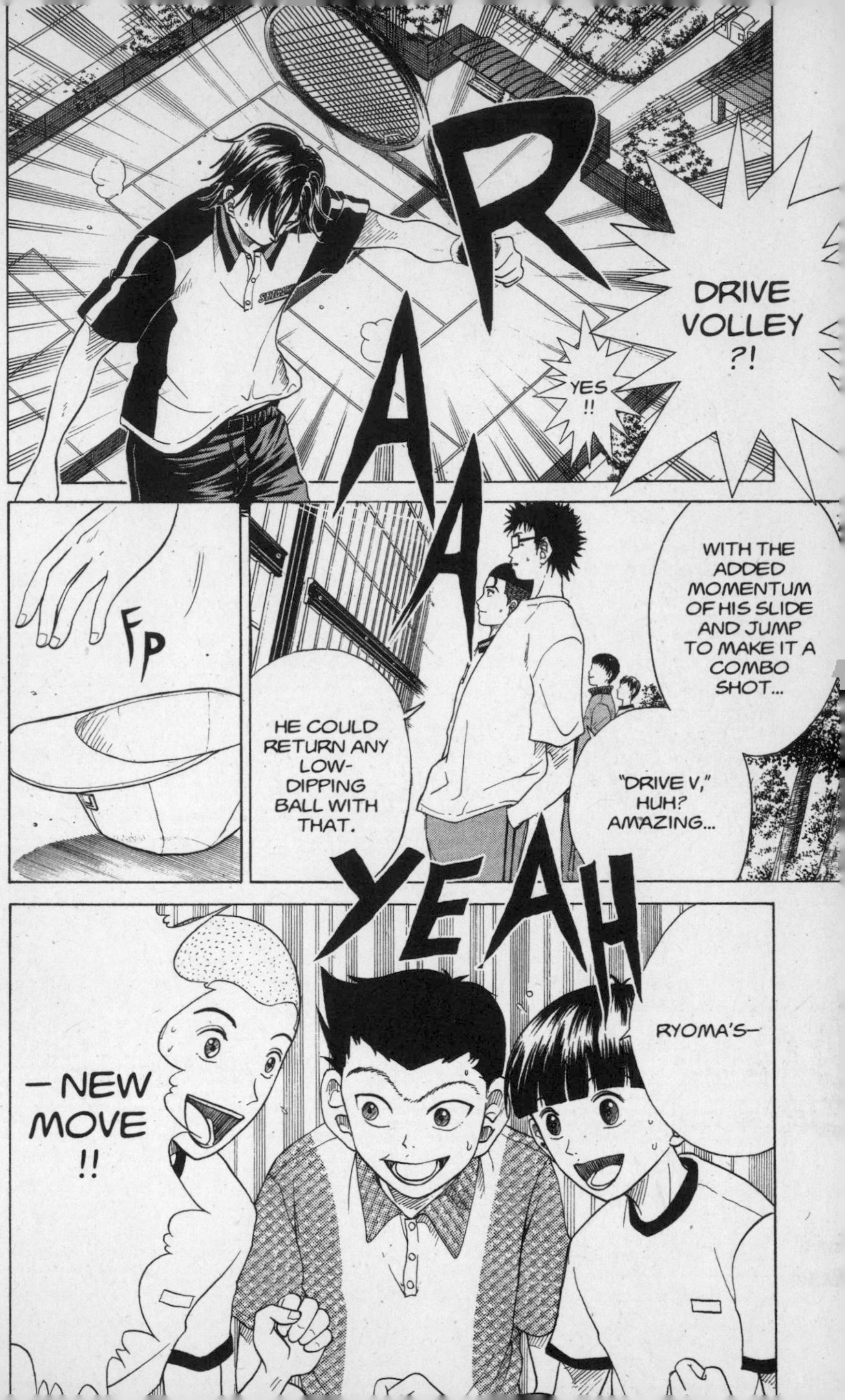
DRIVE VOLLEY ?!
YES !!
RAAA
WITH THE ADDED MOMENTUM OF HIS SLIDE AND JUMP TO MAKE IT A COMBO SHOT...
"DRIVE V," HUH? AMAZING...
HE COULD RETURN ANY LOW-DIPPING BALL WITH THAT.
FP
YEAH
RYOMA'S—
—NEW MOVE !!

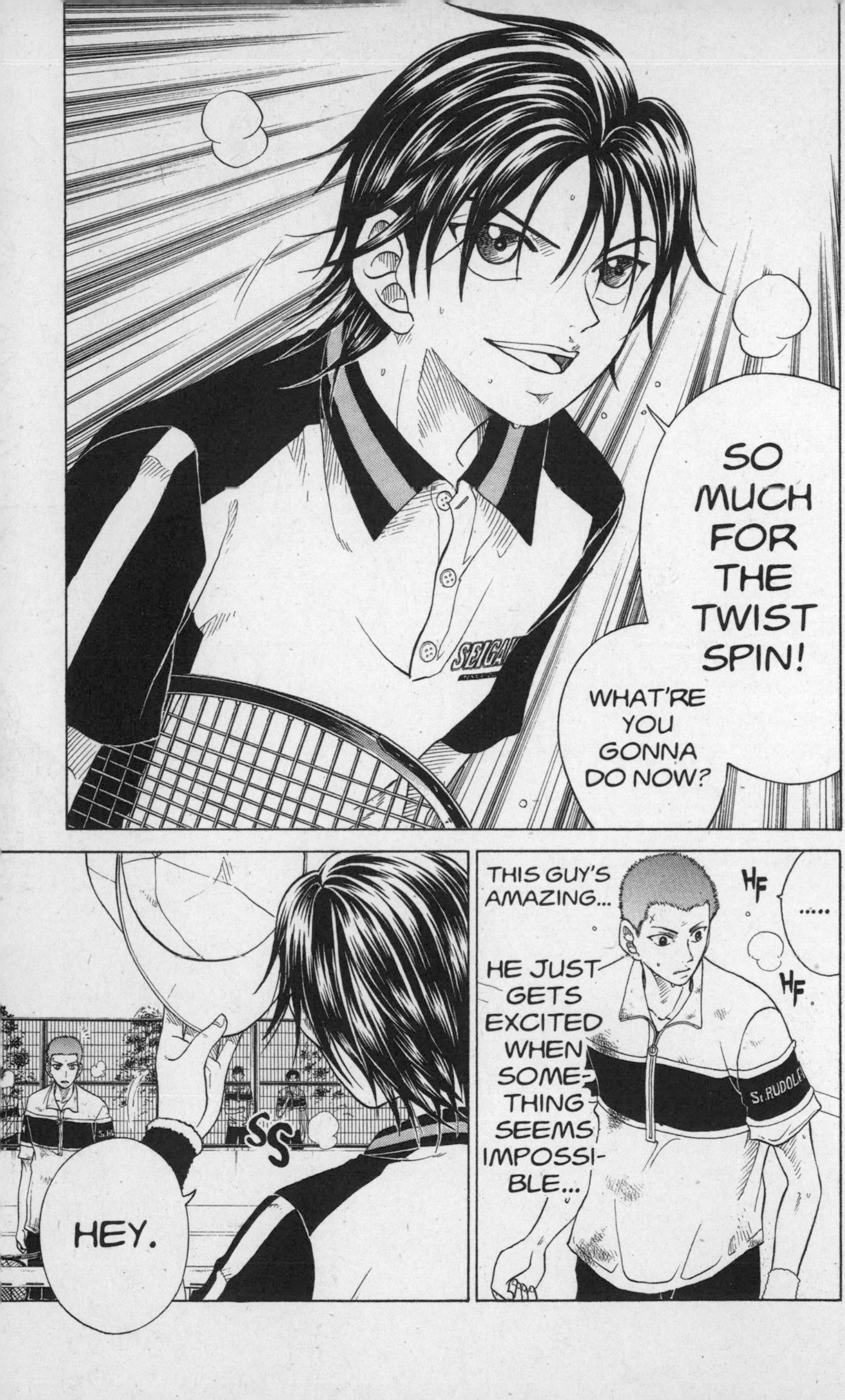
SO MUCH FOR THE TWIST SPIN!
WHAT'RE YOU GONNA DO NOW?
.....
HF
HF
THIS GUY'S AMAZING...
HE JUST GETS EXCITED WHEN SOME-THING SEEMS IMPOSSI-BLE...
SS
HEY.

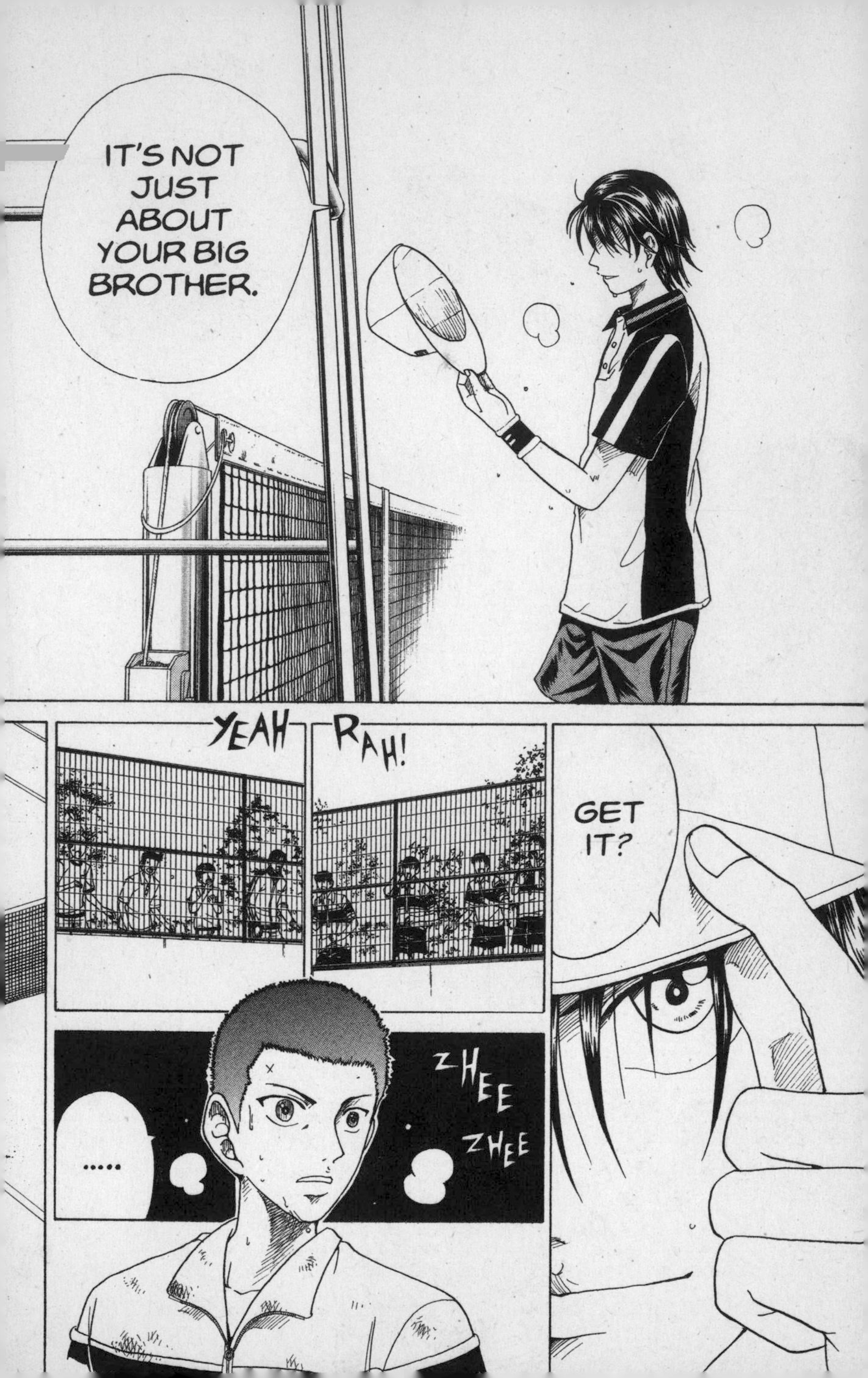
IT'S NOT JUST ABOUT YOUR BIG BROTHER.
GET IT?
RAH!
YEAH
ZHEE
ZHEE
.....

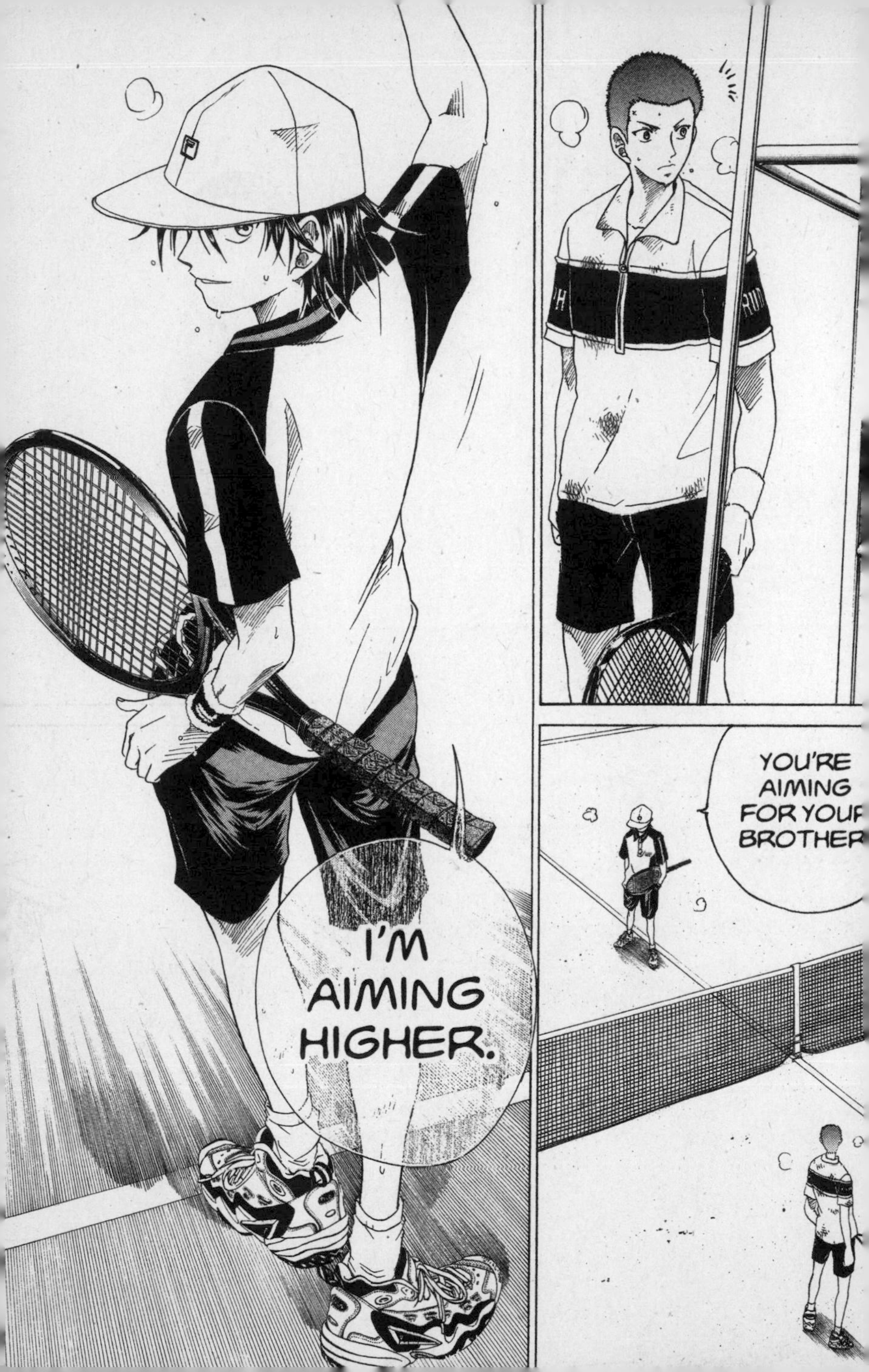
YOU'RE AIMING FOR YOUR BROTHER
I'M AIMING HIGHER.

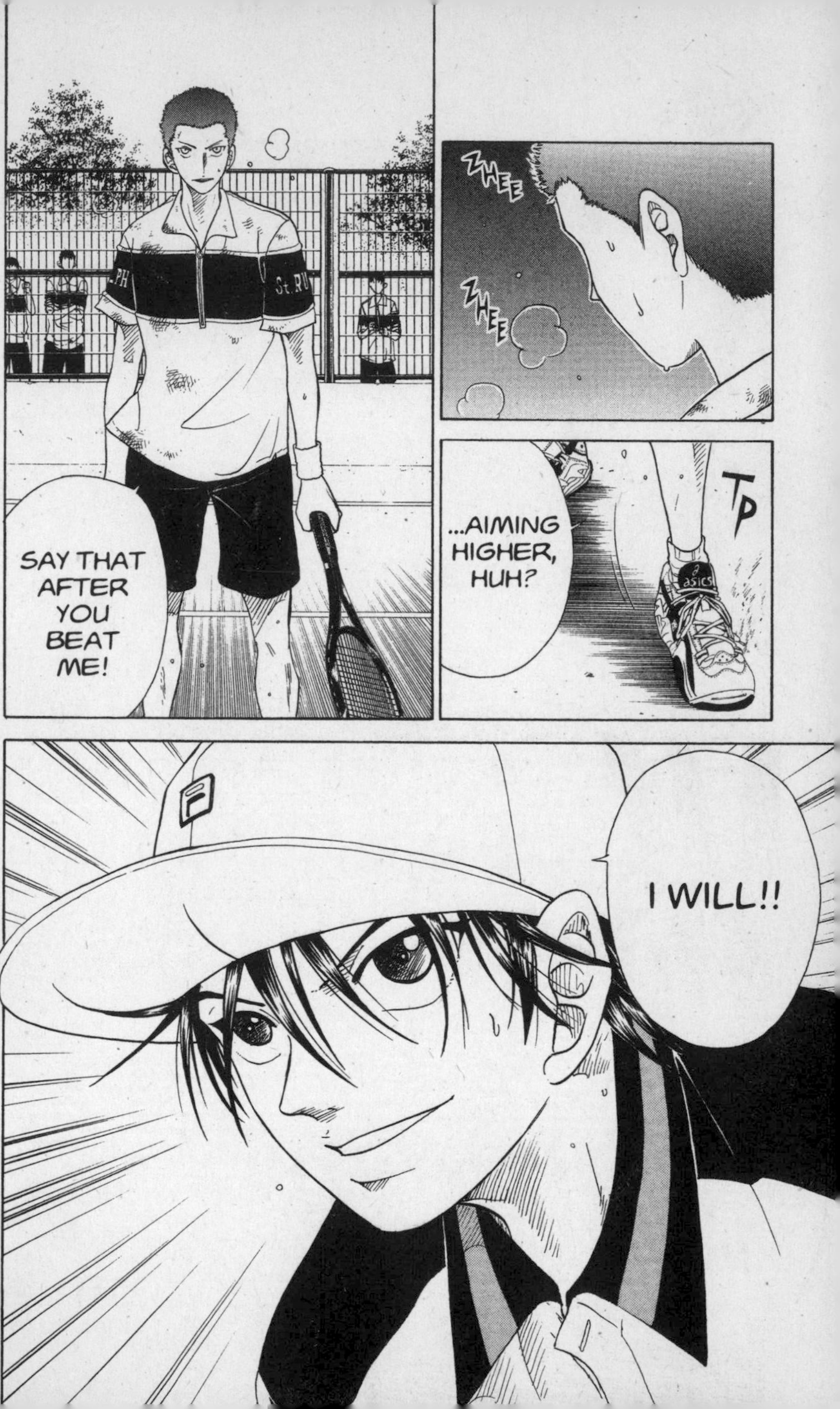
ZHEE
ZHEE
...AIMING HIGHER, HUH?
TP
SAY THAT AFTER YOU BEAT ME!
I WILL!!

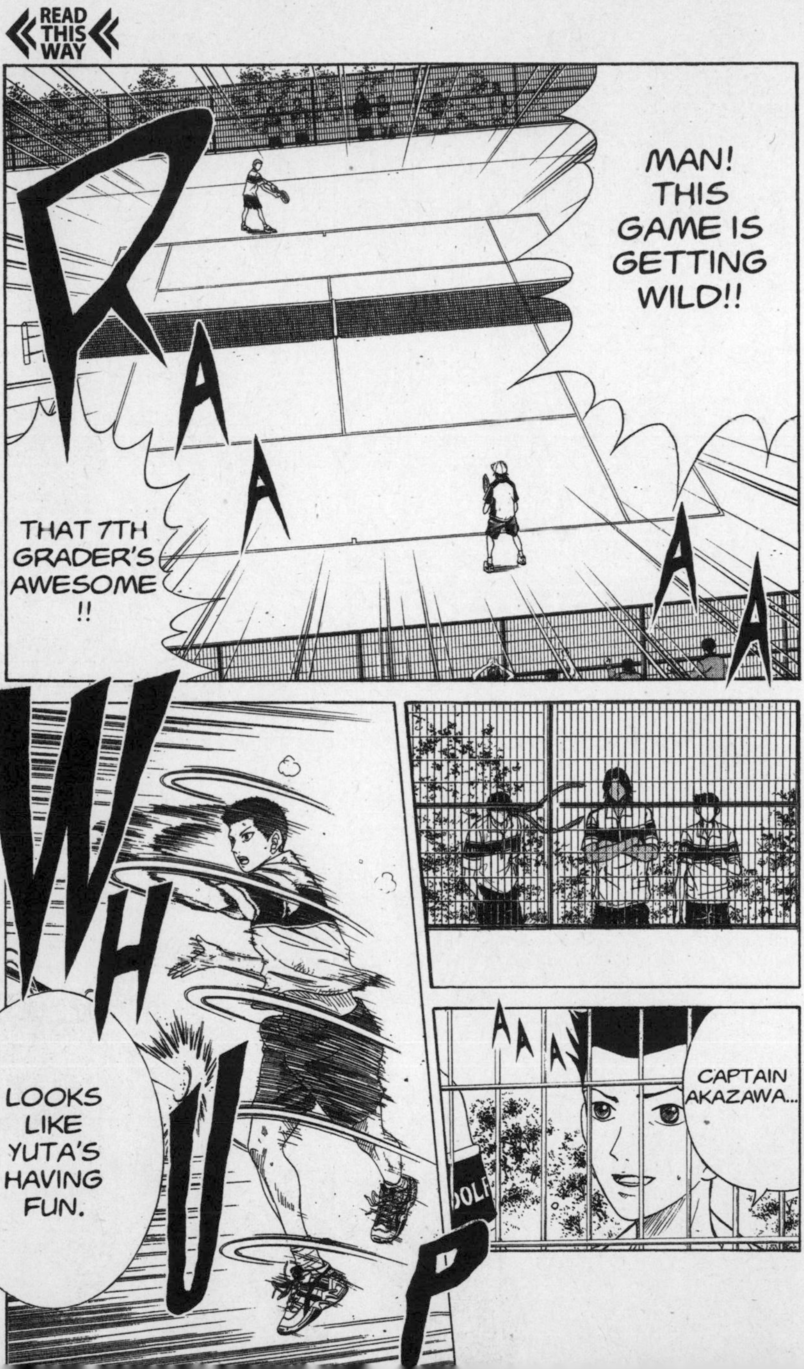
READ THIS WAY
RAAAAA
MAN! THIS GAME IS GETTING WILD!!
THAT 7TH GRADER'S AWESOME !!
CAPTAIN AKAZAWA...
AAA
WHUP
LOOKS LIKE YUTA'S HAVING FUN.

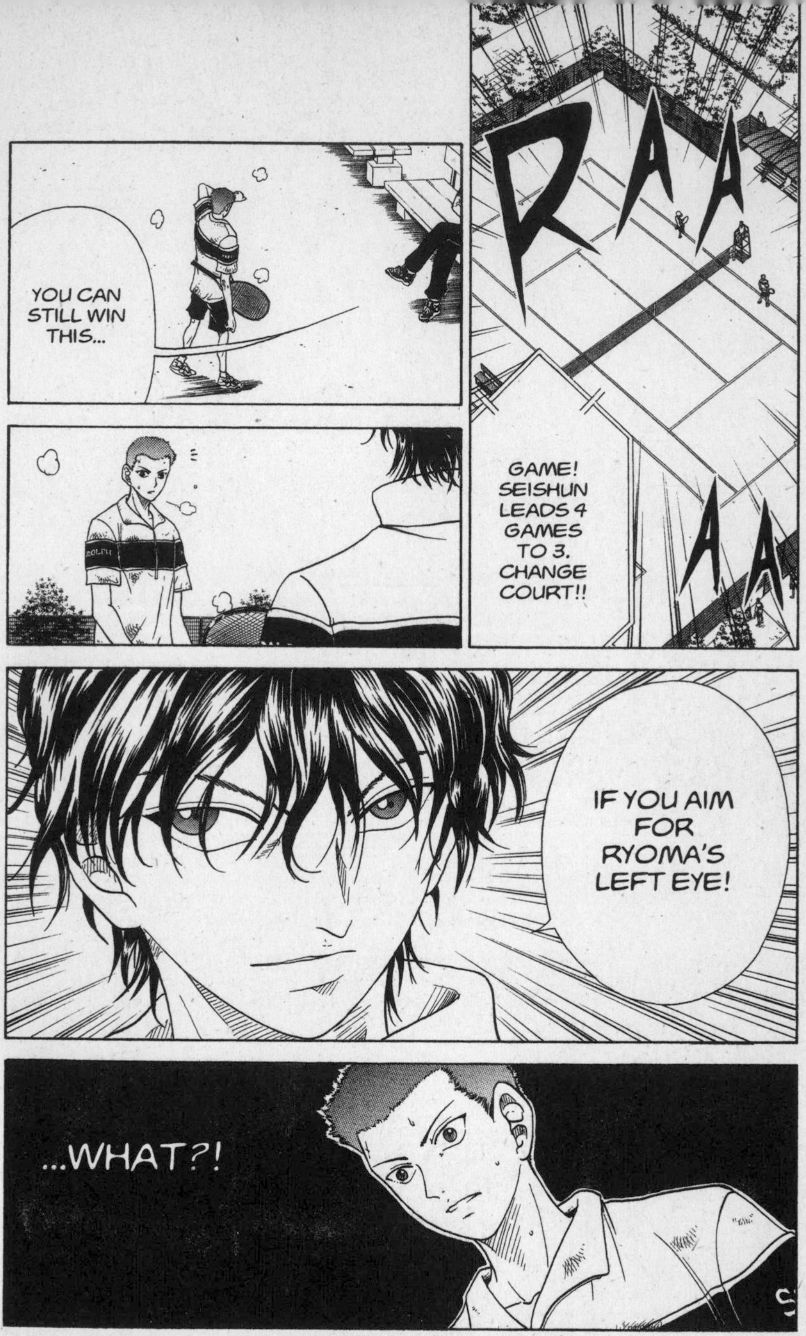

RAA
AA
GAME! SEISHUN LEADS 4 GAMES TO 3. CHANGE COURT!!
YOU CAN STILL WIN THIS...
IF YOU AIM FOR RYOMA'S LEFT EYE!
...WHAT?!

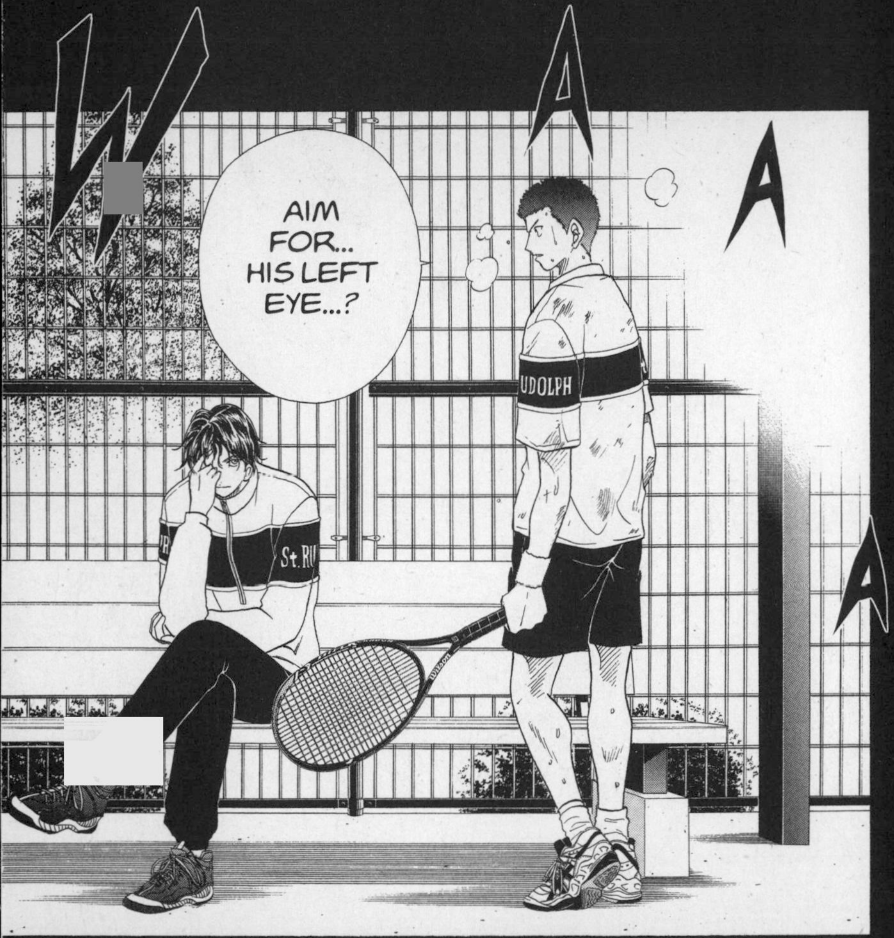
WAAA
AIM FOR... HIS LEFT EYE...?

GENIUS 74: NO FOOLING

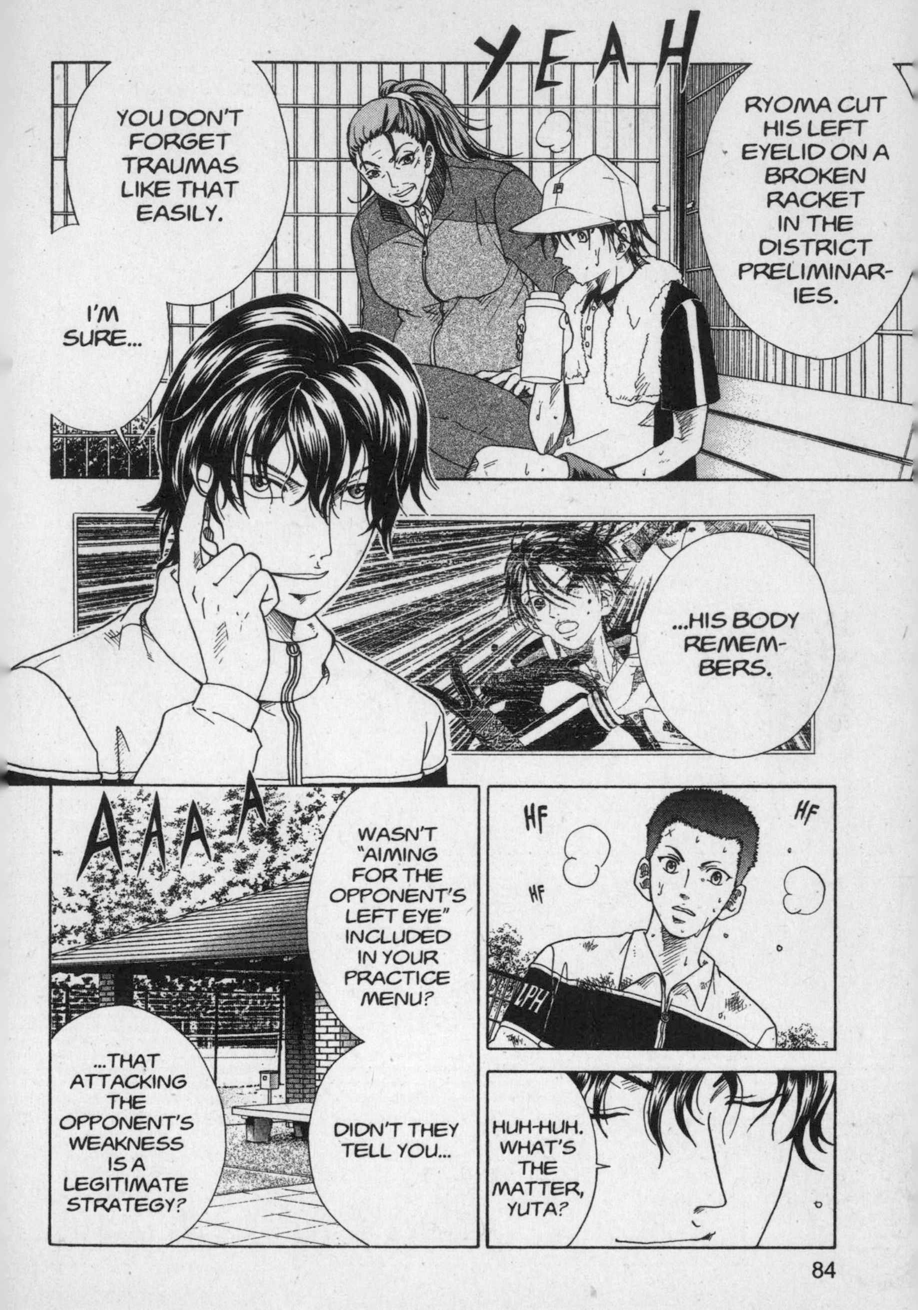
YEAH
RYOMA CUT HIS LEFT EYELID ON A BROKEN RACKET IN THE DISTRICT PRELIMINAR-IES.
YOU DON'T FORGET TRAUMAS LIKE THAT EASILY.
I'M SURE...
...HIS BODY REMEM-BERS.
HF
HF
HF
HUH-HUH. WHAT'S THE MATTER, YUTA?
AAAA
WASN'T "AIMING FOR THE OPPONENT'S LEFT EYE" INCLUDED IN YOUR PRACTICE MENU?
DIDN'T THEY TELL YOU...
...THAT ATTACKING THE OPPONENT'S WEAKNESS IS A LEGITIMATE STRATEGY?

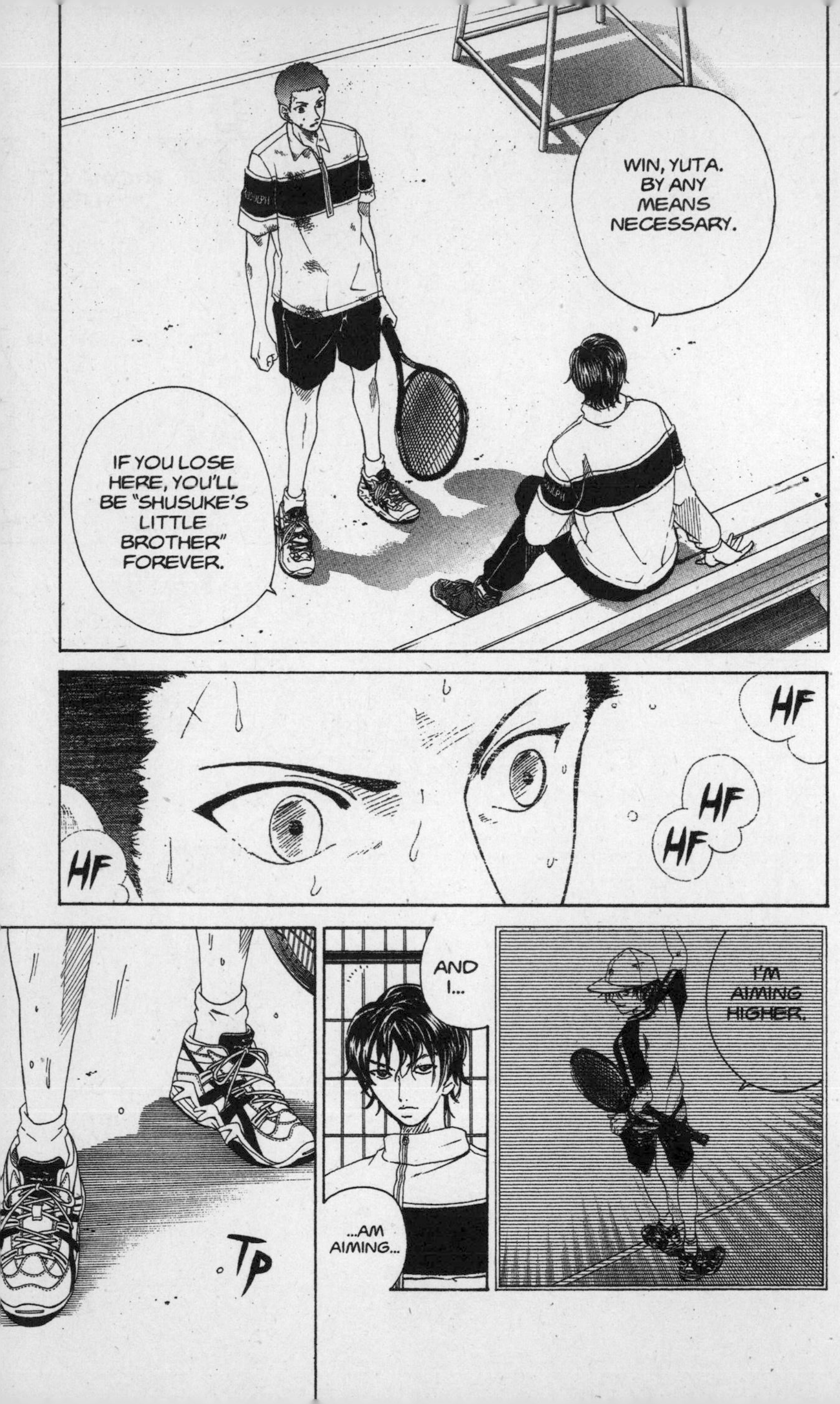
WIN, YUTA. BY ANY MEANS NECESSARY.
IF YOU LOSE HERE, YOU'LL BE "SHUSUKE'S LITTLE BROTHER" FOREVER.
HF
HF
HF
HF
I'M AIMING HIGHER.
AND I...
...AM AIMING...
TP

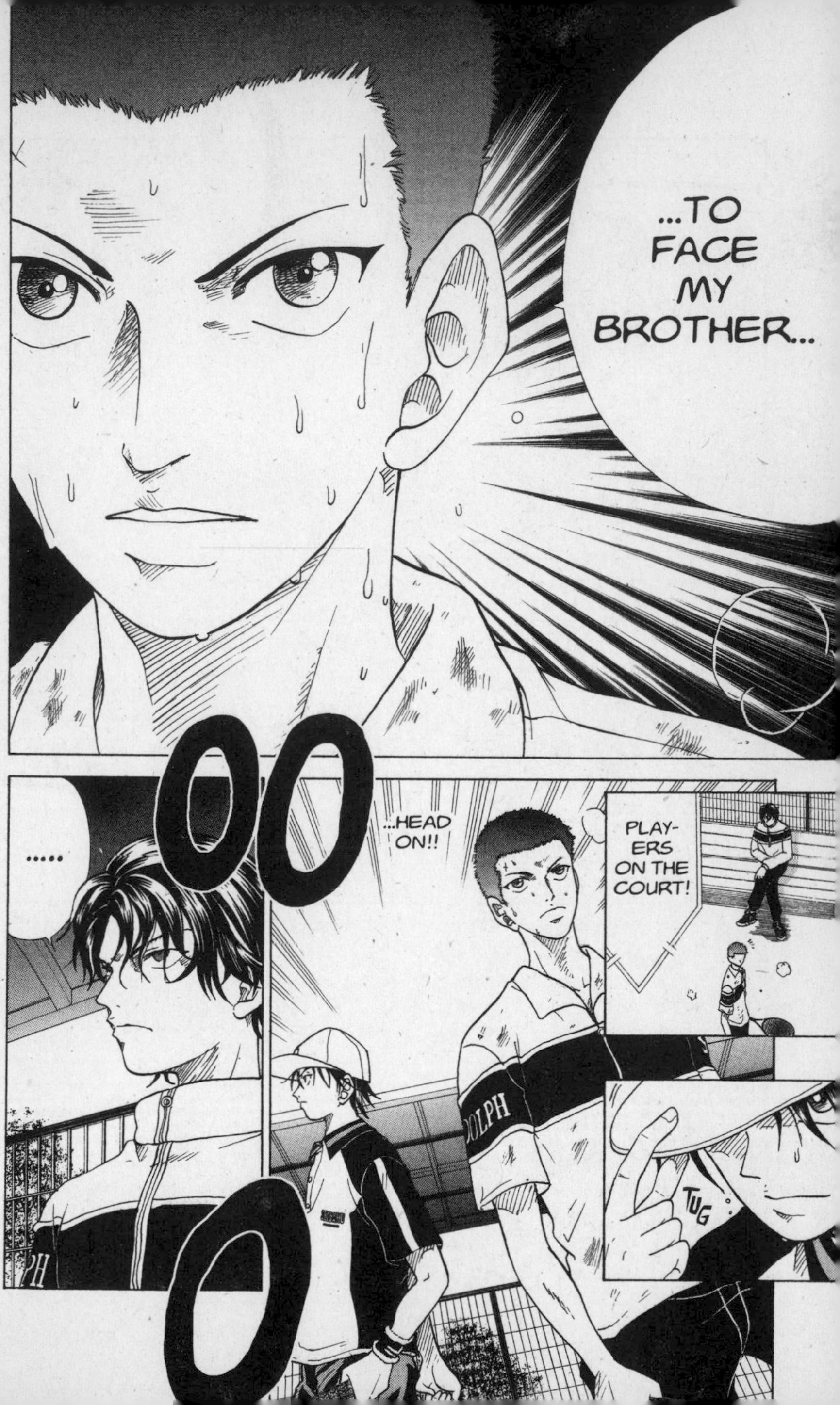
...TO FACE MY BROTHER...
PLAY-ERS ON THE COURT!
TUG
...HEAD ON!!
OO
.....
O

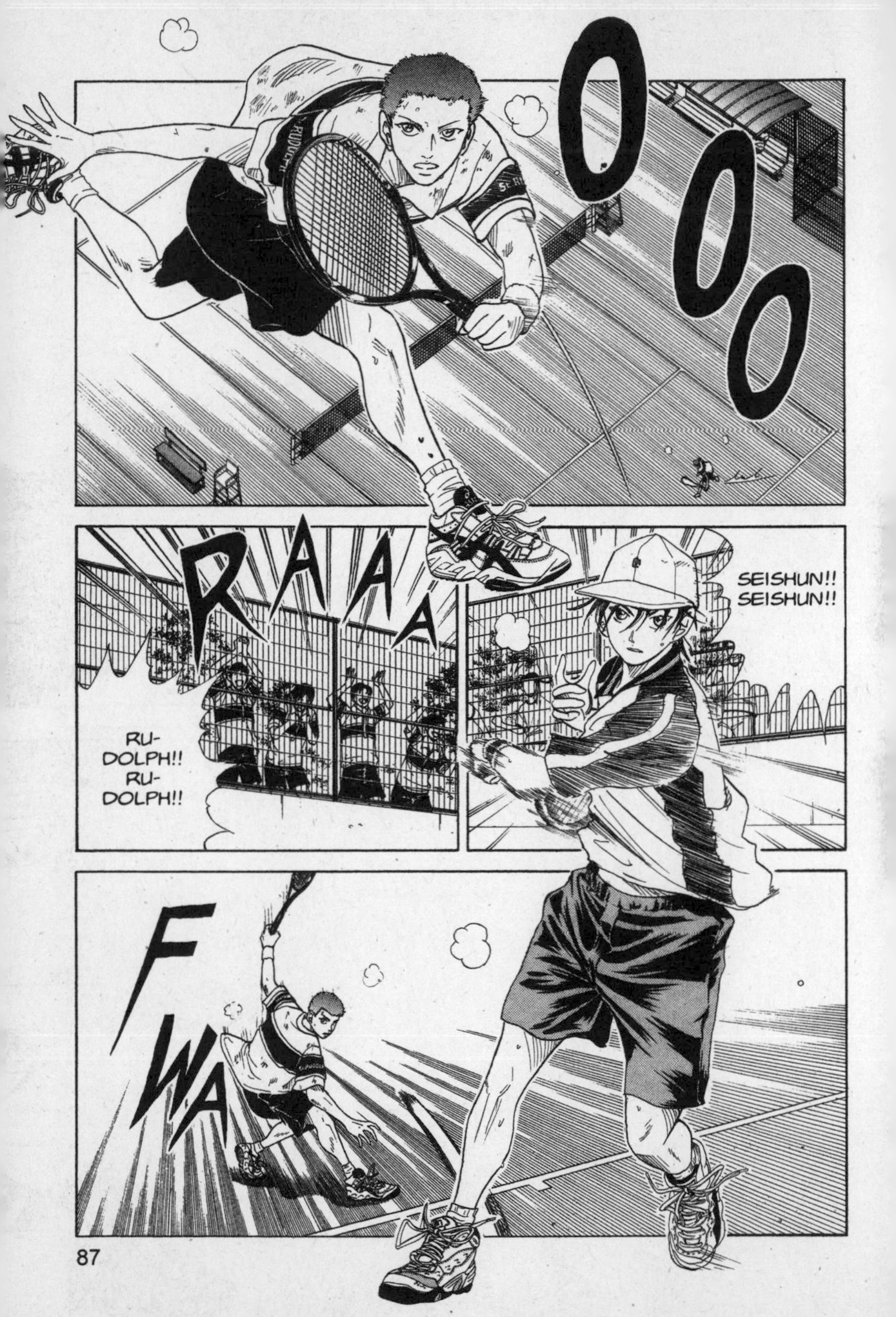
OOOO
SEISHUN!! SEISHUN!!
RAAAA
RU-DOLPH!! RU-DOLPH!!
FWA

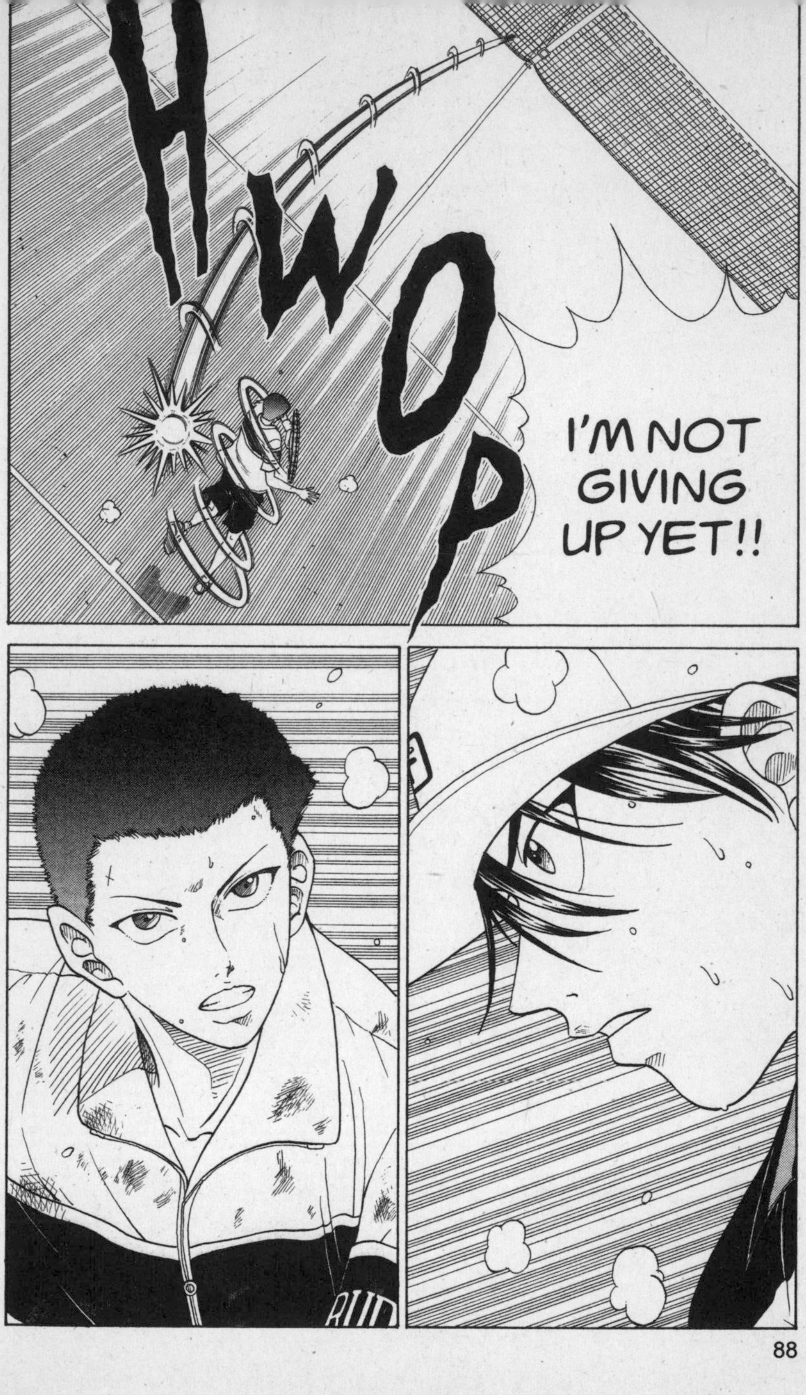
HWOP
I'M NOT GIVING UP YET!!

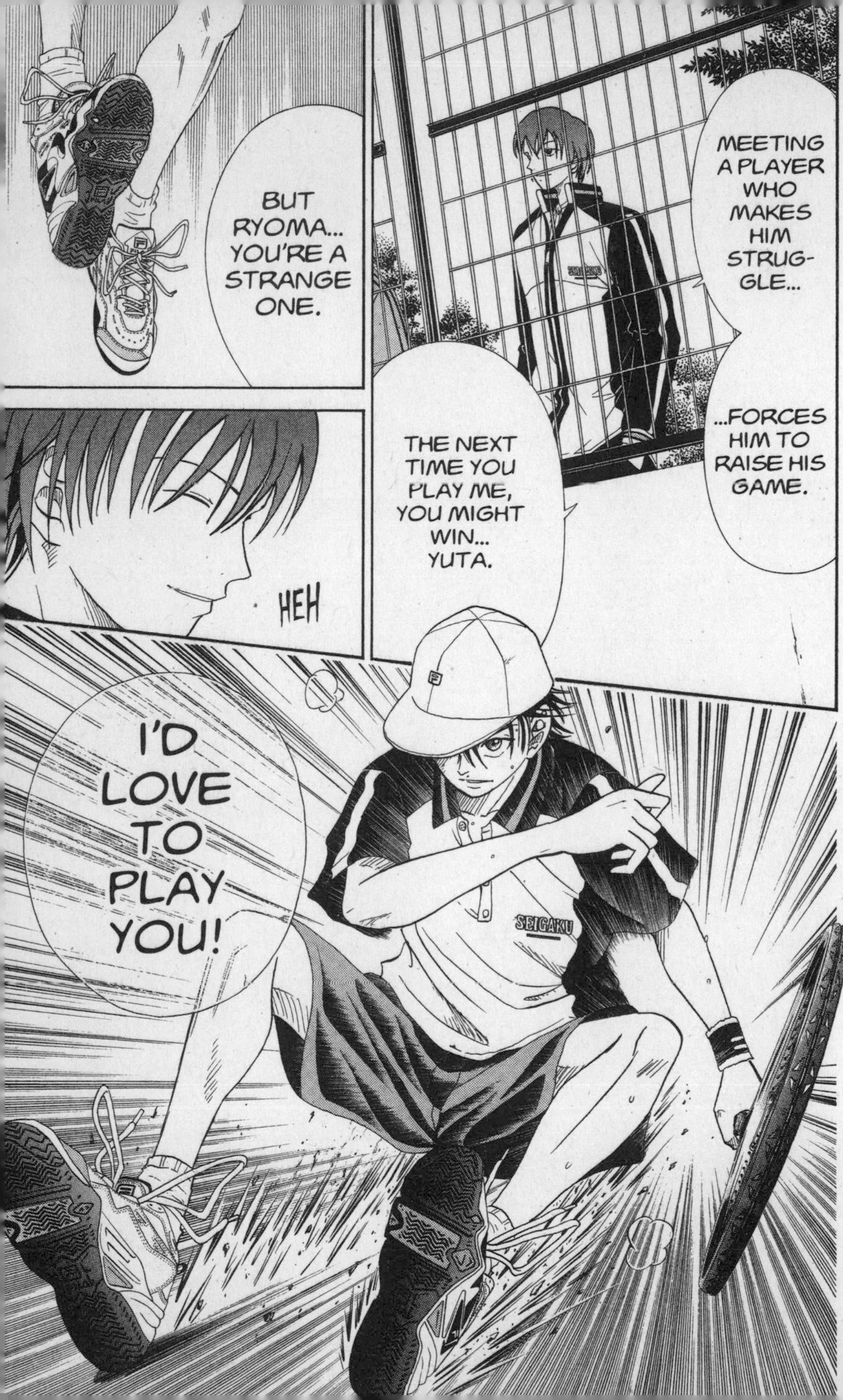
MEETING A PLAYER WHO MAKES HIM STRUG-GLE...
...FORCES HIM TO RAISE HIS GAME.
THE NEXT TIME YOU PLAY ME, YOU MIGHT WIN... YUTA.
BUT RYOMA... YOU'RE A STRANGE ONE.
HEH
I'D LOVE TO PLAY YOU!

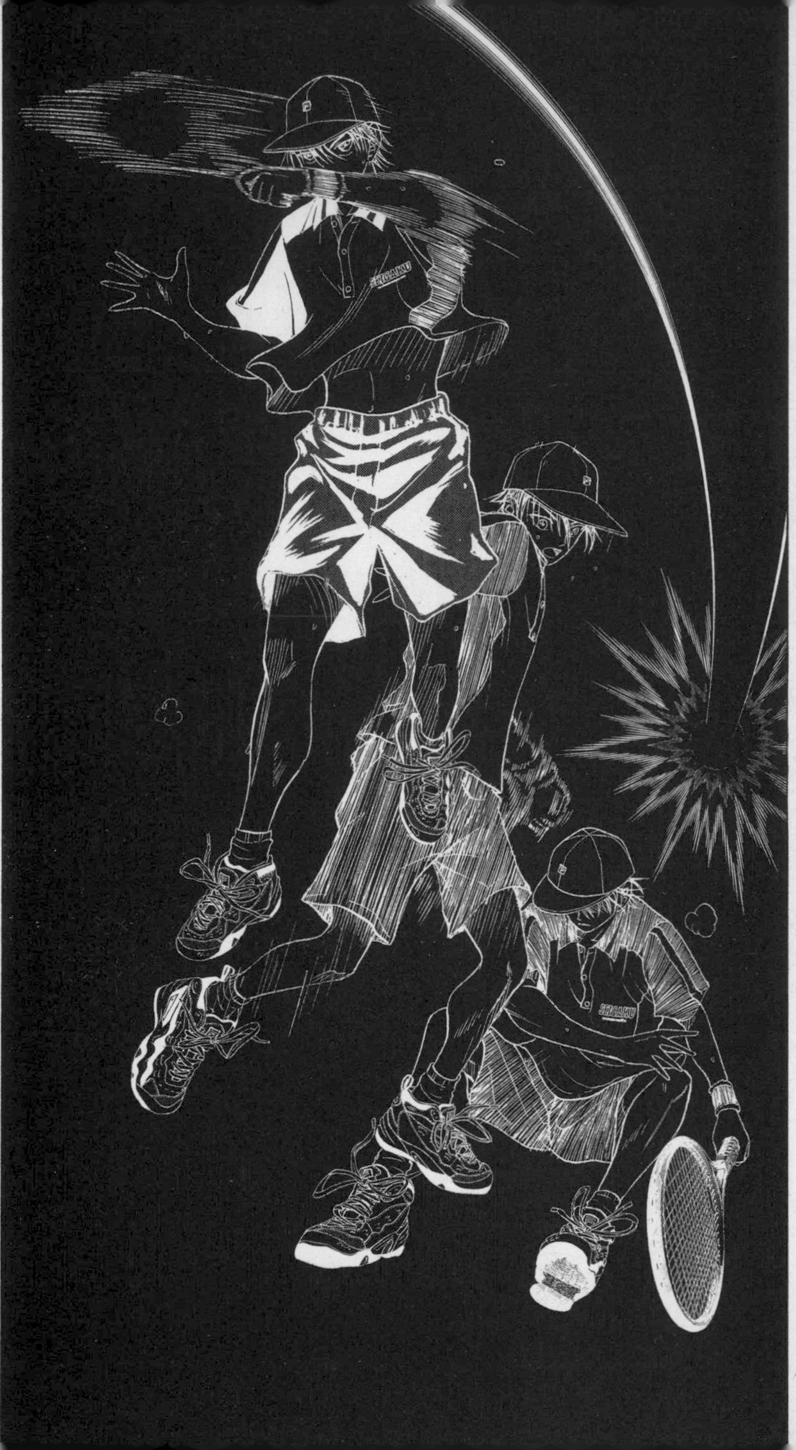
SEIGAKU
SEIGAKU

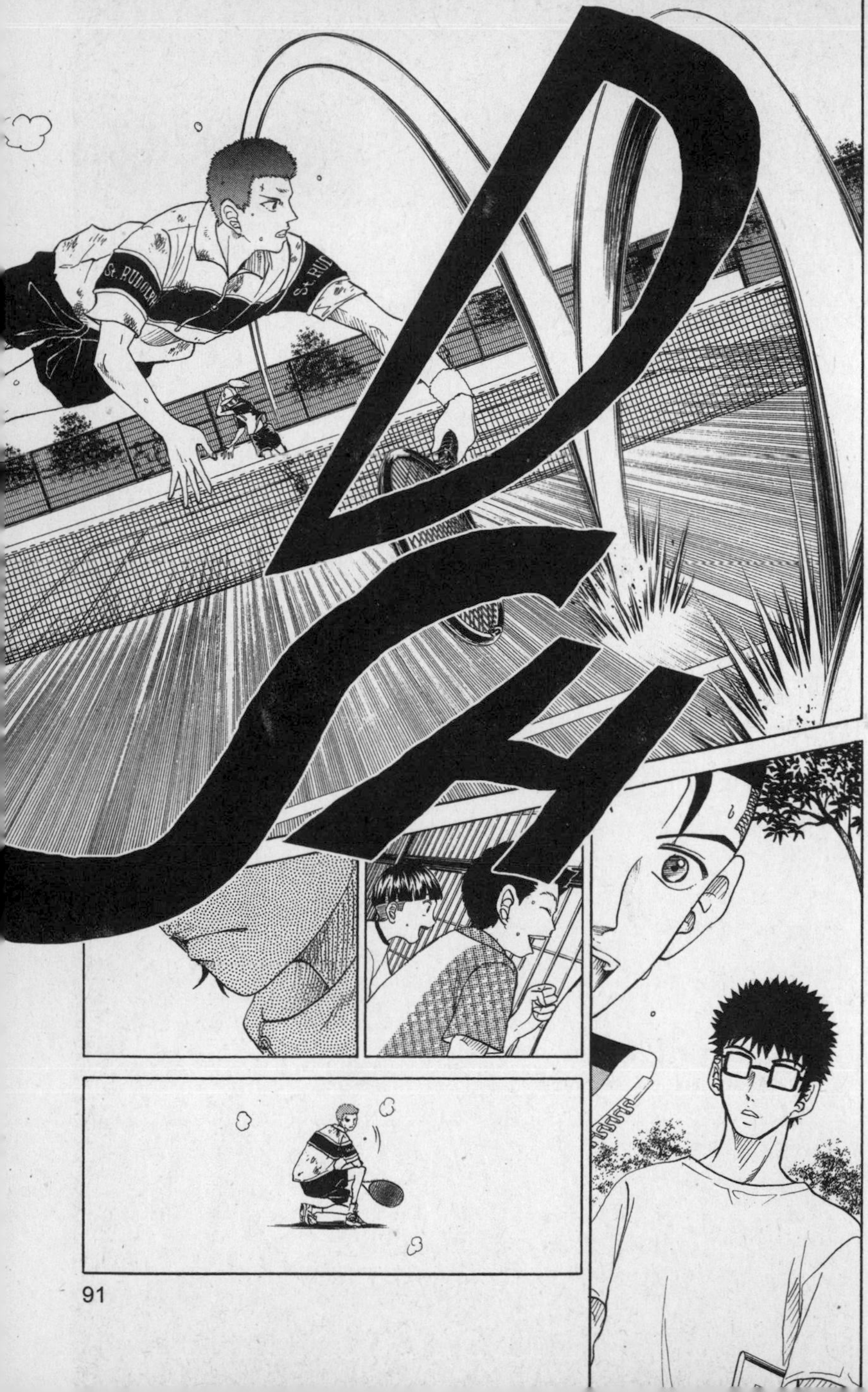
St. RUDOLPH

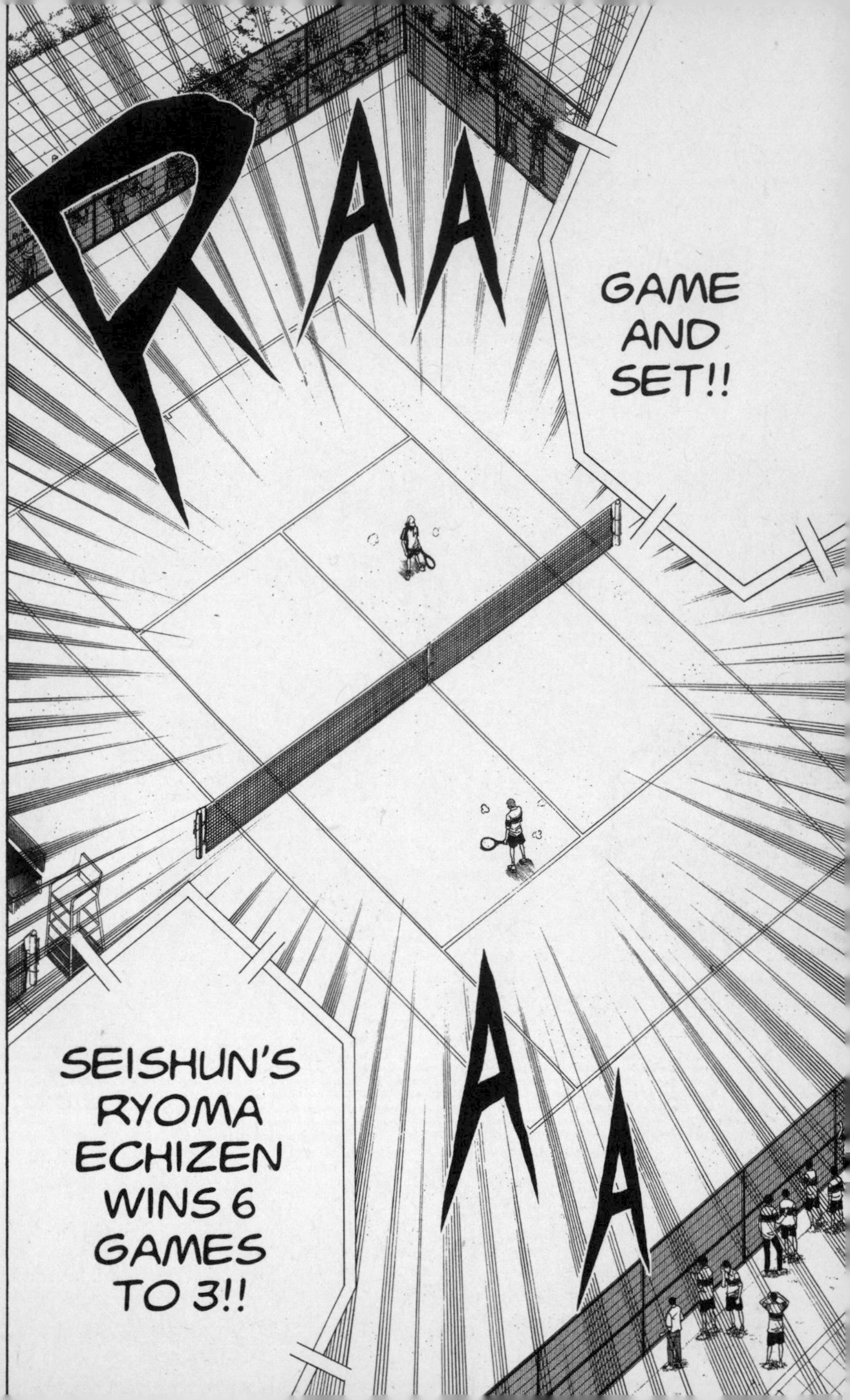
GAME AND SET!!
RAA
AAA
SEISHUN'S RYOMA ECHIZEN WINS 6 GAMES TO 3!!

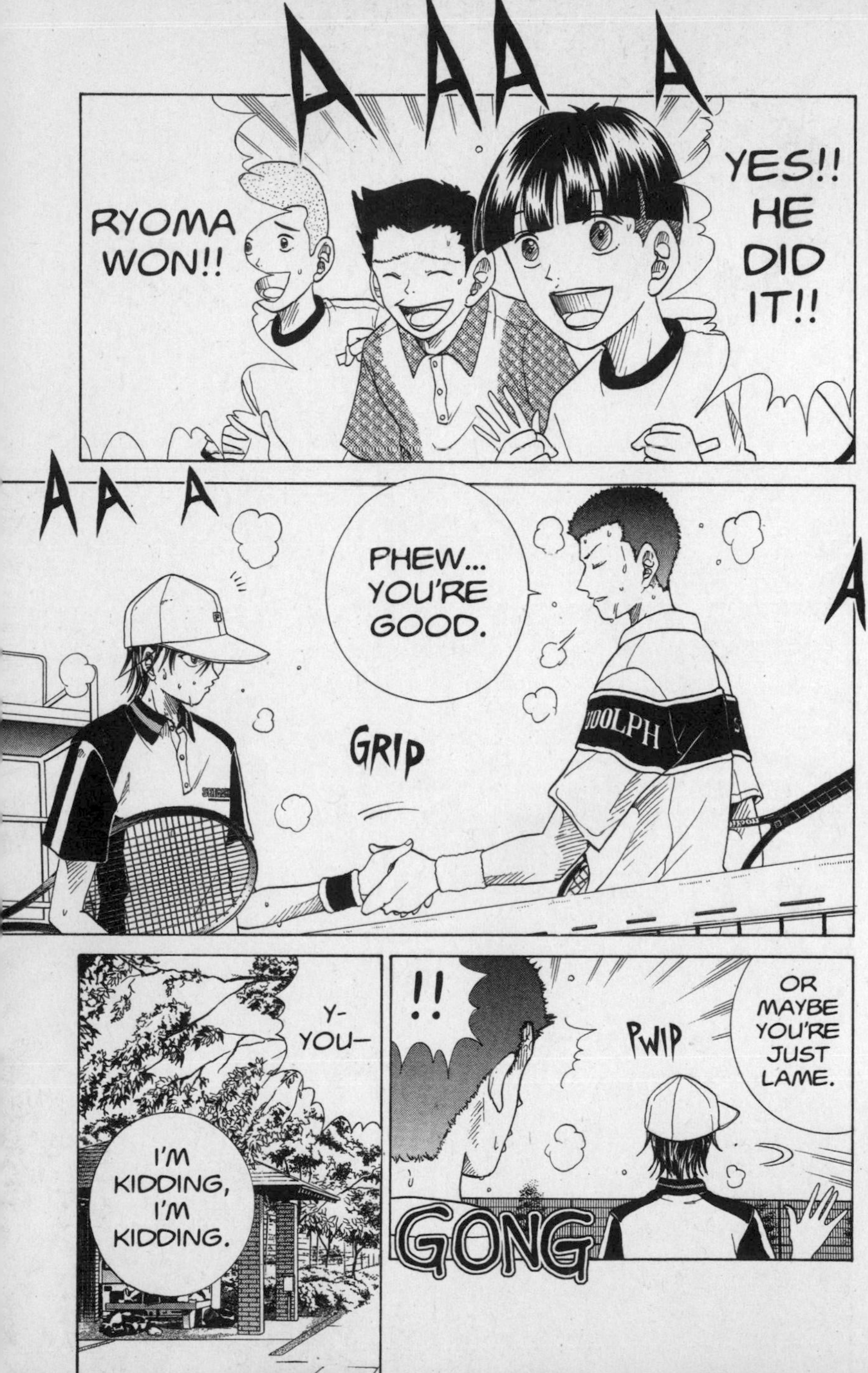
A A A A
YES!! HE DID IT!!
RYOMA WON!!
A A A A
PHEW... YOU'RE GOOD.
GRIP
OR MAYBE YOU'RE JUST LAME.
PWIP
!!
GONG
Y- YOU-
I'M KIDDING, I'M KIDDING.

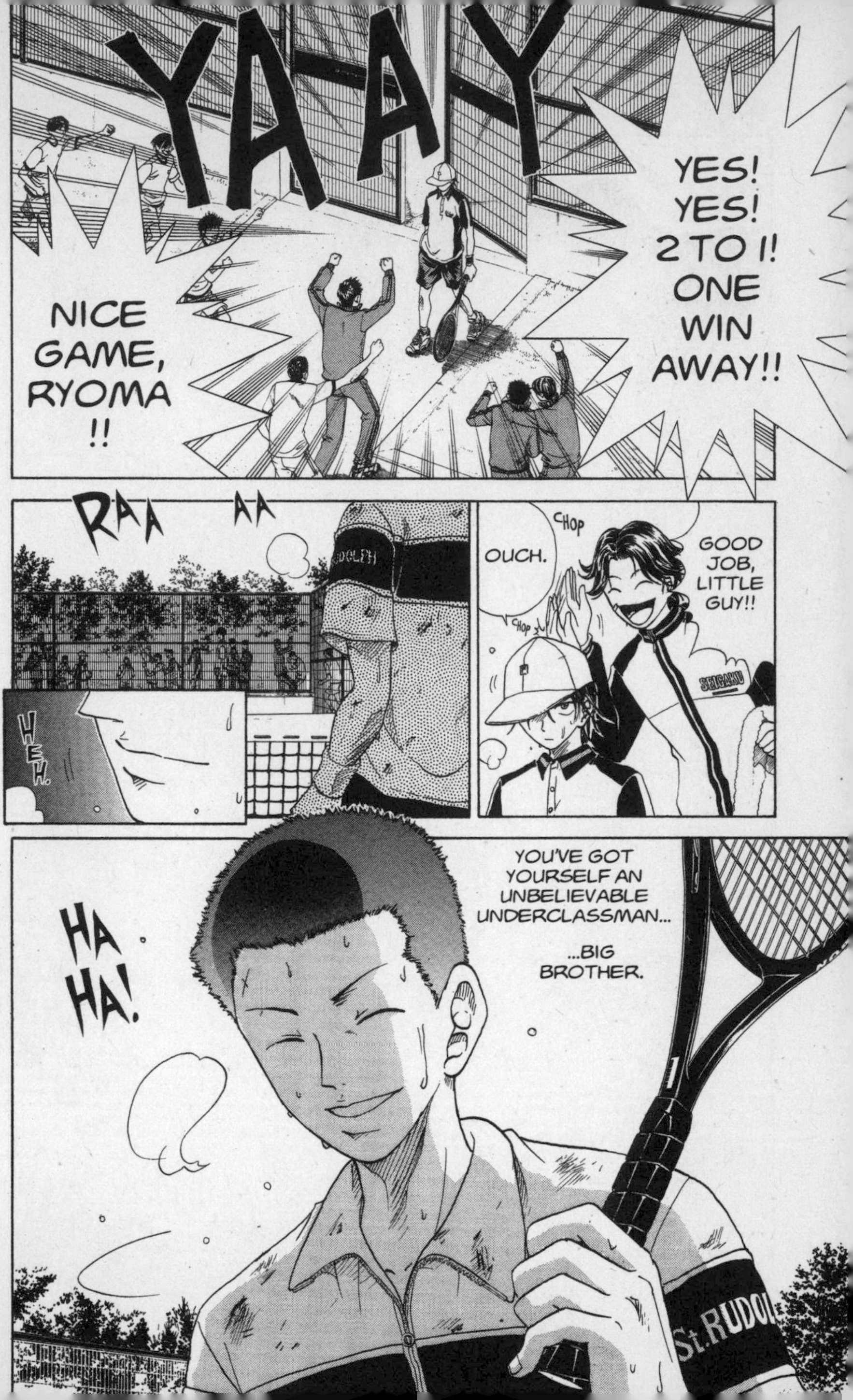
YAAY
YES! YES! 2 TO 1! ONE WIN AWAY!!
NICE GAME, RYOMA !!
GOOD JOB, LITTLE GUY!!
CHOP
OUCH.
CHOP
RAAAA
HEH.
YOU'VE GOT YOURSELF AN UNBELIEVABLE UNDERCLASSMAN...
...BIG BROTHER.
HA HA!

READ THIS WAY

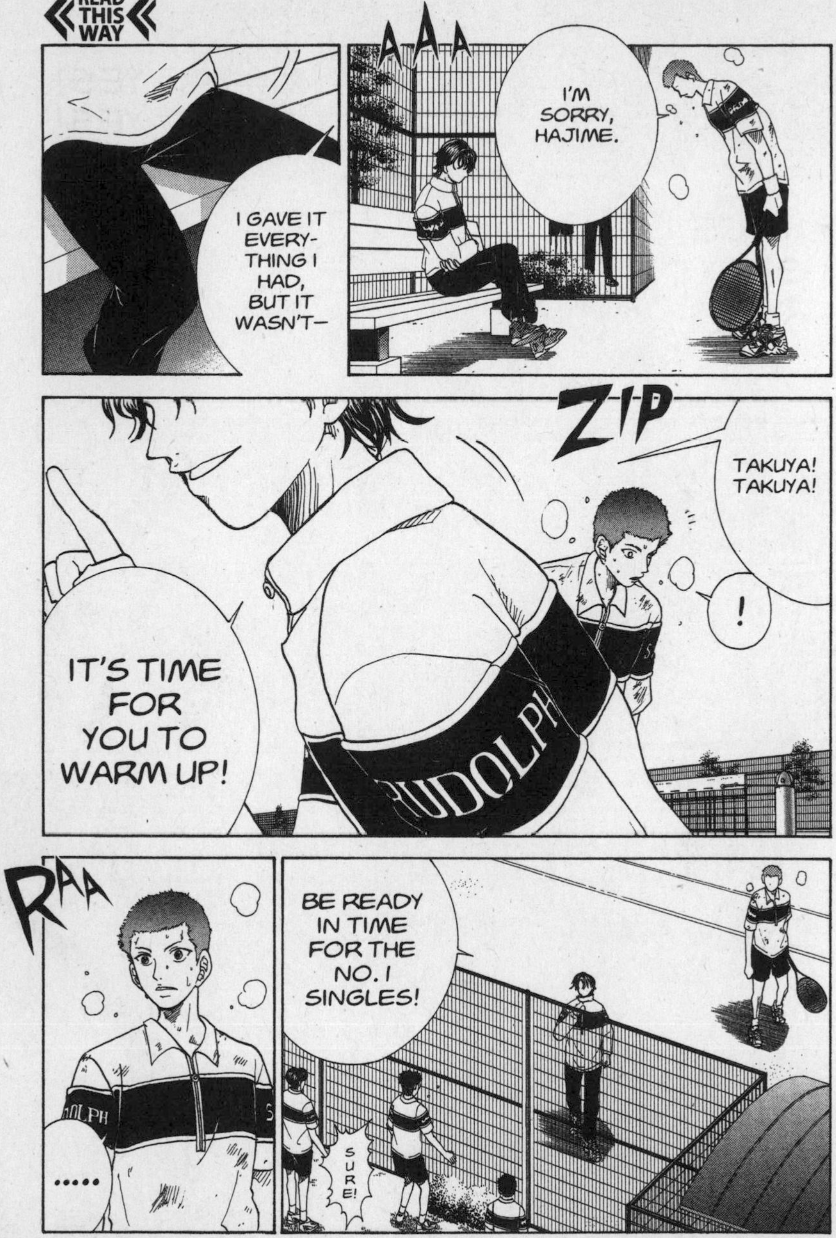

AAA
I'M SORRY, HAJIME.
I GAVE IT EVERYTHING I HAD, BUT IT WASN'T—
ZIP
TAKUYA! TAKUYA!
!
IT'S TIME FOR YOU TO WARM UP!
BE READY IN TIME FOR THE NO. 1 SINGLES!
SURE!
RAA
.....

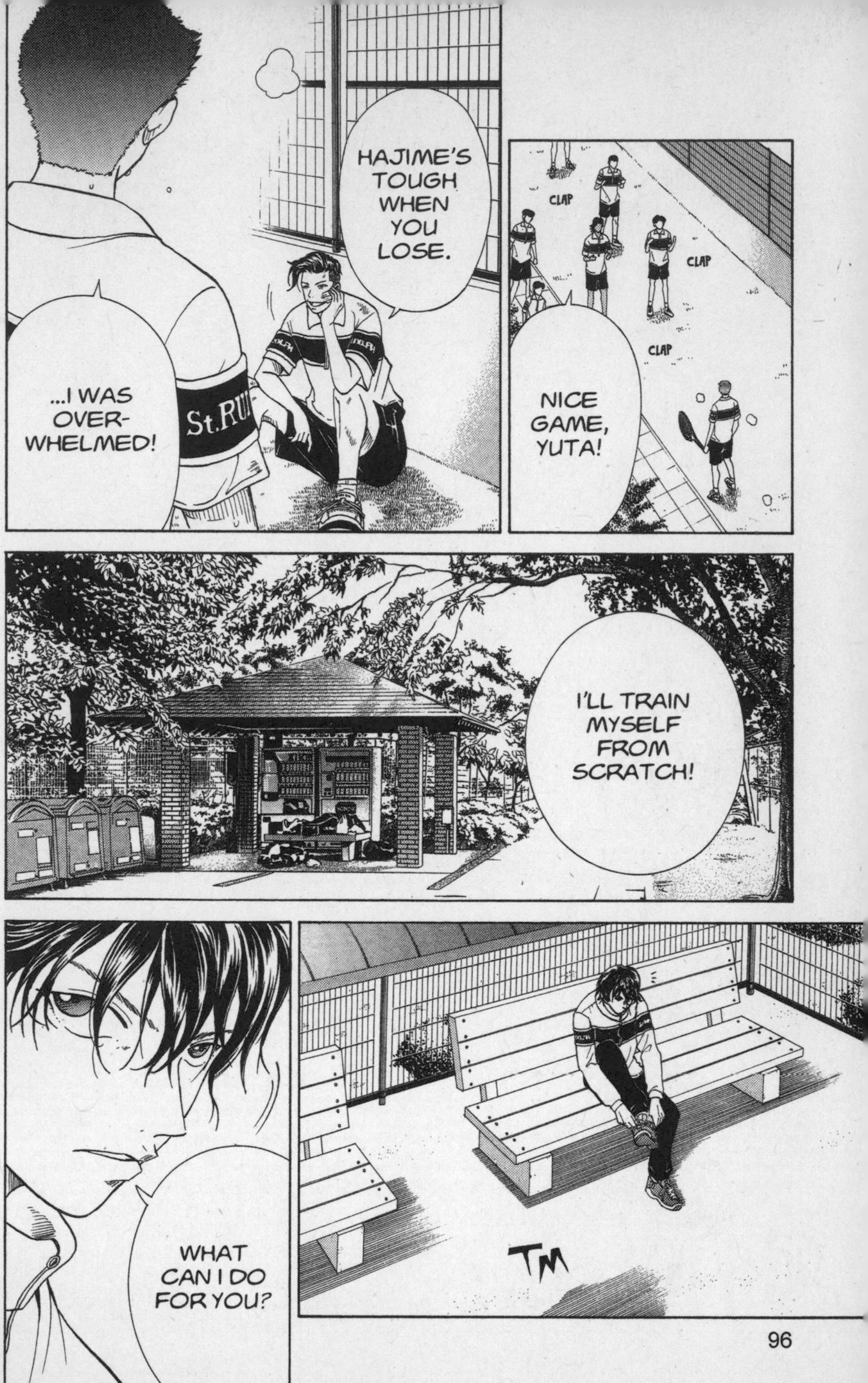
CLAP
CLAP
CLAP
NICE GAME, YUTA!
HAJIME'S TOUGH WHEN YOU LOSE.
...I WAS OVER-WHELMED!
I'LL TRAIN MYSELF FROM SCRATCH!
TM
WHAT CAN I DO FOR YOU?

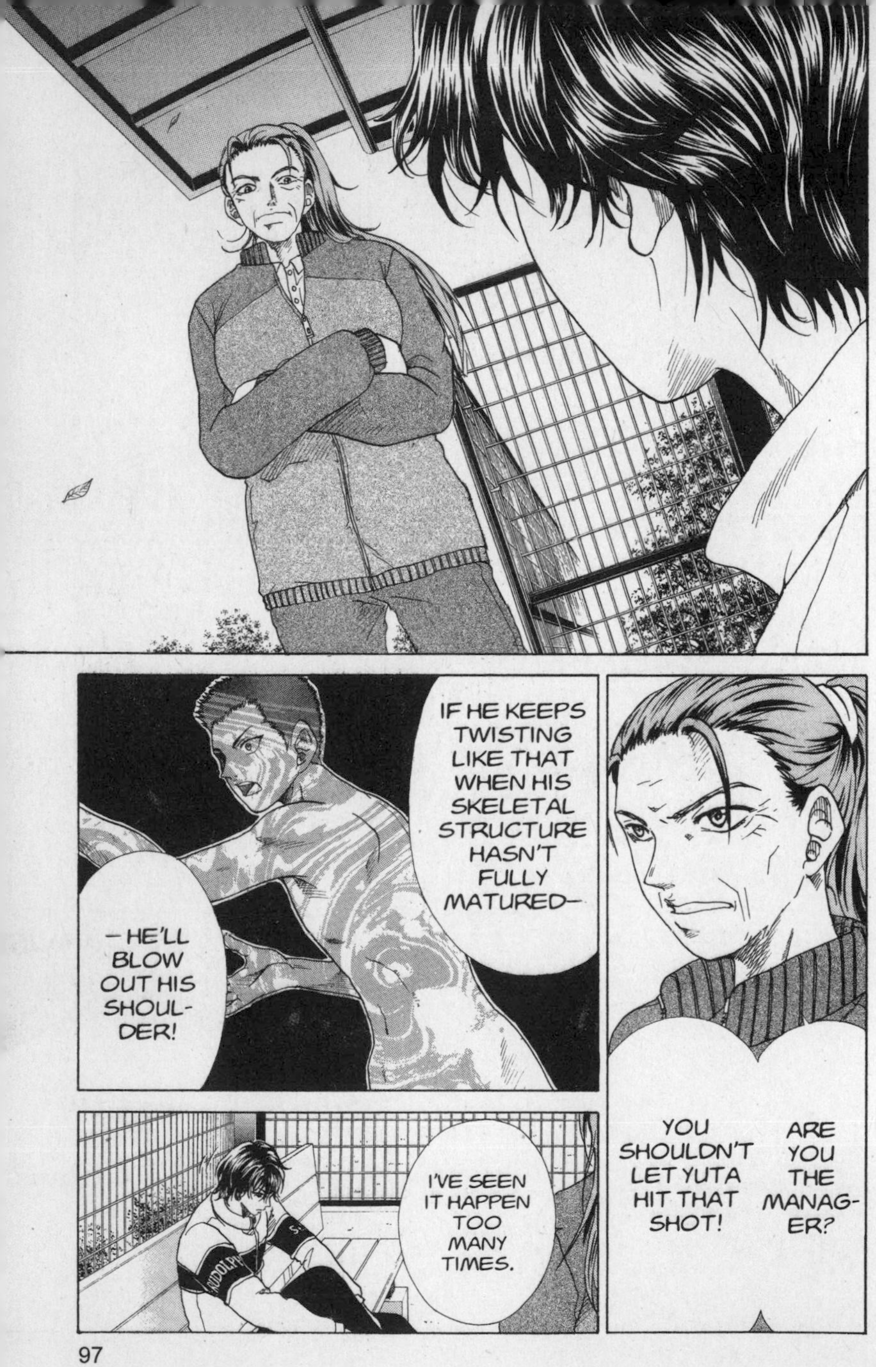
ARE YOU THE MANAG-ER?
YOU SHOULDN'T LET YUTA HIT THAT SHOT!
IF HE KEEPS TWISTING LIKE THAT WHEN HIS SKELETAL STRUCTURE HASN'T FULLY MATURED—
—HE'LL BLOW OUT HIS SHOUL-DER!
I'VE SEEN IT HAPPEN TOO MANY TIMES.

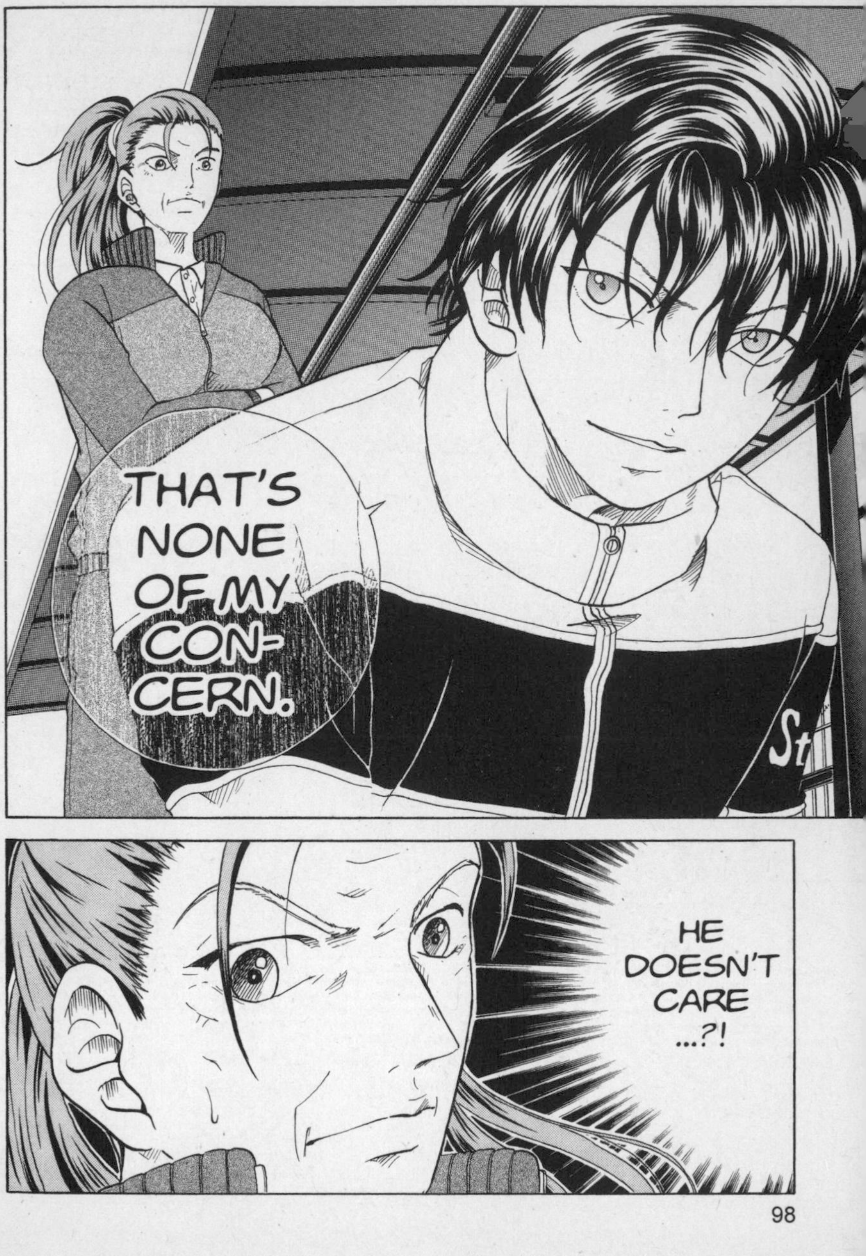
THAT'S NONE OF MY CON- CERN.
HE DOESN'T CARE ...?!

READ THIS WAY

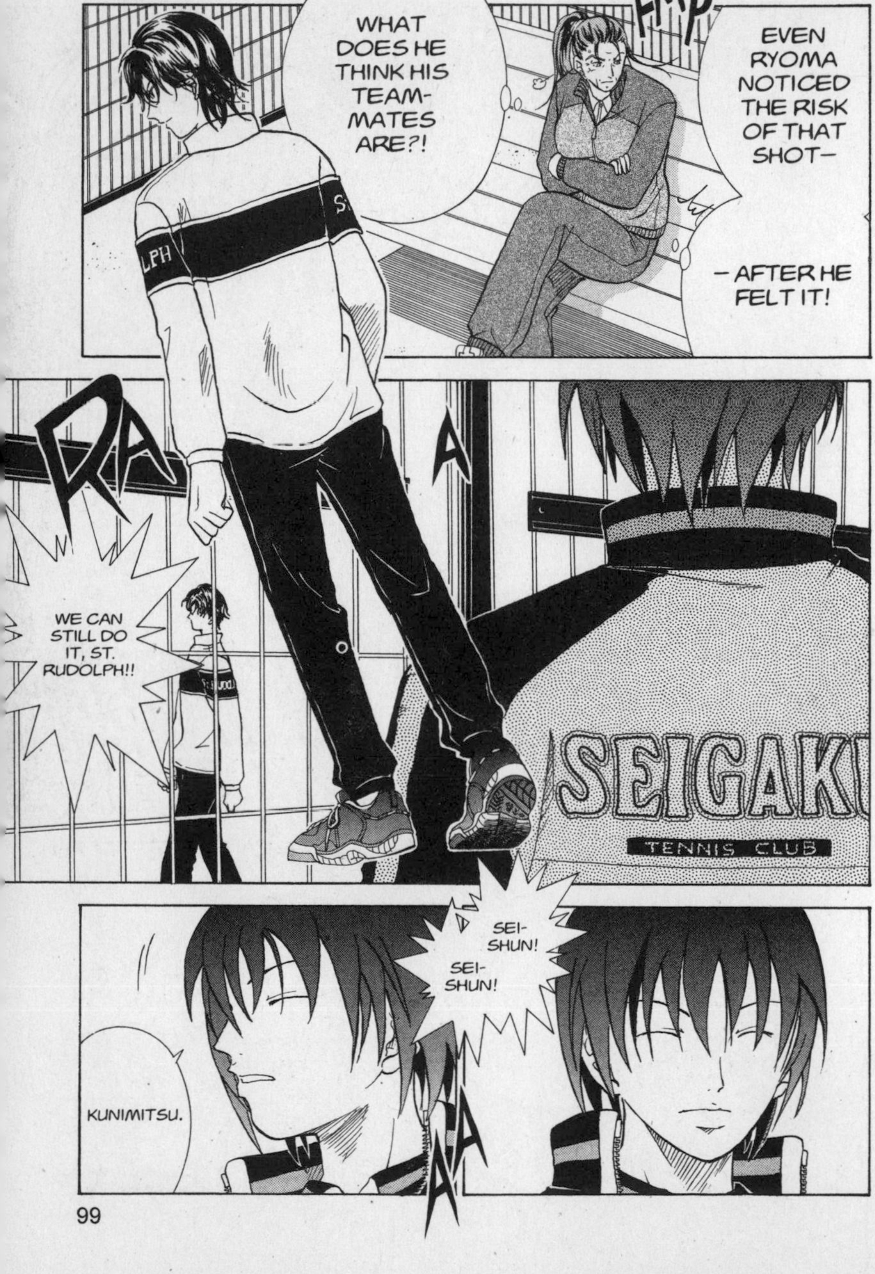
FMP
EVEN RYOMA NOTICED THE RISK OF THAT SHOT—
—AFTER HE FELT IT!
WHAT DOES HE THINK HIS TEAM-MATES ARE?!
DA
A
SEIGAKU
TENNIS CLUB
WE CAN STILL DO IT, ST. RUDOLPH!!
SEI-SHUN!
SEI-SHUN!
KUNIMITSU.

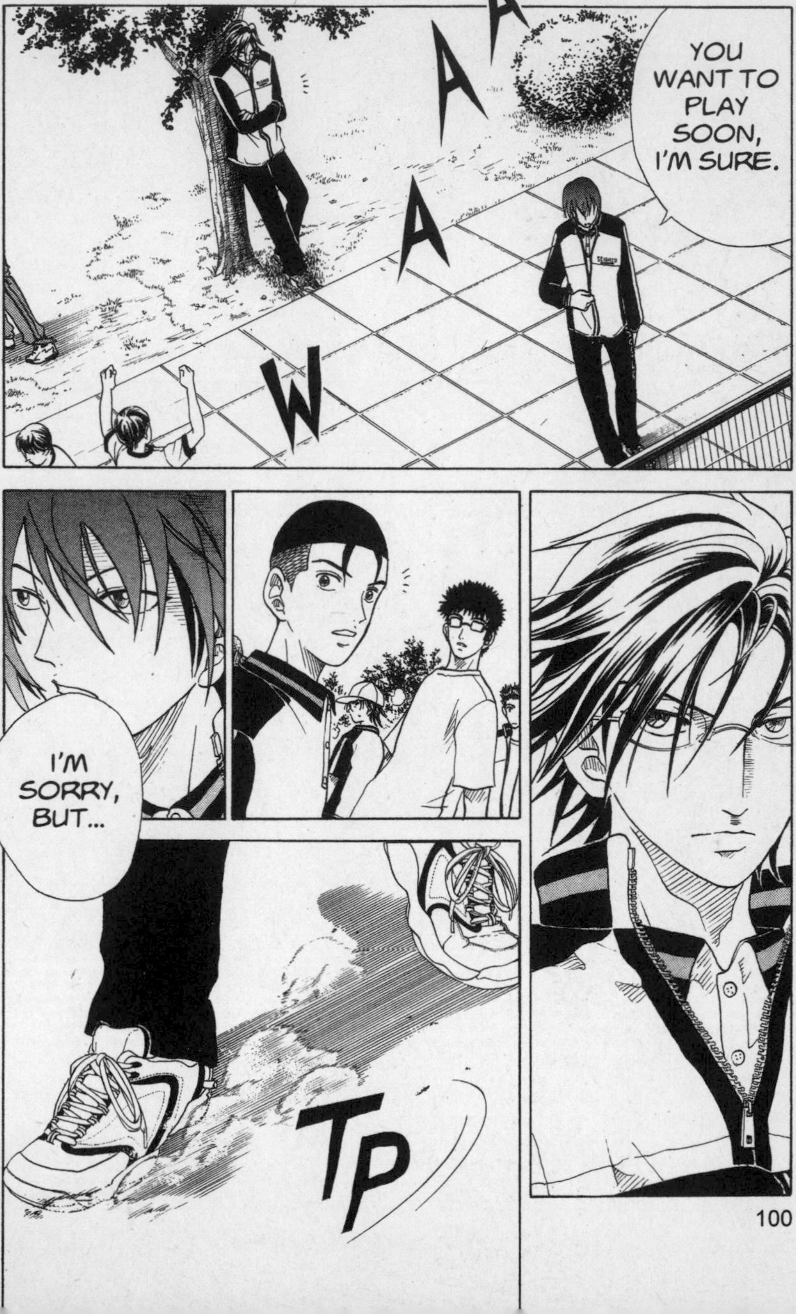
YOU WANT TO PLAY SOON, I'M SURE.
WAAAA
I'M SORRY, BUT...
TP

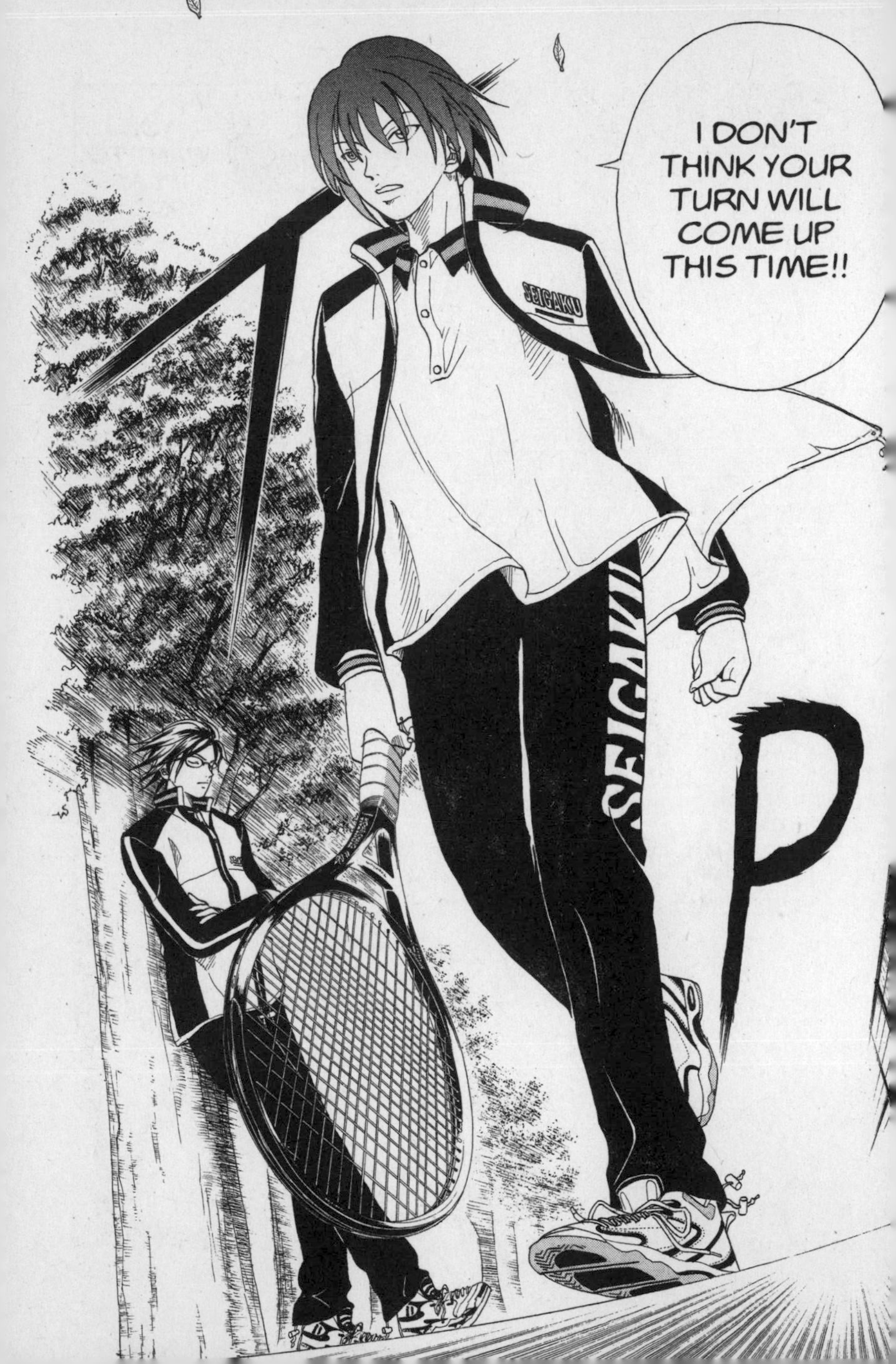
I DON'T THINK YOUR TURN WILL COME UP THIS TIME!!
SEIGAKU
SEIGAKU
P

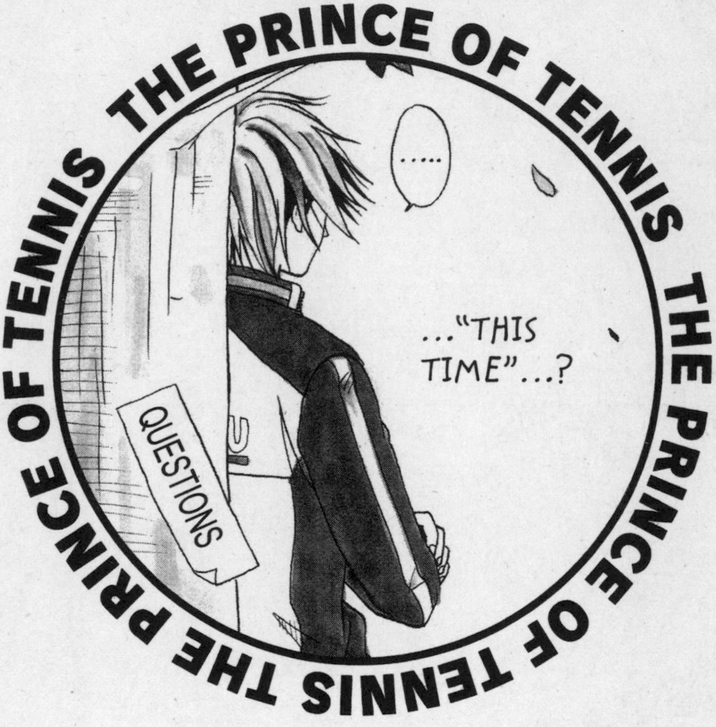
THE PRINCE OF TENNIS THE PRINCE OF TENNIS THE PRINCE OF TENNIS
......
..."THIS TIME"...?
QUESTIONS

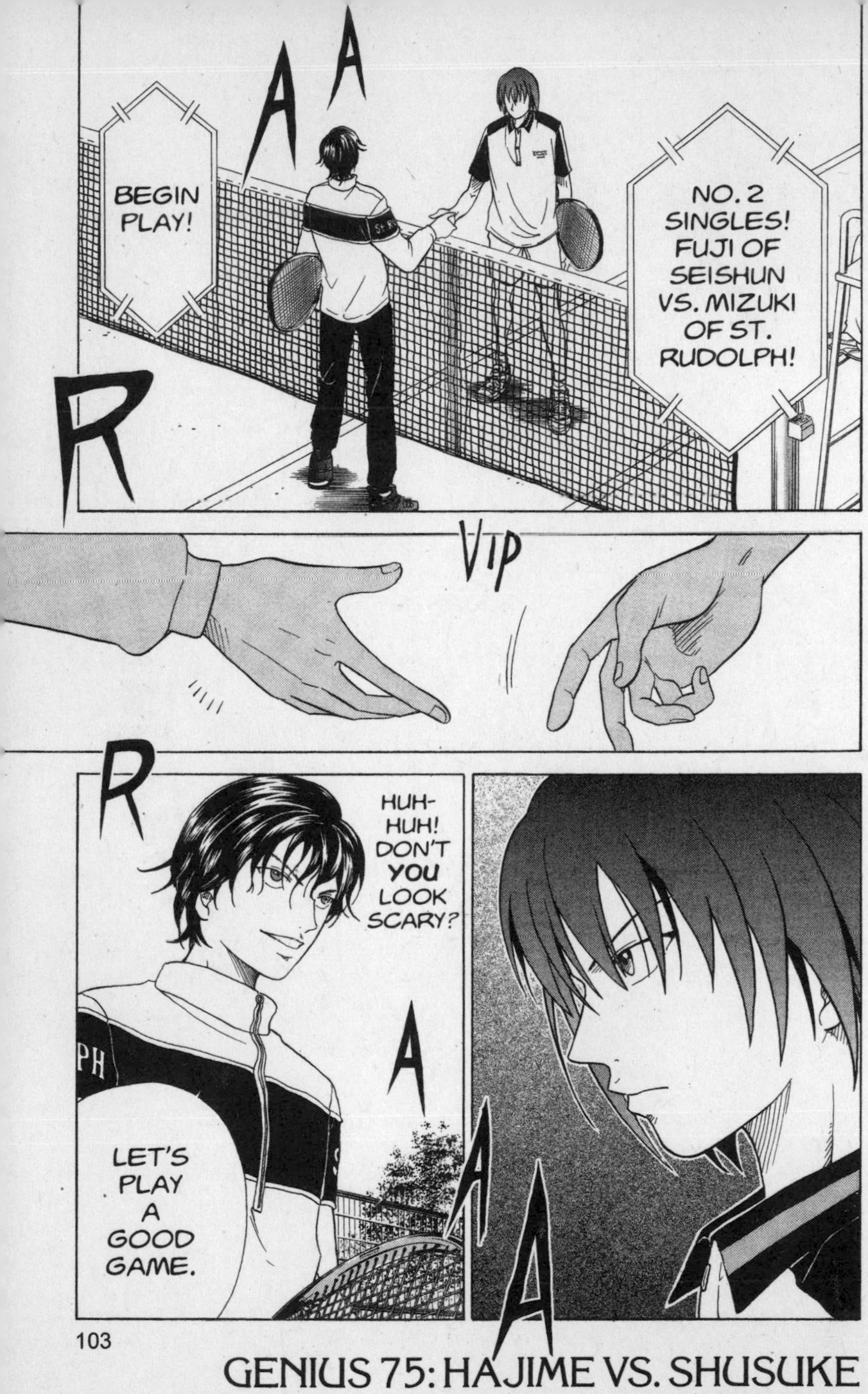
NO. 2 SINGLES! FUJI OF SEISHUN VS. MIZUKI OF ST. RUDOLPH!
BEGIN PLAY!
VIP
HUH-HUH! DON'T YOU LOOK SCARY?
LET'S PLAY A GOOD GAME.

GENIUS 75: HAJIME VS. SHUSUKE

GENIUS 75: HAJIME VS. SHUSUKE

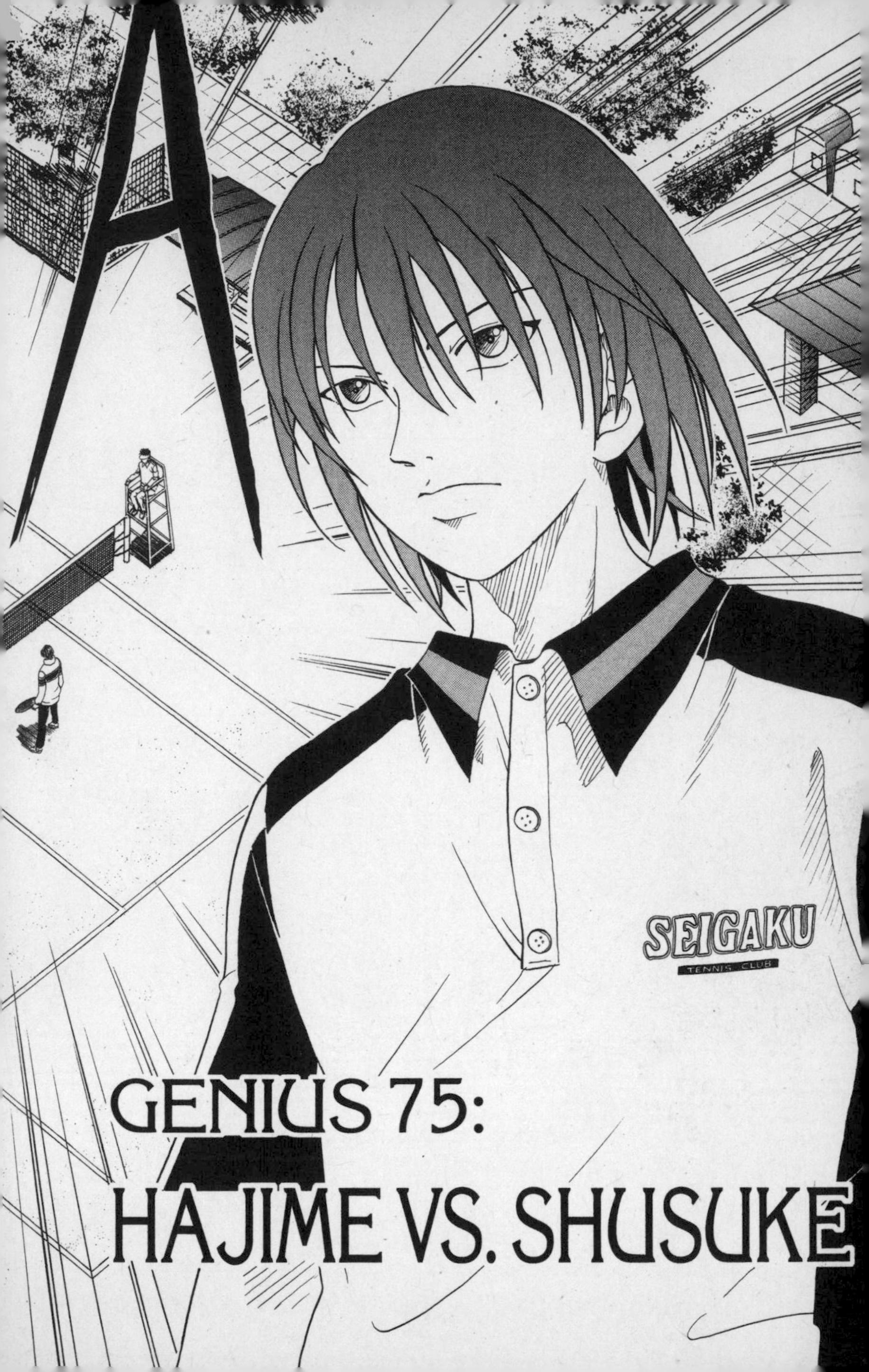
SEIGAKU
TENNIS CLUB

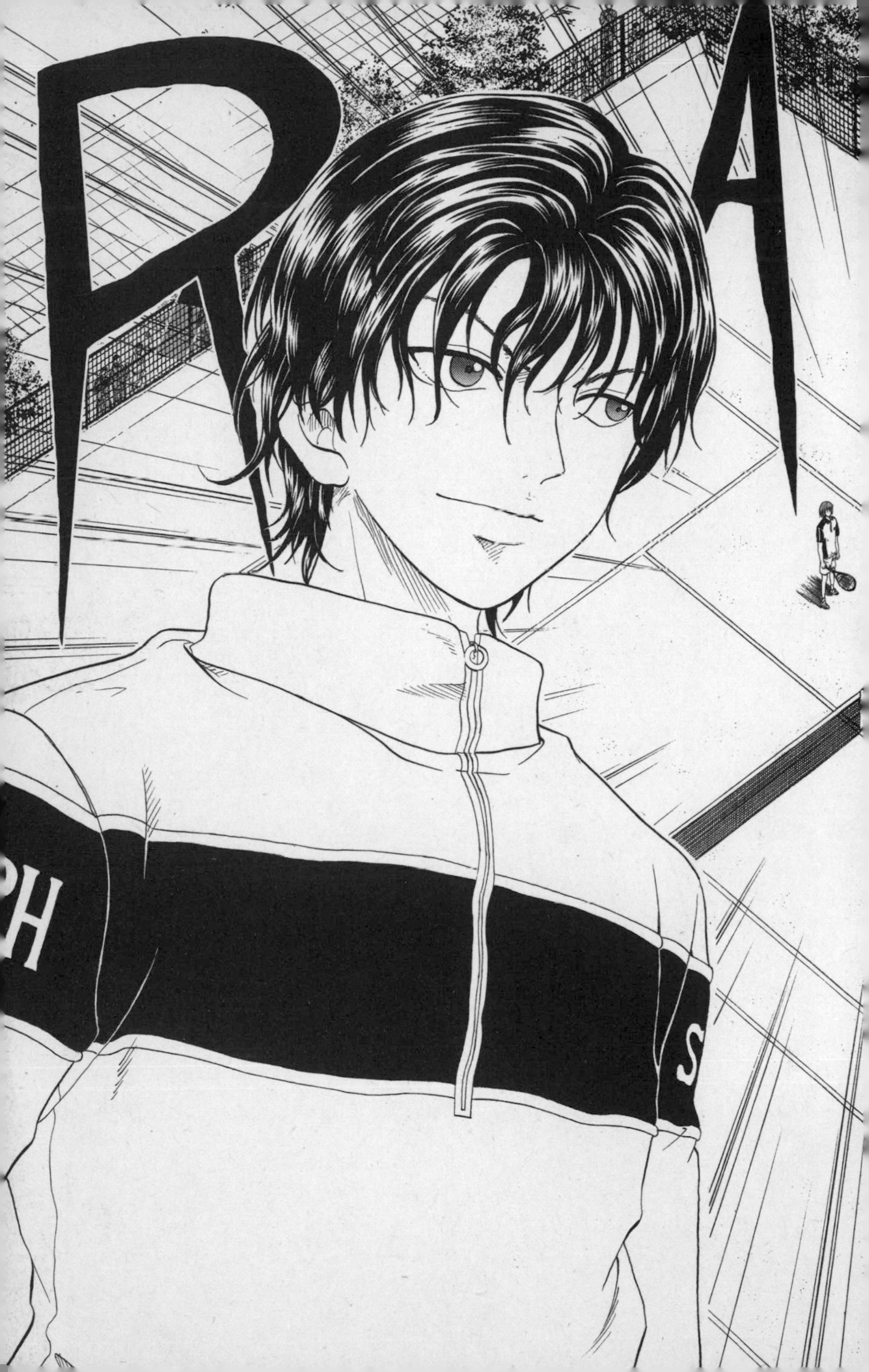
PA

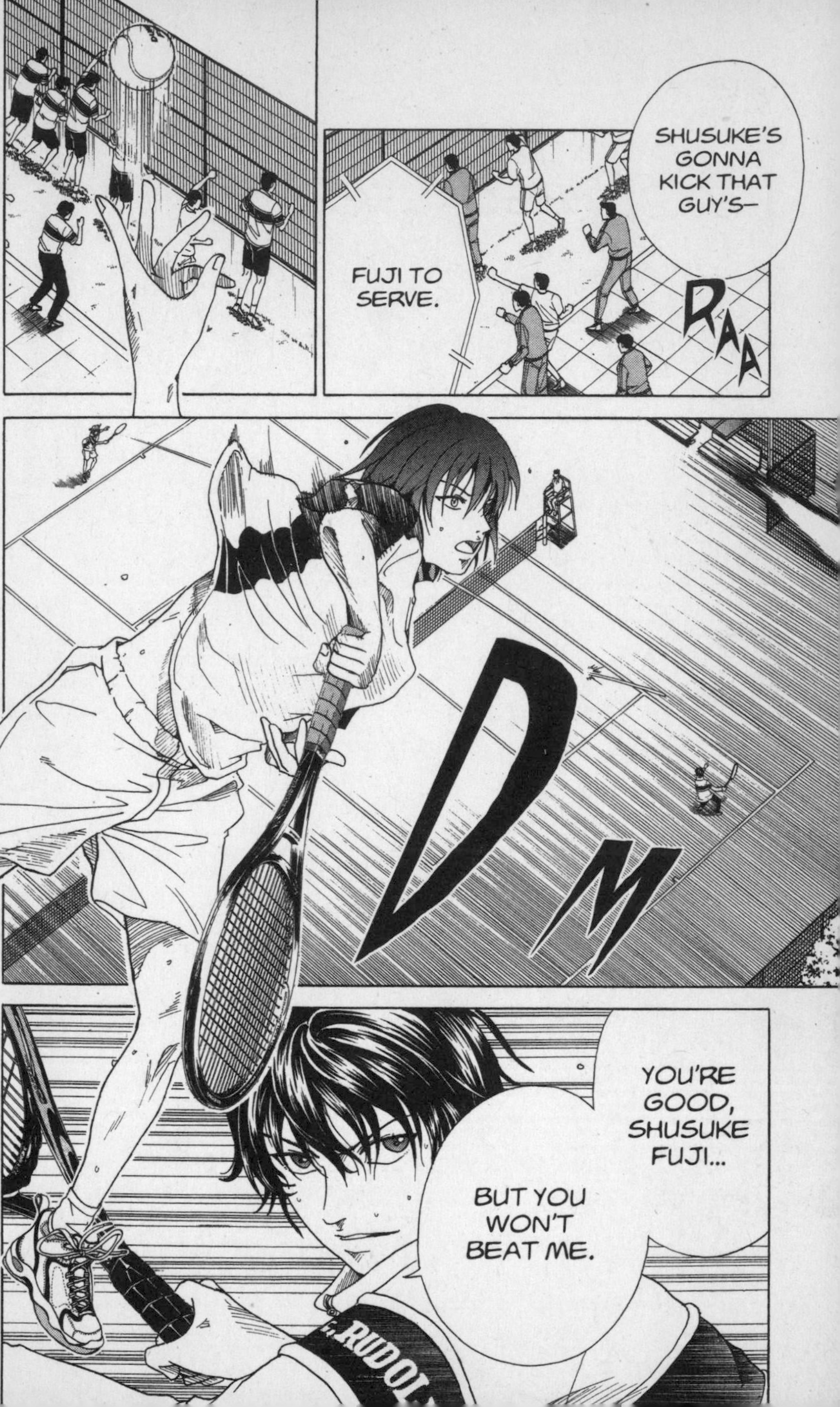
SHUSUKE'S GONNA KICK THAT GUY'S—
FUJI TO SERVE.
DAA
DM
YOU'RE GOOD, SHUSUKE FUJI...
BUT YOU WON'T BEAT ME.

READ THIS WAY

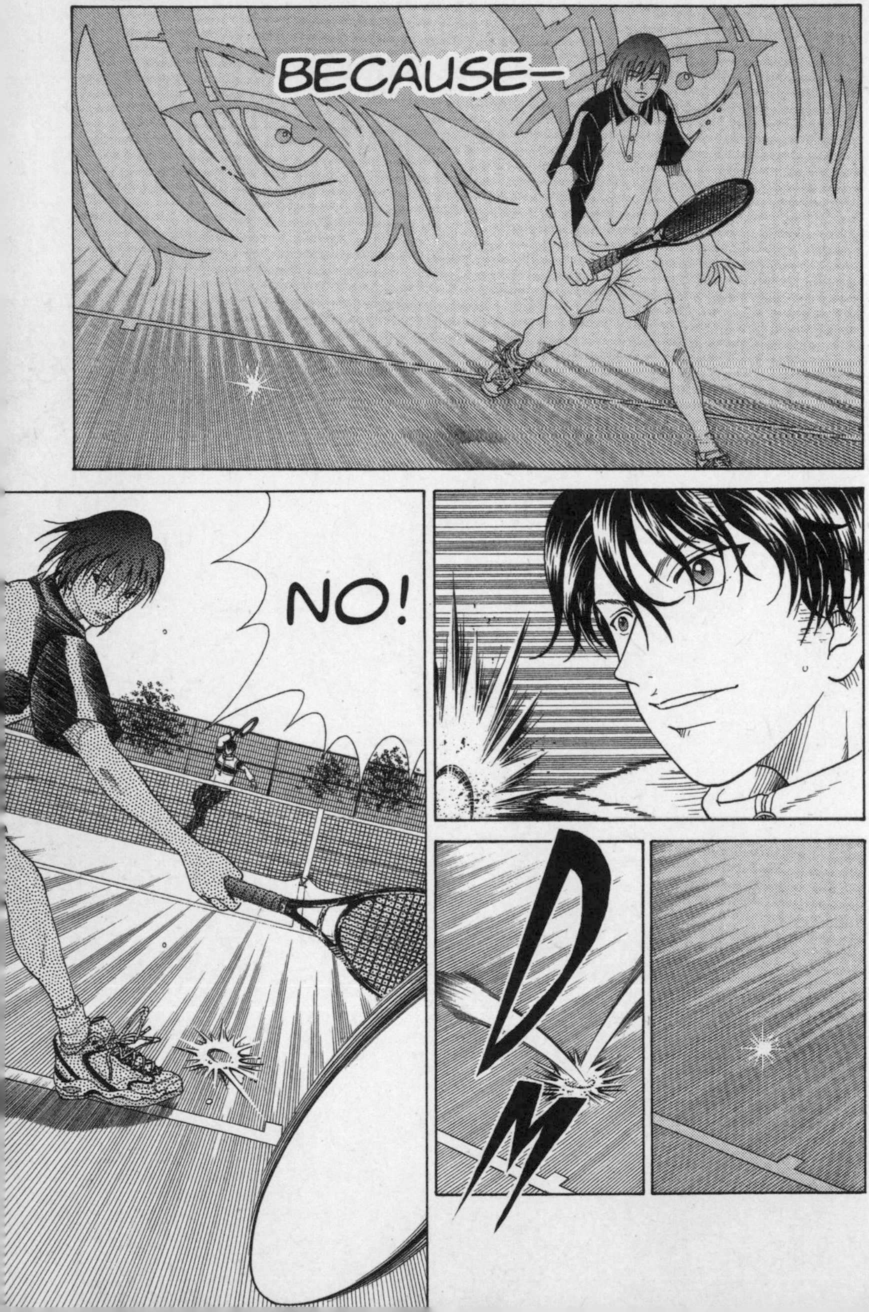
BECAUSE—
NO!
DM

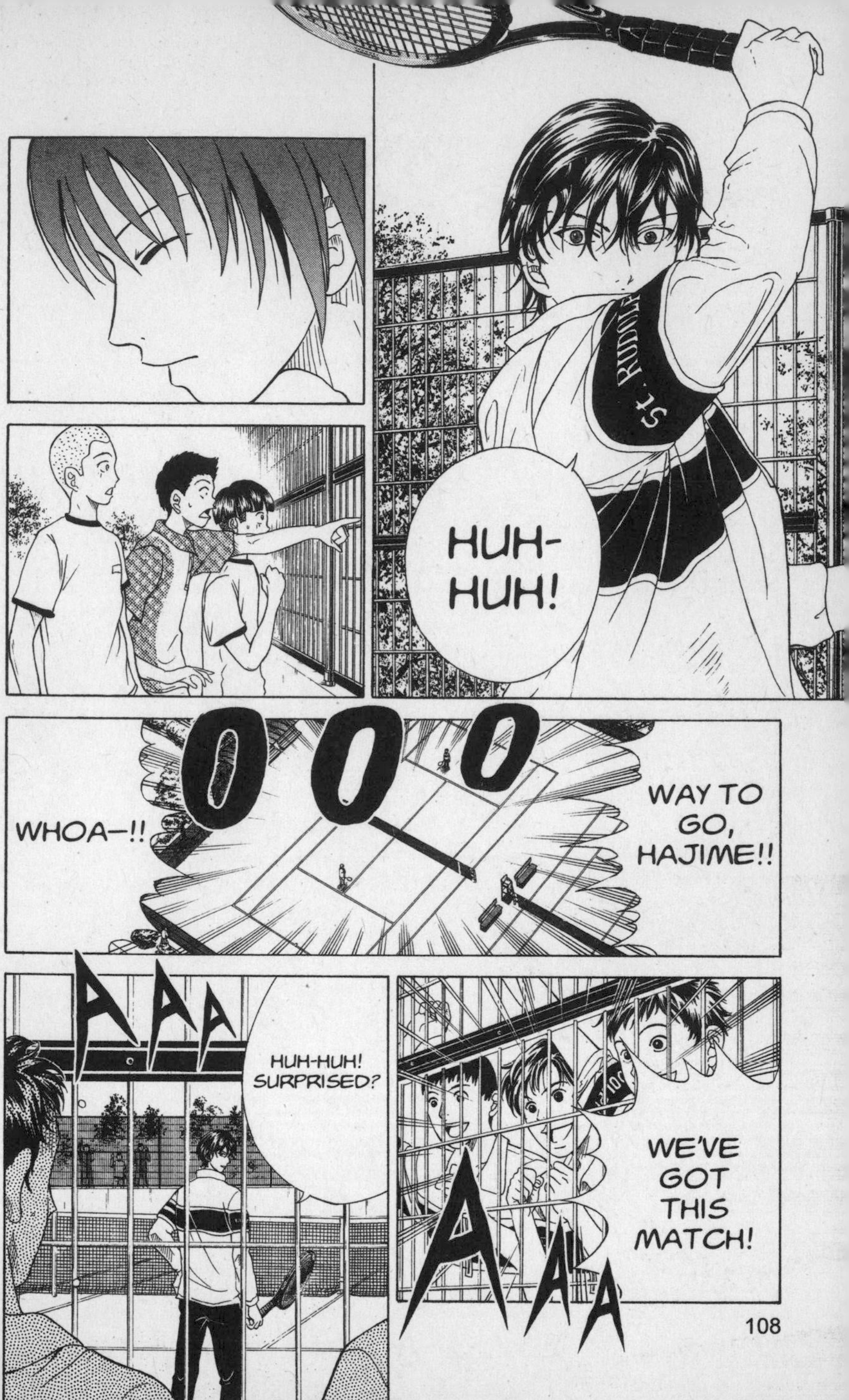
HUH-
HUH!
WAY TO
GO,
HAJIME!!
OOO
WHOA–!!
WE'VE
GOT
THIS
MATCH!
AAAA
HUH-HUH!
SURPRISED?
AAA

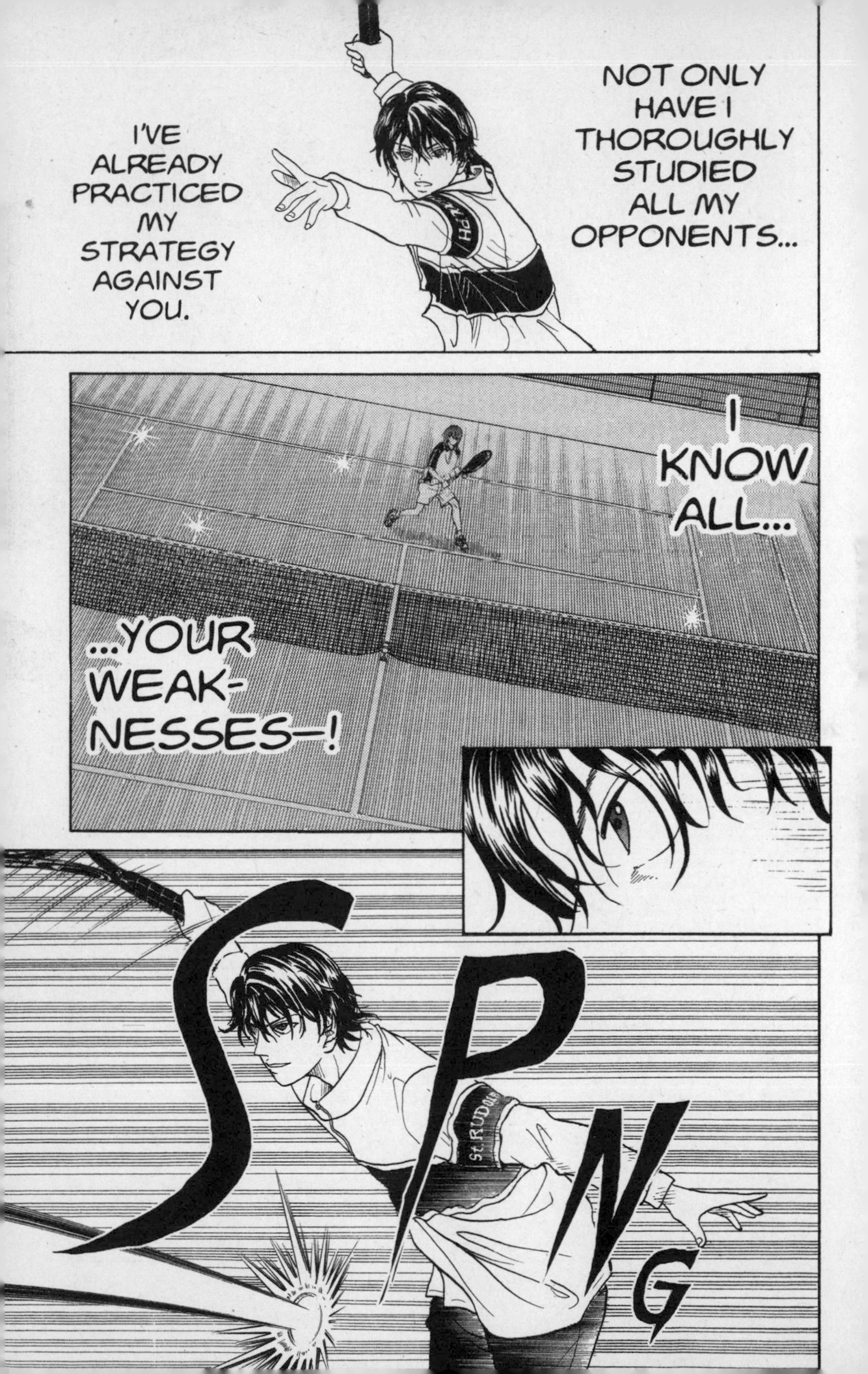
NOT ONLY HAVE I THOROUGHLY STUDIED ALL MY OPPONENTS...
I'VE ALREADY PRACTICED MY STRATEGY AGAINST YOU.
I KNOW ALL...
...YOUR WEAK-NESSES—!
SPNG

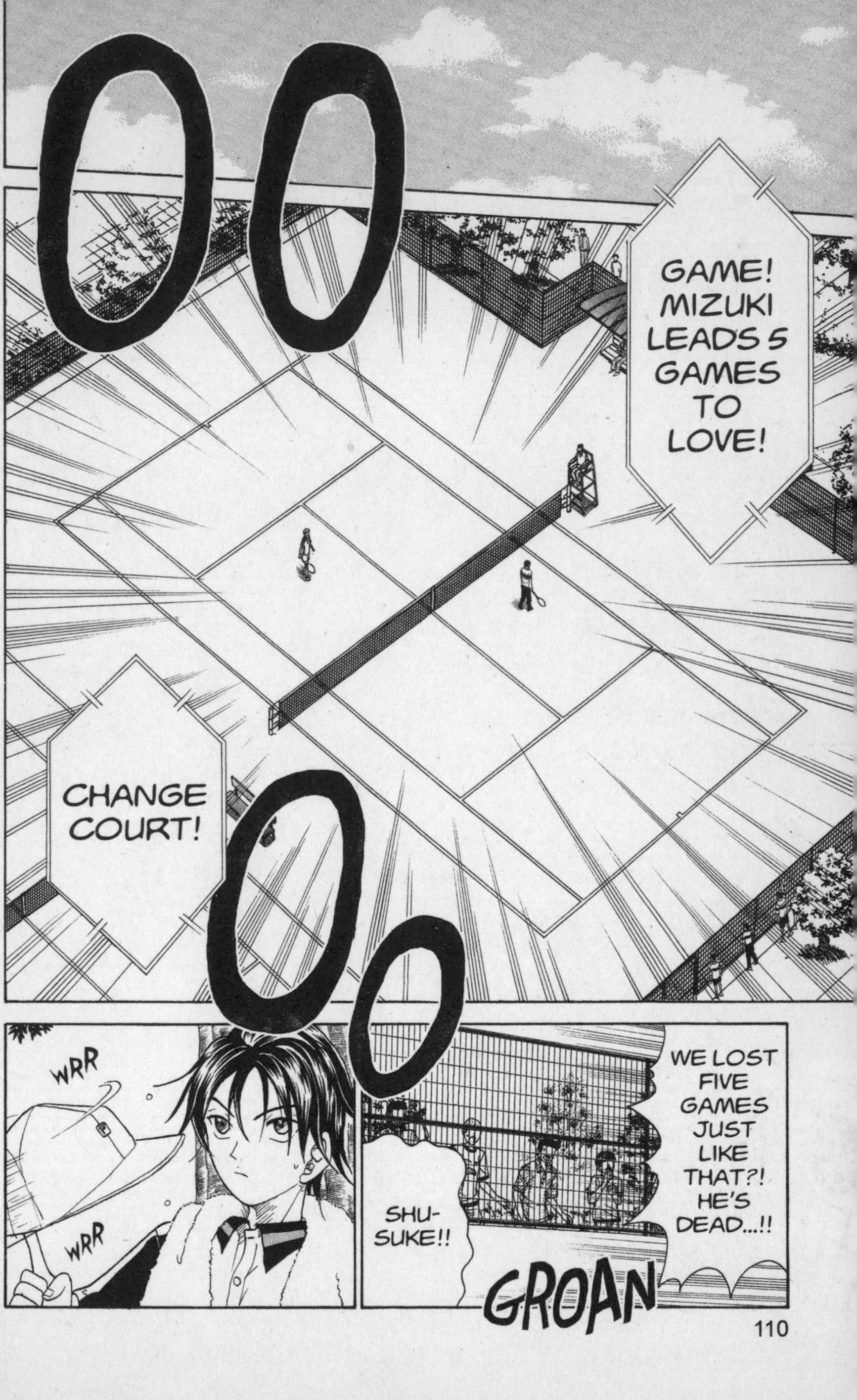
GAME! MIZUKI LEADS 5 GAMES TO LOVE!
CHANGE COURT!
WE LOST FIVE GAMES JUST LIKE THAT?! HE'S DEAD...!!
SHU-SUKE!!
GROAN
WRR
WRR

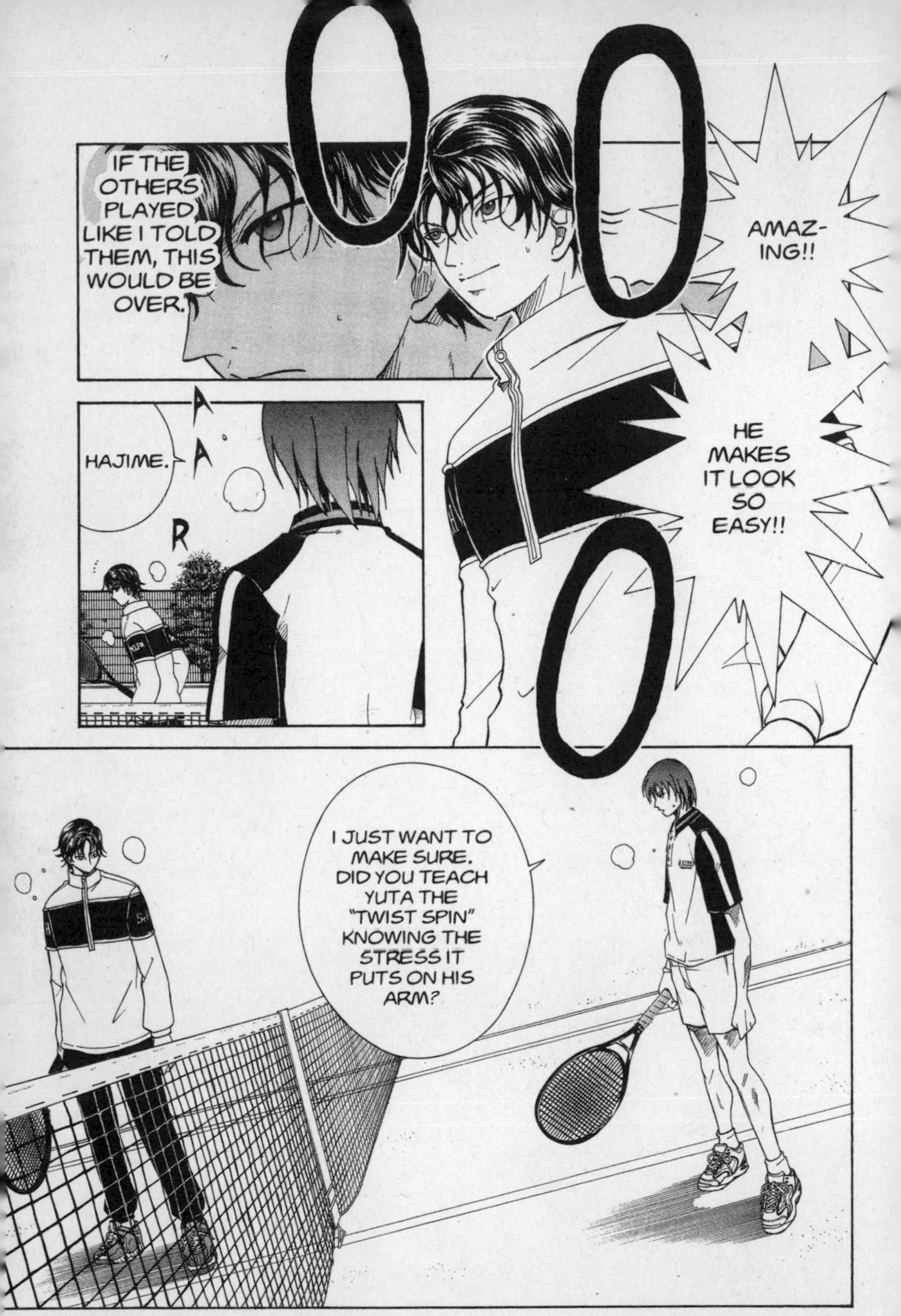
AMAZ-ING!!
HE MAKES IT LOOK SO EASY!!
IF THE OTHERS PLAYED LIKE I TOLD THEM, THIS WOULD BE OVER.
HAJIME.
I JUST WANT TO MAKE SURE. DID YOU TEACH YUTA THE "TWIST SPIN" KNOWING THE STRESS IT PUTS ON HIS ARM?

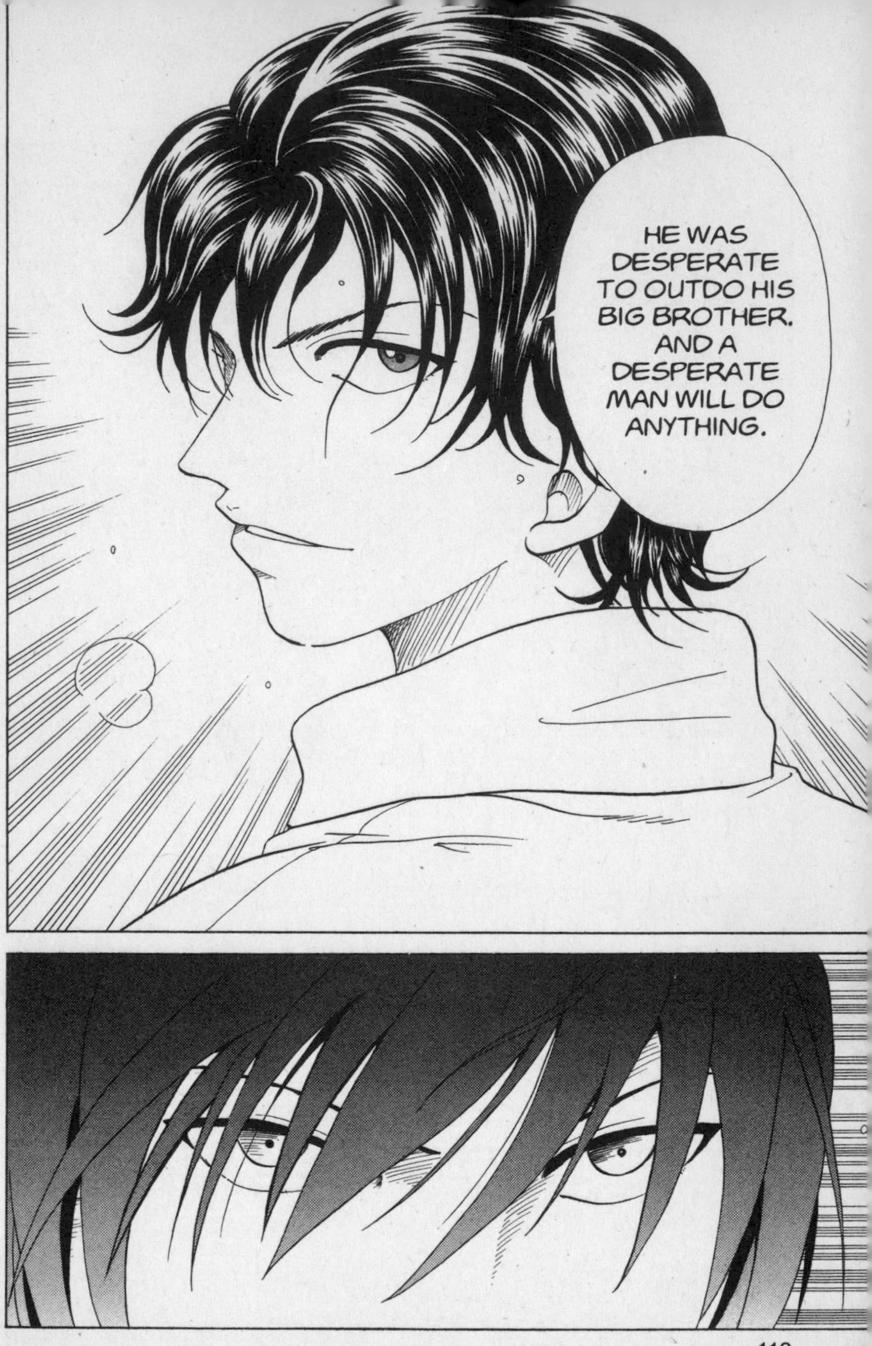
HE WAS DESPERATE TO OUTDO HIS BIG BROTHER. AND A DESPERATE MAN WILL DO ANYTHING.

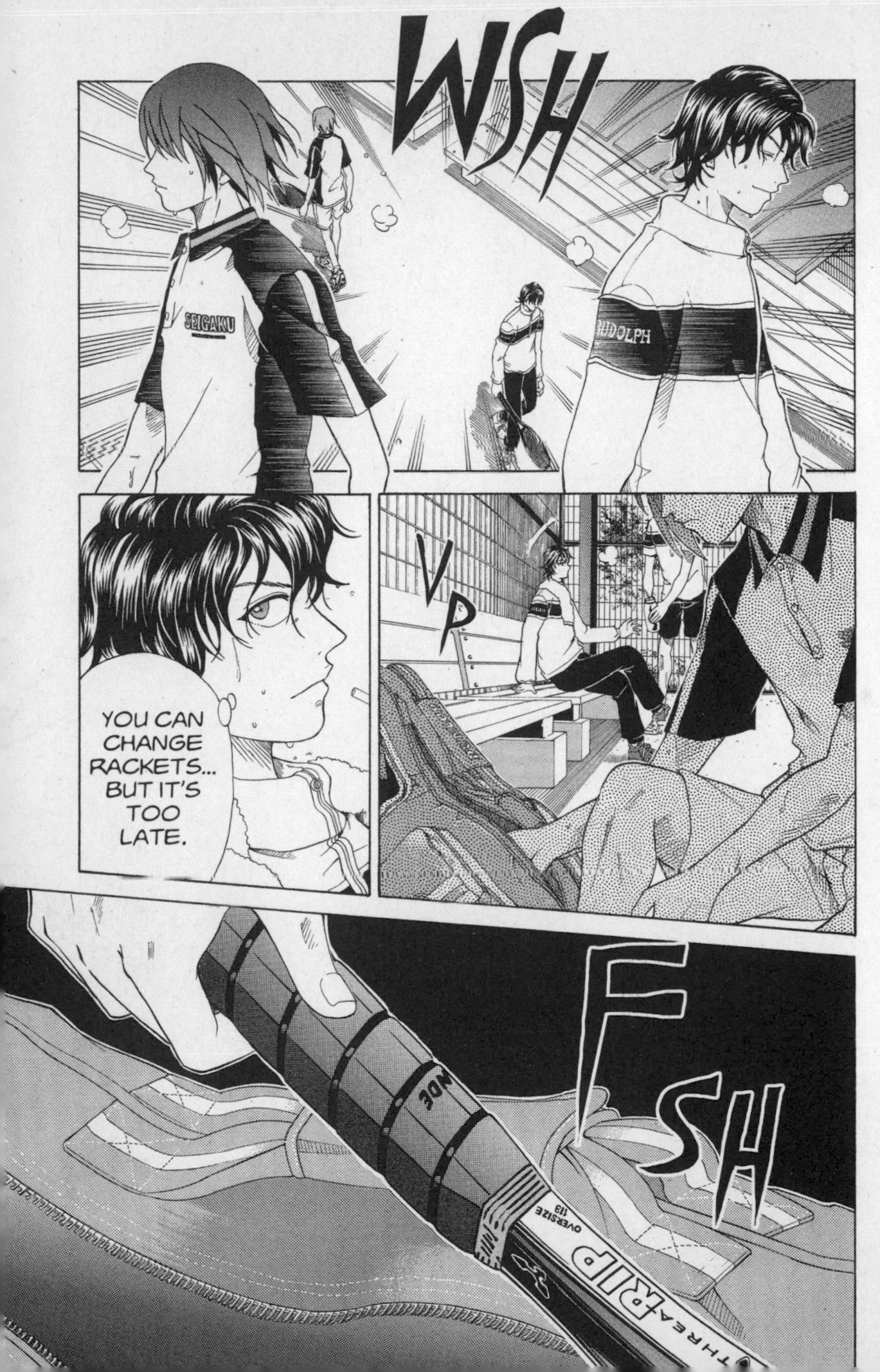
WSH
SEIGAKU
VP
YOU CAN CHANGE RACKETS... BUT IT'S TOO LATE.
FSH

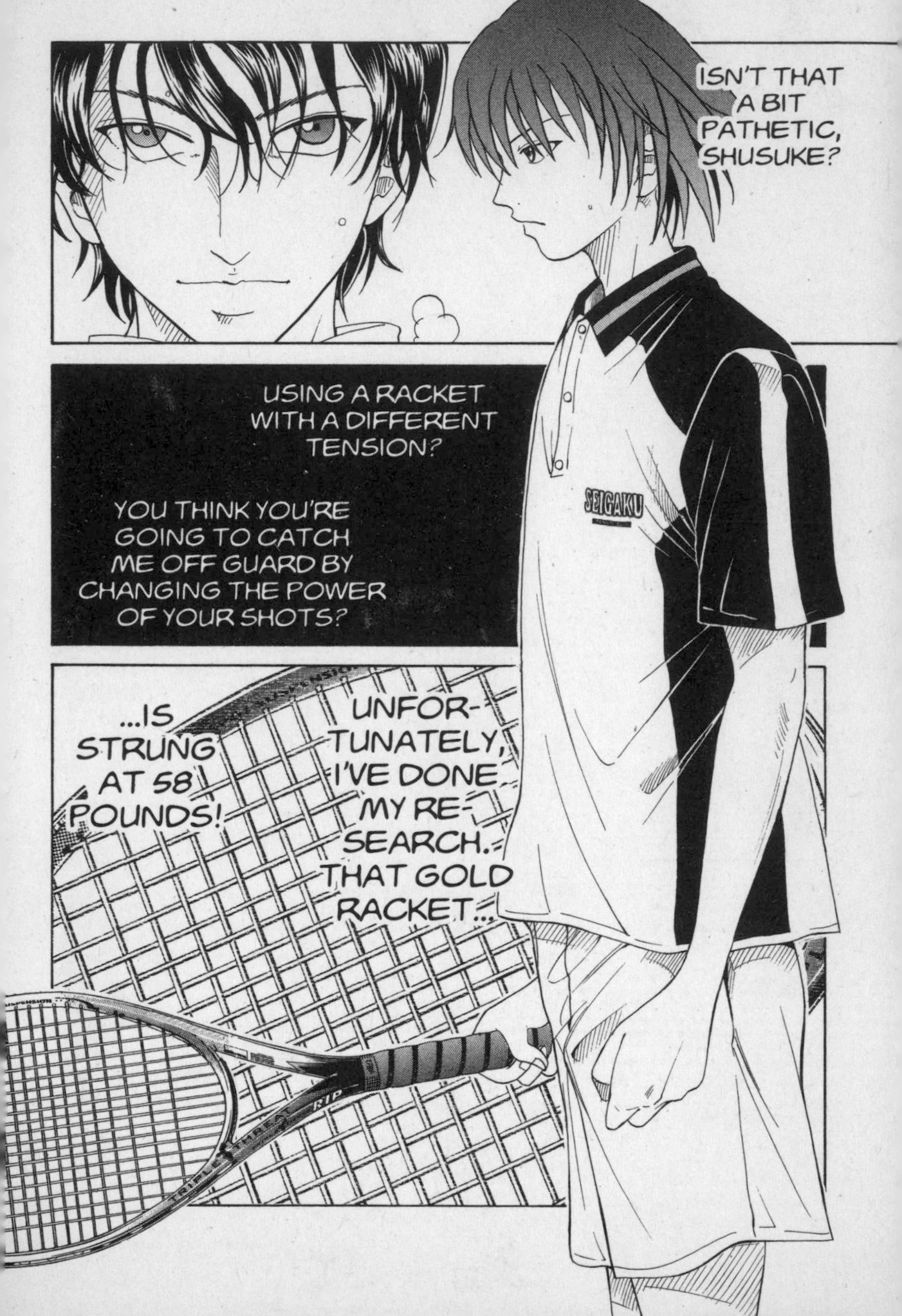
ISN'T THAT A BIT PATHETIC, SHUSUKE?
USING A RACKET WITH A DIFFERENT TENSION?
YOU THINK YOU'RE GOING TO CATCH ME OFF GUARD BY CHANGING THE POWER OF YOUR SHOTS?
SEIGAKU
UNFOR-TUNATELY, I'VE DONE MY RE-SEARCH. THAT GOLD RACKET...
...IS STRUNG AT 58 POUNDS!

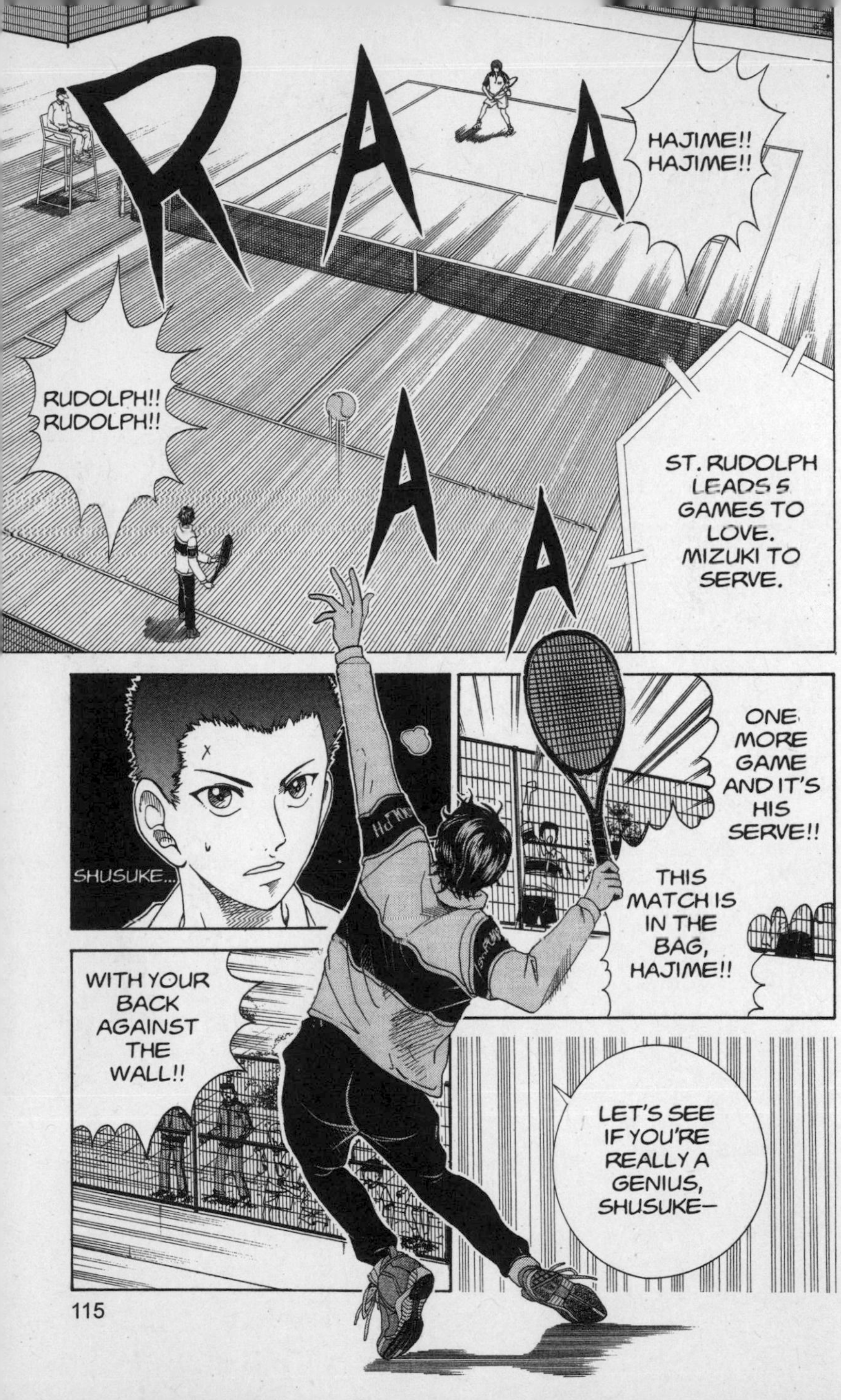
HAJIME!! HAJIME!!
RAAAAA
ST. RUDOLPH LEADS 5 GAMES TO LOVE. MIZUKI TO SERVE.
RUDOLPH!! RUDOLPH!!
ONE MORE GAME AND IT'S HIS SERVE!!
THIS MATCH IS IN THE BAG, HAJIME!!
SHUSUKE...
LET'S SEE IF YOU'RE REALLY A GENIUS, SHUSUKE—
WITH YOUR BACK AGAINST THE WALL!!

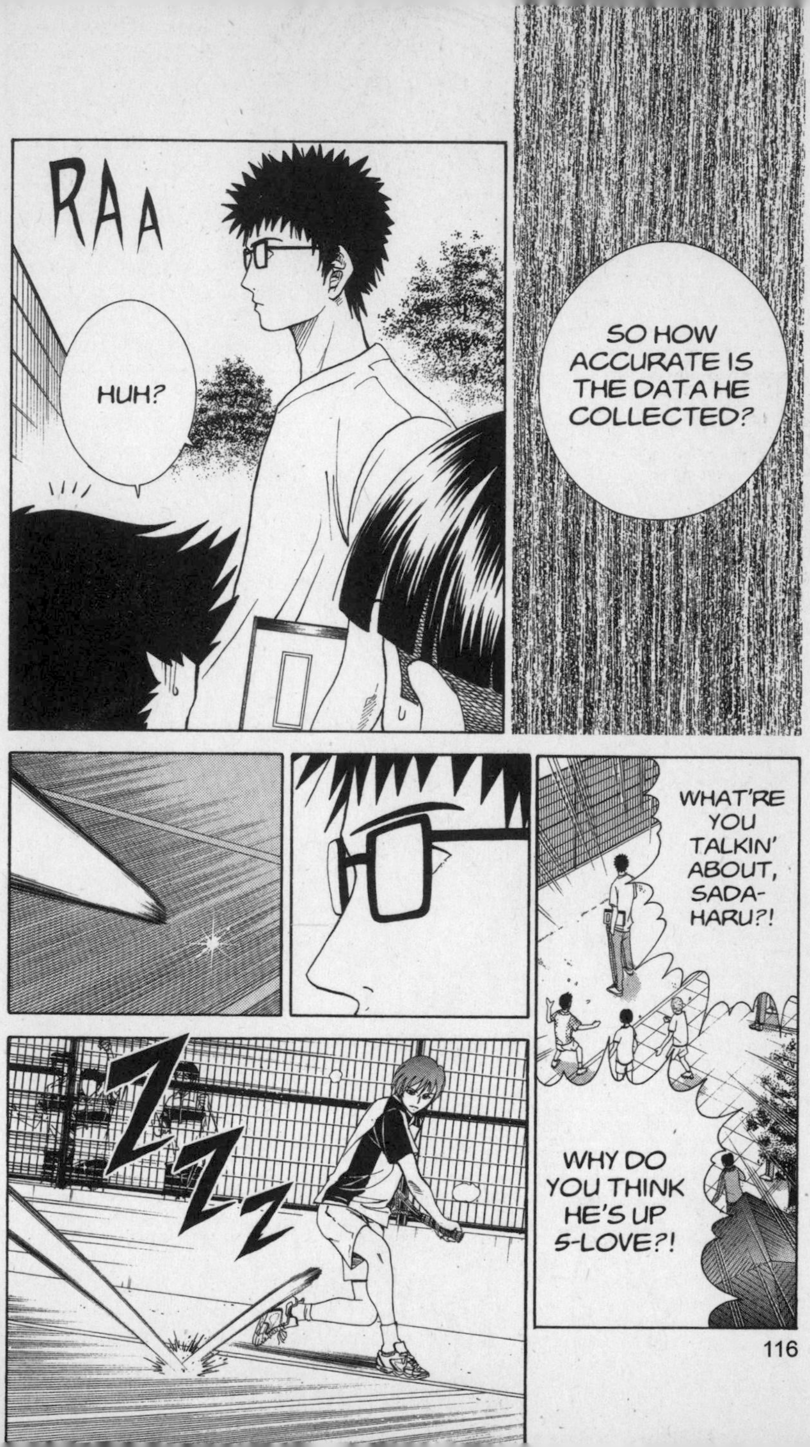
SO HOW ACCURATE IS THE DATA HE COLLECTED?
RAA
HUH?
WHAT'RE YOU TALKIN' ABOUT, SADA-HARU?!
WHY DO YOU THINK HE'S UP 5-LOVE?!
ZZZZ

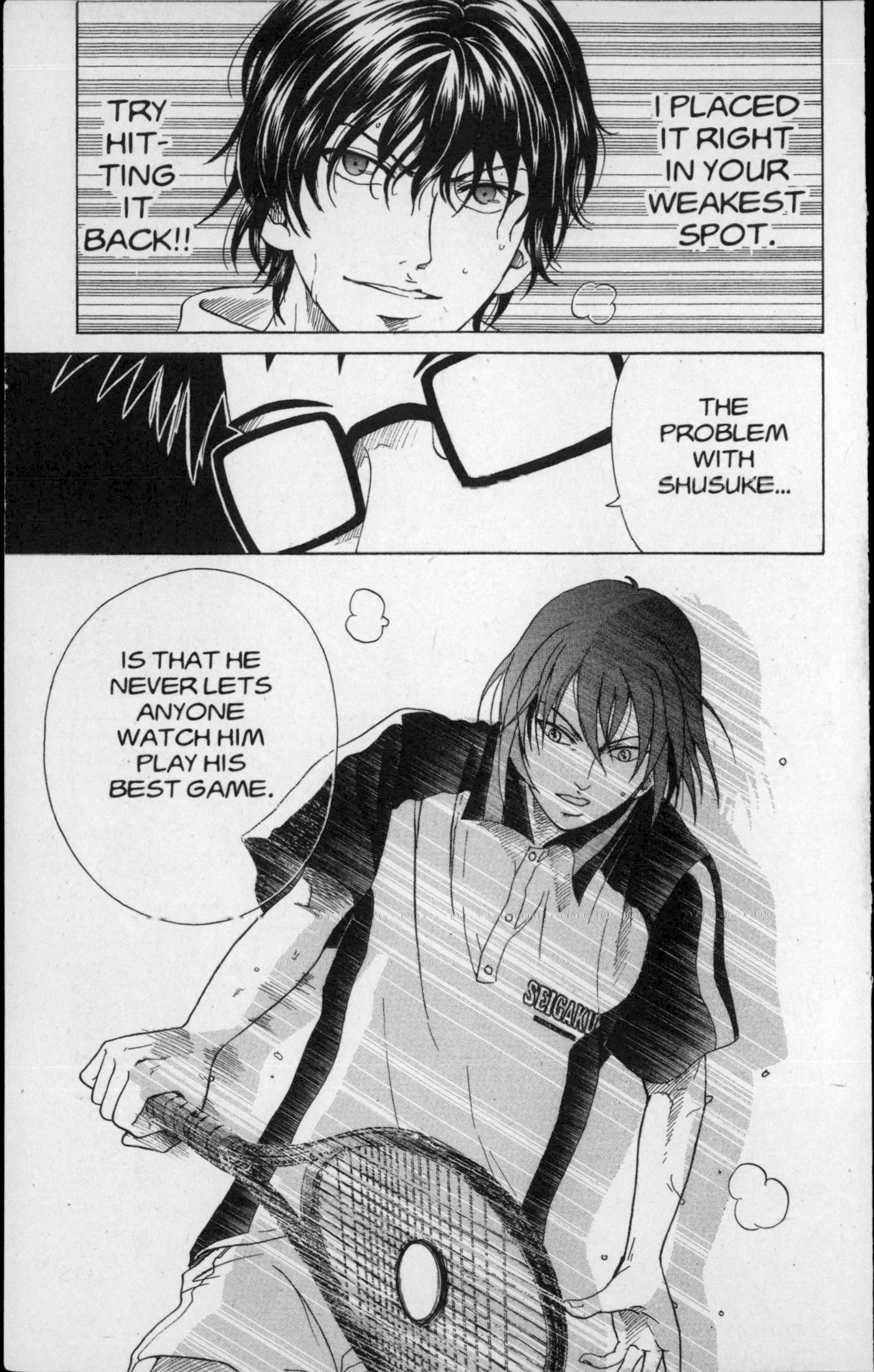
I PLACED IT RIGHT IN YOUR WEAKEST SPOT.
TRY HIT-TING IT BACK!!
THE PROBLEM WITH SHUSUKE...
IS THAT HE NEVER LETS ANYONE WATCH HIM PLAY HIS BEST GAME.
SEIGAKU

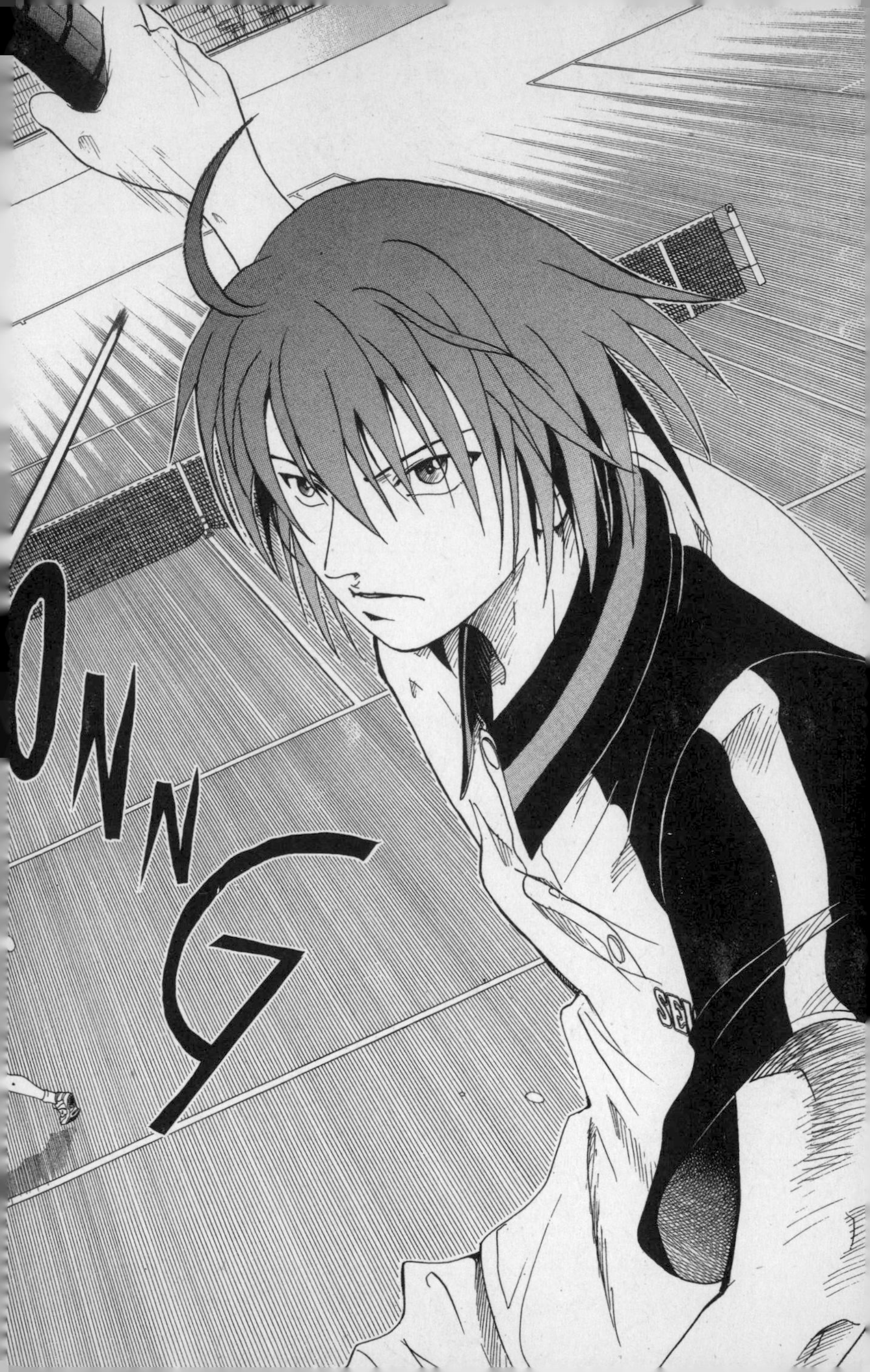
ONNG

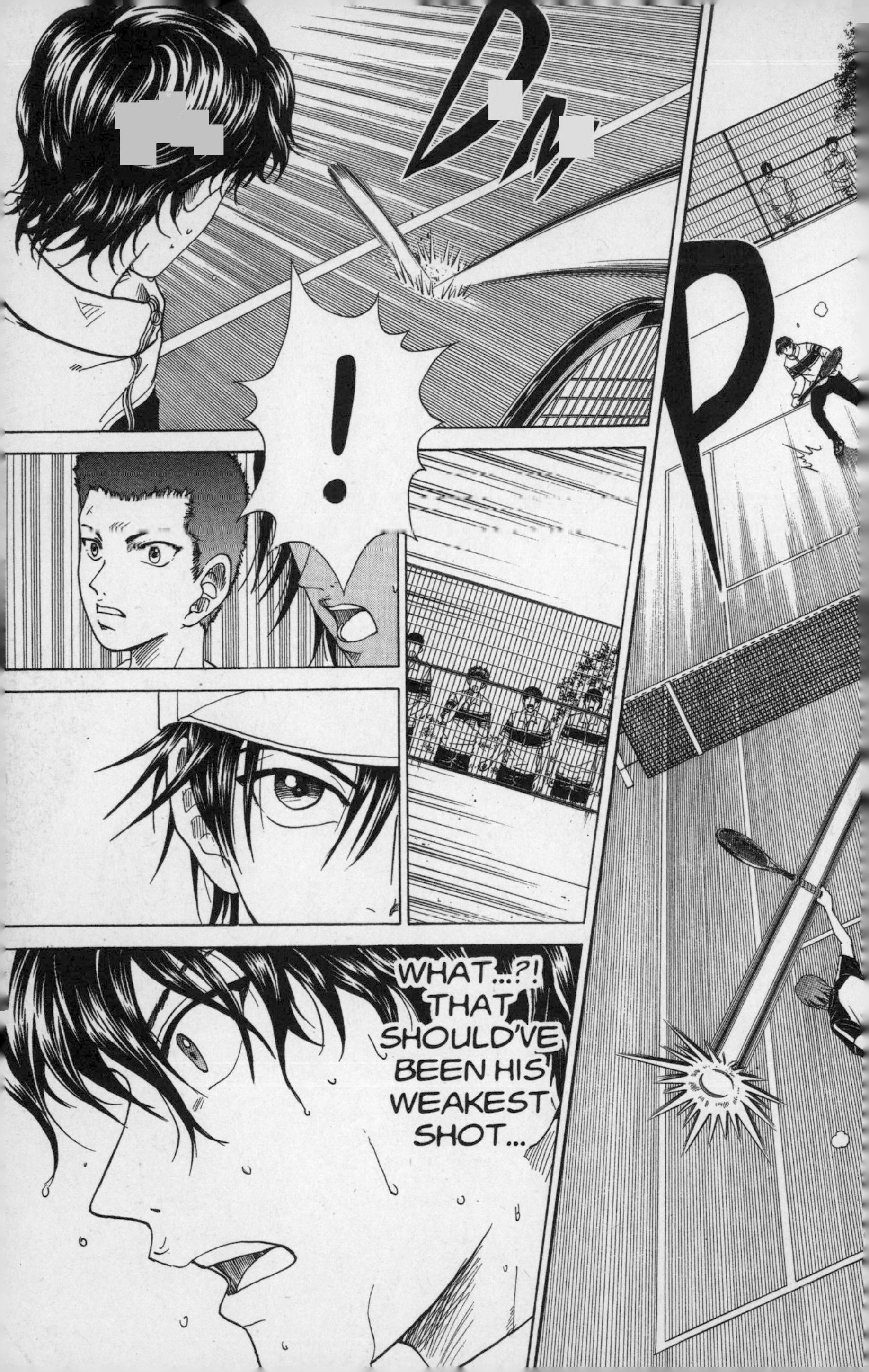
!
WHAT...?! THAT SHOULD'VE BEEN HIS WEAKEST SHOT...

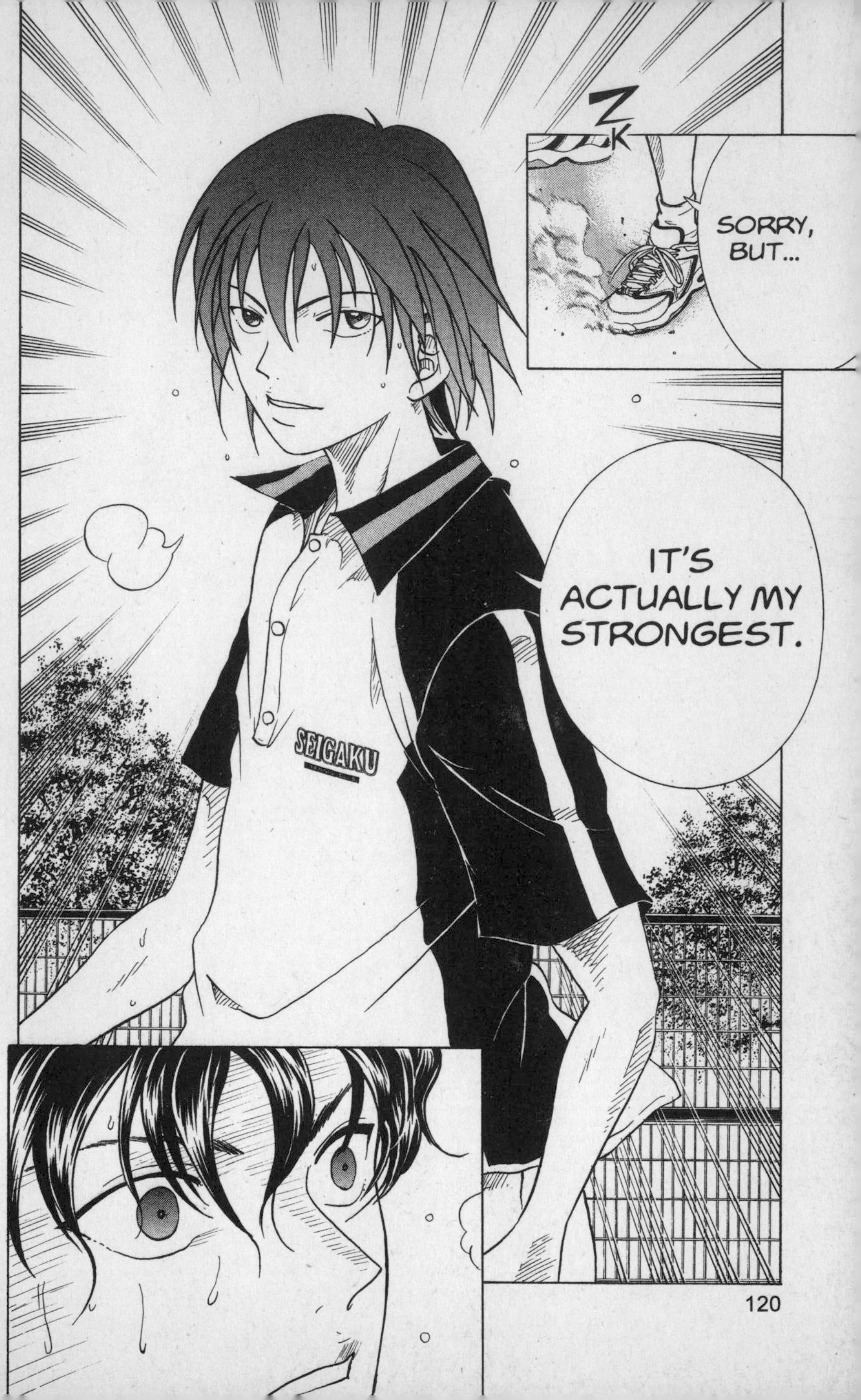
ZK
SORRY, BUT...
IT'S ACTUALLY MY STRONGEST.

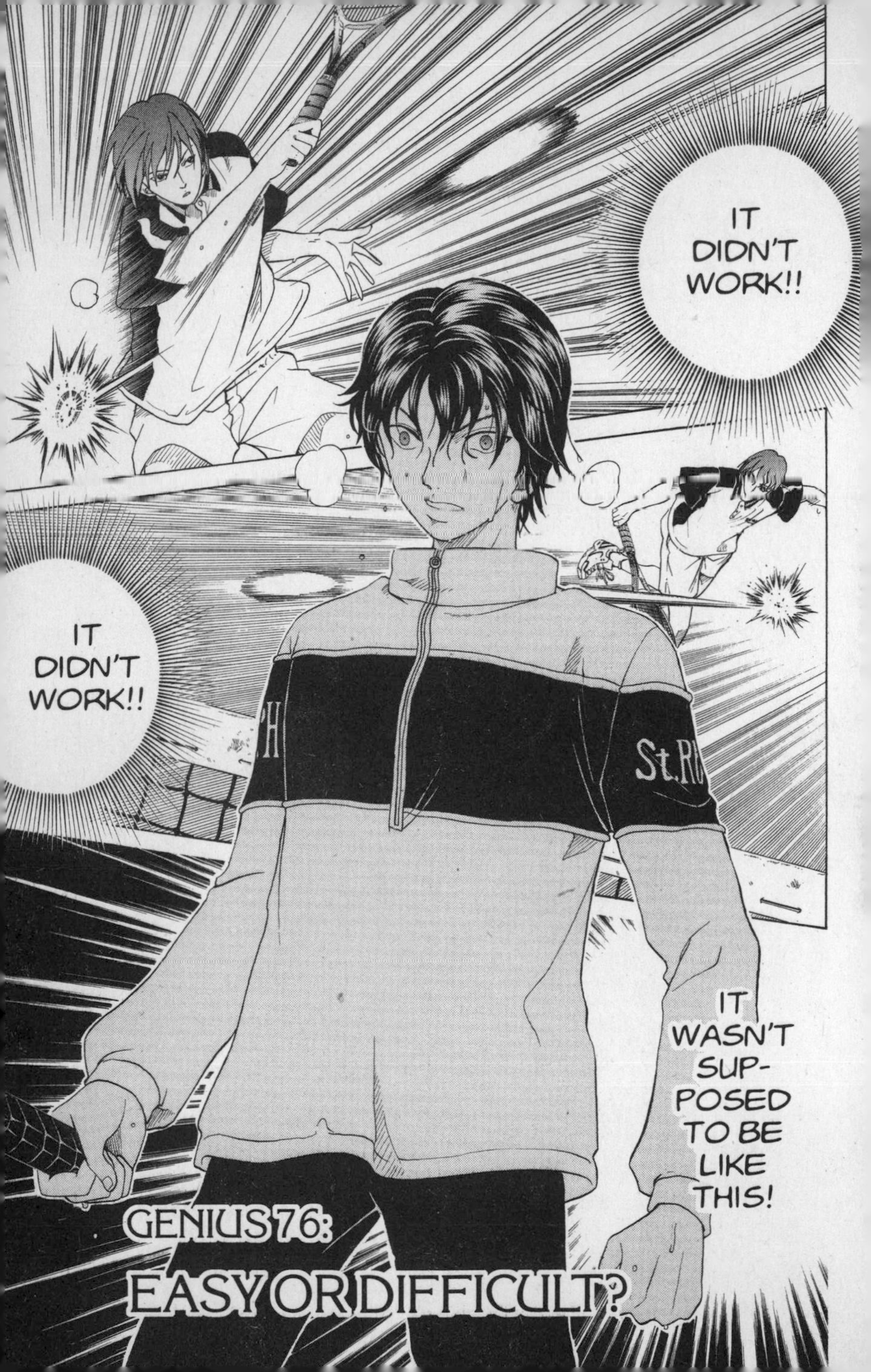
IT DIDN'T WORK!!
IT DIDN'T WORK!!
IT WASN'T SUP-POSED TO BE LIKE THIS!
GENIUS 76:
EASY OR DIFFICULT?

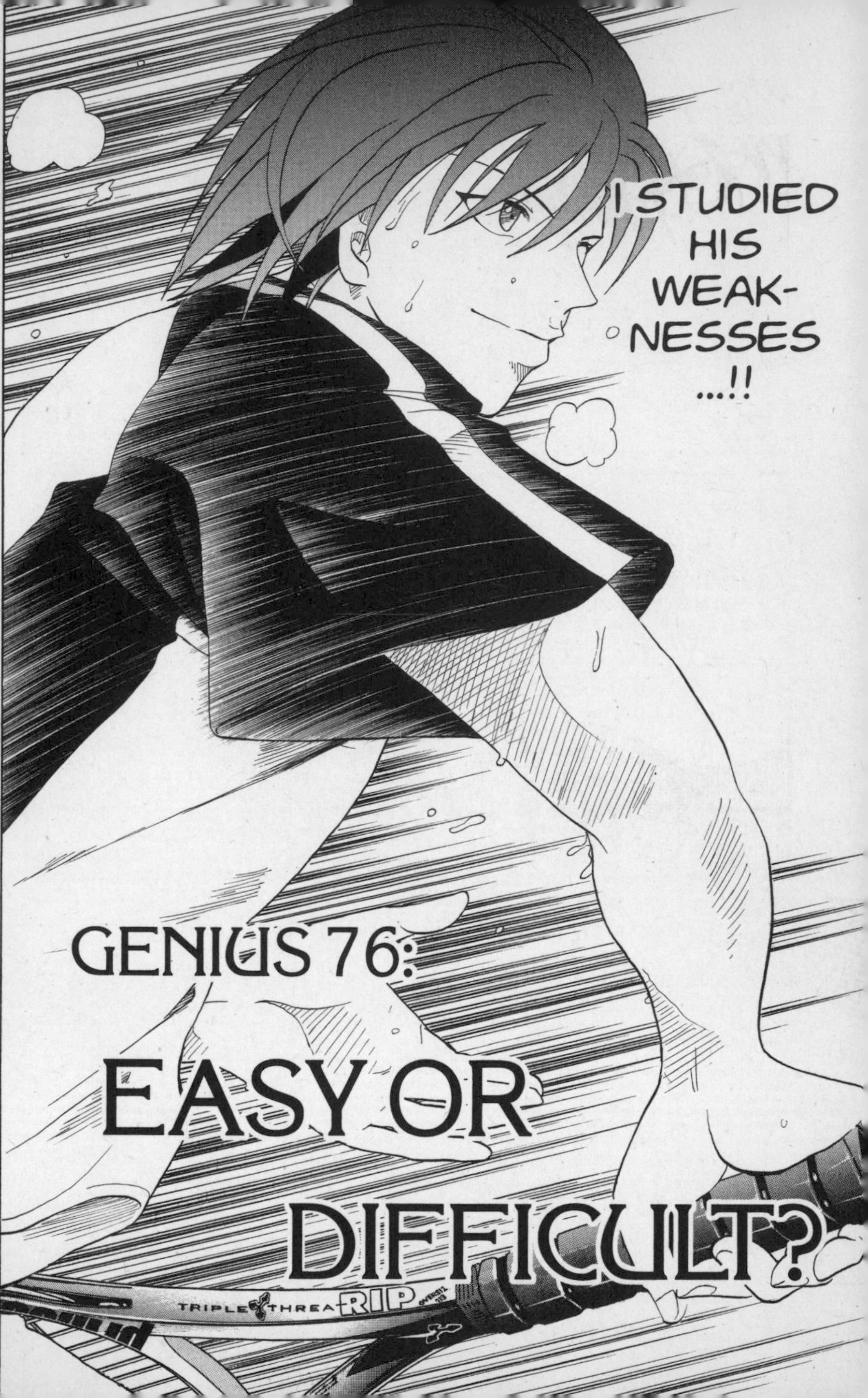
I STUDIED HIS WEAK-NESSES ...!!
GENIUS 76:
EASY OR DIFFICULT?
TRIPLE THREAT RIP

READ THIS WAY

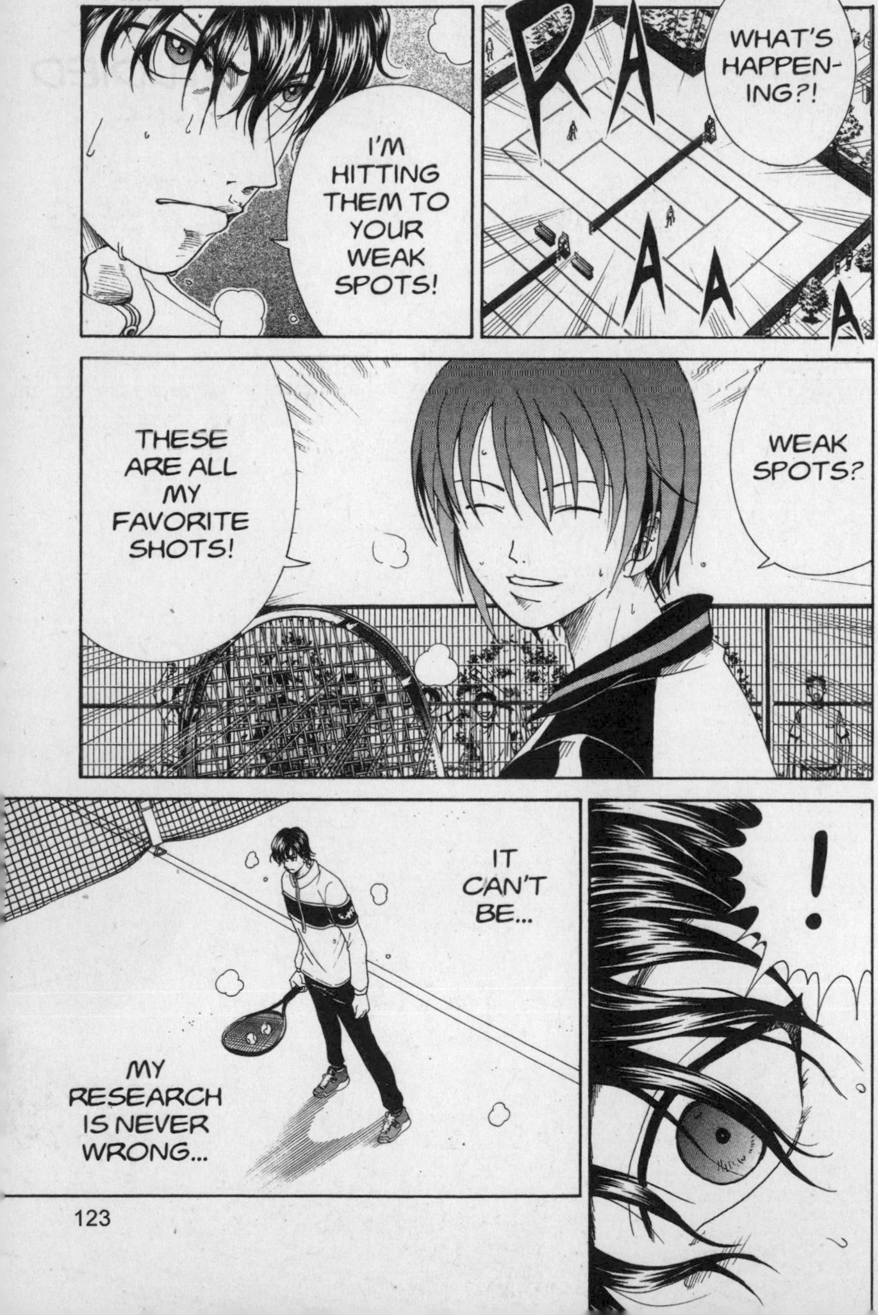

RAAAA
WHAT'S HAPPENING?!
I'M HITTING THEM TO YOUR WEAK SPOTS!
WEAK SPOTS?
THESE ARE ALL MY FAVORITE SHOTS!
!
IT CAN'T BE...
MY RESEARCH IS NEVER WRONG...

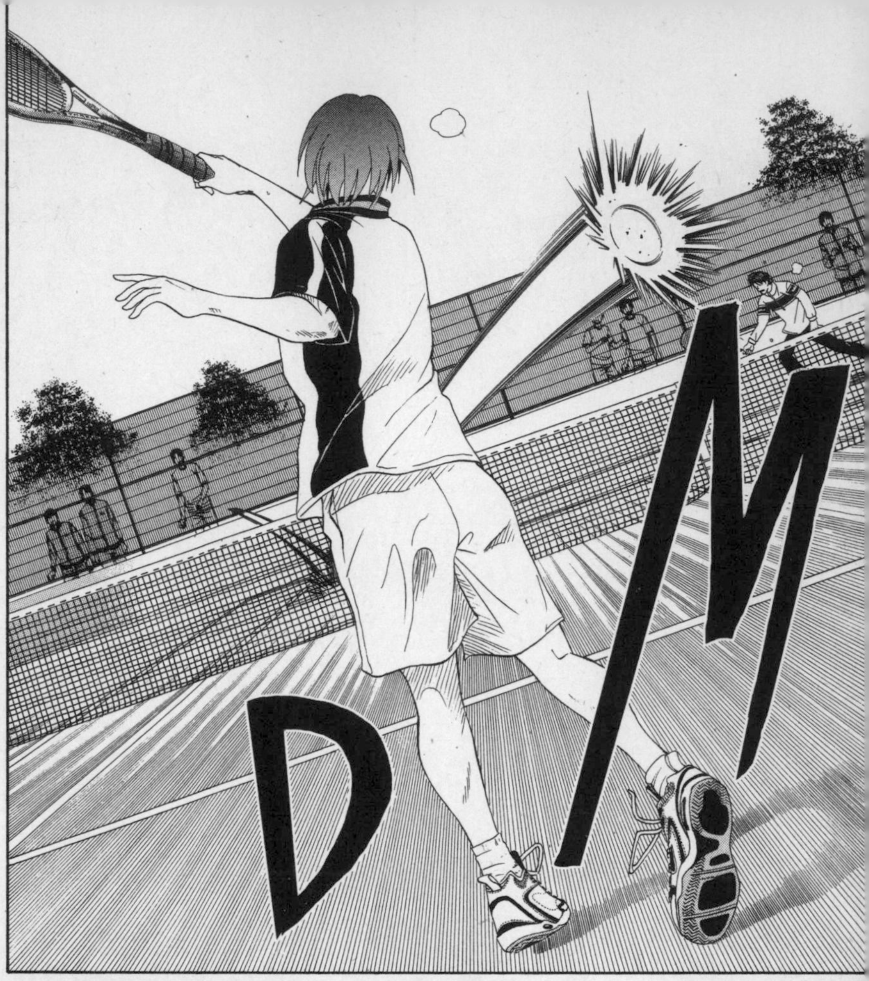
DM

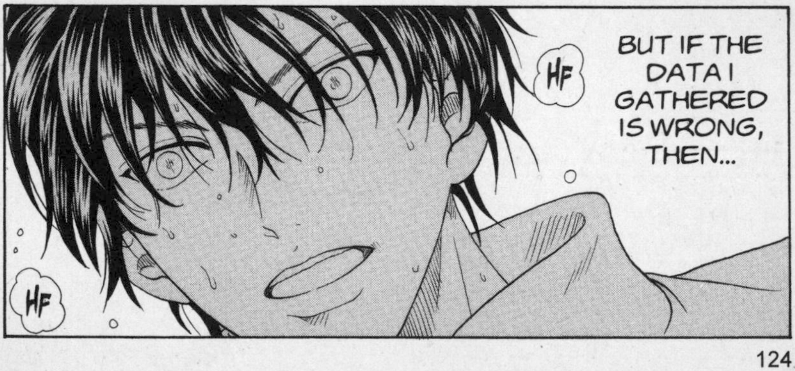
BUT IF THE DATA I GATHERED IS WRONG, THEN...
HF
HF

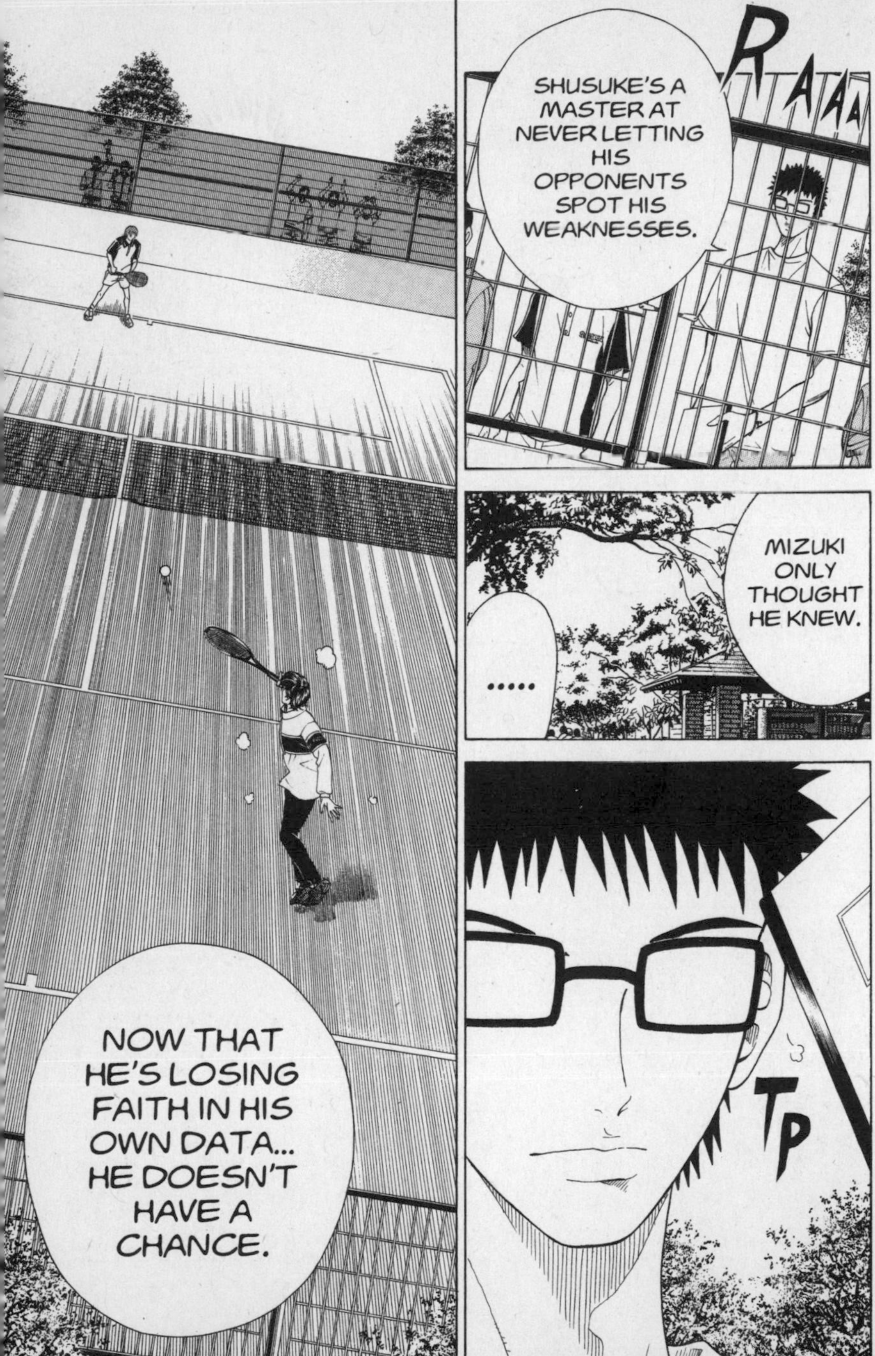
RAAA
SHUSUKE'S A MASTER AT NEVER LETTING HIS OPPONENTS SPOT HIS WEAKNESSES.
MIZUKI ONLY THOUGHT HE KNEW.
.....
TP
NOW THAT HE'S LOSING FAITH IN HIS OWN DATA... HE DOESN'T HAVE A CHANCE.

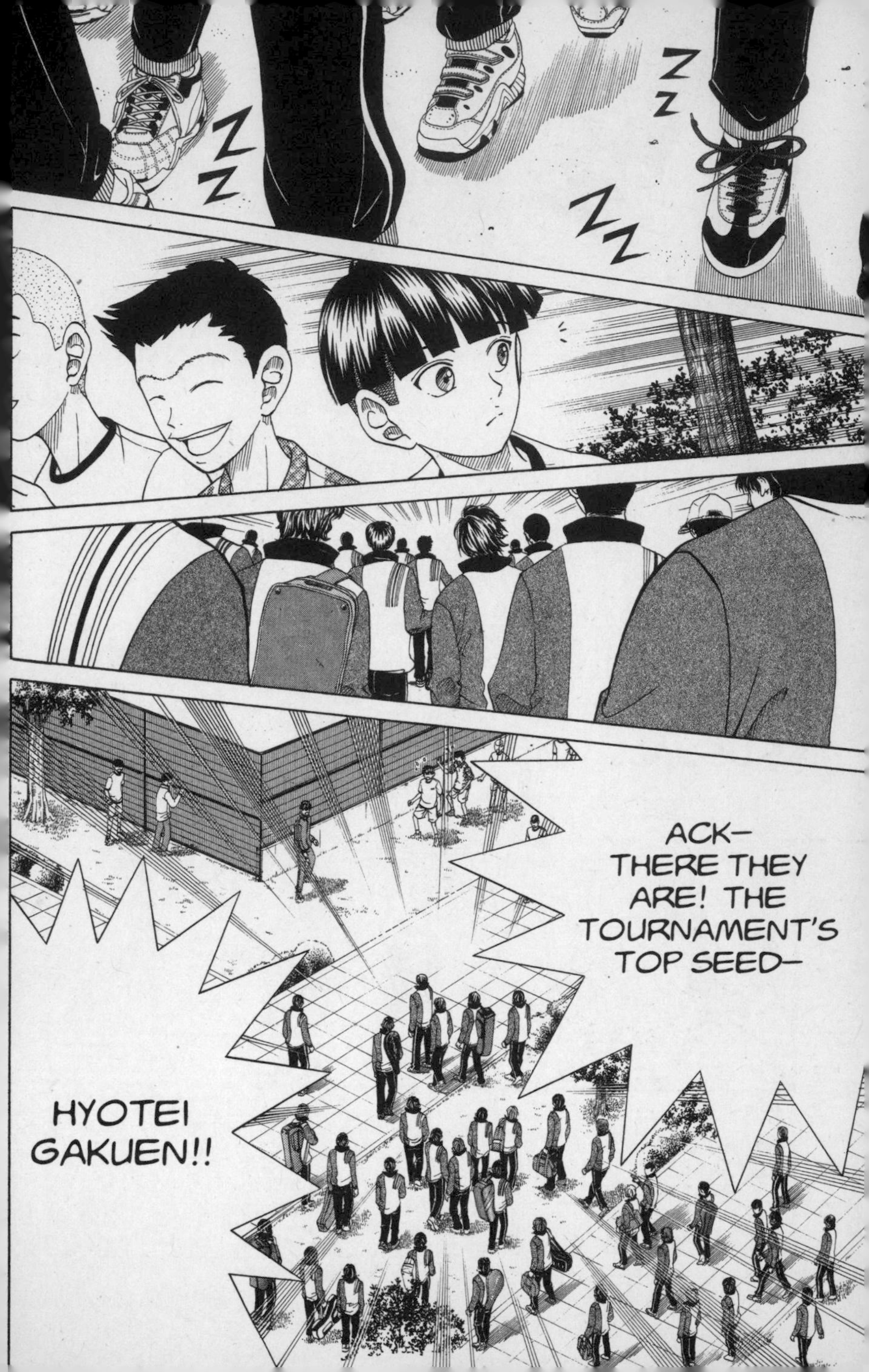
ACK— THERE THEY ARE! THE TOURNAMENT'S TOP SEED—
HYOTEI GAKUEN!!

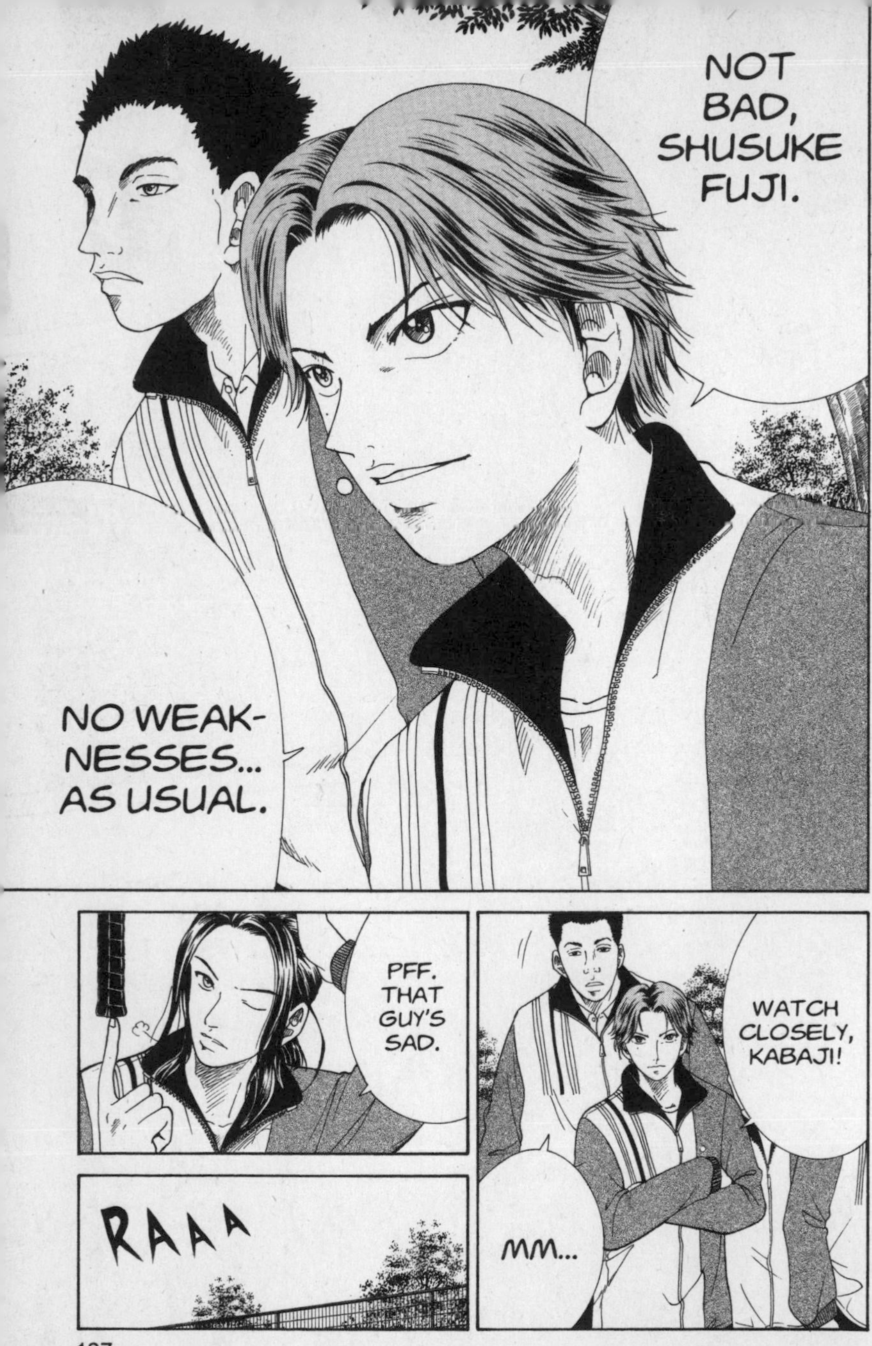
NOT BAD, SHUSUKE FUJI.
NO WEAK-NESSES... AS USUAL.
WATCH CLOSELY, KABAJI!
MM...
PFF. THAT GUY'S SAD.
RAAA

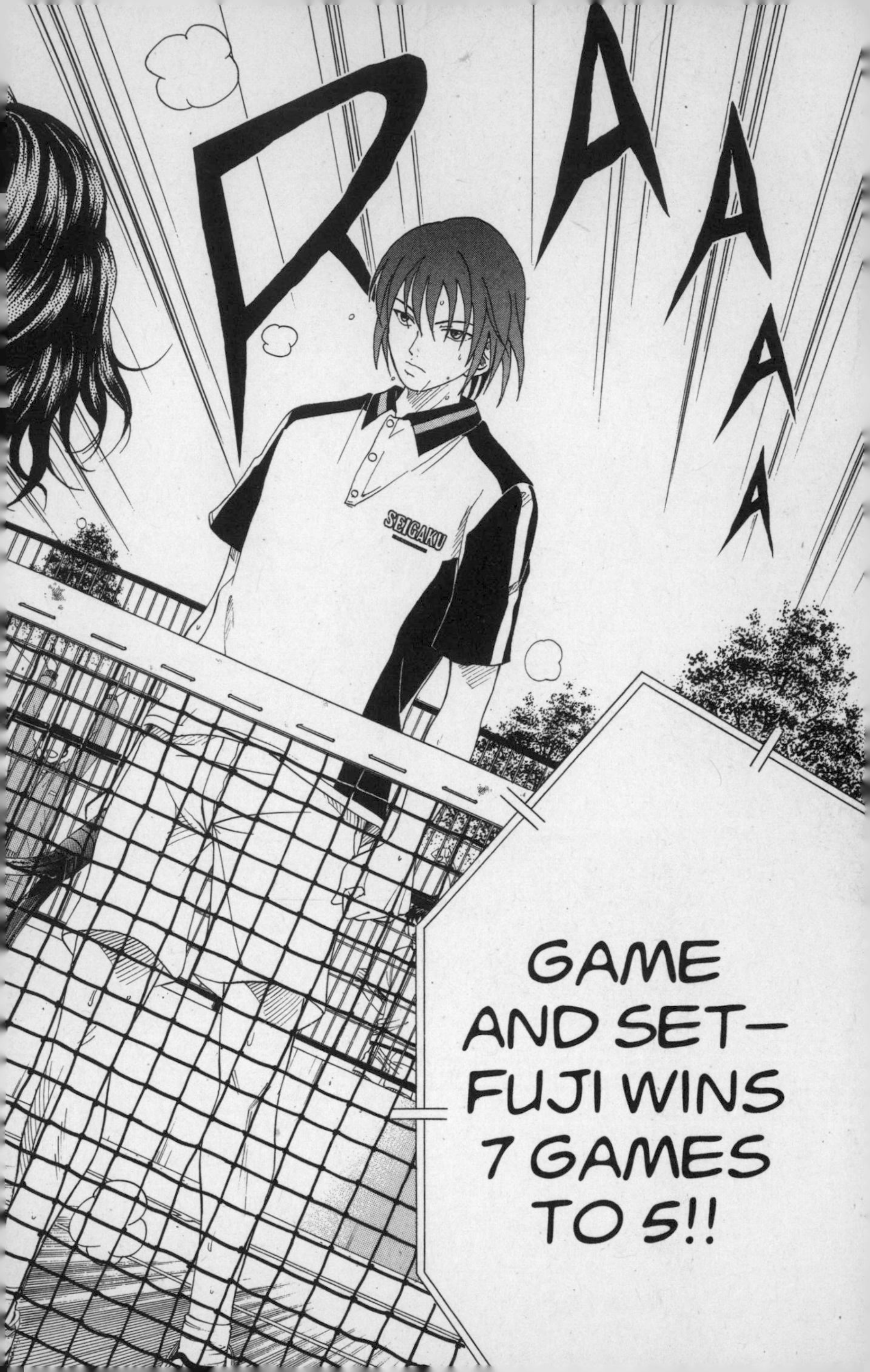
RAAAAA
SEIGAKU
GAME AND SET— FUJI WINS 7 GAMES TO 5!!

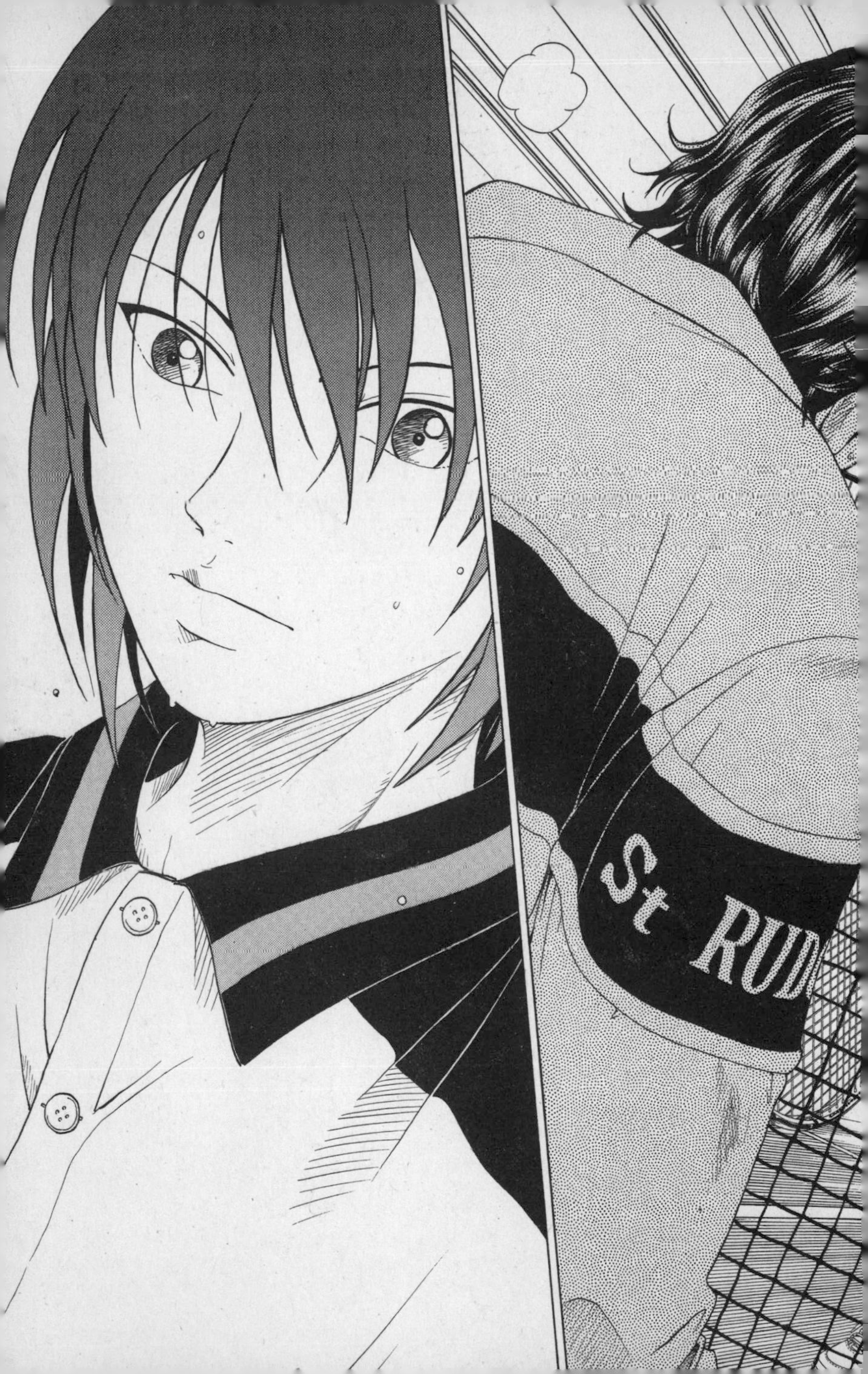
St RUD

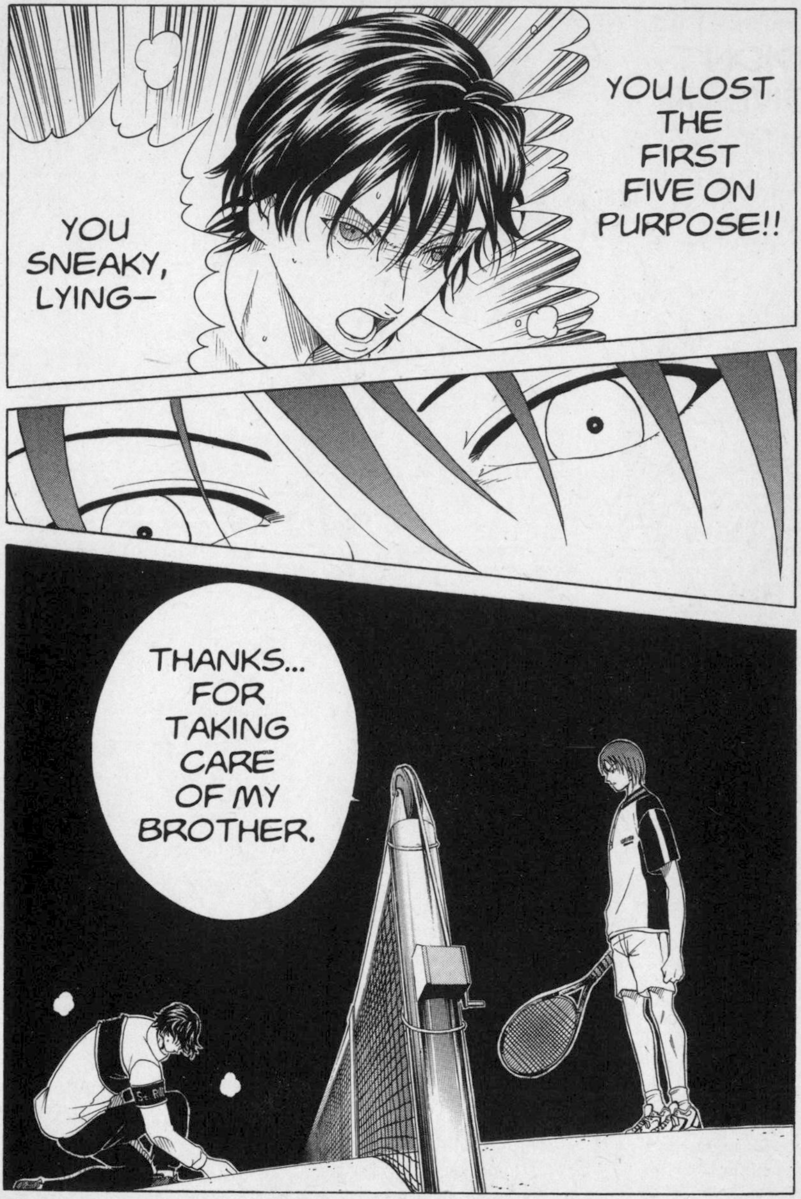
YOU LOST THE FIRST FIVE ON PURPOSE!!
YOU SNEAKY, LYING—
THANKS... FOR TAKING CARE OF MY BROTHER.

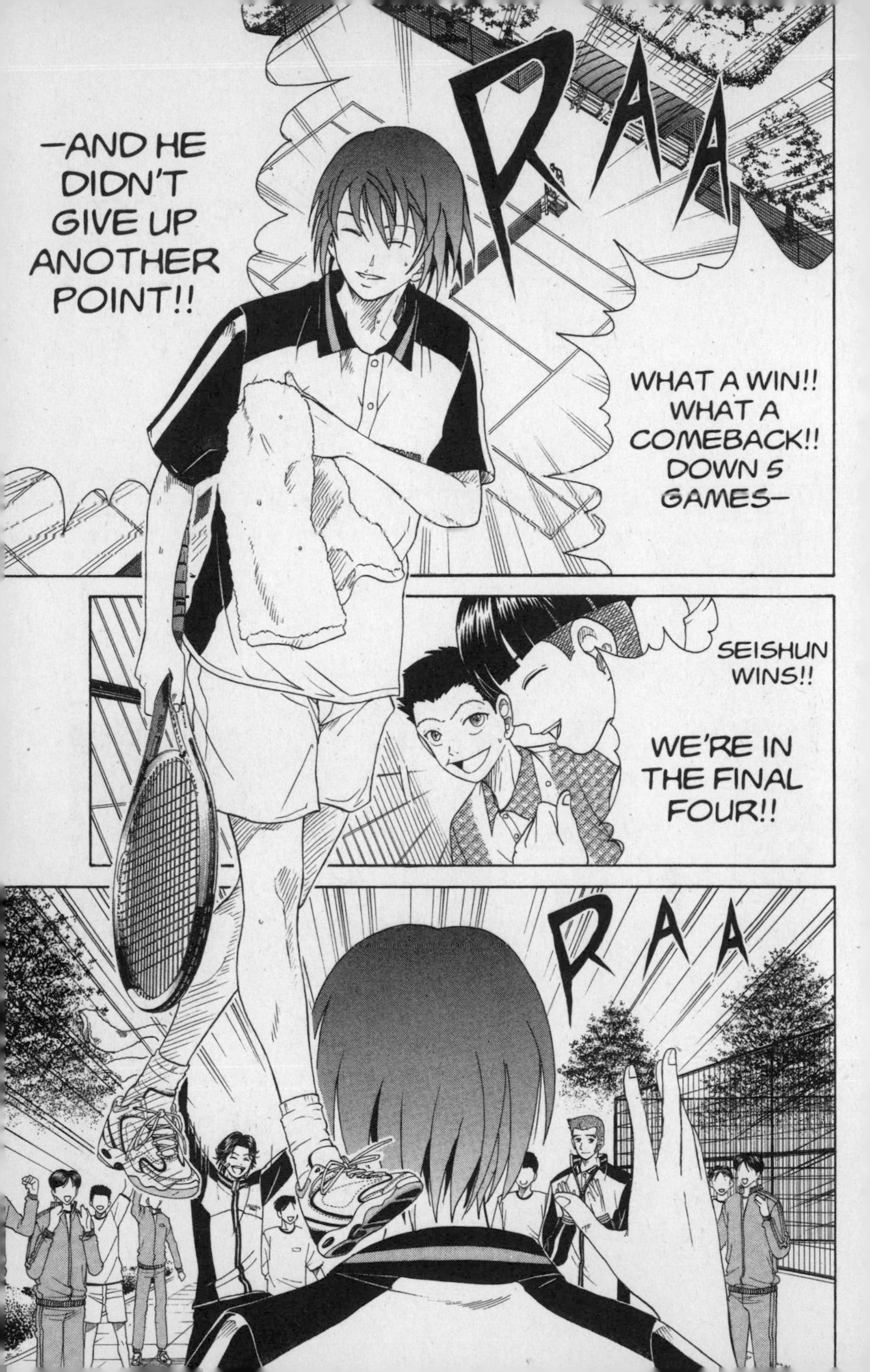
RAA
WHAT A WIN!! WHAT A COMEBACK!! DOWN 5 GAMES—
—AND HE DIDN'T GIVE UP ANOTHER POINT!!
SEISHUN WINS!!
WE'RE IN THE FINAL FOUR!!
RAA

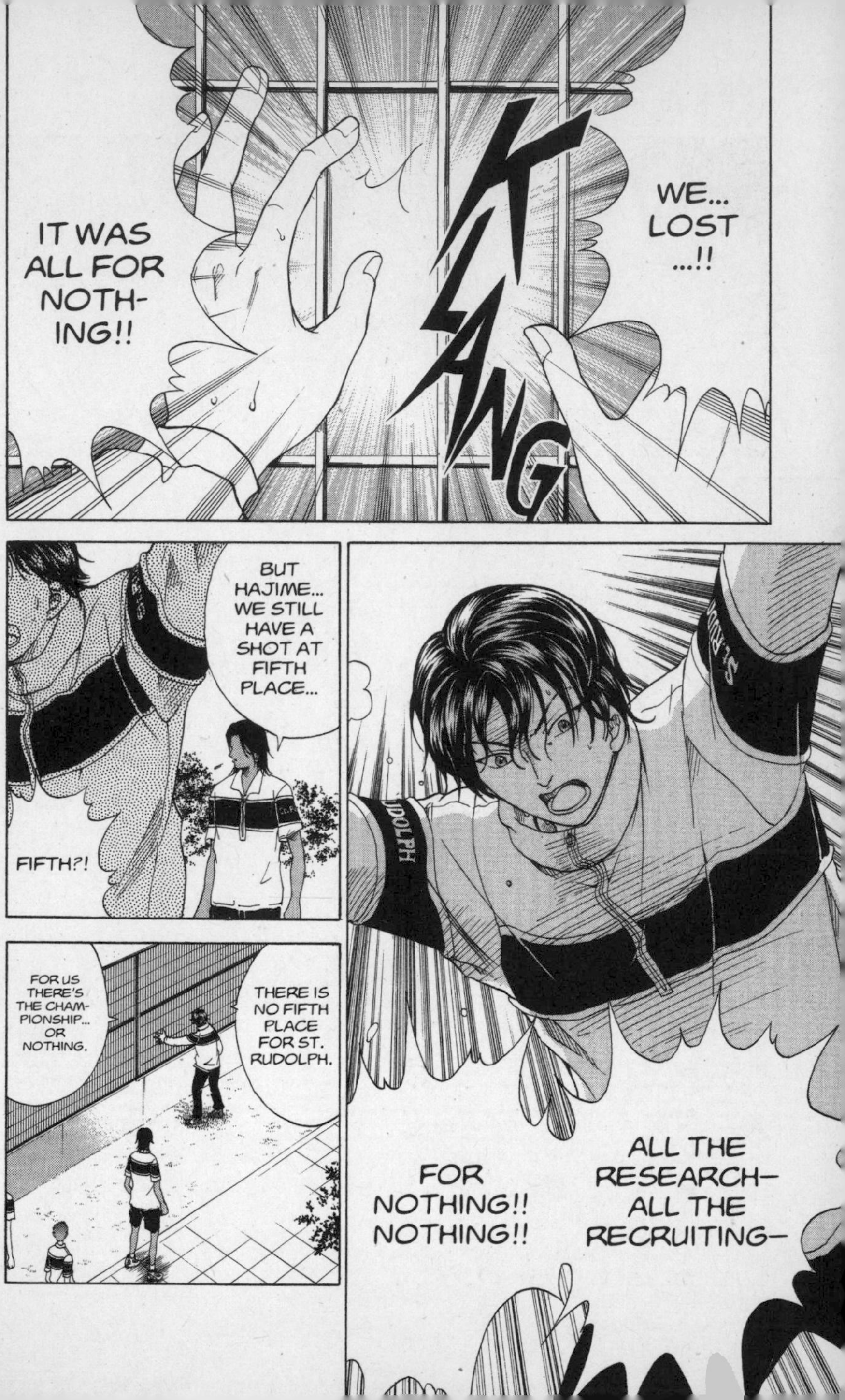
WE... LOST ...!!
KLANG
IT WAS ALL FOR NOTHING!!
ALL THE RESEARCH— ALL THE RECRUITING—
FOR NOTHING!! NOTHING!!
BUT HAJIME... WE STILL HAVE A SHOT AT FIFTH PLACE...
FIFTH?!
THERE IS NO FIFTH PLACE FOR ST. RUDOLPH.
FOR US THERE'S THE CHAMPIONSHIP... OR NOTHING.

READ THIS WAY

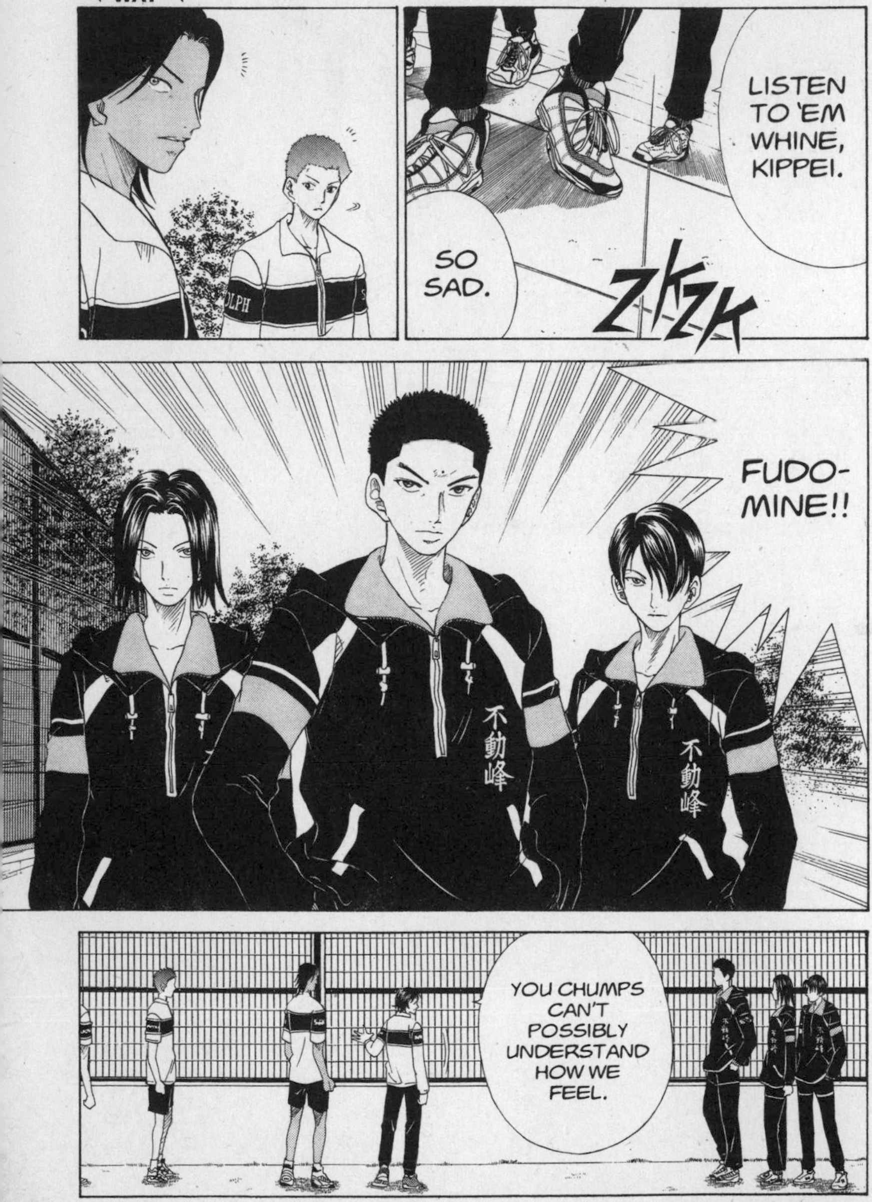
LISTEN TO 'EM WHINE, KIPPEI.
SO SAD.
ZKZK
FUDO-MINE!!
不動峰
不動峰
YOU CHUMPS CAN'T POSSIBLY UNDERSTAND HOW WE FEEL.

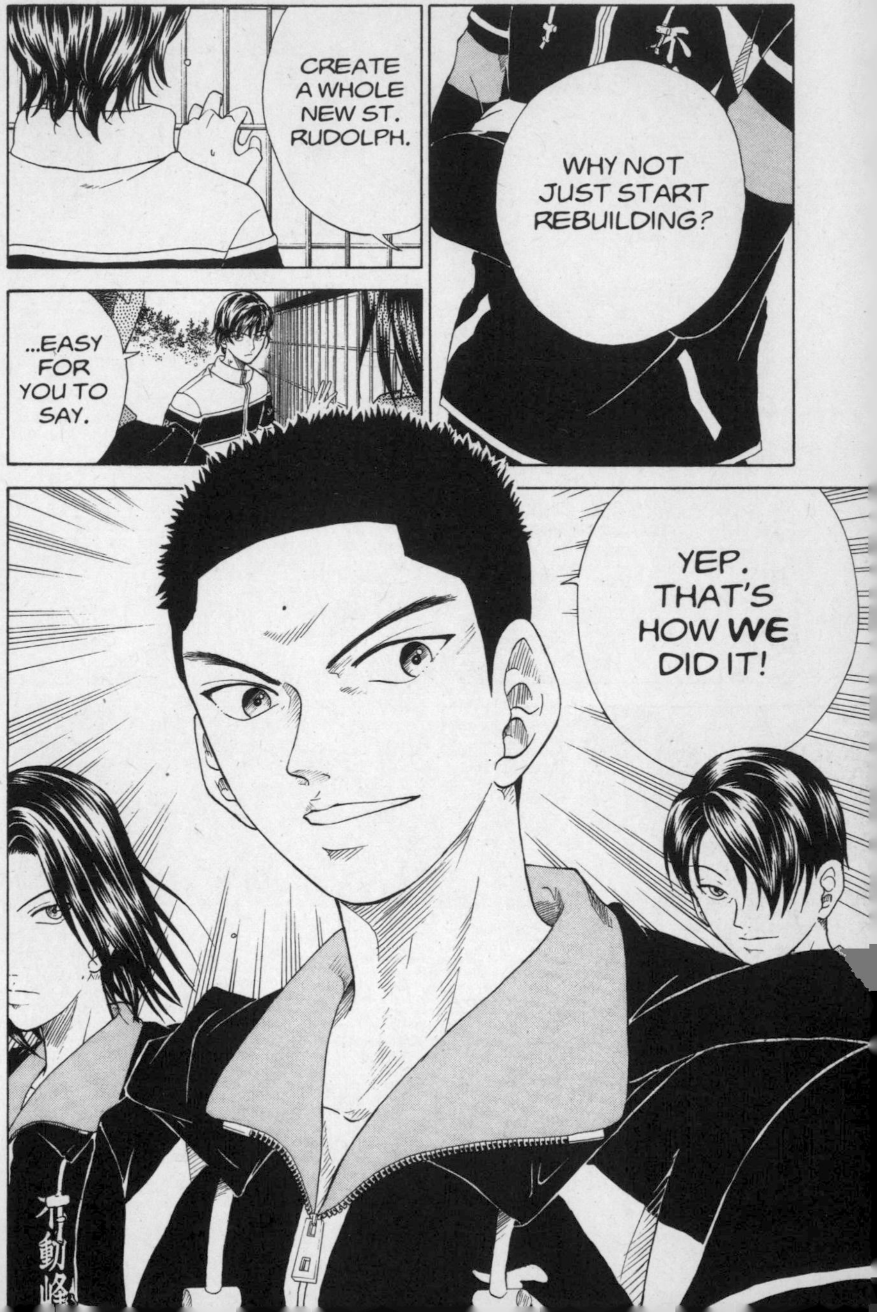
WHY NOT JUST START REBUILDING?
CREATE A WHOLE NEW ST. RUDOLPH.
...EASY FOR YOU TO SAY.
YEP. THAT'S HOW **WE** DID IT!
不動峰

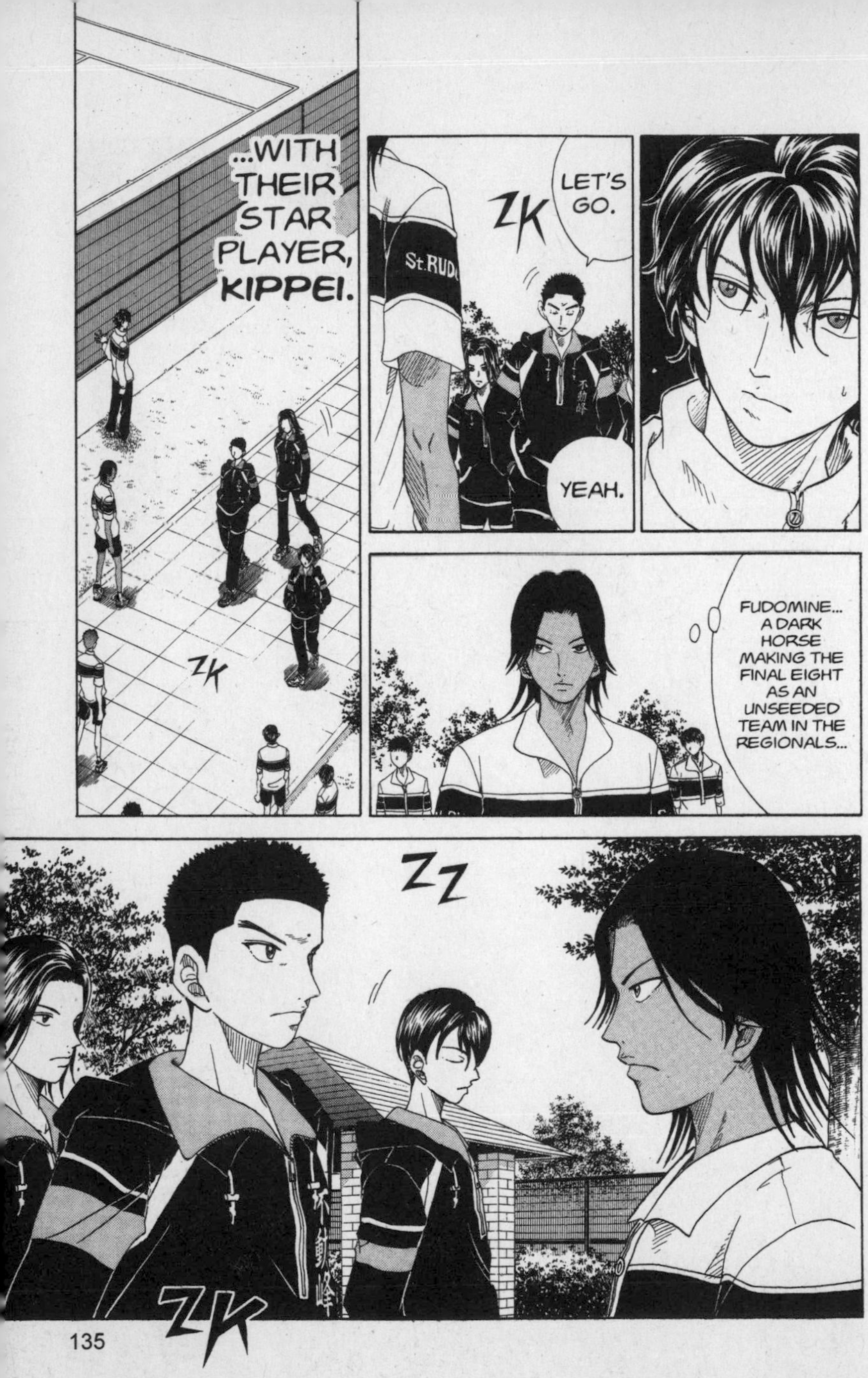
LET'S GO.
ZK
YEAH.
FUDOMINE... A DARK HORSE MAKING THE FINAL EIGHT AS AN UNSEEDED TEAM IN THE REGIONALS...
...WITH THEIR STAR PLAYER, KIPPEI.
ZK
ZZ
ZK

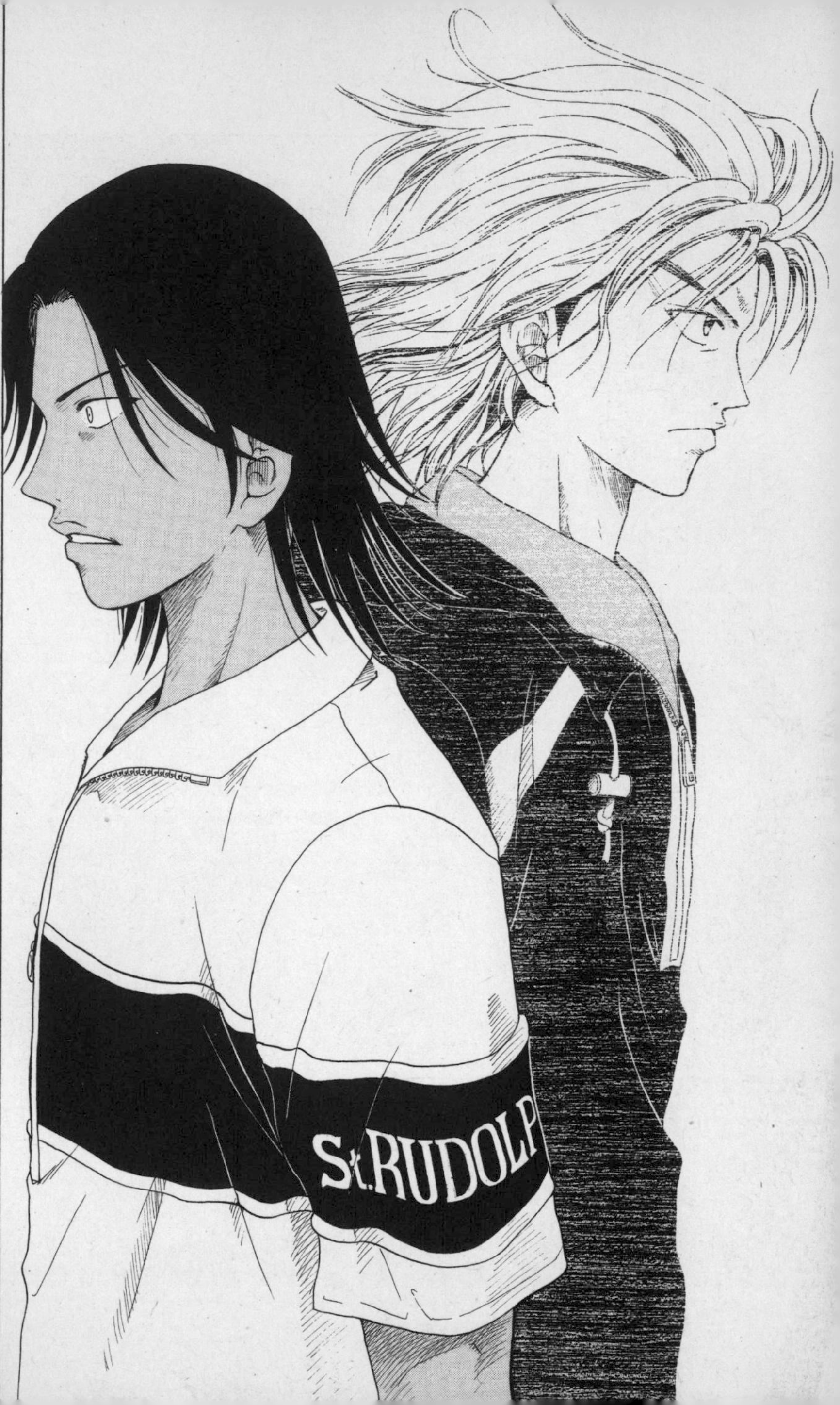
St.RUDOLP

READ THIS WAY

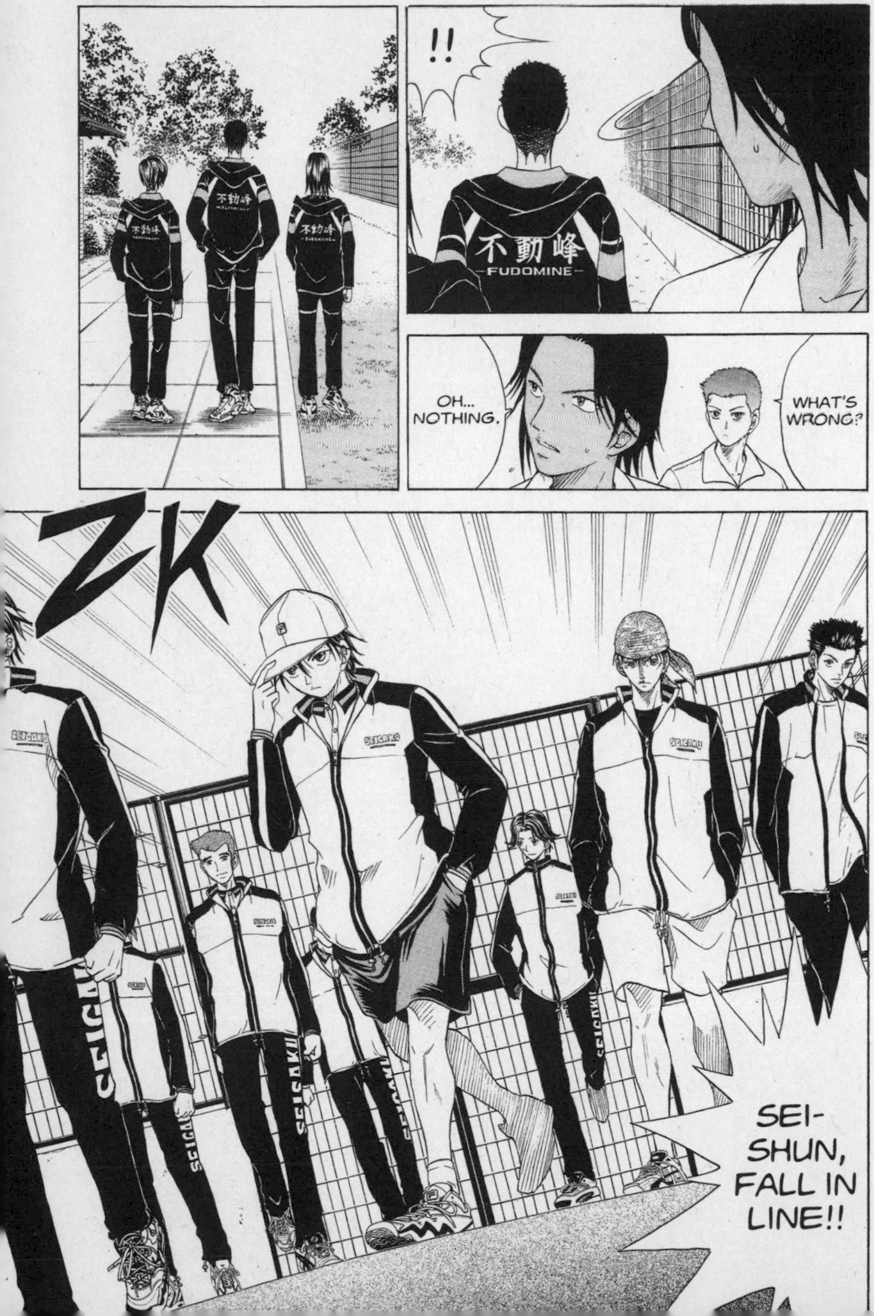
!!
不動峰
—FUDOMINE—
WHAT'S WRONG?
OH... NOTHING.
ZK
SEI-SHUN, FALL IN LINE!!

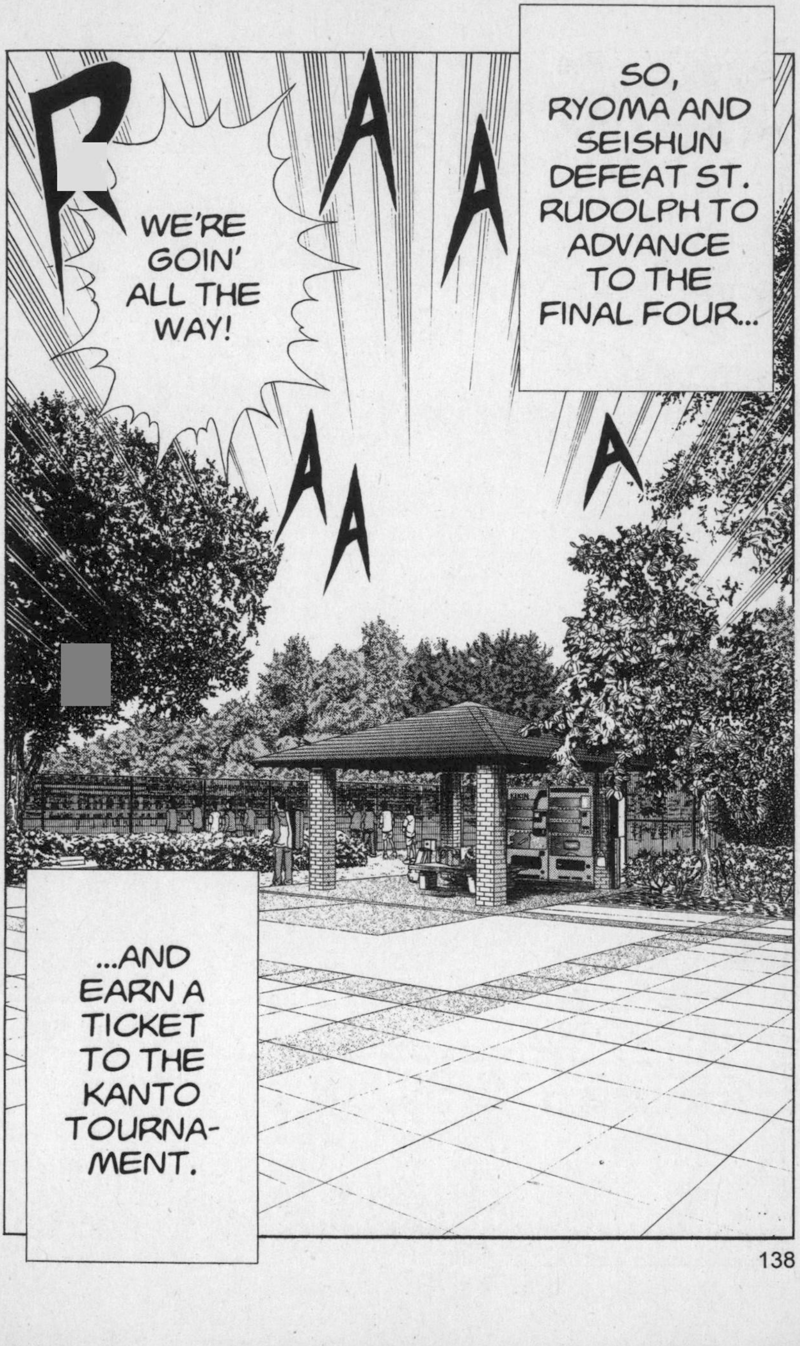
SO, RYOMA AND SEISHUN DEFEAT ST. RUDOLPH TO ADVANCE TO THE FINAL FOUR...
RAAAAA
WE'RE GOIN' ALL THE WAY!
...AND EARN A TICKET TO THE KANTO TOURNAMENT.

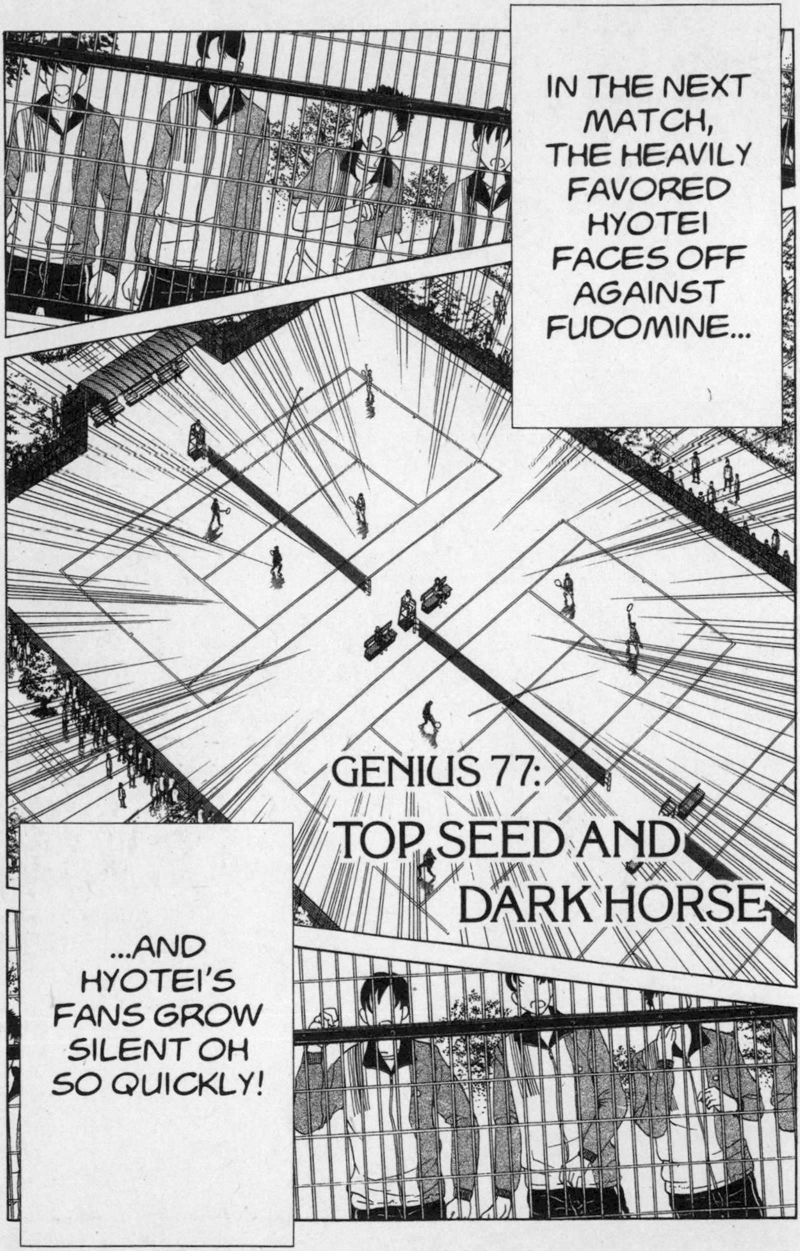
IN THE NEXT MATCH, THE HEAVILY FAVORED HYOTEI FACES OFF AGAINST FUDOMINE...
GENIUS 77:
TOP SEED AND DARK HORSE
...AND HYOTEI'S FANS GROW SILENT OH SO QUICKLY!

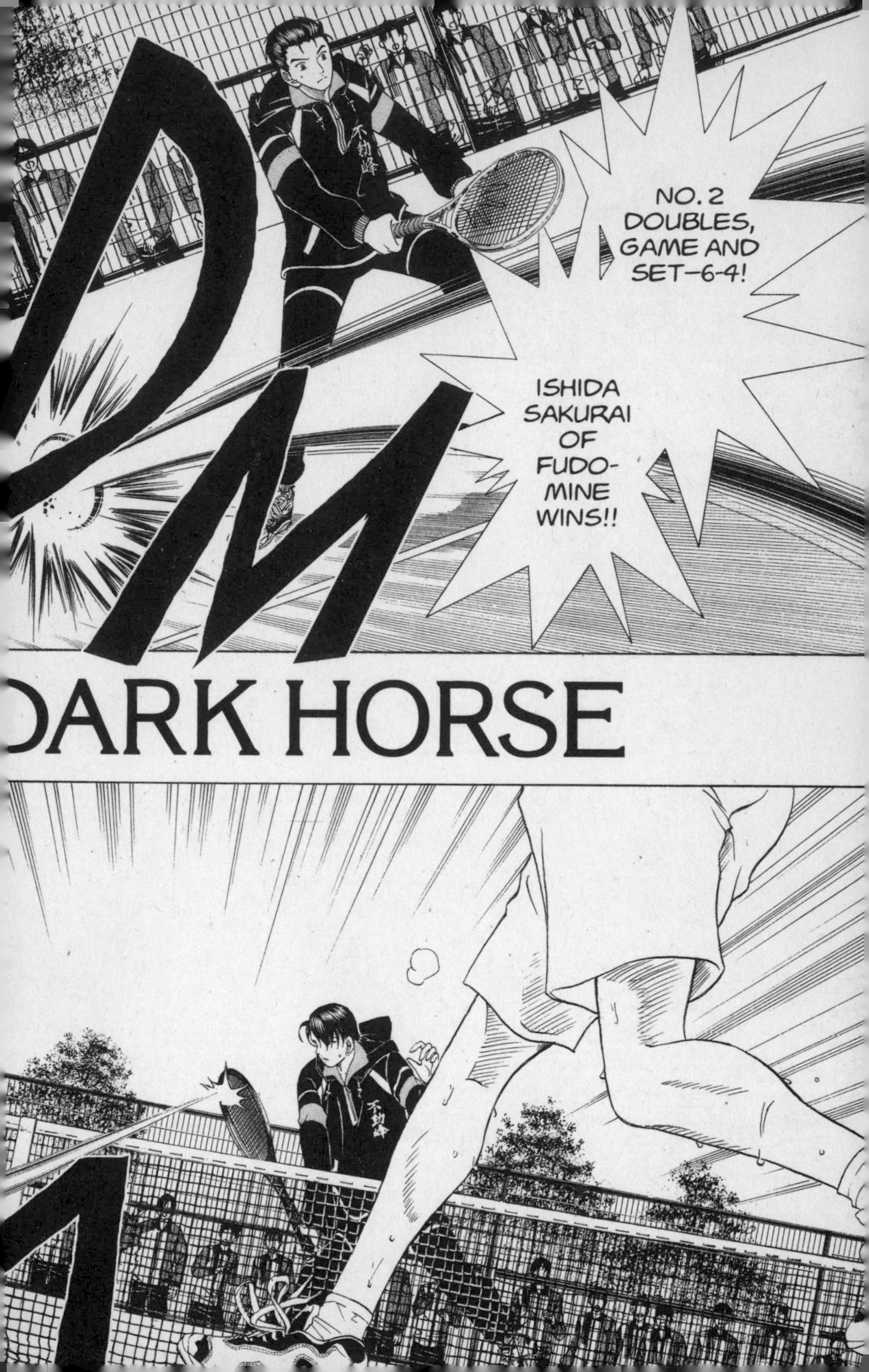
NO. 2 DOUBLES, GAME AND SET—6-4!
ISHIDA SAKURAI OF FUDO-MINE WINS!!
DARK HORSE

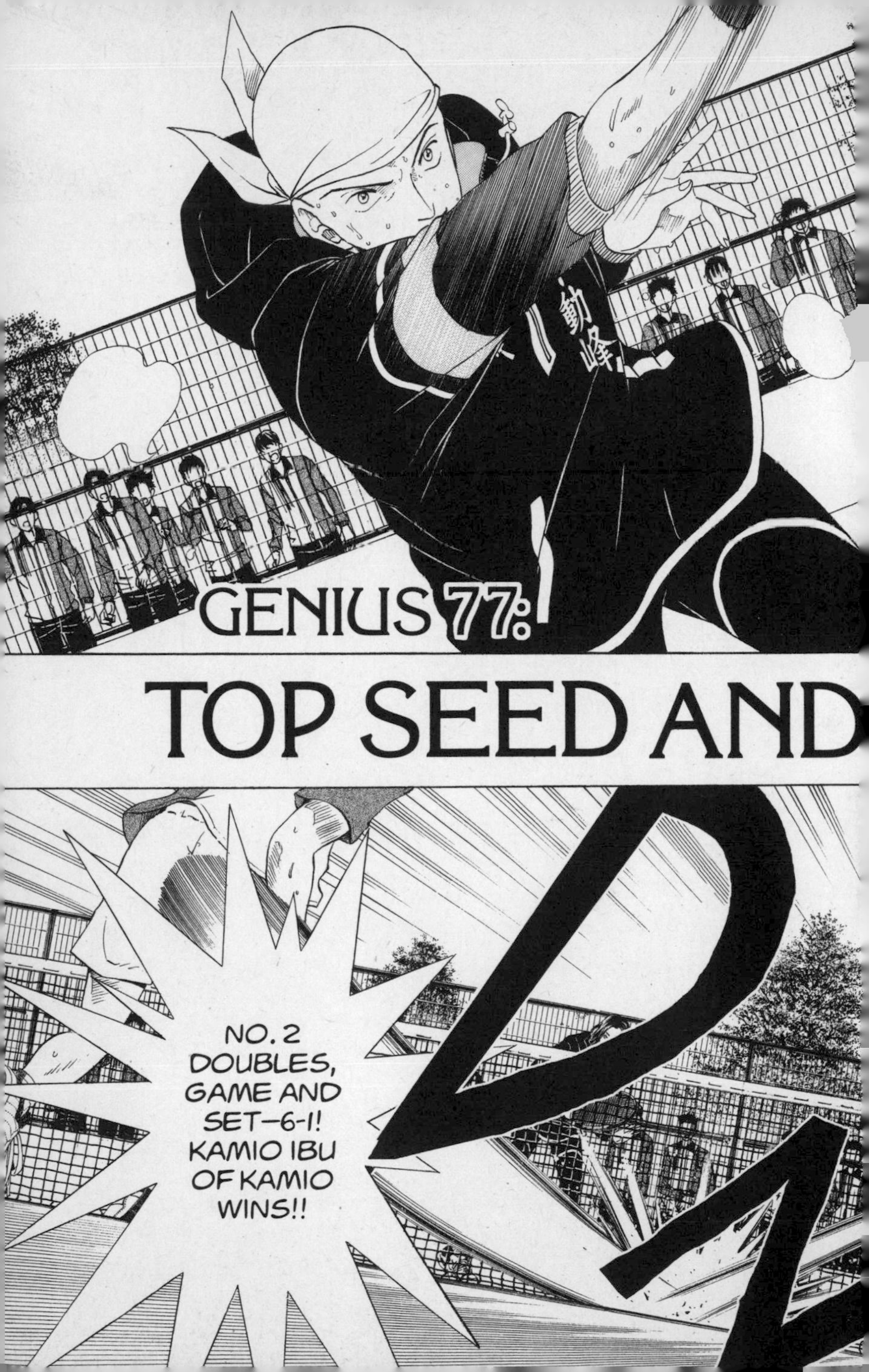
GENIUS 77:
TOP SEED AND
NO. 2 DOUBLES, GAME AND SET—6-1! KAMIO IBU OF KAMIO WINS!!

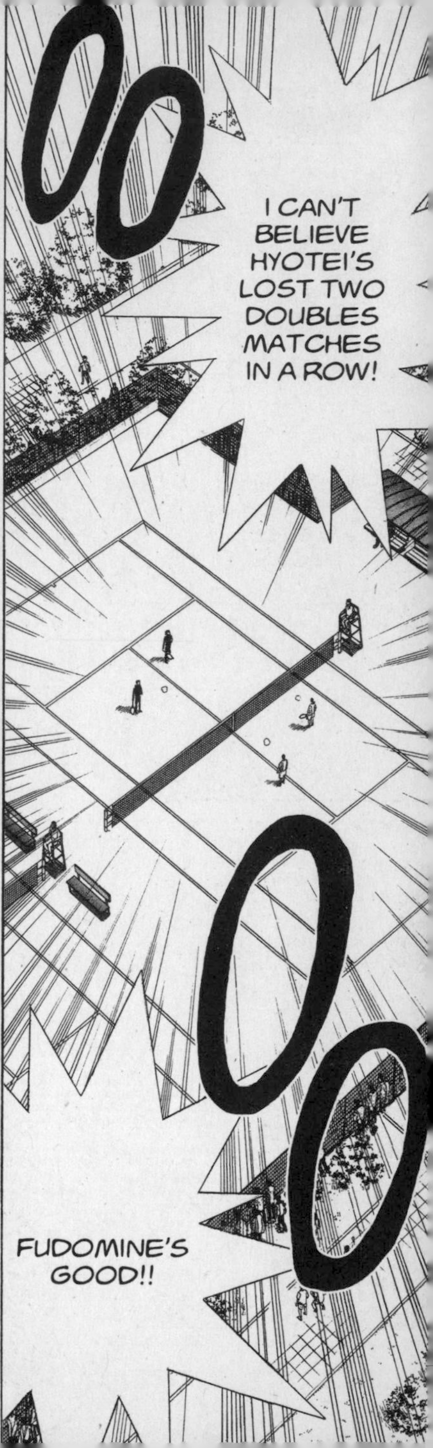
OO
I CAN'T BELIEVE HYOTEI'S LOST TWO DOUBLES MATCHES IN A ROW!
OOO
FUDOMINE'S GOOD!!

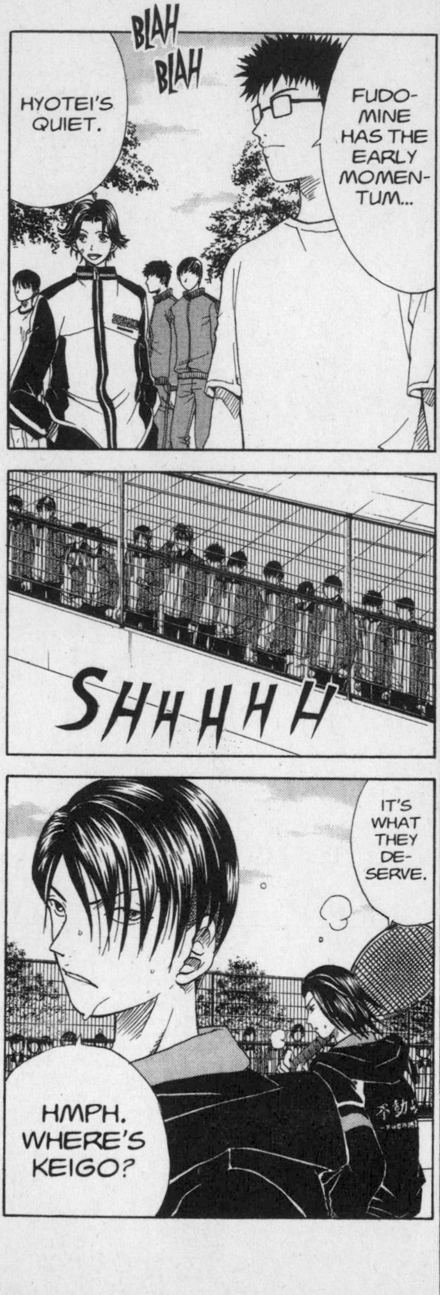
FUDO-MINE HAS THE EARLY MOMEN-TUM...
BLAH BLAH
HYOTEI'S QUIET.
SHHHHH
IT'S WHAT THEY DE-SERVE.
HMPH. WHERE'S KEIGO?

READ THIS WAY

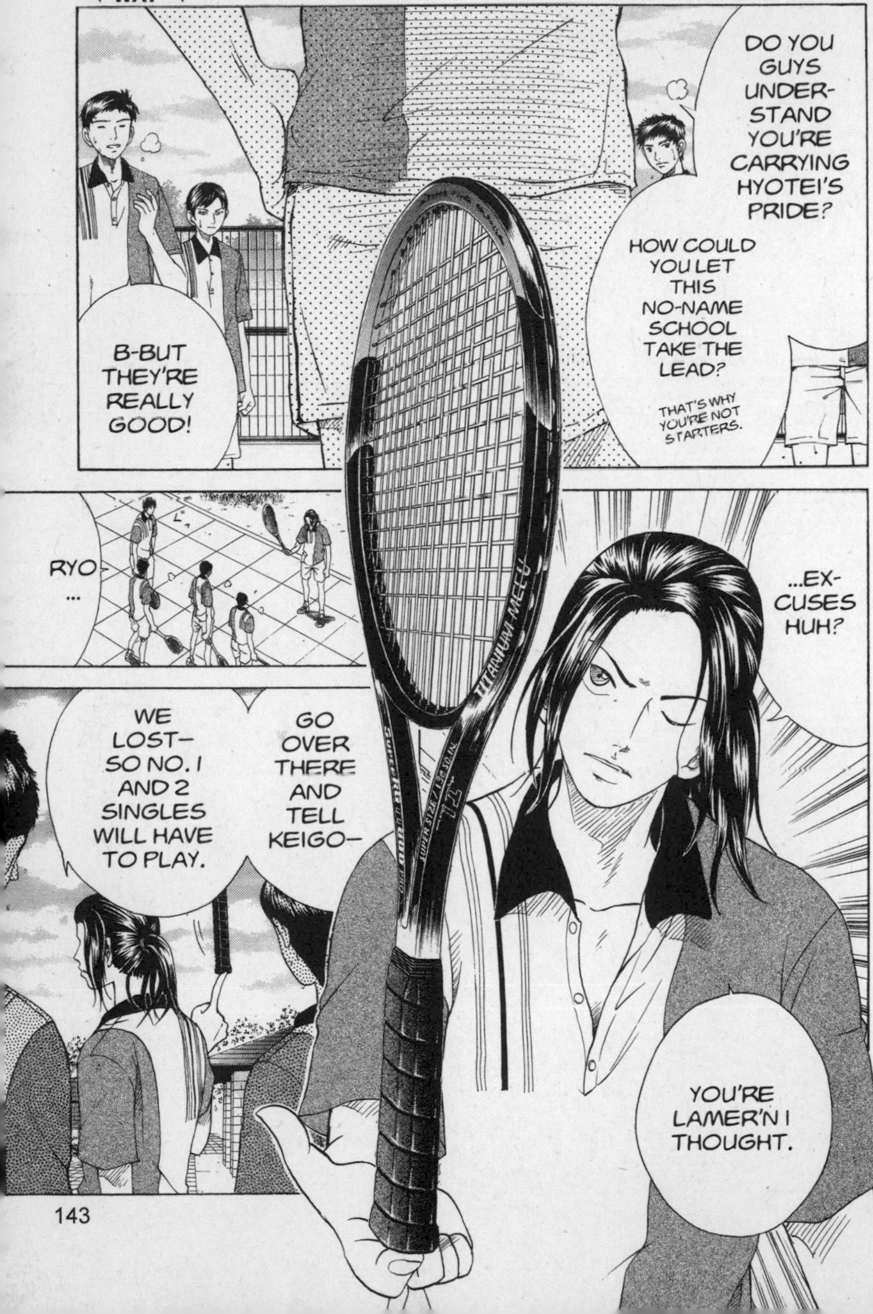

DO YOU GUYS UNDER-STAND YOU'RE CARRYING HYOTEI'S PRIDE?
HOW COULD YOU LET THIS NO-NAME SCHOOL TAKE THE LEAD?
THAT'S WHY YOU'RE NOT STARTERS.
B-BUT THEY'RE REALLY GOOD!
...EX-CUSES HUH?
YOU'RE LAMER'N I THOUGHT.
RYO-...
GO OVER THERE AND TELL KEIGO—
WE LOST— SO NO. 1 AND 2 SINGLES WILL HAVE TO PLAY.

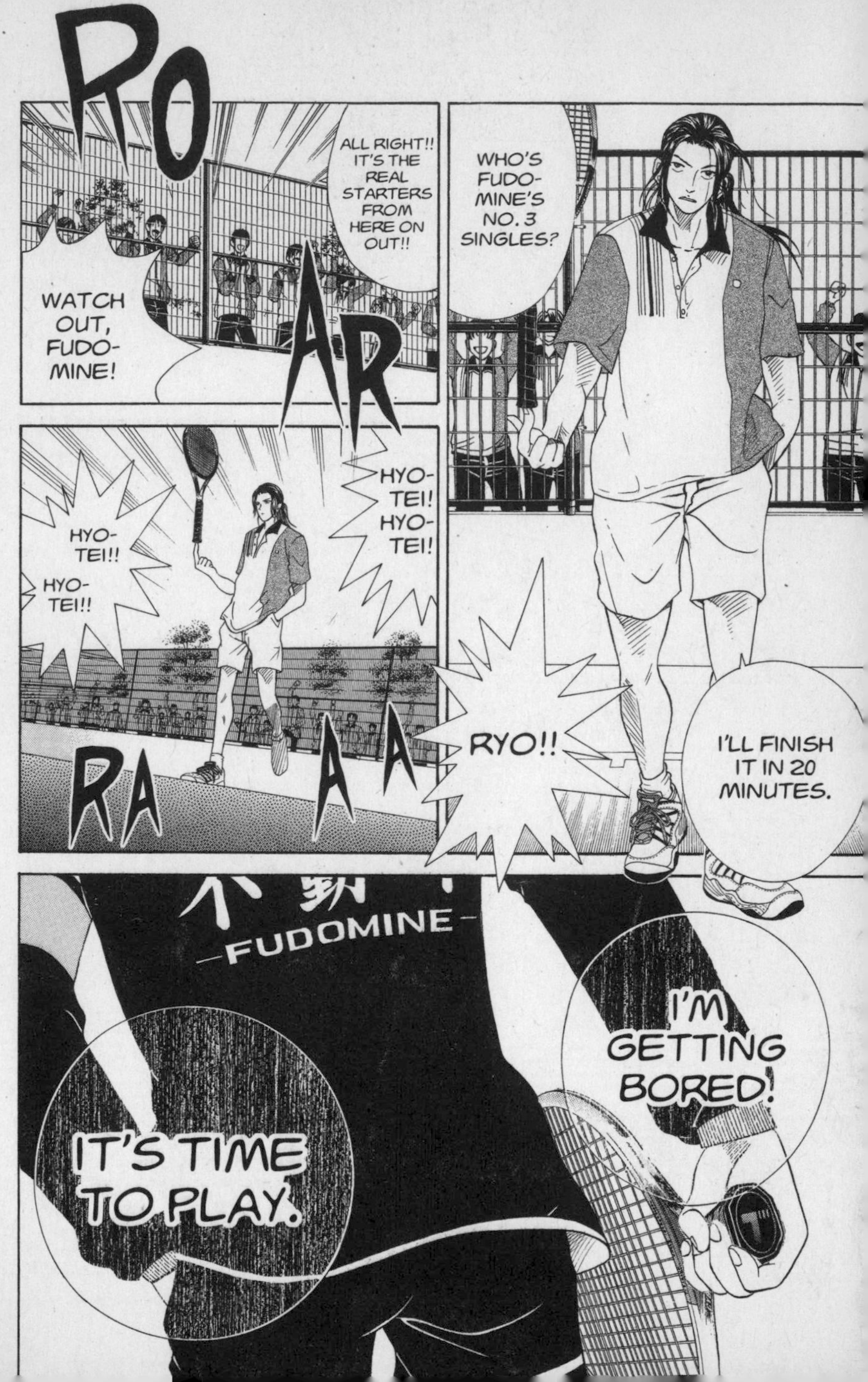
WHO'S FUDOMINE'S NO. 3 SINGLES?
I'LL FINISH IT IN 20 MINUTES.
RO
AR
ALL RIGHT!! IT'S THE REAL STARTERS FROM HERE ON OUT!!
WATCH OUT, FUDOMINE!
HYOTEI! HYOTEI!
HYOTEI!!
HYOTEI!!
RA
A
A
RYO!!
FUDOMINE
I'M GETTING BORED!
IT'S TIME TO PLAY.

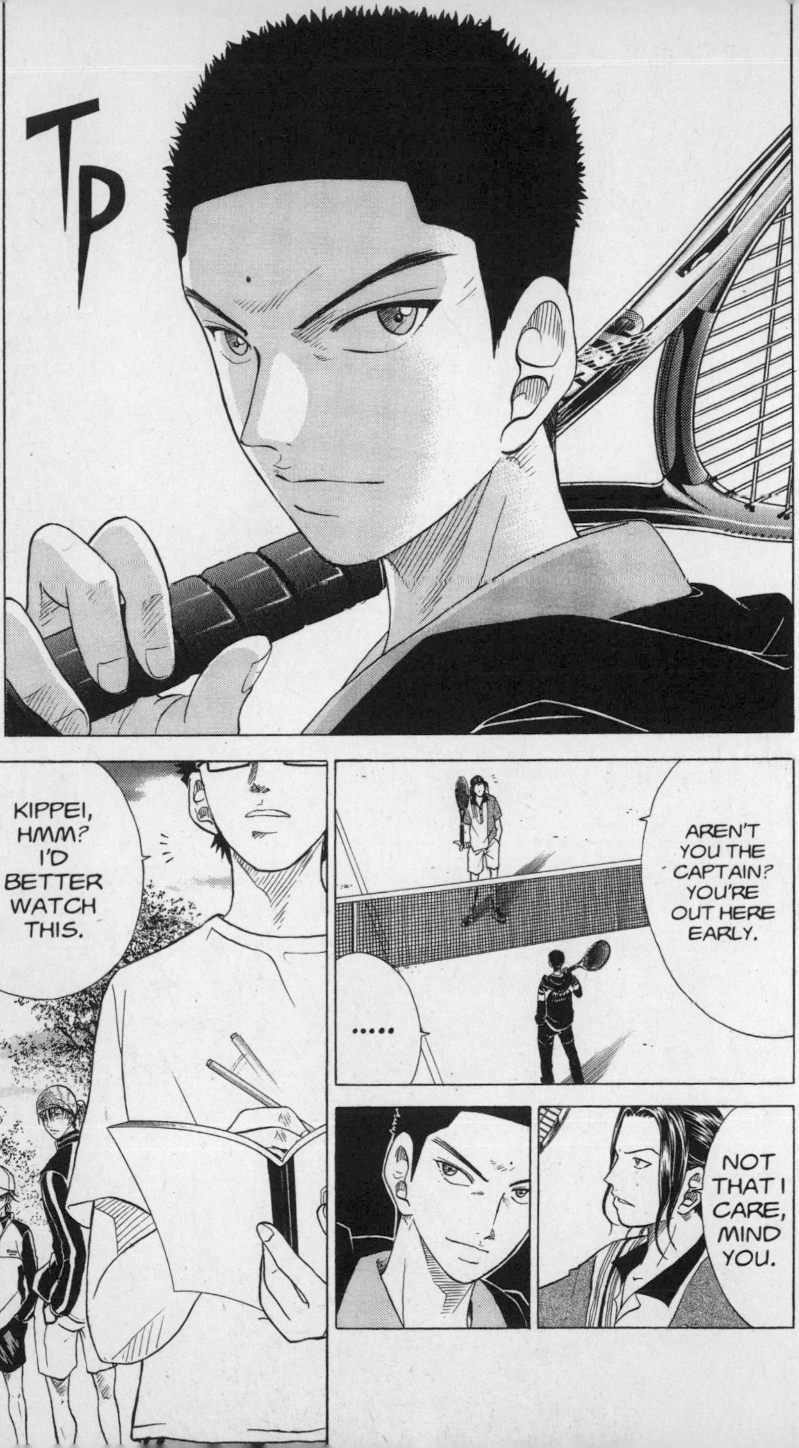
TP
AREN'T YOU THE CAPTAIN? YOU'RE OUT HERE EARLY.
.....
NOT THAT I CARE, MIND YOU.
KIPPEI, HMM? I'D BETTER WATCH THIS.

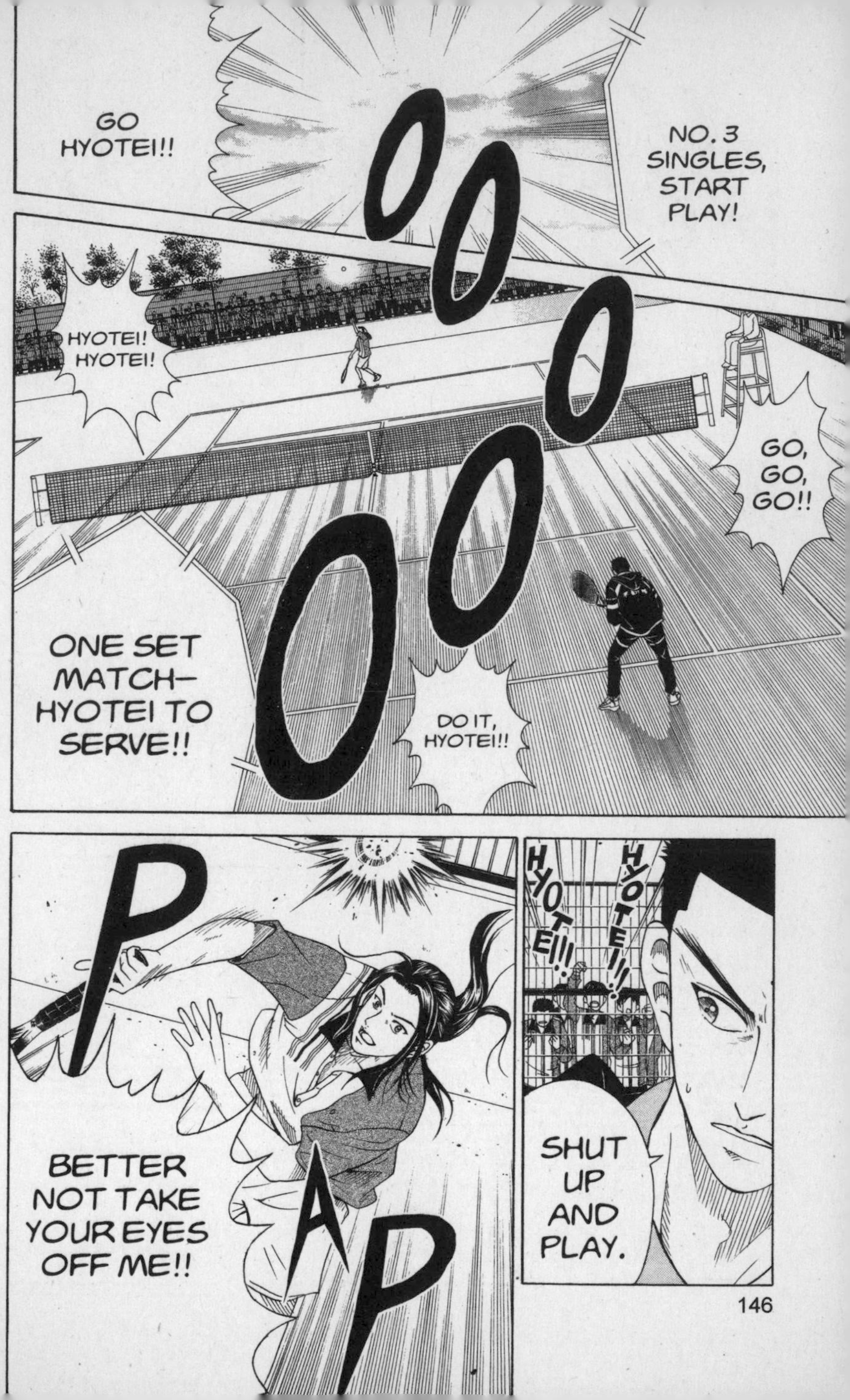
NO. 3 SINGLES, START PLAY!
GO HYOTEI!!
OOOOOO
GO, GO, GO!!
HYOTEI! HYOTEI!
ONE SET MATCH— HYOTEI TO SERVE!!
DO IT, HYOTEI!!
HYOTEI!!!
HYOTEI!!!
SHUT UP AND PLAY.
PAP
BETTER NOT TAKE YOUR EYES OFF ME!!

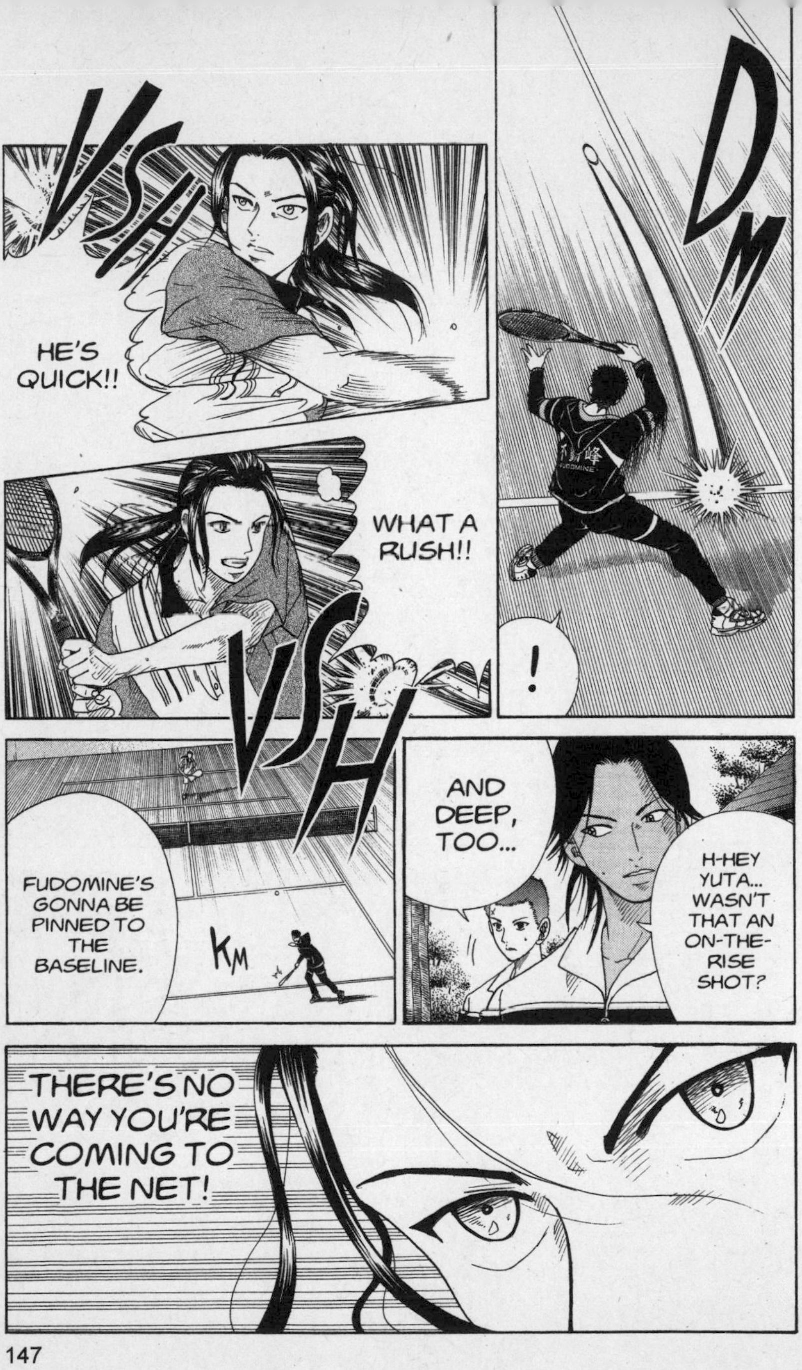
DM
!
VSH
HE'S QUICK!!
WHAT A RUSH!!
VSH
H-HEY YUTA... WASN'T THAT AN ON-THE-RISE SHOT?
AND DEEP, TOO...
FUDOMINE'S GONNA BE PINNED TO THE BASELINE.
KM
THERE'S NO WAY YOU'RE COMING TO THE NET!

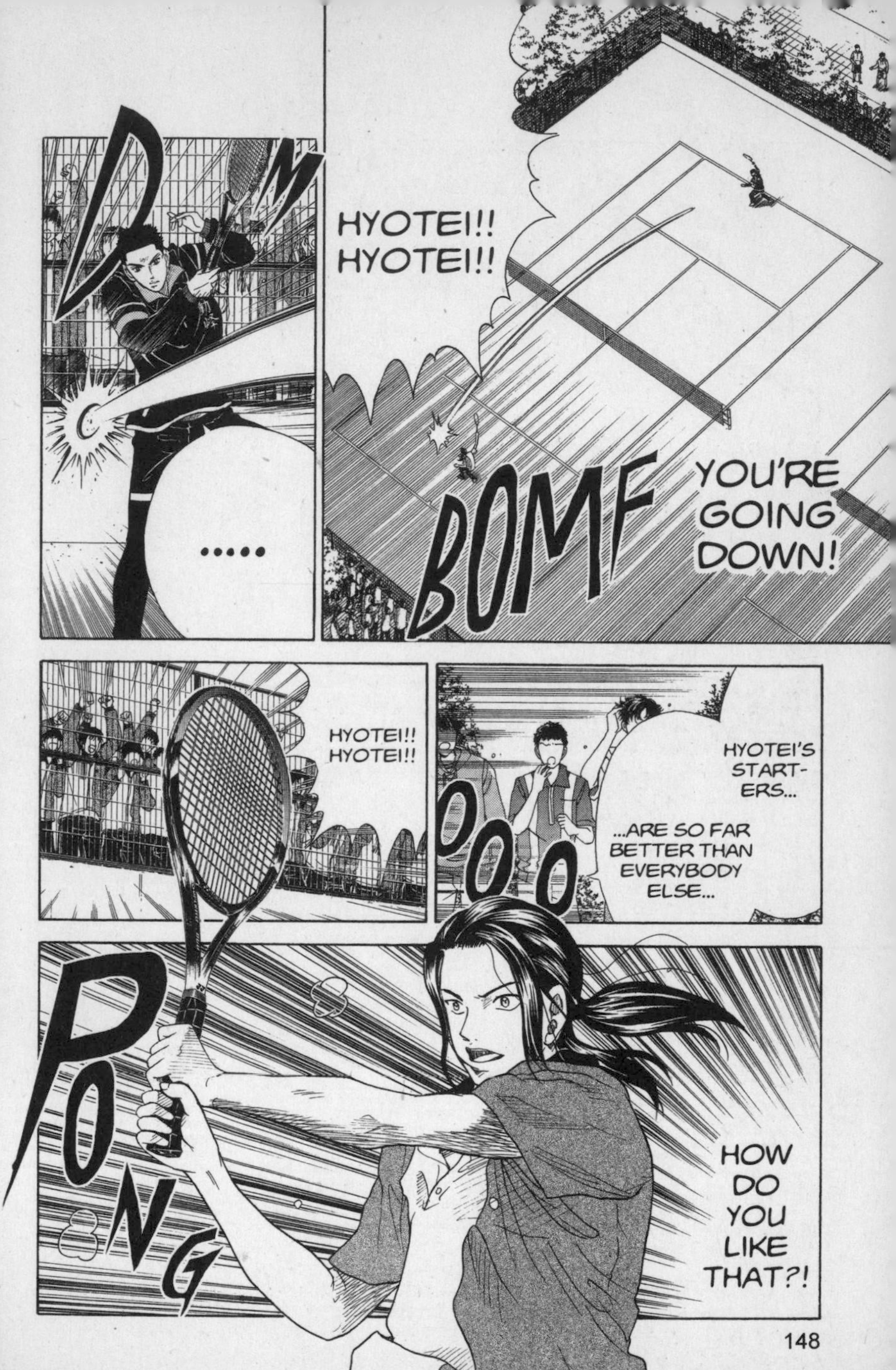
HYOTEI!! HYOTEI!!
BOMF
YOU'RE GOING DOWN!
.....
HYOTEI'S START-ERS...
...ARE SO FAR BETTER THAN EVERYBODY ELSE...
OOO
HYOTEI!! HYOTEI!!
PONG
HOW DO YOU LIKE THAT?!

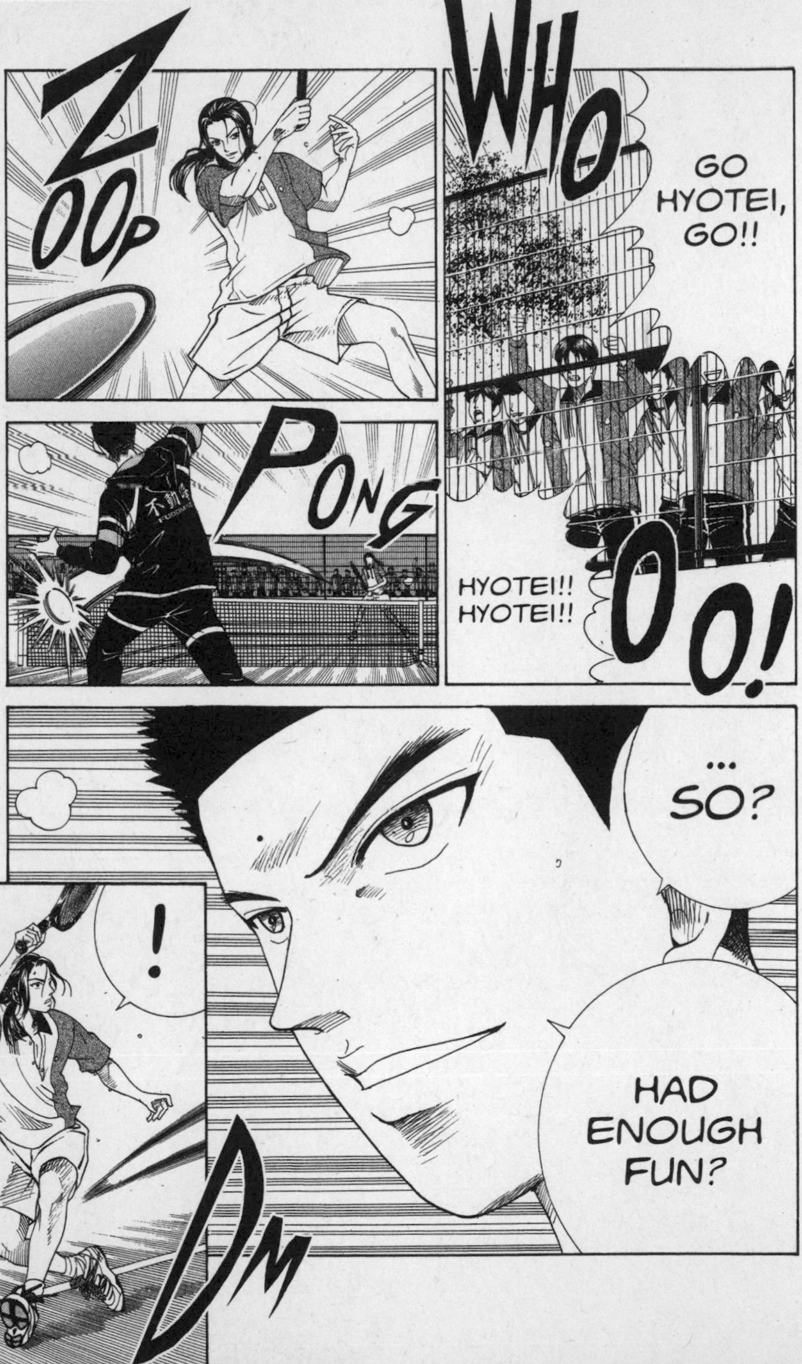
WHOOO!
GO HYOTEI, GO!!
HYOTEI!! HYOTEI!!
ZOOP
PONG
... SO?
HAD ENOUGH FUN?
!
DM

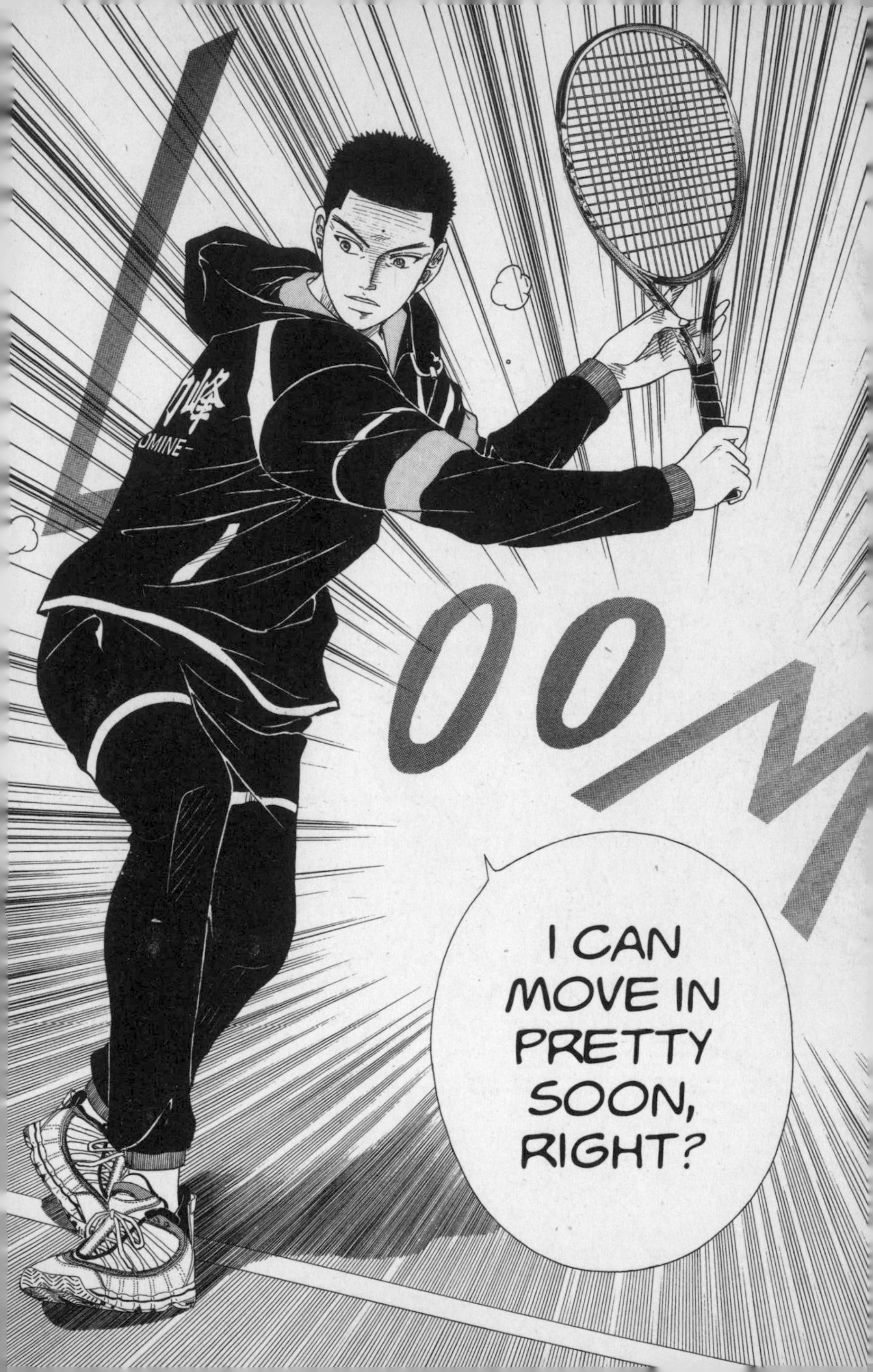

-OMINE-
OOM
I CAN MOVE IN PRETTY SOON, RIGHT?

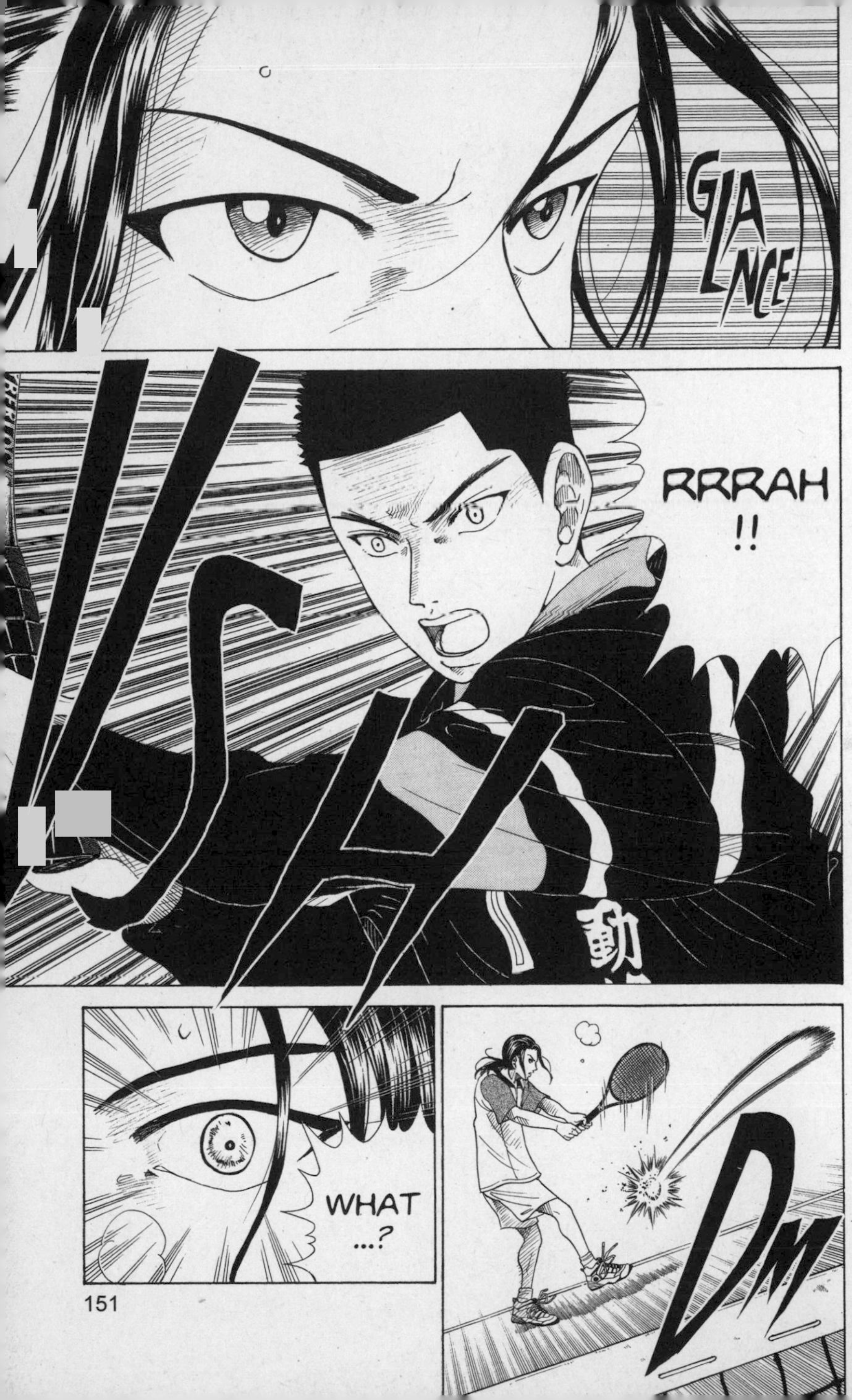
GLANCE
RRRAH !!
WHAT ...?

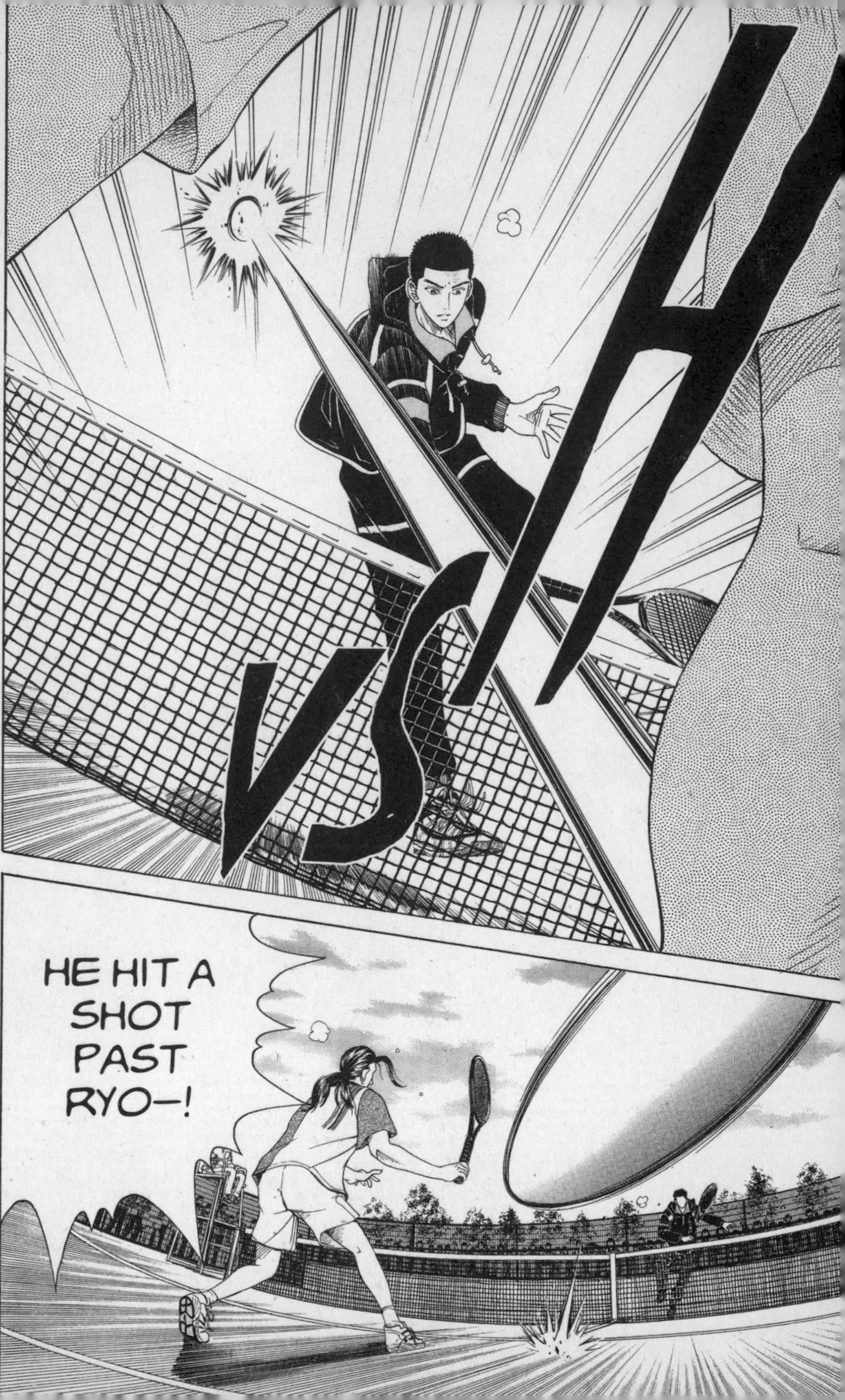

VSH
HE HIT A SHOT PAST RYO--!

READ THIS WAY

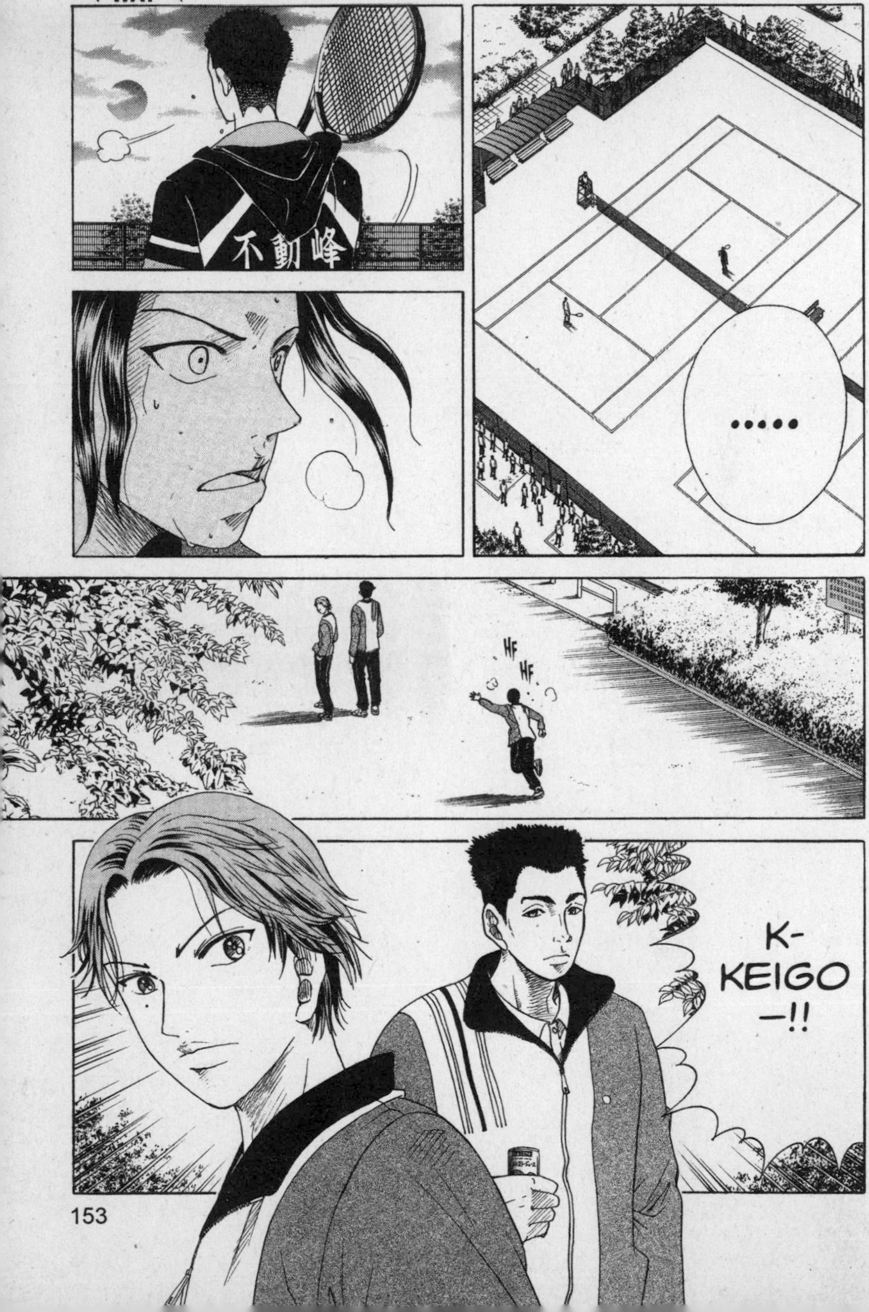
.....
HF HF
K-KEIGO—!!

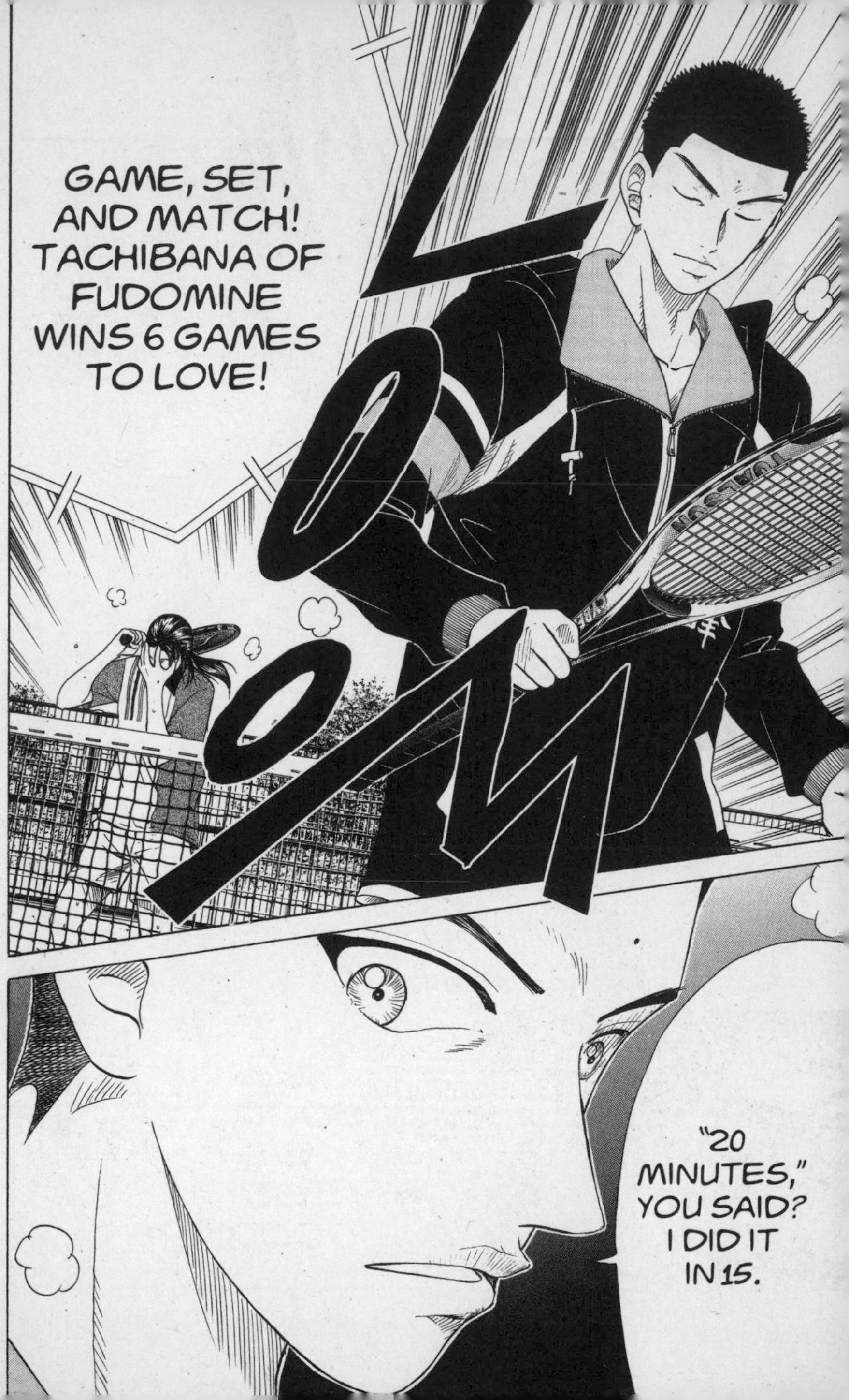
GAME, SET, AND MATCH! TACHIBANA OF FUDOMINE WINS 6 GAMES TO LOVE!
ZOOM
"20 MINUTES," YOU SAID? I DID IT IN 15.

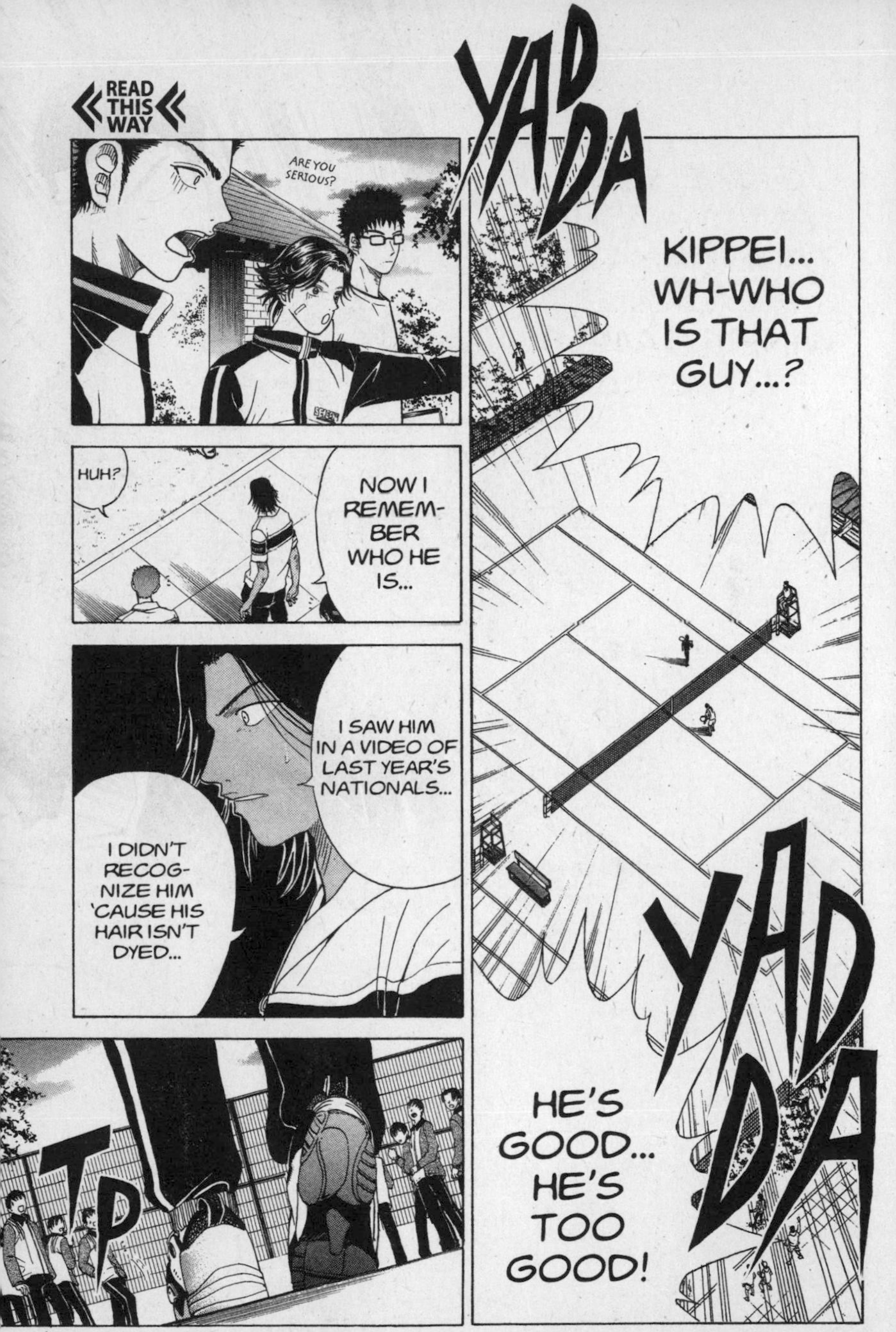
READ THIS WAY
YAD
DA
KIPPEI... WH-WHO IS THAT GUY...?
YAD
DA
HE'S GOOD... HE'S TOO GOOD!
ARE YOU SERIOUS?
NOW I REMEMBER WHO HE IS...
HUH?
I SAW HIM IN A VIDEO OF LAST YEAR'S NATIONALS...
I DIDN'T RECOGNIZE HIM 'CAUSE HIS HAIR ISN'T DYED...
TP

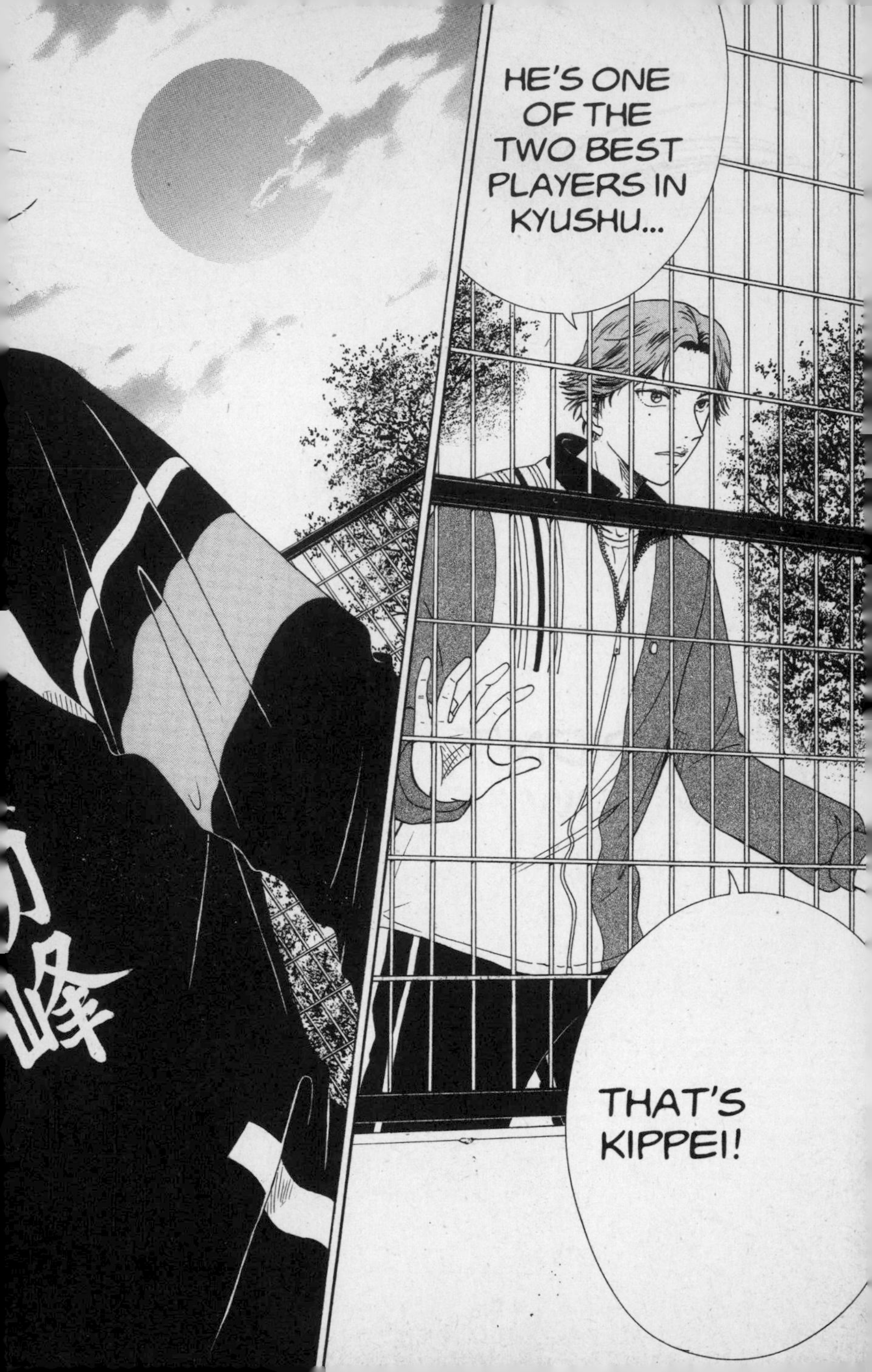
HE'S ONE OF THE TWO BEST PLAYERS IN KYUSHU...
THAT'S KIPPEI!

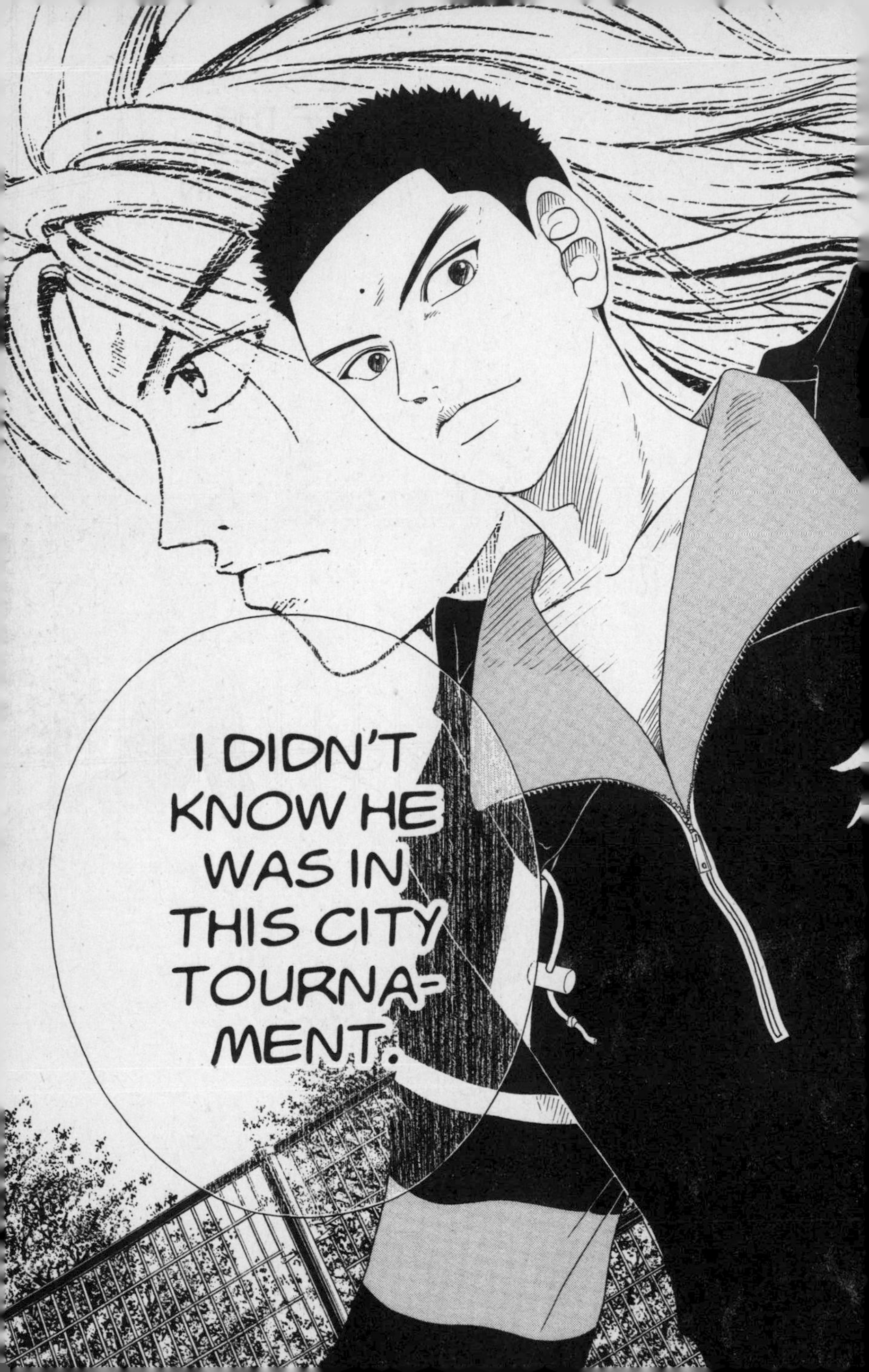
I DIDN'T KNOW HE WAS IN THIS CITY TOURNAMENT.

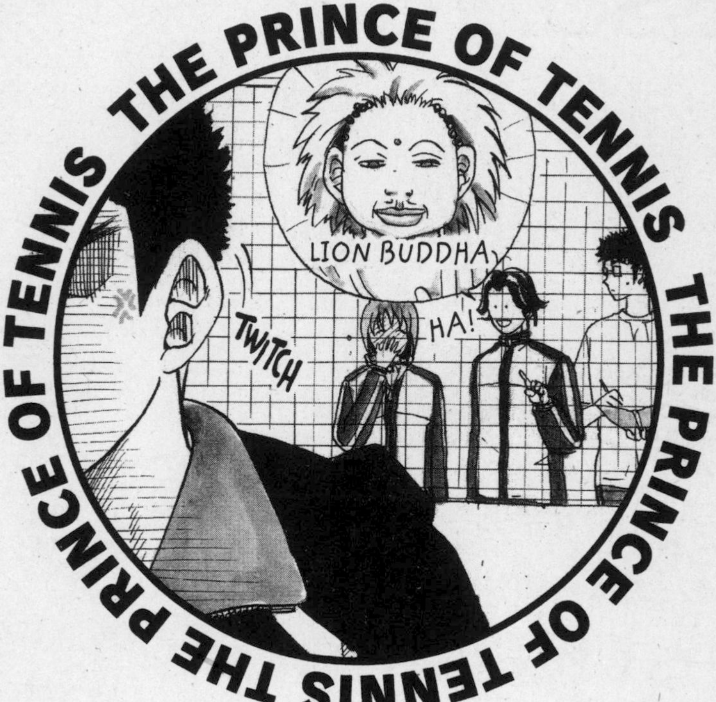
THE PRINCE OF TENNIS THE PRINCE OF TENNIS THE PRINCE OF TENNIS
LION BUDDHA
HA!
TWITCH

GENIUS 78: RENEWED RESOLVE

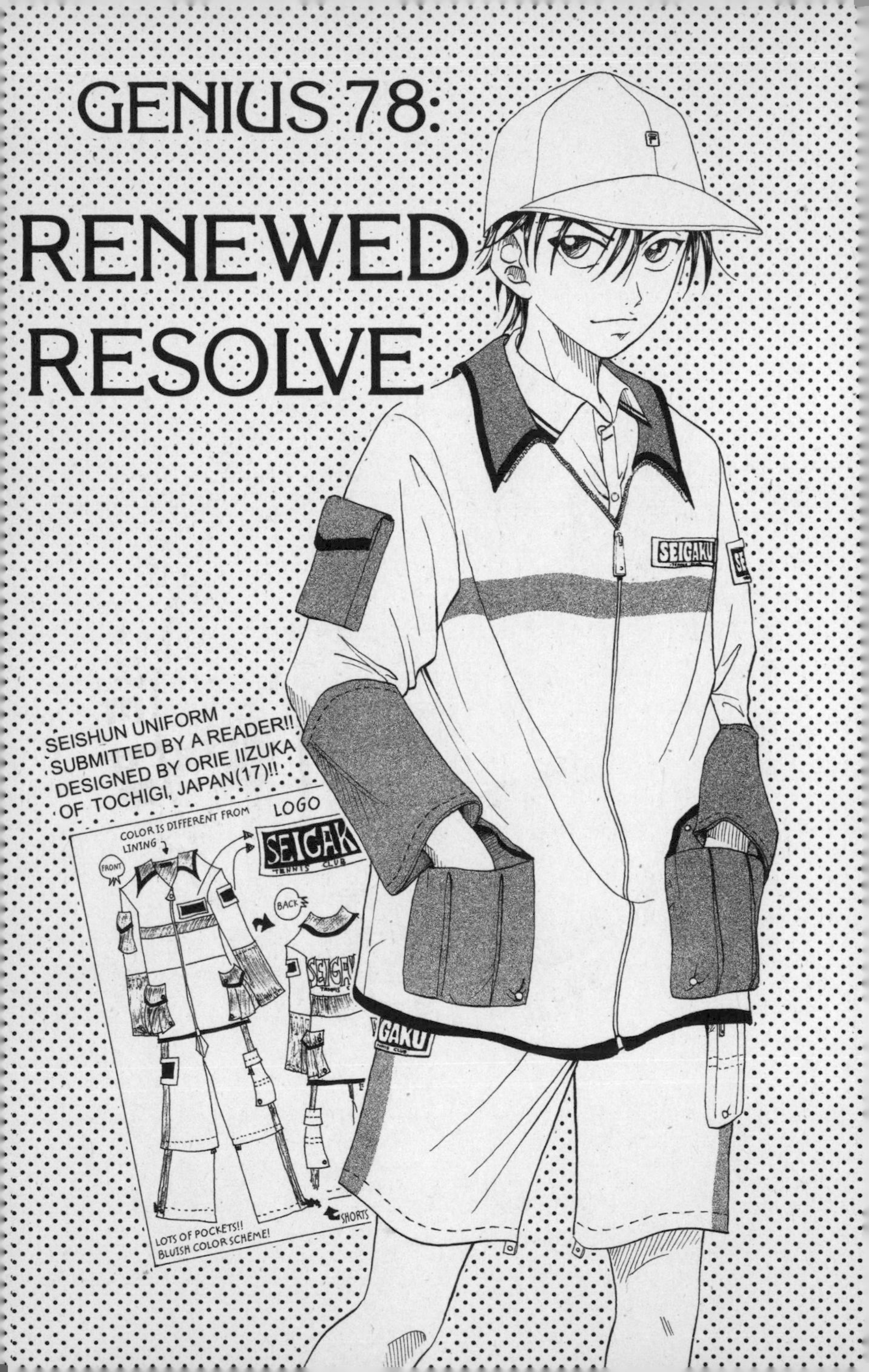
SEIGAKU
SEISHUN UNIFORM SUBMITTED BY A READER!! DESIGNED BY ORIE IIZUKA OF TOCHIGI, JAPAN(17)!!
LOGO
COLOR IS DIFFERENT FROM LINING
SEIGAK TENNIS CLUB
FRONT
BACK
SHORTS
LOTS OF POCKETS!! BLUISH COLOR SCHEME!

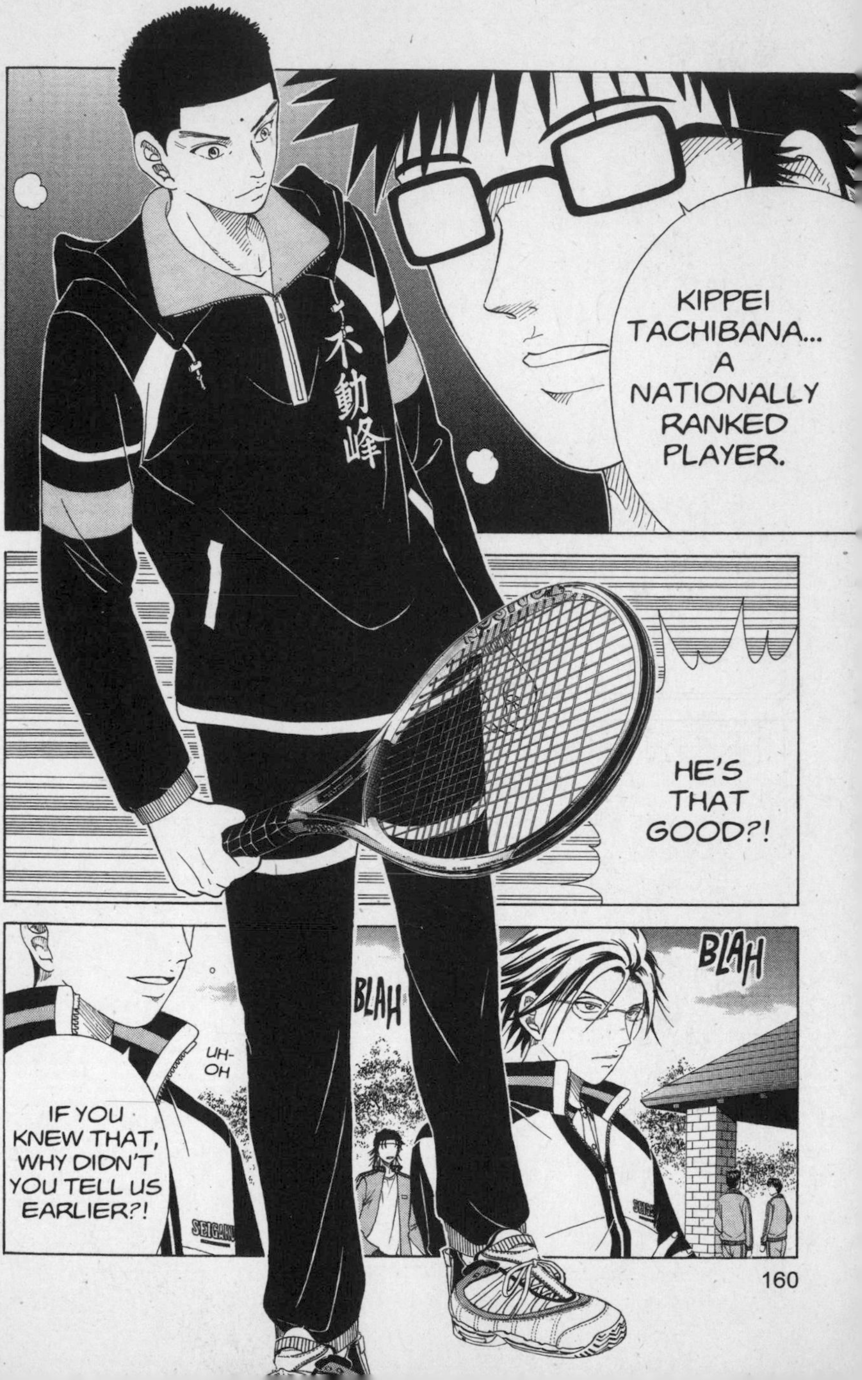
KIPPEI TACHIBANA... A NATIONALLY RANKED PLAYER.
不動峰
HE'S THAT GOOD?!
BLAH
BLAH
UH-OH
IF YOU KNEW THAT, WHY DIDN'T YOU TELL US EARLIER?!
SEIGAKU

READ THIS WAY

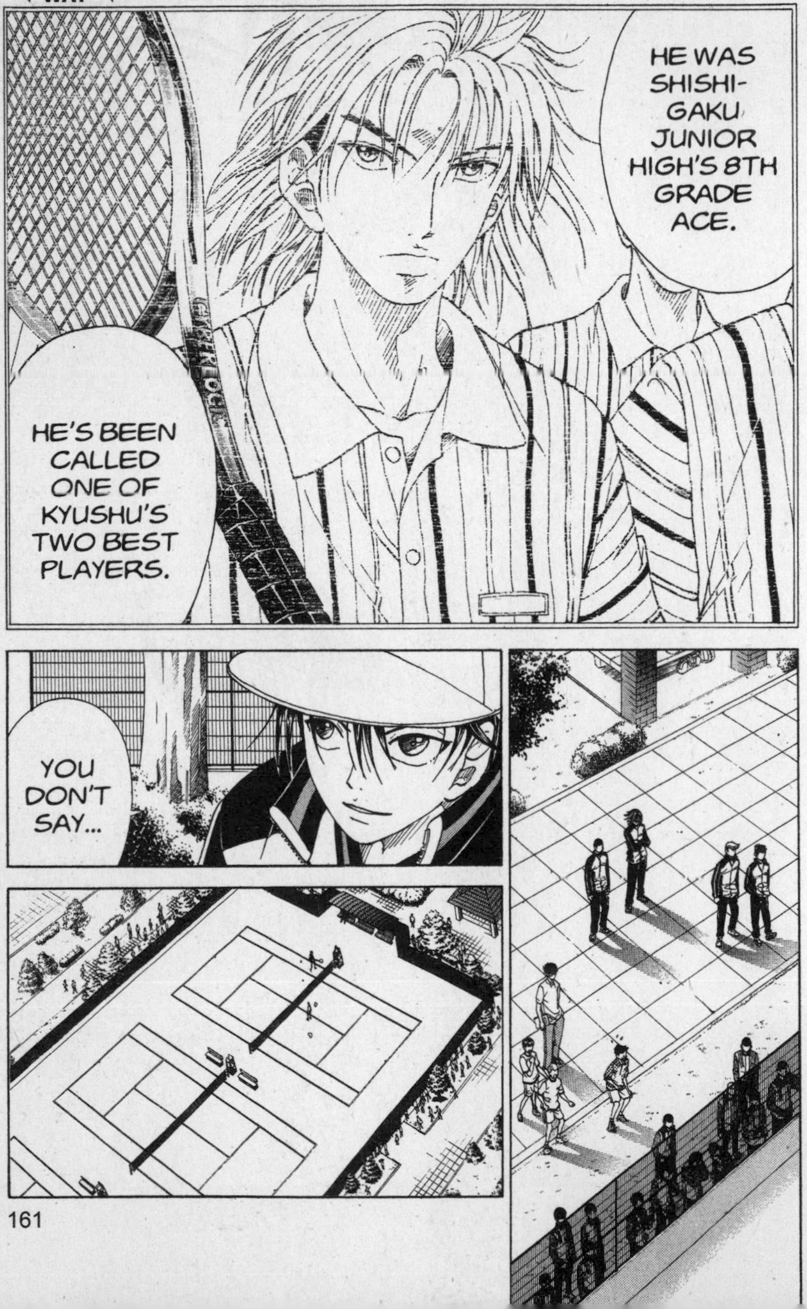
HE WAS SHISHI-GAKU JUNIOR HIGH'S 8TH GRADE ACE.
HE'S BEEN CALLED ONE OF KYUSHU'S TWO BEST PLAYERS.
YOU DON'T SAY...

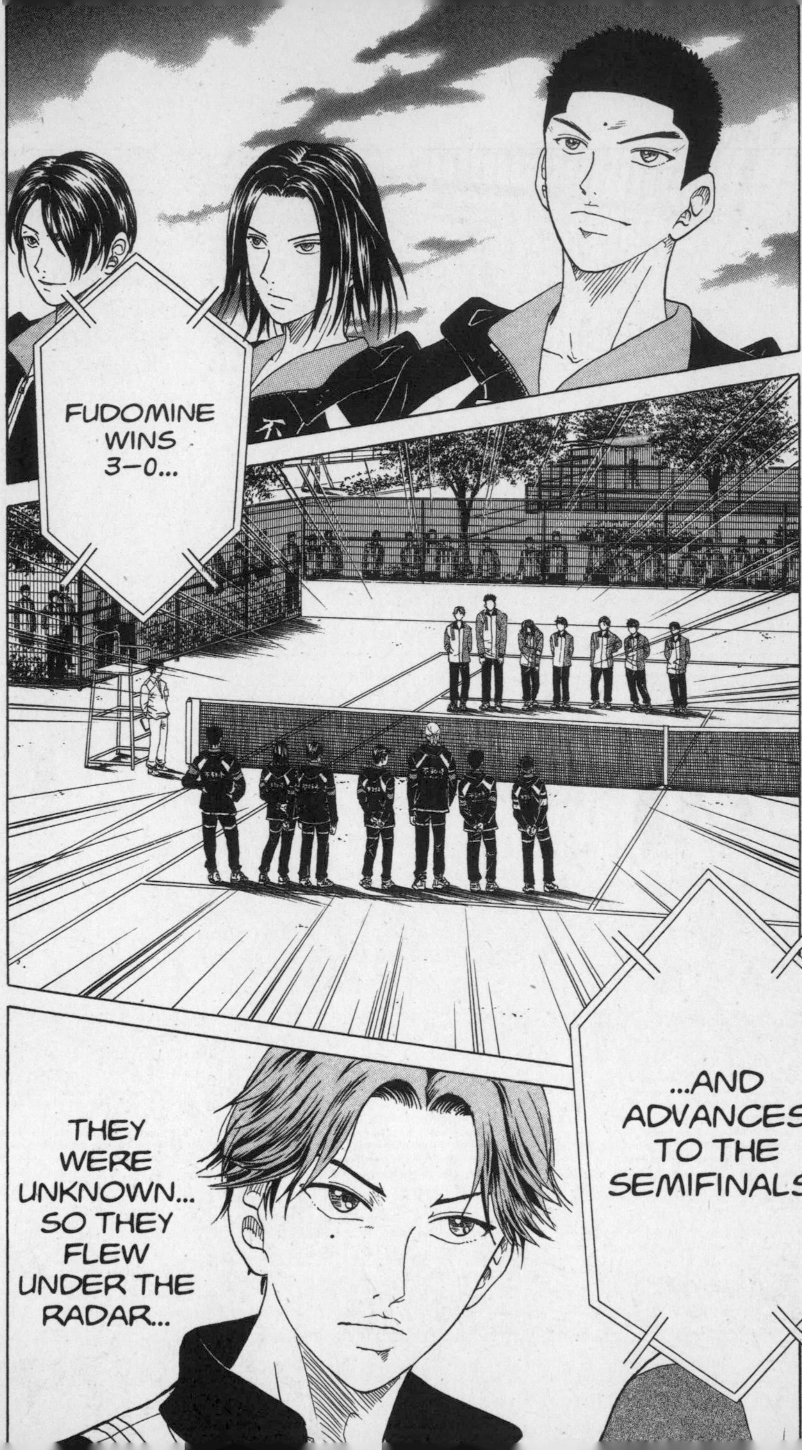
FUDOMINE WINS 3–0...
...AND ADVANCES TO THE SEMIFINALS!
THEY WERE UNKNOWN... SO THEY FLEW UNDER THE RADAR...

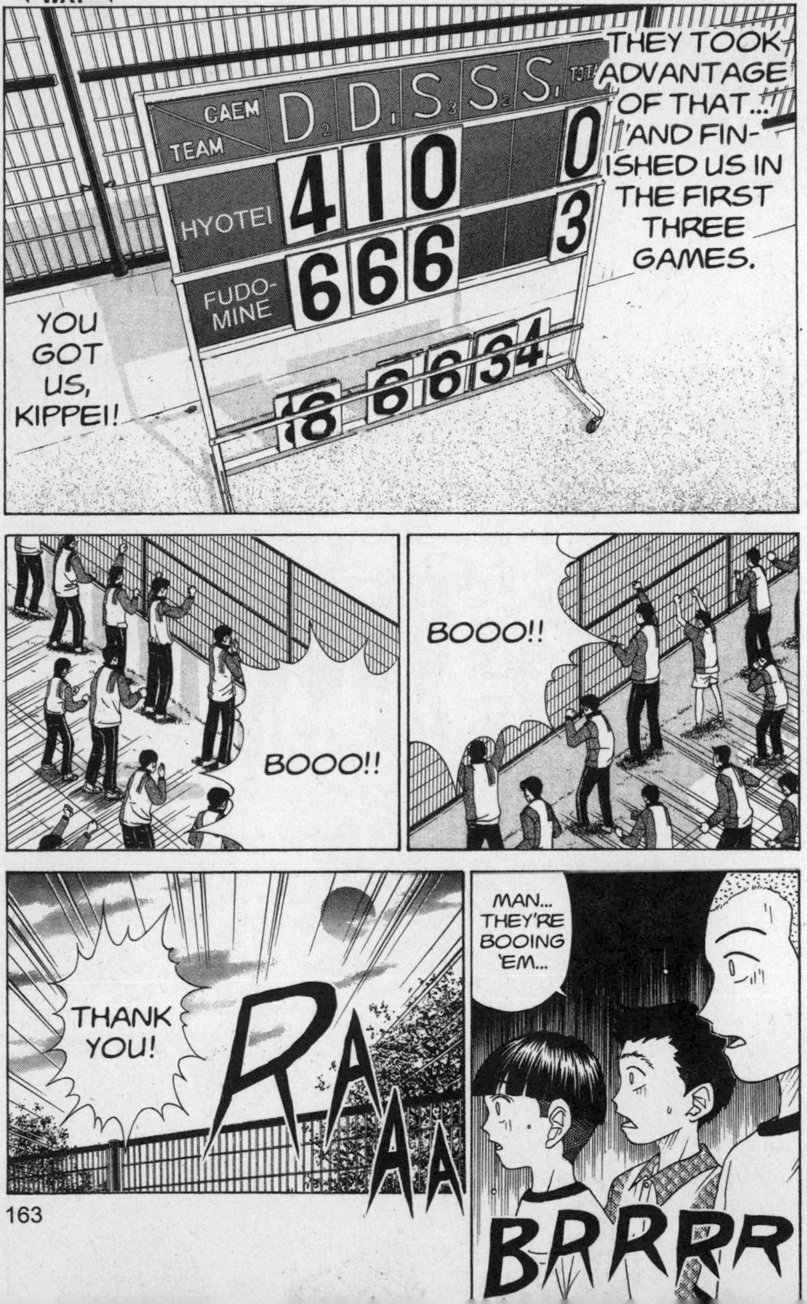
THEY TOOK ADVANTAGE OF THAT...!! AND FINISHED US IN THE FIRST THREE GAMES.
TEAM
HYOTEI
FUDO-MINE
YOU GOT US, KIPPEI!
BOOO!!
BOOO!!
MAN... THEY'RE BOOING 'EM...
BRRRR
THANK YOU!
RAAAA

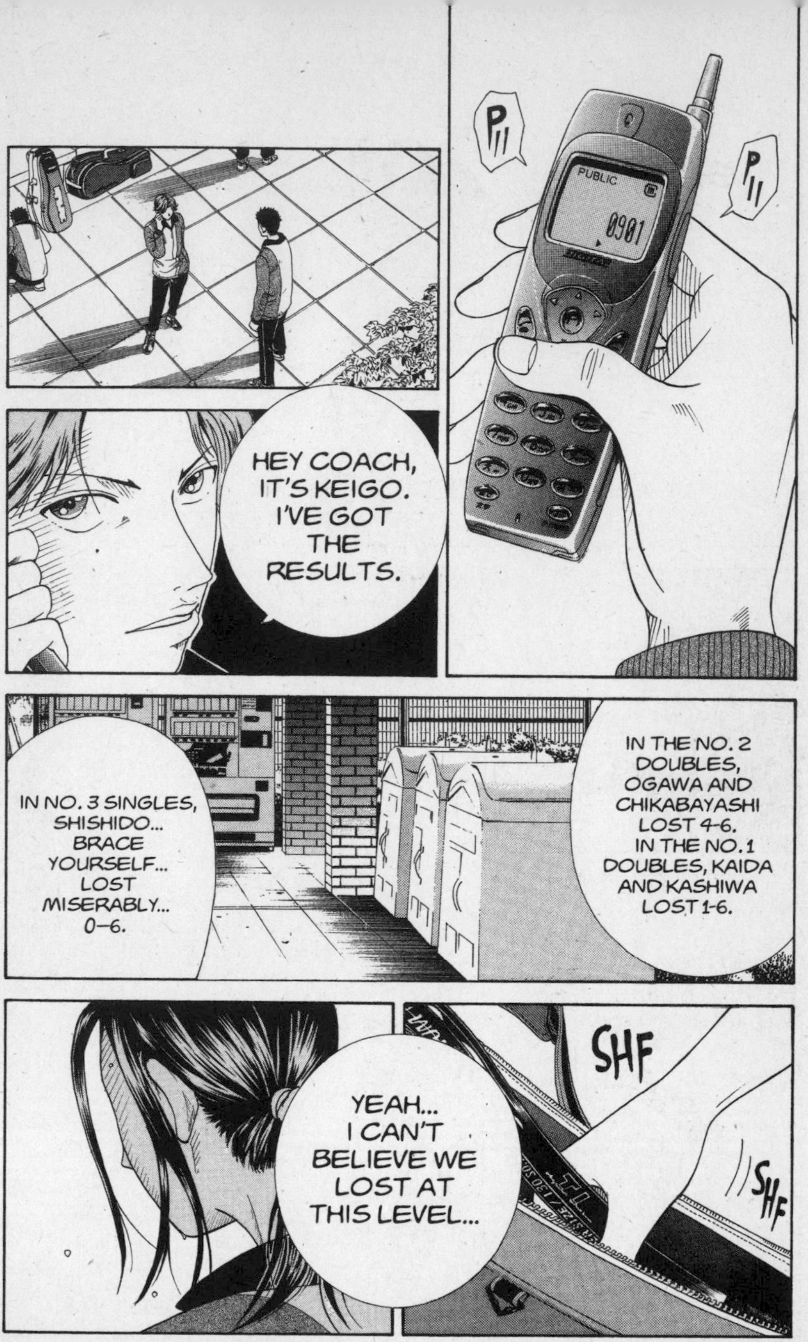
PII
PII
PUBLIC
0901
HEY COACH, IT'S KEIGO. I'VE GOT THE RESULTS.
IN THE NO. 2 DOUBLES, OGAWA AND CHIKABAYASHI LOST 4-6. IN THE NO. 1 DOUBLES, KAIDA AND KASHIWA LOST 1-6.
IN NO. 3 SINGLES, SHISHIDO... BRACE YOURSELF... LOST MISERABLY... 0–6.
SHF
SHF
YEAH... I CAN'T BELIEVE WE LOST AT THIS LEVEL...

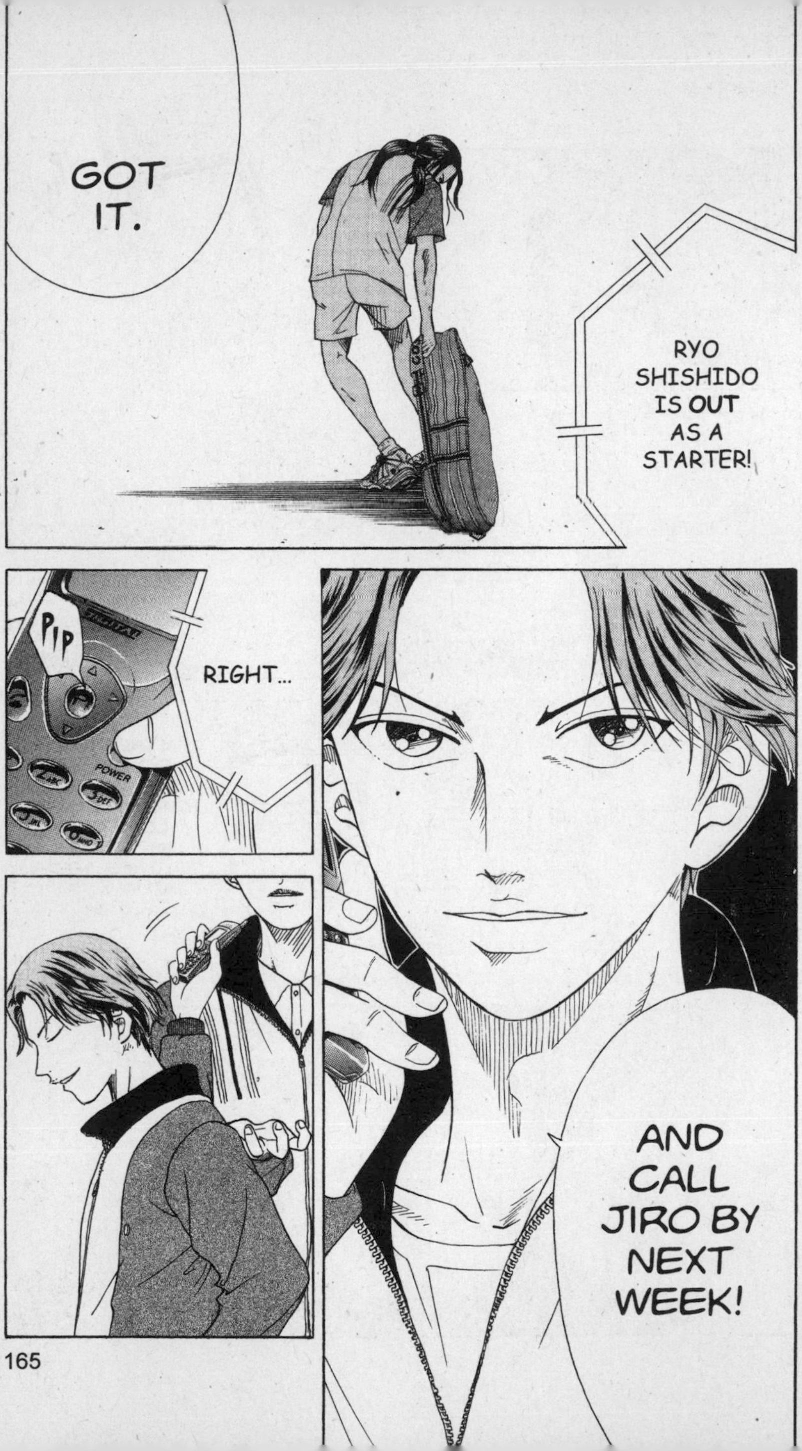
RYO SHISHIDO IS OUT AS A STARTER!
GOT IT.
AND CALL JIRO BY NEXT WEEK!
PIP
RIGHT...

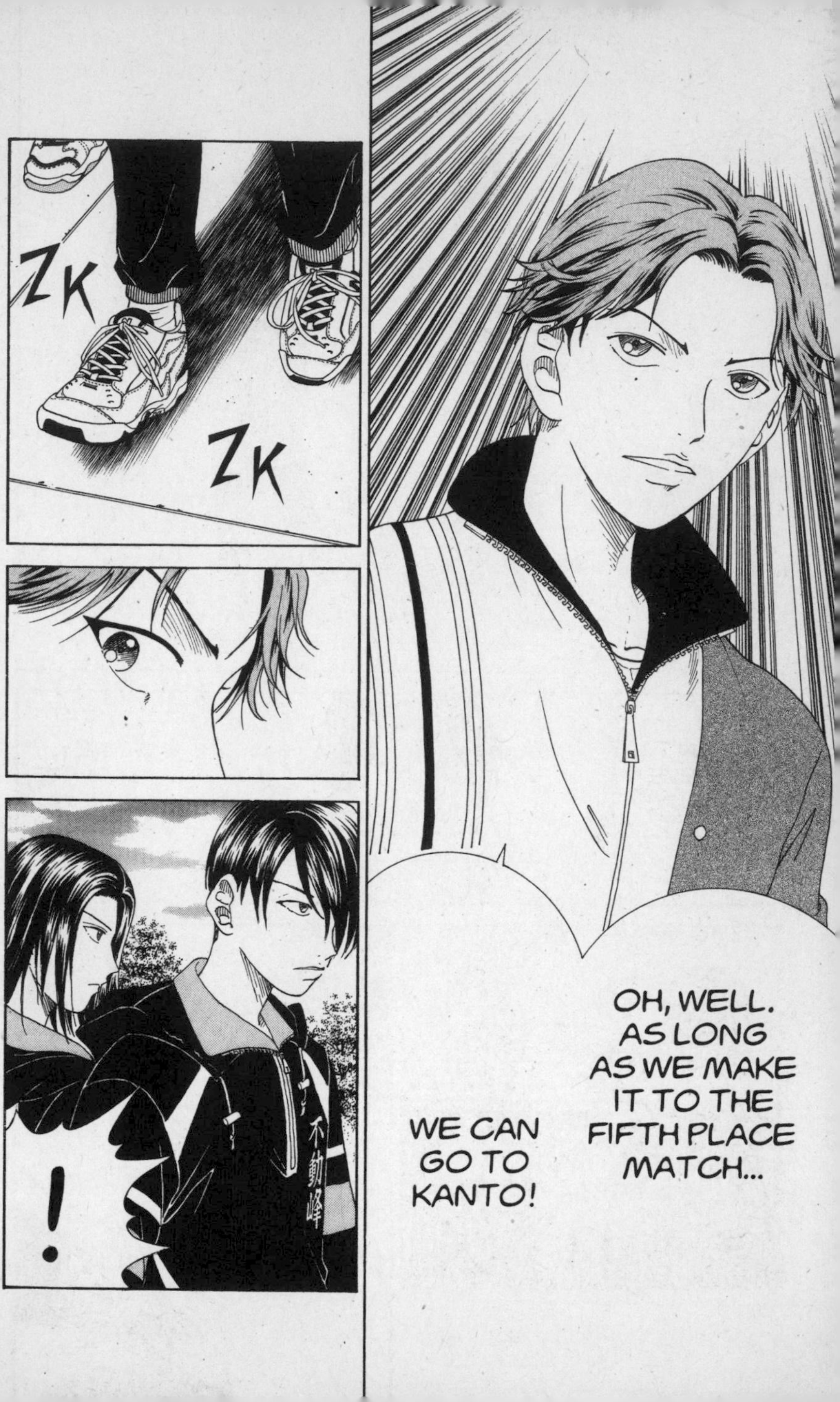
OH, WELL. AS LONG AS WE MAKE IT TO THE FIFTH PLACE MATCH...
WE CAN GO TO KANTO!
ZK
ZK
!
不動峰

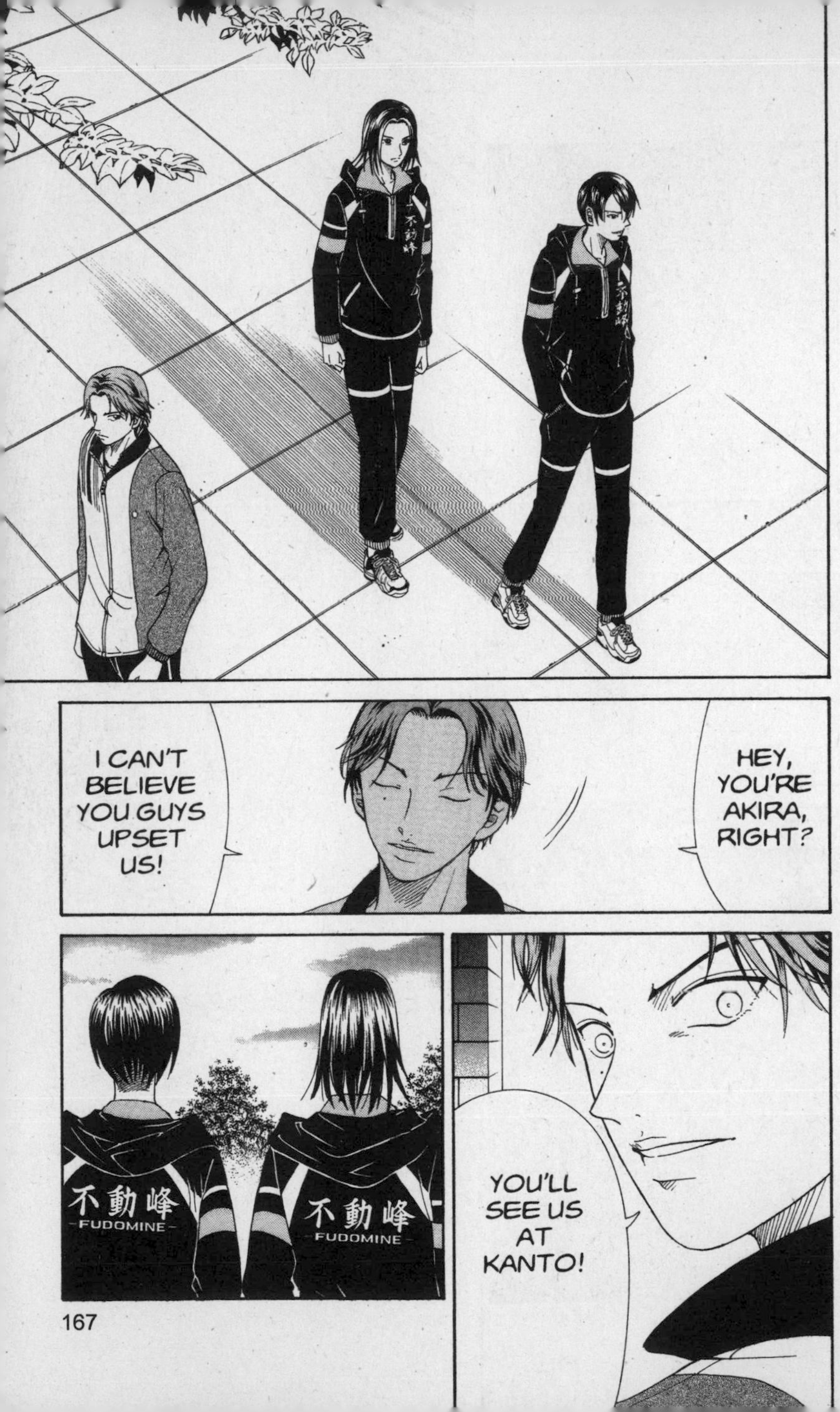

HEY, YOU'RE AKIRA, RIGHT?
I CAN'T BELIEVE YOU GUYS UPSET US!
YOU'LL SEE US AT KANTO!
不動峰 -FUDOMINE-
不動峰 -FUDOMINE-

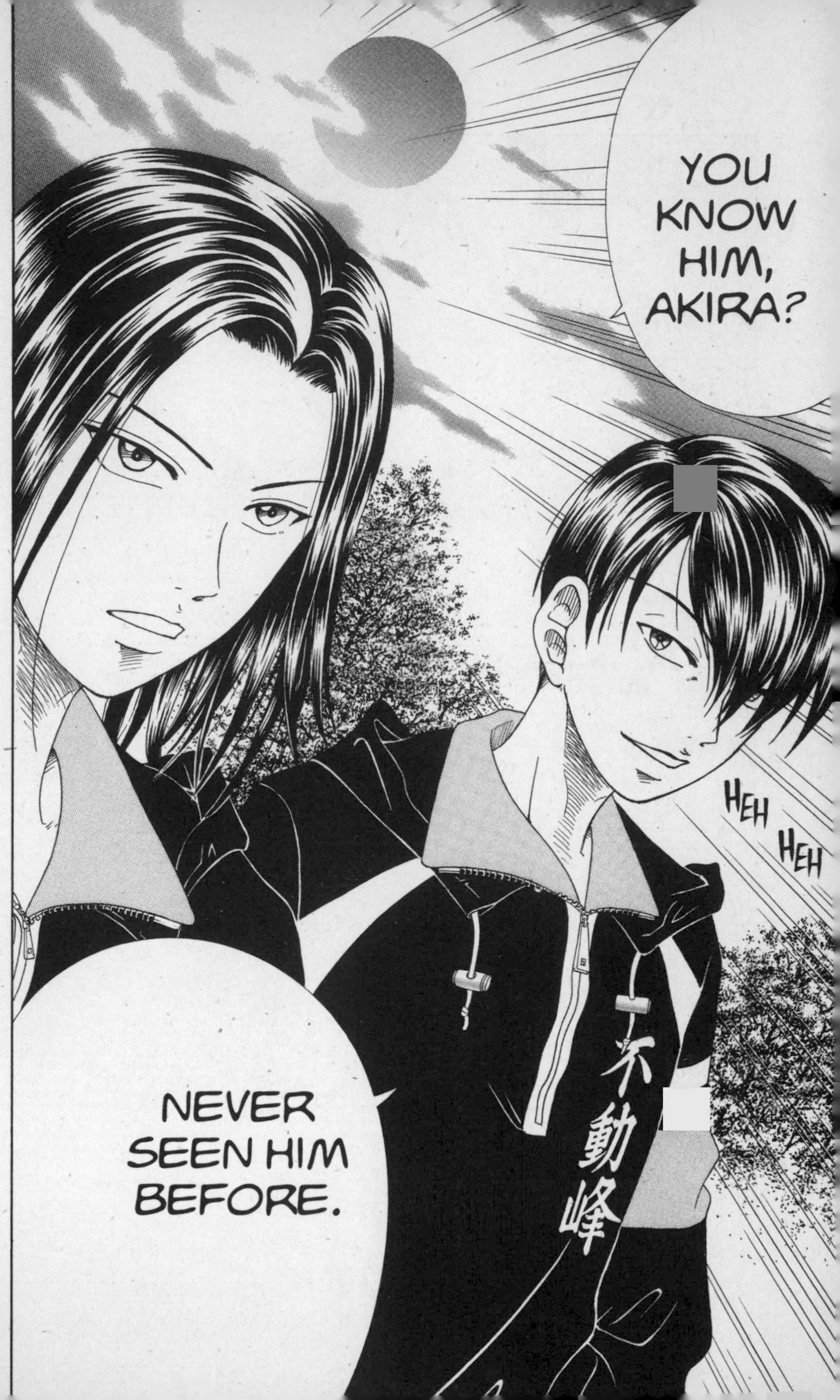
YOU KNOW HIM, AKIRA?
HEH HEH
不動峰
NEVER SEEN HIM BEFORE.

READ THIS WAY

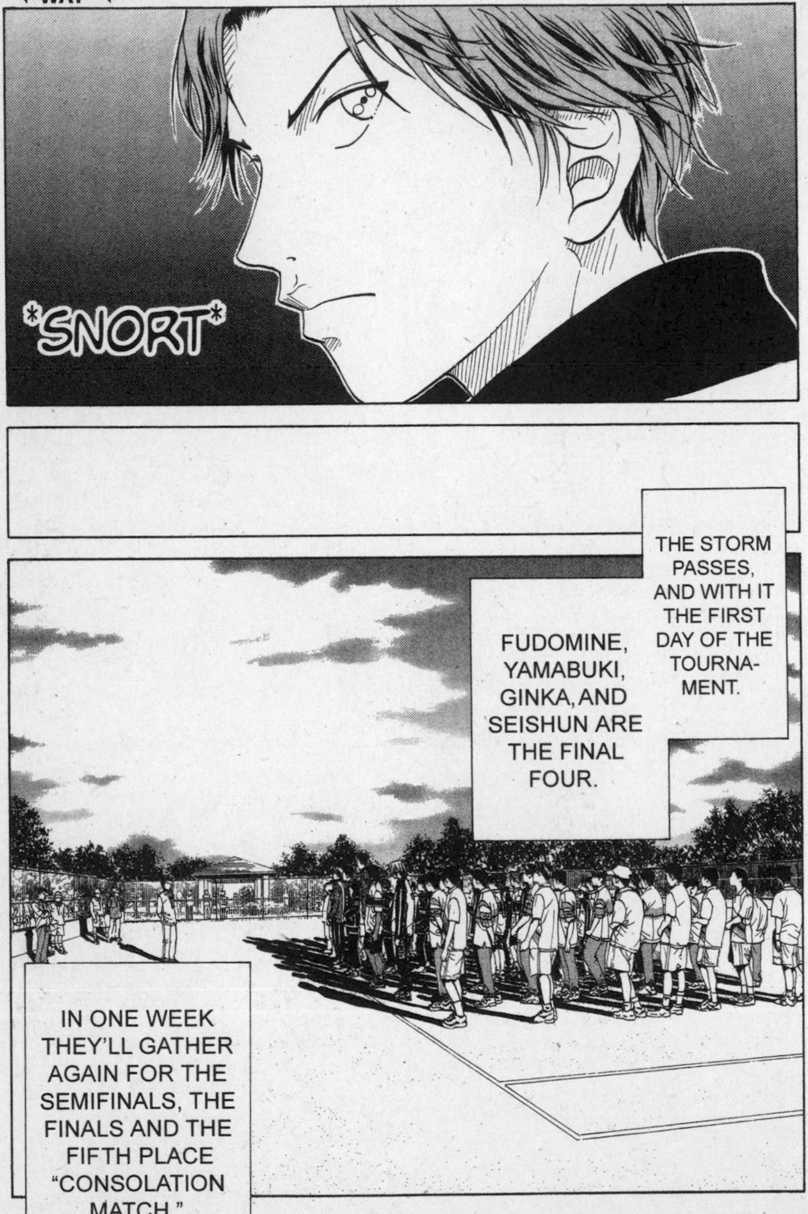
SNORT
THE STORM PASSES, AND WITH IT THE FIRST DAY OF THE TOURNA-MENT.
FUDOMINE, YAMABUKI, GINKA, AND SEISHUN ARE THE FINAL FOUR.
IN ONE WEEK THEY'LL GATHER AGAIN FOR THE SEMIFINALS, THE FINALS AND THE FIFTH PLACE "CONSOLATION MATCH."

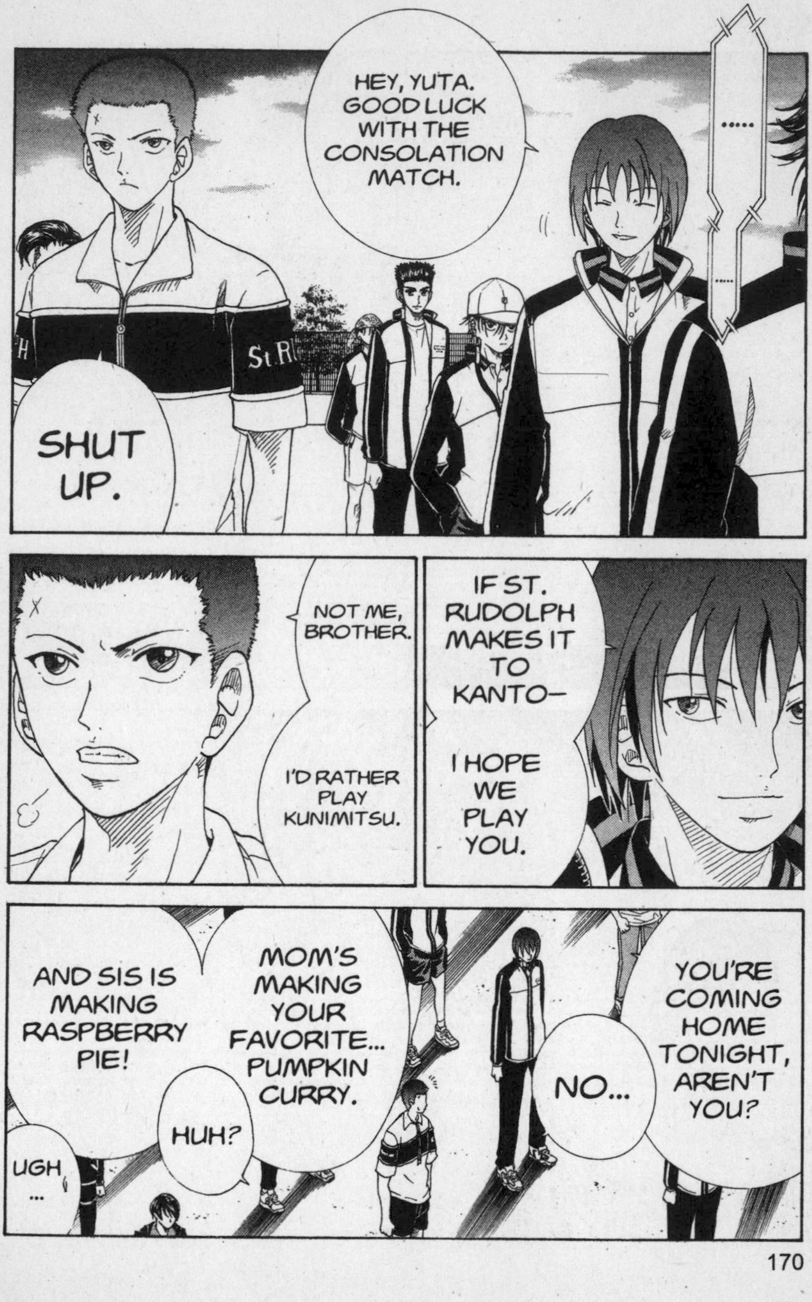
.....
.....
HEY, YUTA. GOOD LUCK WITH THE CONSOLATION MATCH.
SHUT UP.
IF ST. RUDOLPH MAKES IT TO KANTO—
I HOPE WE PLAY YOU.
NOT ME, BROTHER.
I'D RATHER PLAY KUNIMITSU.
YOU'RE COMING HOME TONIGHT, AREN'T YOU?
NO...
MOM'S MAKING YOUR FAVORITE... PUMPKIN CURRY.
HUH?
AND SIS IS MAKING RASPBERRY PIE!
UGH...

READ THIS WAY

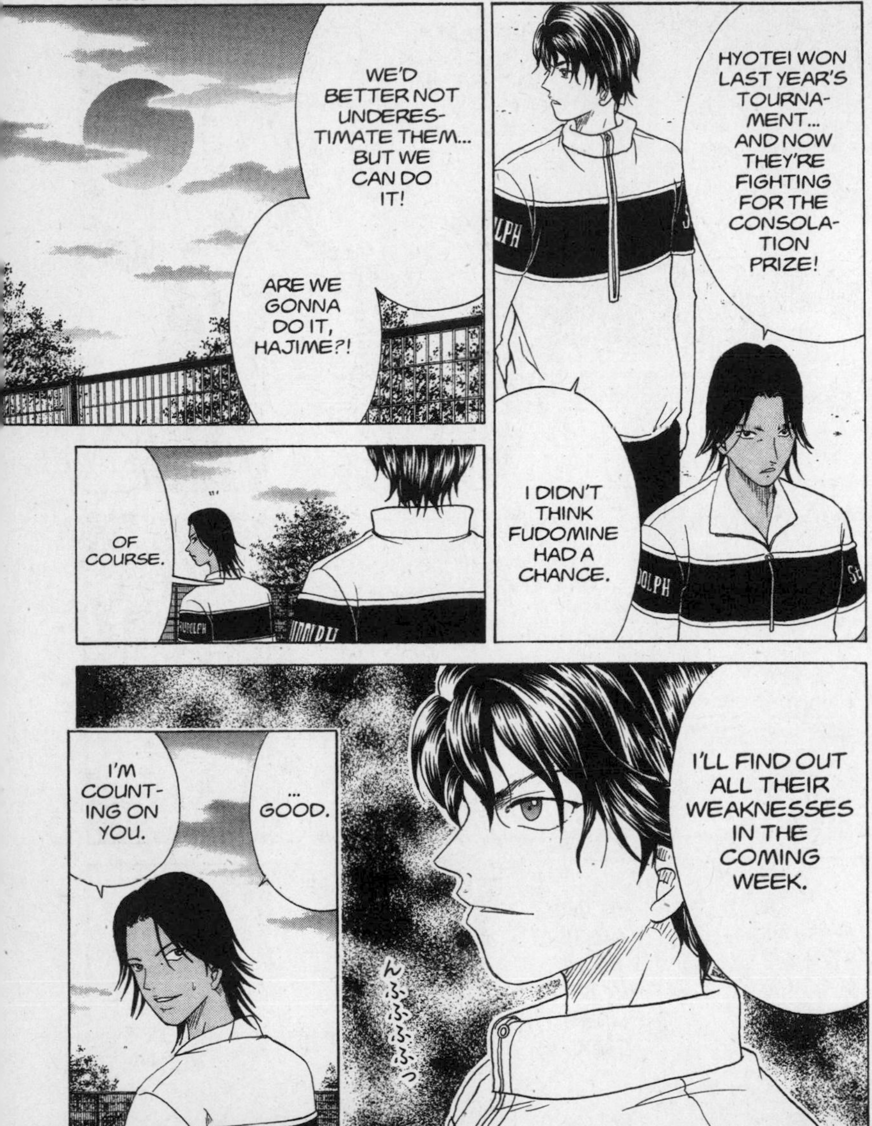
HYOTEI WON LAST YEAR'S TOURNAMENT... AND NOW THEY'RE FIGHTING FOR THE CONSOLATION PRIZE!
I DIDN'T THINK FUDOMINE HAD A CHANCE.
WE'D BETTER NOT UNDERESTIMATE THEM... BUT WE CAN DO IT!
ARE WE GONNA DO IT, HAJIME?!
OF COURSE.
I'LL FIND OUT ALL THEIR WEAKNESSES IN THE COMING WEEK.
んふふふっ
...GOOD.
I'M COUNTING ON YOU.

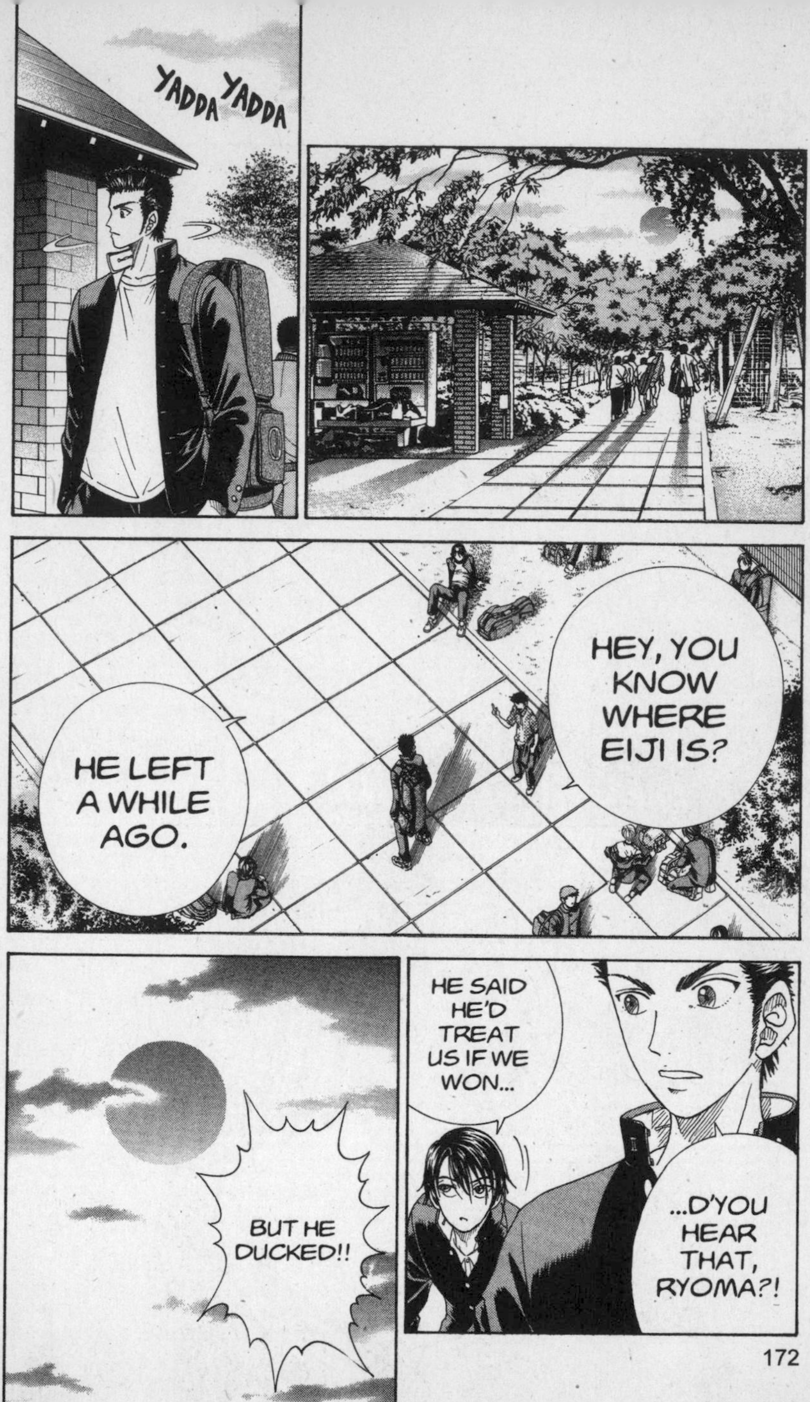
YADDA YADDA
HEY, YOU KNOW WHERE EIJI IS?
HE LEFT A WHILE AGO.
HE SAID HE'D TREAT US IF WE WON...
...D'YOU HEAR THAT, RYOMA?!
BUT HE DUCKED!!

READ THIS WAY

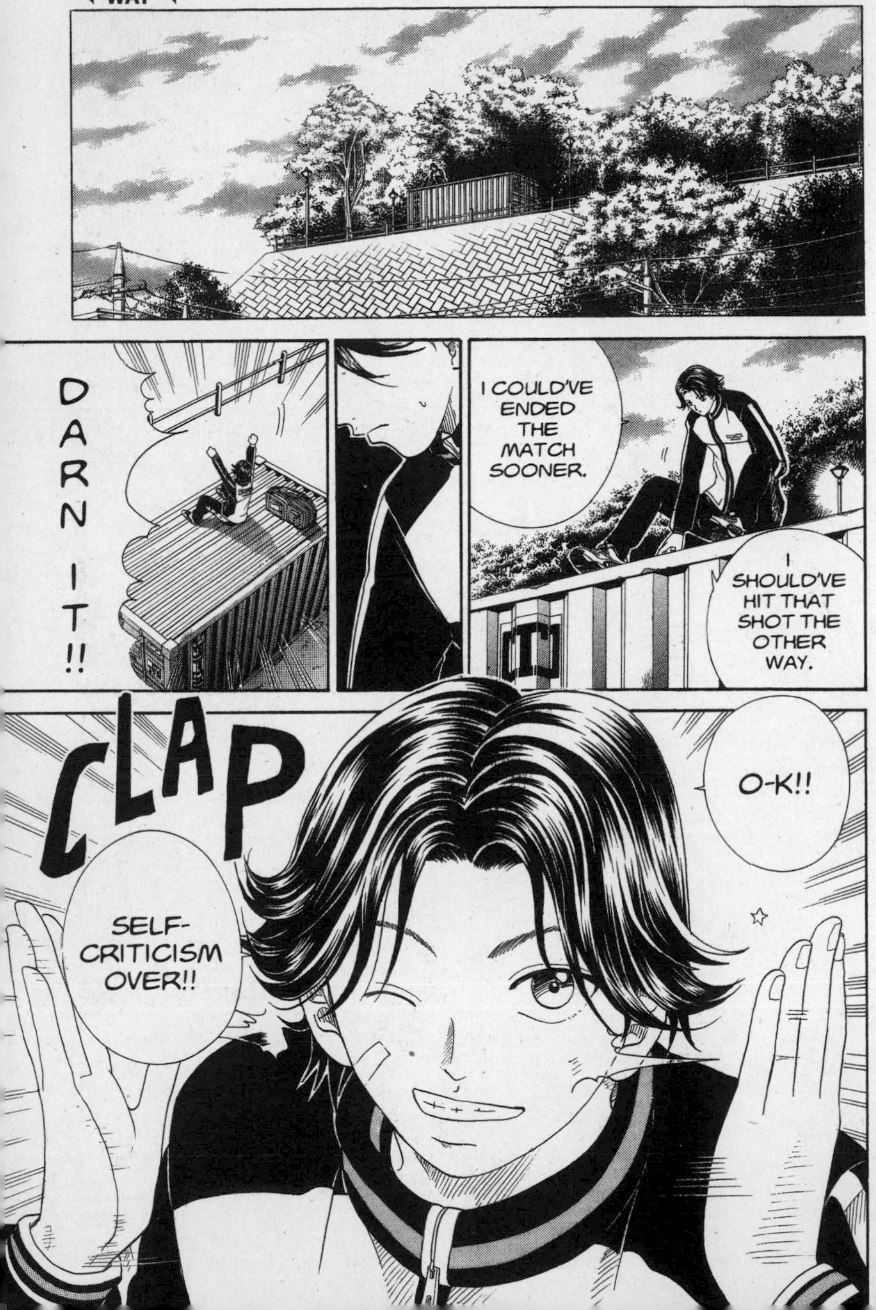
I COULD'VE ENDED THE MATCH SOONER.
I SHOULD'VE HIT THAT SHOT THE OTHER WAY.
DARN IT!!
O-K!!
CLAP
SELF-CRITICISM OVER!!

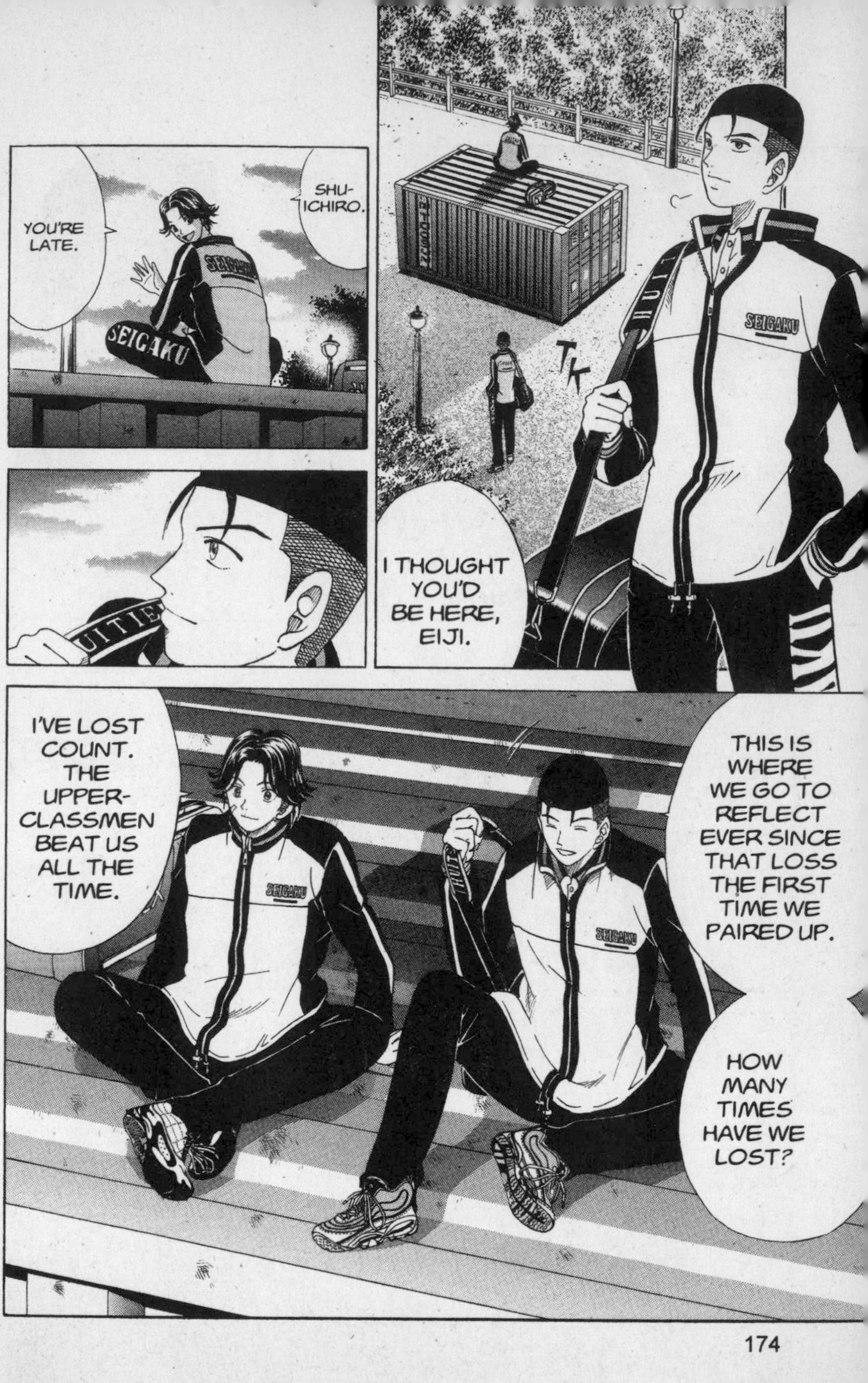
TK
I THOUGHT YOU'D BE HERE, EIJI.
SHU-ICHIRO.
YOU'RE LATE.
THIS IS WHERE WE GO TO REFLECT EVER SINCE THAT LOSS THE FIRST TIME WE PAIRED UP.
HOW MANY TIMES HAVE WE LOST?
I'VE LOST COUNT. THE UPPER-CLASSMEN BEAT US ALL THE TIME.

READ THIS WAY

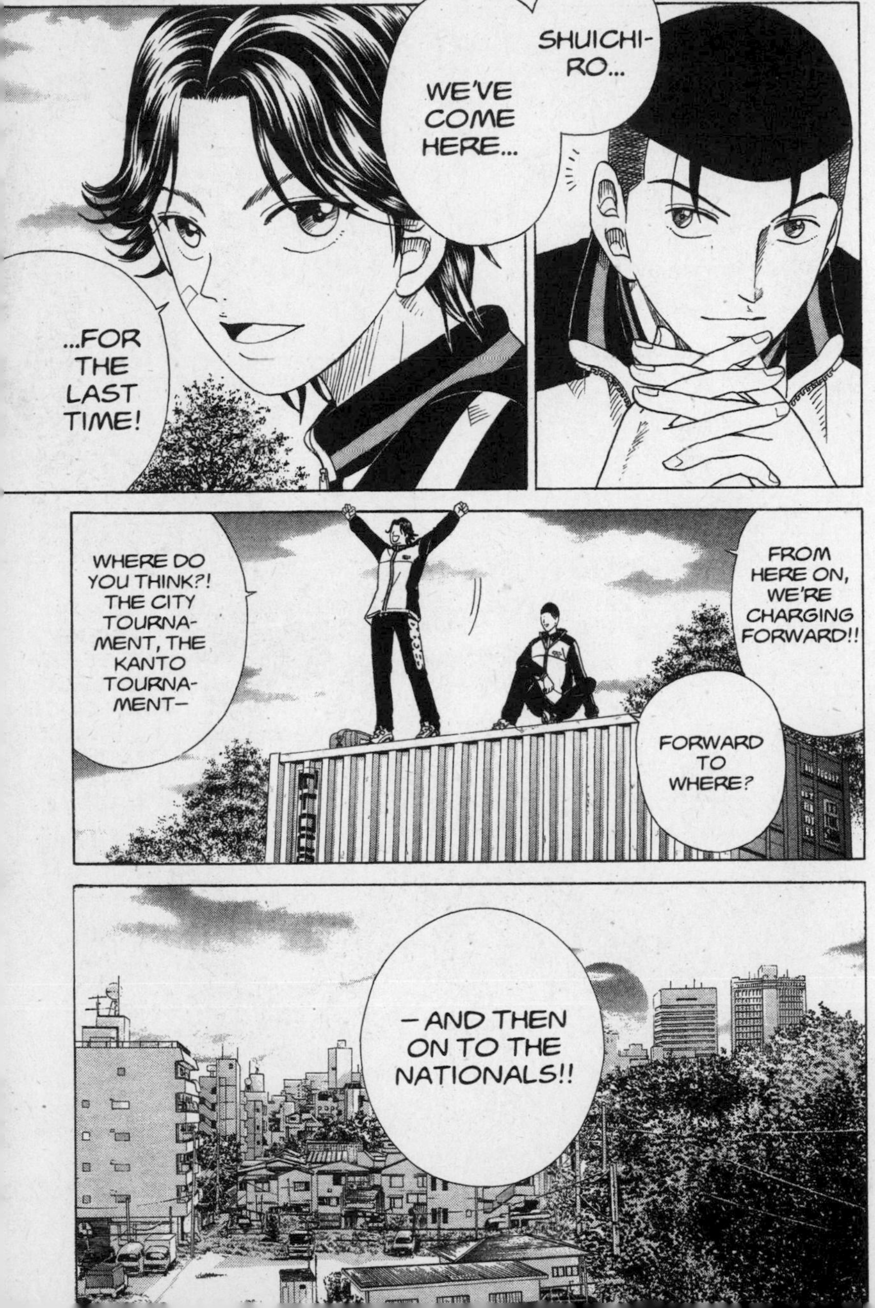
SHUICHI-RO...
WE'VE COME HERE...
...FOR THE LAST TIME!
FROM HERE ON, WE'RE CHARGING FORWARD!!
FORWARD TO WHERE?
WHERE DO YOU THINK?! THE CITY TOURNA-MENT, THE KANTO TOURNA-MENT—
—AND THEN ON TO THE NATIONALS!!

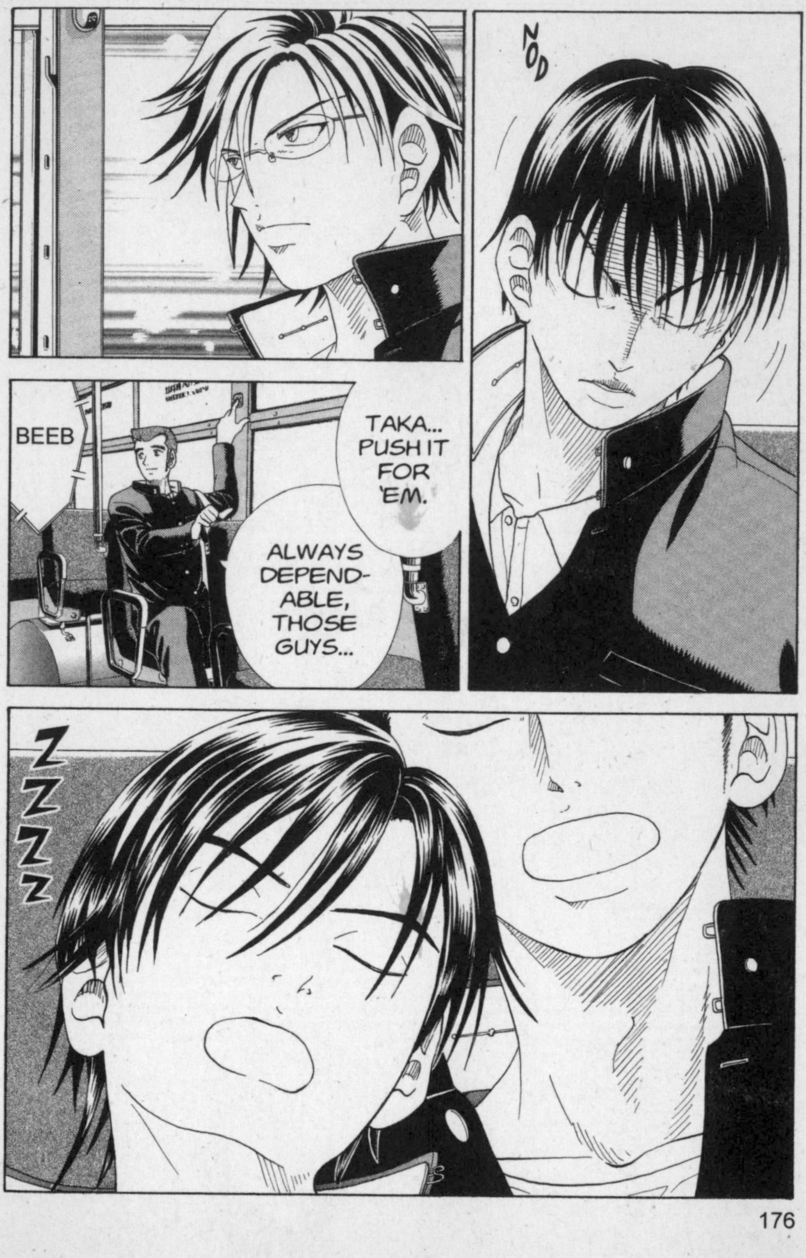
NOD
TAKA... PUSH IT FOR 'EM.
ALWAYS DEPEND-ABLE, THOSE GUYS...
BEEB
ZZZZ

READ THIS WAY

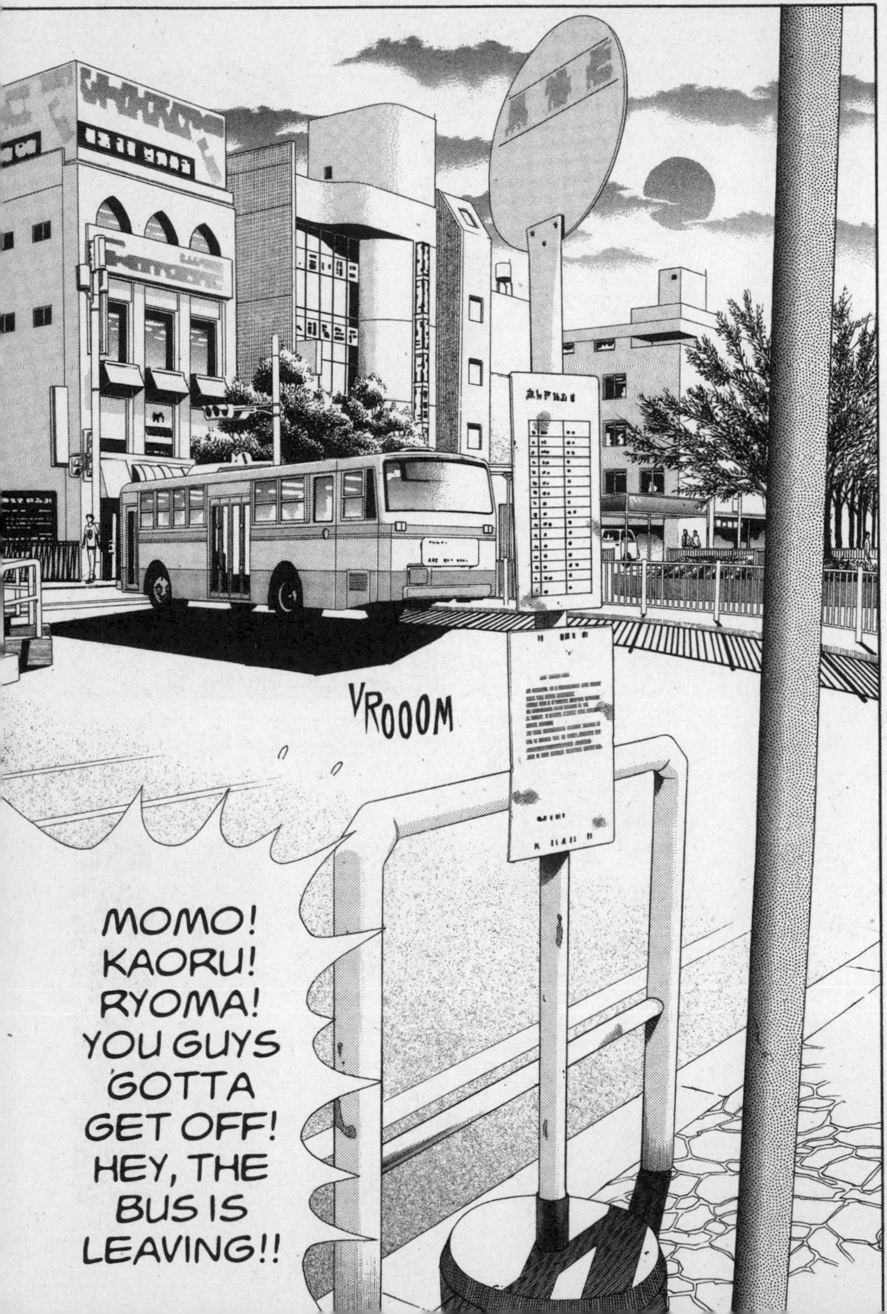
VROOOM
MOMO! KAORU! RYOMA! YOU GUYS GOTTA GET OFF! HEY, THE BUS IS LEAVING!!

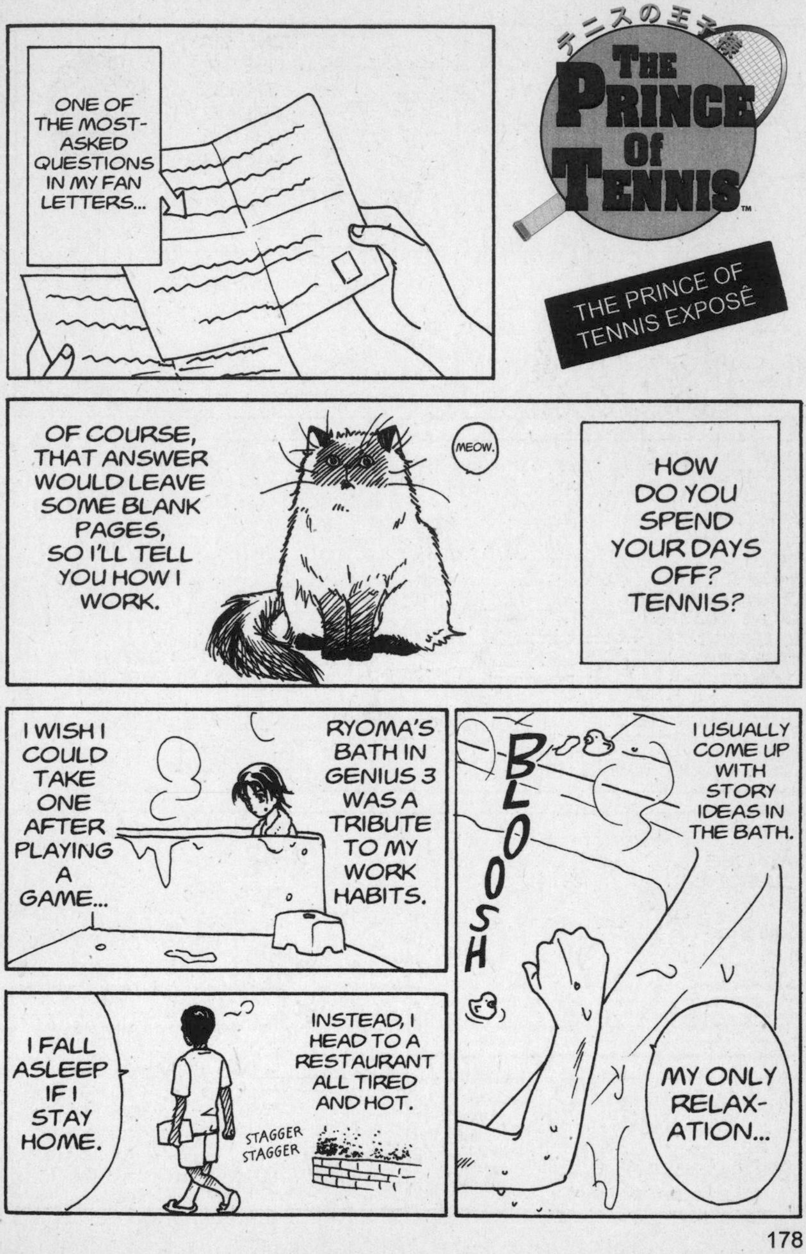
テニスの王子様
THE PRINCE OF TENNIS™
THE PRINCE OF TENNIS EXPOSÊ
ONE OF THE MOST-ASKED QUESTIONS IN MY FAN LETTERS...
HOW DO YOU SPEND YOUR DAYS OFF? TENNIS?
MEOW.
OF COURSE, THAT ANSWER WOULD LEAVE SOME BLANK PAGES, SO I'LL TELL YOU HOW I WORK.
I USUALLY COME UP WITH STORY IDEAS IN THE BATH.
BLOOOSH
MY ONLY RELAX-ATION...
RYOMA'S BATH IN GENIUS 3 WAS A TRIBUTE TO MY WORK HABITS.
I WISH I COULD TAKE ONE AFTER PLAYING A GAME...
INSTEAD, I HEAD TO A RESTAURANT ALL TIRED AND HOT.
STAGGER STAGGER
I FALL ASLEEP IF I STAY HOME.

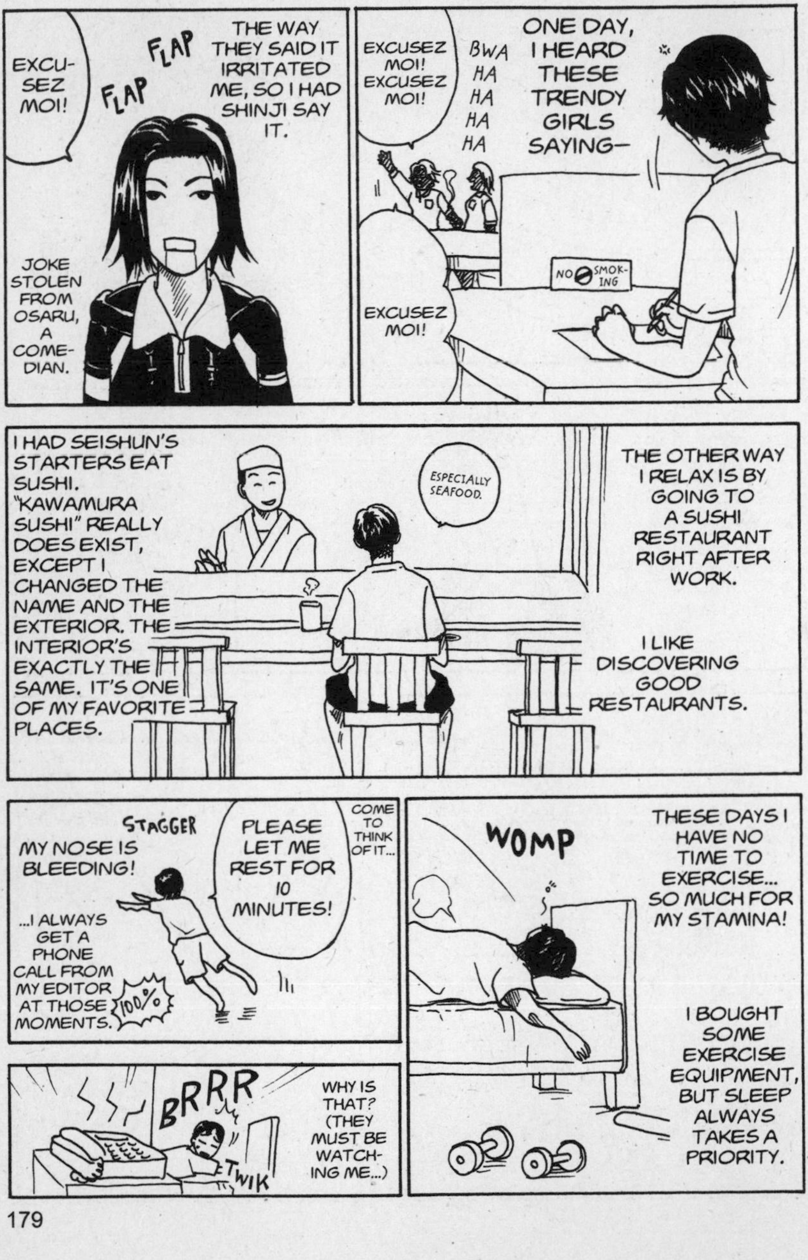
ONE DAY, I HEARD THESE TRENDY GIRLS SAYING—
BWA HA HA HA HA
EXCUSEZ MOI! EXCUSEZ MOI!
NO SMOKING
EXCUSEZ MOI!
THE WAY THEY SAID IT IRRITATED ME, SO I HAD SHINJI SAY IT.
FLAP
FLAP
EXCUSEZ MOI!
JOKE STOLEN FROM OSARU, A COMEDIAN.
THE OTHER WAY I RELAX IS BY GOING TO A SUSHI RESTAURANT RIGHT AFTER WORK.
ESPECIALLY SEAFOOD.
I LIKE DISCOVERING GOOD RESTAURANTS.
I HAD SEISHUN'S STARTERS EAT SUSHI. "KAWAMURA SUSHI" REALLY DOES EXIST, EXCEPT I CHANGED THE NAME AND THE EXTERIOR. THE INTERIOR'S EXACTLY THE SAME. IT'S ONE OF MY FAVORITE PLACES.
THESE DAYS I HAVE NO TIME TO EXERCISE... SO MUCH FOR MY STAMINA!
WOMP
I BOUGHT SOME EXERCISE EQUIPMENT, BUT SLEEP ALWAYS TAKES A PRIORITY.
COME TO THINK OF IT...
PLEASE LET ME REST FOR 10 MINUTES!
STAGGER
MY NOSE IS BLEEDING!
...I ALWAYS GET A PHONE CALL FROM MY EDITOR AT THOSE MOMENTS.
100%
WHY IS THAT? (THEY MUST BE WATCHING ME...)
BRRR
TWIK

SEISHUN QUESTION BOX

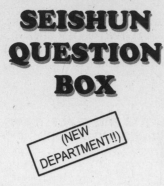

(NEW DEPARTMENT!!)

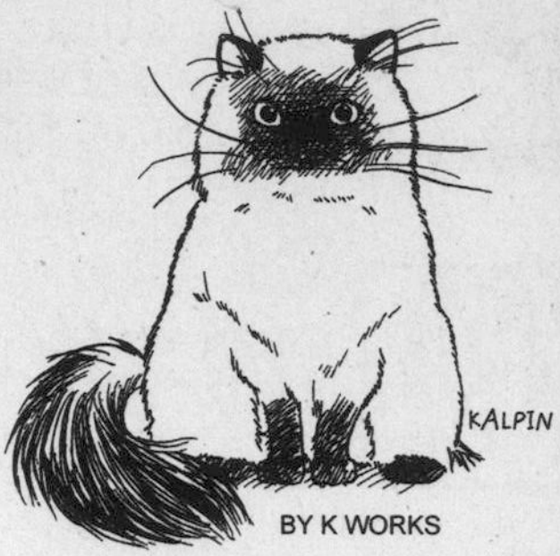
KALPIN

BY K WORKS

THANK YOU FOR ALL YOUR WARM LETTERS!! I'VE DECIDED TO HAVE THE CHARACTERS THEMSELVES ANSWER SOME OF THE MOST FREQUENTLY ASKED QUESTIONS!!

Q : I'M A BIG FAN OF EIJI! SEEING HIS ELDER SISTER IN GENIUS 21 MADE ME WANT TO KNOW MORE ABOUT HIS FAMILY!
(FUKUOKA, FUKUOKA Y.M)

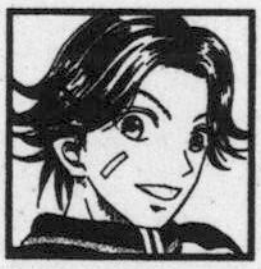

YES! I'M HONORED TO BE THE FIRST!

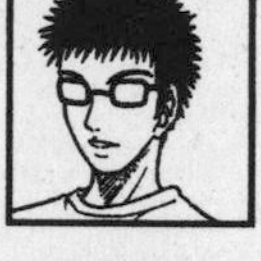

I'LL TELL YOU WHAT HIS FAMILY IS LIKE...

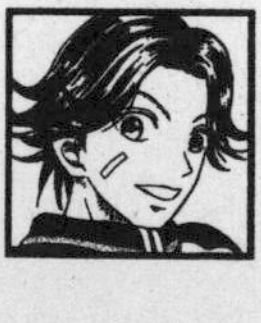

SHUT UP, SADAHARU! THEY ASKED ME!
(WAVES "GET LOST!")

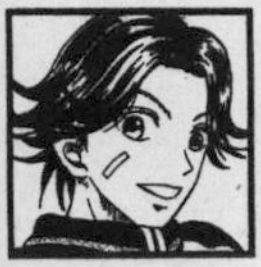

I'M THE YOUNGEST, AND I LIVE WITH MY GRANDPA, GRANDMA, DAD, MOM, TWO OLDER BROTHERS, AND TWO OLDER SISTERS...PLUS MY SISTER'S DOG AND MY MOM'S PARAKEET...

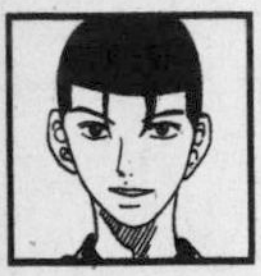

WHEN I HAD DINNER AT EIJI'S PLACE, IT WAS REALLY LIVELY. (MAYBE TOO LIVELY.)

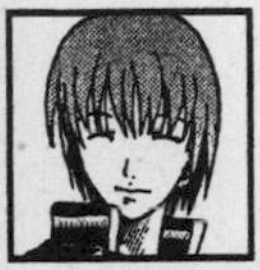

MM. A VERY CHEERFUL FAMILY.

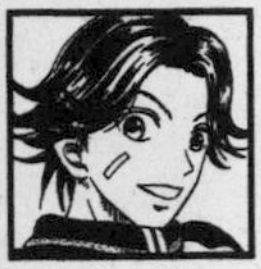

BOTH MY PARENTS LEAVE FOR WORK IN THE MORNING, SO WE SHARE BREAKFAST DUTIES...FOR SEVEN PEOPLE!! I'M EXHAUSTED!!

Q: I STARTED JUNIOR HIGH THIS YEAR AND JOINED THE TENNIS TEAM. BUT WE PRACTICE THE BASICS ALL THE TIME. I CAN'T WAIT TO ACTUALLY HIT A BALL. OUR TEAM PLAYS "SOFT TENNIS"...IS THAT DIFFERENT FROM SEISHUN'S TENNIS?

(SAITAMA, HANNO O.N)

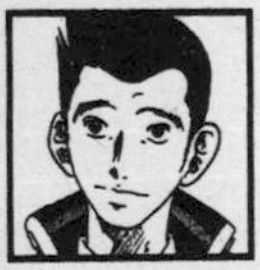

CONGRATULATIONS ON JOINING THE TENNIS TEAM!! (CLAP CLAP.)

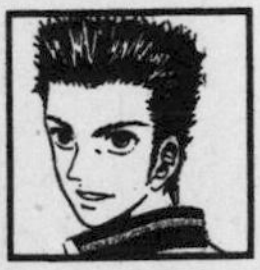

WHEN WE WERE 7TH GRADERS, ALL WE DID WAS PRACTICE THE BASICS, ESPECIALLY OUR SWINGS. IT'S NOTHING EXCITING, BUT IT'S TIRING, HUH?

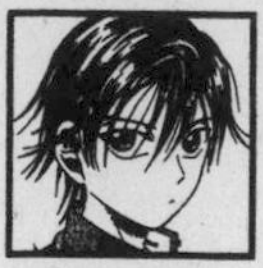

YOU MUST BE KIDDING...

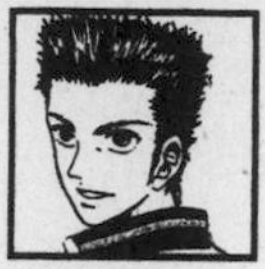

...#. YOU SHUT UP!

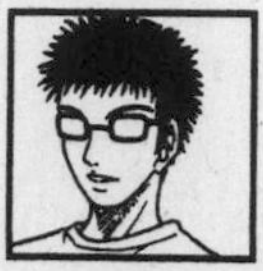

SWINGING IS THE FOUNDATION. YOU'VE GOT TO LEARN TO PAY ATTENTION TO YOUR GRIP AND THE RACKET FACE. GOOD LUCK!

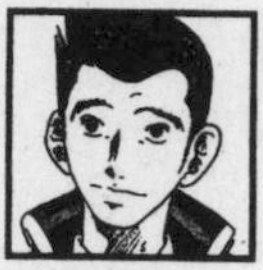

THE SWING IN SOFT TENNIS IS DIFFERENT FROM REGULAR TENNIS, BUT EITHER WAY, THE MOST IMPORTANT THING IS TO HAVE FUN. IT FEELS GOOD WHEN YOU HIT A WINNER, TOO!

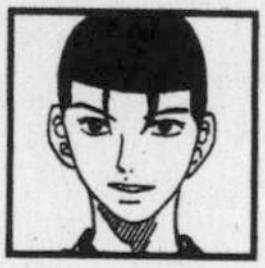

... (REMEMBERING BURNING SERVE)

Q : I LIKE THE "SNAKE"!! TELL ME HOW TO HIT VIPER'S "SNAKE"!!
(AICHI, TOYOAKI K.A)

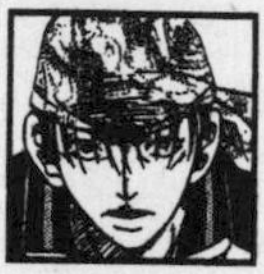

I'M NOT "VIPER."

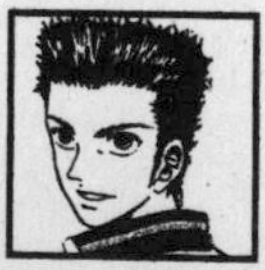

C'MON, TELL HIM, VI—**KAORU.** YOU'RE POPULAR!!

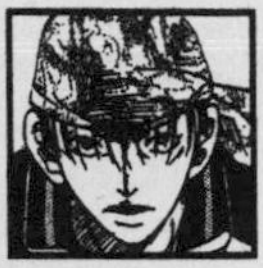

SHUT UP!! HOW DO I HIT IT? I JUST GO "RRRAR" WHEN I HIT THE BALL! (IN "SNAKE" POSITION.)

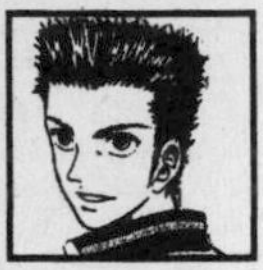

WHAT KIND OF ANSWER IS THAT?

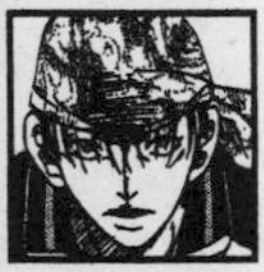

THEN HOW DO YOU HIT YOUR "DUNK SMASH"?!

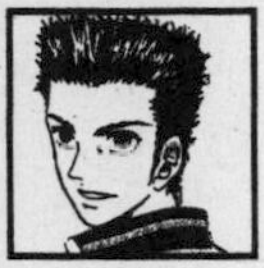

WELL, WHEN THEY HIT IT HIGH, I GO "KABOOM!" (SWINGS HIGH.)

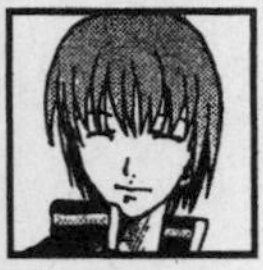

KAORU'S "SNAKE" REQUIRES SKILL, SO NOT MANY PEOPLE IN SEISHUN CAN HIT IT. (SMILES.)

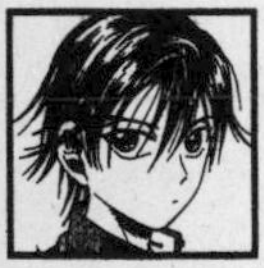

OH, I WOULDN'T SAY THAT... (KAORU GLARES.)

Q : IS THE CAPTAIN REALLY A JUNIOR HIGH STUDENT? I DON'T BELIEVE IT.
(SHIZUOKA, GOTEMBA T.O.)

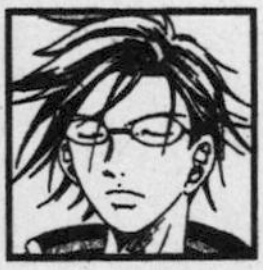

... (EVERYBODY TURNS AROUND AND LAUGHS)

In the Next Volume...

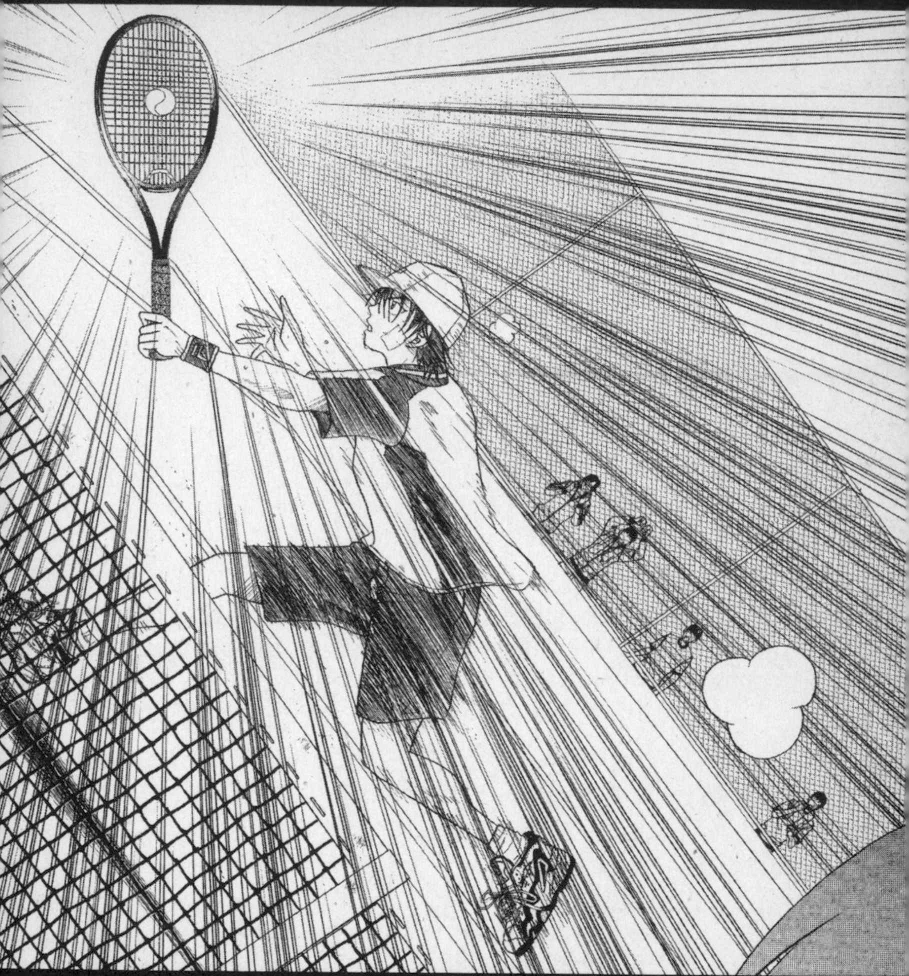

A little ego goes a long way. With Team Captain Kunimitsu scheduling intra-squad games to prepare Seishun Academy's players for the City Tournament, there's no telling what kind of trouble the feisty players can get themselves into. For starters, what possessed The Prince of Tennis Ryoma Echizen to smash his way through an intense practice match against Shusuke?!

Available in November 2005